# Islamic Cont

This volume brings together some of the finest writings on the Muslims of Indian subcontinent and the role of Islamic symbols and identities in public life. It highlights the extent to which Muslims, like their Hindu counterparts, have been engaged in recent times in renewing and rethinking the historic traditions of their faiths.

The essays are united in the challenge they offer to the negative stereotypes that are current, for example, that Islam is inevitably politically militant, that Muslim women are particularly oppressed, or that Islam is a static tradition. The essays in contrast show the Islamic scholars of India and Pakistan as people engaged with issues of the modern world and, pragmatically driven in their socio-political activities. What also remains constant in all the essays is the focus on individual Muslim lives, giving the volume the feel of a vibrant oral history.

The author argues that, for the most part, there has been an absence of 'Islamist politics' or movements in the colonial period and thereafter in India. Instead, there is a wide evidence of a firm commitment to democratic secularism and a-political spiritual renewal. She cautions that the over-emphasis on jihad-oriented movements in Afghanistan and Pakistan should not eclipse the more enduring and pervasive patterns of Islamic activity in South Asia. Nor should they distract from other constructive activities of the Muslims of the subcontinent like—education of boys and girls, moral and spiritual guidance, cultivation of Greco-Arabic medicine, poetry, and production of pilgrimage accounts.

**Barbara D. Metcalf** is Alice Freeman Palmer Professor of History, University of Michigan, USA. Her interest in South Asian history goes back nearly forty years, and her publications include *Islamic Revival in British India: Deoband, 1860–1900*, (second edition with new introduction, OUP 2002), and *Perfecting Women: Maulana Ashraf 'Ali Thanawi's Bibishti Zewar* (OIP 2002).

# Islamic Contestations
## Essays on Muslims in India and Pakistan

*Barbara D. Metcalf*

**OXFORD**
UNIVERSITY PRESS

# OXFORD
UNIVERSITY PRESS

Oxford University Press is a department of the University of Oxford.
It furthers the University's objective of excellence in research, scholarship,
and education by publishing worldwide. Oxford is a registered trademark of
Oxford University Press in the UK and in certain other countries

Published in India by
Oxford University Press
YMCA Library Building, 1 Jai Singh Road, New Delhi 110001, India

First Edition published in 2004
Oxford India Paperbacks 2006

ISBN-13: 978-0-19-568513-8
ISBN-10: 0-19-568513-X

Typeset in Garamond (TTF) 10.5/12
by Excellent Laser Typesetters, Pitampura, Delhi 110 034
Printed in India by Repro Knowledgecast Limited, Thane

# Contents

# Acknowledgements

Chapter 1 first published in *Modern Asian Studies*, 12, 1 (1978): 11–34.

Chapter 2 first published in Muhammad Khalid Masud and David S. Powers, eds. *Islamic Legal Interpretation: Muftis and their Fatwas*, pp. 184–92. Cambridge: Harvard University Press, 1996.

Chapter 4 first published in Zoya Hasan, ed. *Forging Identities: Gender, Communities and the State*, pp. 1–21. Delhi: Kali for Women, 1994.

Chapter 5 first published in *Modern Asian Studies*, 19, 1 (1985): 1–28.

Chapter 6 first published in Robert E. Frykenberg, ed. *Delhi Through the Ages*, pp. 299–315. Delhi: Oxford University Press, 1985.

Chapter 7 first published in Hartmut Lehmann and Peter van der Veer, eds. *The Religious Morality of the Nation State*, pp. 129–43. Princeton: Princeton University Press, 1998.

Chapter 8 first published in *The Journal of Asian Studies*, 54, 4 (1995): 1–17.

Chapter 9 first published in Peter Merkl and Ninian Smart, eds. *Religion and Politics in the Modern World*, pp. 170–90. New York: New York University Press, 1982.

Chapter 10 first published in William R. Roff, ed. *Islam and the Politics of Meaning*, pp. 132–59. London: Croom Helm and Berkeley: University of California Press, 1987.

0viii ACKNOWLEDGEMENTS

Chapter 11 first published in Craig Calhoun, Paul Price, and Ashley Timmer, eds. *Understanding September 11*, pp. 53–66. New York: The New Press, 2002.

Chapter 12 first published in *Journal of South Asian and Middle Eastern Studies*, 1, 2 (1997): 68–74.

Chapter 13 first published in Dale Eickleman and James Piscatori, eds. *Muslim Travellers: Pilgrimage, Migration and the Religious Imagination*, pp. 85–107. London: Routledge; and Berkeley: University of California Press, 1990.

Chapter 14 first published in Robert Folkenflik, ed. *Autobiography and Self-Representation*, pp. 149–67. Stanford: Stanford University Press, 1993.

Chapter 15 first published in *The Journal of Asian Studies*, 54, 2 (1995): 474–80.

# Introduction

The essays in this volume, written over the last quarter century, are a product of an interest in India that now spans almost four decades.[1] In writing on Muslims, I opted to focus on a relatively little studied, but demographically very substantial, segment of the subcontinental population. At the same time I chose a population neglected among those 'rightly' studied only in the Middle East. To add to my somewhat contrarian perspective, I sought throughout to show Muslims, especially the so-called 'mullas', as engaged with issues of the modern world and not simply a blind reactionaries, as they are conventionally described. In my work I have emphasized, moreover, that the traditionally educated Muslim leadership in the colonial period, far from being 'fanatic', were pragmatically driven in their socio-political activities, acting, as I have written elsewhere, 'within the complex world of opportunities and constraints, motivations, and tastes they [typically] shared' with non-Muslims as well.[2]

That pragmatism, in the colonial period and in the independent Republic of India as well, meant an absence, for the most part, of anything that could be labelled 'Islamic politics' in the sense of political theories or ideologies intended to create polities organized on the basis of divinely revealed principles. The Pakistan movement should not be considered 'Islamic': it was a movement for a secular, liberal democracy, although once the country was established there certainly were voices that sought to create an Islamically ordered state (Chapters 9 and 10). Outsiders to this field are typically astonished to learn, in contrast, that what is arguably the largest Islamic movement to emerge in the Indian subcontinent in the twentieth century was one that focused on internal spiritual renewal. The emergence of jihad-oriented movements in Afghanistan and Pakistan at the turn of the twenty-first century (Chapter 11) should not eclipse what have been more enduring and more pervasive patterns of Islamic activity in South Asia. These have been obscured, in the first place, by an 'Orientalism', reinforced by some modern reform movements that relegates Muslims whose primary languages were neither Arabic nor Persian to the margins of scholarly work. They have been further distorted by widespread pejorative stereotypes about Muslims and Islam, in general.

After the events of 11 September 2001 and the subsequent 'war on terrorism', an unsought justification for my choice of field presented itself, namely, contemporary relevance. As someone who had studied the history of the Deoband movement, the sectarian orientation claimed by the Taliban and their supporters in Pakistan, I was consulted often by reporters and others struggling to make sense of the organizational and ideological context of the unfolding events. I had also studied the Tablighi Jama'at, a movement that had emerged among Deobandis in the colonial period, a little-known movement that seemed to turn up with puzzling frequency in the lives of those in the United States allegedly involved in terrorism.

The essays below, as well as my writing as a whole, however, do not deal directly with the contemporary situation but with a range of historical themes. Several describe movements of socio-religious reform with their focus on self-realization and self-improvement, and their quest of respect and self-respect, that ran through Indian movements of all religious groups in the colonial period. Other essays study the role of Muslims in the Indian nationalist movement, or their programmes and ideologies in the independent states that emerged after 1947. These stories of the Deobandis and other South Asian Muslims offer rich material for demonstrating the way substantial numbers of people have chosen to order their lives from the late nineteenth century onwards. Theirs are stories that merit historical study on their own.

A striking characteristic of these stories is the variety of interpretations of their religious traditions that Muslims have produced to guide and justify their behaviour in modern times. The Muslims described in these essays, belonging to different movements and schools, may diverge widely from each other in everything from ritual behaviour to political strategies. Moreover, even those who share a sectarian label may differ among themselves, and depart dramatically from their predecessors at a later period of time. The word 'contestation' in the title of this volume is intended to point to the extent to which Muslims, like their Hindu counterparts, have been engaged in recent times in renewing and rethinking the historic traditions of their faiths. 'Contestation' points both to actual debates among Muslims and to the multiple dialogues with Islamic texts and symbols undertaken by individuals and groups.

Outsiders and Muslims themselves, like most participants in historic religious traditions, often speak as if their tradition, in this case 'Islam', offered a single standard and single interpretation. While 'Islam' as such may never change, however, both theorists and Muslims themselves have recognized that historic religious traditions act as 'discursive traditions' whose institutions and symbols are interpreted afresh in changing contexts.[3] Maulana Husain Ahmad Madani (1879–1958), discussed briefly in Chapter 11, was one of those who were explicit in articulating the responsibility of Muslims in addressing themselves to history and shifting contexts in the process of finding the appropriate models of behaviour. As he pointed out, if a teaching of Islam as central to the faith as the canonical prayer had multiple variations depending on such contextual issues as whether a Muslim was travelling or settled, sick or well, disabled or fit, how much more must Islamic teachings in relation to governance and interaction with non-Muslims vary depending on historical circumstances? How much more, in other words, must an Islamic political stance be based on assessment of the historical context and not on theory?[4]

Given the variety that emerges from the process of interpretation, let alone from behaviours based less clearly on the tradition itself, it is not surprising that the modern period of social, cultural, and political change has seen a proliferation of distinctive intellectual positions and ideologies. Few generalizations about Islam and Muslims hold up across these essays, even dealing as they do with Muslims of a specific geographic region. They challenge the stereotypes that Islam is inevitably politically militant, that Muslim women are particularly oppressed, or that Islam is a static tradition, sunk in medievalism. There may indeed be militancy, oppression, or stasis, but that is not the whole story, and Muslims themselves have challenged positions they themselves characterize with such terms.

A great deal of what is described here, therefore, does not deal with issues that have so absorbed Western observers. The worlds of Muslims discussed here involve much beyond nationalism and politics, for example, including a rich affective, and relational life, described here primarily among men. They often entail passionate quests for spiritual progress and realization. They engage creative realms from poetry to bodily healing. As Dipesh Chakrabarty has argued for the historical worlds of Indians in the twentieth century in general, they include, as actors, divinities, and holy personages from the beyond.[5]

This does not mean that a 'subaltern' realm or an 'inner sphere' has existed beyond the reach of colonial culture and institutions. Indeed, what is striking in many cases is the extent to which thinkers steeped in traditional learning and operating only in the vernacular participate in projects and deal with issues better known to have been current among the elite who knew English. This is exemplified not only in the Deoband movement in general, but, for example, in the guidance text for women I discuss below. This text's author was one of the great scholars and sufis of the twentieth century, a man who rarely left the country town in which he received the disciples and petitioners who, in part thanks to the new rail line, came to him in droves. He knew no English. Yet when at the turn of the twentieth century, he wrote a guidance manual for women, he not only participated in the discussion of issues related to gender, but also implicitly engaged with the concerns relating to authenticity and individual self-realization that permeated cultural life in these decades.[6]

In the remainder of this introduction, I first provide an autobiographical description of the institutional context in which my interest in these subjects evolved. In so doing, I elaborate on my first book-length projects—the history of Deoband, a collaborative project on moral formation and authority, and the related study of this influential guidance text for women—which set the foundation for many of the articles included here. I hope this personal account is of general interest, in part because it is an example of the way post-war international and area studies programmes in the United States shaped scholarship on what had been little studied areas of the world. The second part of the introduction reviews, and comments on, the themes of the articles that follow.

## 'My Life: A Fragment'

In writing about a fragment of my career, I borrow the title of a wonderful memoir written by a leading Indian political figure of the 1920s.[7] In his memoir, Muhammad Ali marvellously recreated his experience of mastering the English language and immersing himself in British higher education and cultural life. I only wish that I could report anything like his 'cross-cultural' success, let alone that I could write as well as he. There was little in my early life to predict that I would spend my adult life focused on a geographic area halfway round the world, growing up as I did in working class Philadelphia, with family members—apart from a stepfather who had seen service in World War II—whose most distant travel was by train to the Jersey shore. My interests were to be very much a product of changing times.

Neither my high school nor undergraduate college four decades back offered any teaching on India or, indeed, on non-Western areas at all. Yet my public high school is worth describing simply because it implicitly encouraged an international, albeit European, perspective. It was a remarkable institution: an all-city school focused on college preparation for girls, an anomaly (now ended) in American state schooling. One significant aspect of that school was its implicit 'multiculturalism' *avant la lettre*: I mixed with girls of recent immigrant backgrounds, not least in my case Europeans who had fled Hitler's tyranny, and my world was immeasurably widened as it would not have been had I gone to a neighbourhood high school. A second aspect of that school that shaped me profoundly was its spectacularly good language teaching. There is, of course, a gendered dimension to this that needs to be criticized: I barely did science at all. But the rigorous training I had in Latin, French, and Spanish made me imagine not only other times and places, but made me imagine myself differently. It made me think that I could try on another person, be a kind of cultural chameleon, something that no doubt happened as I interacted with people of different educational and class backgrounds than those I had grown up with. It is worth calling attention to the school's demographic mix and its emphasis on languages given that the United States

today—in contrast to most of the world—asks so little of its high
school and college students in terms of language study.

After high school, in the early 1960s, I attended Swarthmore
College. Even if Eurocentric, my first history course focused on
world history, and I subsequently studied 'the expansion of
Europe', followed by an honours seminar on the British Empire.
This last course was taught by a visiting lecturer, Jean Kopytoff,
a specialist in the history of Sierra Leone, just back from celebrating Nigerian independence, and committed to history from the side
of the ruled, not simply a history limited to the actions of the
ruling class. An important point to me personally, as well as to
the field if one believes that fields need both women and men, was
the fact that I had as a role model a woman historian. At Berkeley,
when I began doctoral studies in 1966, there was not a single
woman faculty member in either the History Department or
what became the Department of South/Southeast Asian Studies.[8]
A perhaps surprising number of my cohort at Swarthmore went
on to careers that involved Asia or the 'non-West' generally.
Swarthmore was a politically left, intellectual hothouse, with many
students of that Kennedy era profoundly engaged with pressing
social issues, not least at this time the civil rights movement. There
was a sense that the study of what came to be called 'the Third
World' could be part of that engagement.

I began my graduate work by completing a master's degree at
the University of Wisconsin. It was Jean Kopytoff who urged me
to continue my studies with (her fellow Swarthmore alumnus)
Philip Curtin—who would emerge as one of the pre-eminent historian of Africa in the United States. Curtin had pioneered a new
graduate programme called 'Comparative Tropical History', a
programme that produced several generations of scholars special-
izing in South Asia, Southeast Asia, Africa, and Latin America.
Curtin's vision, so in tune with Kopytoff's, was to immerse students in the interdisciplinary 'area' study of their chosen region
and to look not to Europe for patterns and comparisons but to
other parts of the 'South'. Too much history, he argued, had
been written that attributed all modern change to Europe without
adequate attention to the dynamics of the other parts of the
world. Area studies programmes, with federal government
support, were just emerging in this post-Sputnik era in the mid-
1960s, but Curtin's vision of orienting students to more than

a single area was well ahead of his time. Despite an intellectual enthusiasm for Curtin's approach, there probably was some lingering Anglophilia, rooted no doubt in my bookish childhood, that motivated my choice of India, 'the jewel in the crown', as my primary field of study. My interests, however, before long turned in other directions.

I soon became drawn to the history of Muslims in the Indian subcontinent, a population whose history I came to believe was neglected and misinterpreted. I came to this interest, however, almost by chance. At Wisconsin, once I had chosen India as my focus, I was directed to Hindi as the language I needed to study, and someone vaguely advised me that if I was interested in history I should study Urdu—Hindustani or Hindi using the Persian script—since that would lead me to Persian and hence historical court records. No one would make this suggestion today since the vision of what is included in history is so much more expansive. Urdu as a prose language emerged primarily in the period of the nineteenth and the twentieth centuries as an official language, soon caught up in the debates that created self-conscious religiously defined communities. It was those movements related to Muslim identity and Islam that became my subject.

My graduate training was rather piecemeal. In these early years, language was abysmally taught with linguists figuring out the rules, unable to speak themselves, and 'native speakers' prompted to provide models. I loathed hours spent in language labs listening to tapes of 'phonetic discrimination'. I owe an incalculable debt to Ralph Russell, then of the School of Oriental and African Studies, who generously met me at the end of his day's work during several months in London when I was en route to India to do dissertation research. He insisted that a reading knowledge of a language was insufficient, and pushed me to speak as well as read. As for guidance in my subject area, I was most influenced by Ira Lapidus, a historian of the late medieval Middle East whose breadth and curiosity made him a wonderful interlocutor and reader. I also worked with Hamid Algar, a man of extraordinary learning, and, as a Muslim and, specifically, a Naqshbandi, he was helpful to me in my quest to understand the writings of Muslim scholars and leaders.

The area studies approach that has proven so rich in the United States is the result of foundation and, above all, federal funding to support instruction, colloquia, and other programmes, and critically important graduate fellowships. For a time, it seemed to me odd that someone with interests like mine was supported in graduate school by something called 'National Defense Foreign Language Fellowships'. The value to a society of encouraging study in what may seem unimportant areas, allowing students to take up whatever topic they can justify intellectually, may not have short term 'relevance', but it is critical for fostering research and teaching about the larger world as well as for 'de-provincializing' the core disciplines of the humanities and social sciences.

## Deoband

I don't know what piqued my interest in Deoband initially, but most of the research I have done has built on my initial history of this Islamic madrasa. The Deoband madrasa, a major centre of the 'traditional' Muslim religious leadership in the subcontinent, was often counterposed to a second educational institution, Aligarh, founded at about the same time, taken to be its opposite as the modernizing, westernizing institution. Two points about Deoband in the colonial period were well-known. First, the Deobandis formed no political organization of their own, a stance they continued in independent India. Second, when other Muslim leaders espoused the cause of a separate state for Muslims, articulated at the very end of the colonial era under the aegis of a separate party for Muslims, the Muslim League, for the most part the Deobandis whether as a group or as individuals declined to support them.

What caught my interest in the brief descriptions of Deoband I encountered was a sense of discomfort with the depiction of Deoband as 'traditional'. Here was a school founded only in 1867 that clearly broke with earlier patterns of education. I saw Deoband as a possible case for a critique of modernization theory, which argued that all peoples everywhere were moving toward a form of society, politics, and culture whose script had already been written in the West, and that 'progress' was stimulated only by contact with the West on the part of societies that had, heretofore, been largely stagnant and unchanging.

In 1969 I arrived in Lucknow, the elegant old princely city that is now the capital of the populous north Indian state of Uttar Pradesh, and shortly thereafter I made my first trip to Deoband, by train to Saharanpur, overnight in the Ladies' Retiring Room,

then the first train out the next morning on narrow gauge track
to Deoband. As I disembarked, an elderly bearded man, dressed
in the gray long fitted coat, the sherwani, and cap of the old-
fashioned courtly and educated elite, came forward to greet me.
This was the late Saiyyid Mahbub Rizvi, the archivist and historian
of the school, to whom I had addressed a letter requesting
permission to visit the school and consult its library, who then and
later was generously ready to help me understand the school.
Saiyyid Sahib seated me in his cycle rickshaw, and we proceeded
through the brick streets and lanes to the seminary itself and
directly to the upstairs guest house where I would stay and, in due
course, return several times during the course of my research. I
mostly stayed in that room, making an occasional foray to the
library, from which materials would be sent to me, or to the homes
of teachers or staff of the school. The staff and some of the faculty
would occasionally come to visit.

I was remarkably fortunate in choosing this topic. Deoband
could be studied by a historian because there was an abundance
of records and printed materials. The elders of the school, shaped
by their old world traditions of hospitality and, especially, respect
for scholarship, were generous and helpful to a stranger. There was
also a tradition of openness to outsiders thanks to the school's
involvement in the nationalist movement. The fact that it was a
woman who sought this help seemed more of a problem to
American academics than it was to the Deobandis. I remember an
occasion at the University of Chicago when I was writing up my
dissertation. I presented a talk describing my research and later had
lunch seated next to my host, a political scientist of the Islamic
world. As I described my work on these religious scholars or
'ulama, this person kept repeating, 'but of course the 'ulama will
never talk to you. But of course the ulama will never talk to you'.
He literally could not hear me as I tried to get across that they
had already done so.

Qari Muhammad Tayyib, the grandson of the founder of the
school, was then the school's director. He was an elderly man,
known above all for his Qur'anic recitation as well as for his
spiritual guidance to tens of thousands of disciples across north
India, East Africa, and elsewhere. On every visit, this old man
would slowly come up the stairs to the guest house to see if I, an
unknown student, was comfortable. I also met the lively women

of his household, who rarely went outside the home, but had busy and varied lives, led by Qari Sahib's wife. In Deoband, I got a sense of the everyday life, in part by my 'mistakes' whether of clothing, dream interpretation, or oblivion to 'pollution'.

But what about my thesis concerning the school? From the materials I was able to collect there, I did indeed argue that Aligarh, the so-called modernist school, and Deoband, the 'traditional', in fact shared in fundamentally modern transformations. Both, moreover, were rooted in an indigenous pattern of religious reform that had gained strength at the end of the previous century, a counter to arguments that all change had to come from interaction with Western values or models. Deoband provided a new kind of school, using, to be sure, British models of bureaucratic organization to replace more familiar, more personal models. It used print in ways that furthered an urgency to standardize, to codify, to 'objectify'— to use a term recently coined to suggest this move to self-consciousness and standardization—the meaning of Islam. Deoband, moreover, participated in the new use of Urdu for prose learning, replacing, in many cases, the Persian of the ruling classes and at the same time offering a vernacular language that would serve as a lingua franca over a linguistically plural geographic area.

Qari Sahib, in his memoir of the school, wrote, 'in a time of change, we did not change'. That argument, like the argument of the Aligarh 'modernists' that Deoband is traditional, proved to be part of the historical story and not at all an accurate analysis of what happened in the past. My study of Deoband, in short, provided one of the many examples of how the very concept of 'traditional' becomes part of the self-definition of modernity. It also showed how what is often taken as tradition turns out to be a relatively recent product of the colonial past.

In writing my dissertation, I focused on descriptions of the new institutional structures of this late nineteenth century school in order to show the way Deoband shaped colonial institutions to its own ends. I was also able to do a statistical study of donors to the school, which revealed the large extent to which they represented exactly the kinds of professional and family backgrounds involved with the new westernizing and loyalist movement at Aligarh.

But what my prospectus and outline had left out was what in the end I had learned most about, and what initially strained to find a place in my story: namely, the style of spirituality, the

charismatic leadership, the personal formation, and the miracles
that were seen not only as the fruit of the scholarly learning
the school was known for but also of the personal transformations
that came in the presence of the school's teachers and guides. The
one theme I grew particularly interested in, which shaped further
work I did after the dissertation project, was precisely that of
theories of the person and of personal formation and transformation as understood and taught by these scholars. In this, they were
firmly rooted in the traditions of spiritual realization, usually
termed 'Sufism', that pervade virtually all of Muslim life in the
subcontinent. This emphasis on individual spiritual life and self-
realization, with its own genealogy and vocabulary, emerges as
important to the Hindus as well in the modern period.

## The Joint Committee on South Asia

In the late 1970s, I had the good fortune to be a member of the
SSRC/ACLS's Joint Committee on South Asia.[9] David Szanton,
staff to the committee, was the guiding power behind the committee, bringing his own powerful vision as a Chicago-trained anthropologist to shape a series of remarkably fruitful projects. The
ambitious goals of the committee, as initiated by Szanton, were to
set aside the concepts of Western intellectual and aesthetic systems
in order to seek out patterns of meaning and organization from
within South Asia's own cultural systems.[10] Thanks to the committee, I was able to undertake a project addressing these themes
of personal formation I had become interested in.

One concept that reappears from classical texts with renewed
importance in the present is an emphasis on *adab*, discipline or
deportment, and that became the focus of the project. Teachings
on *adab* deal with such subjects as an objectified self, a 'lower self'
given to indulgence, indiscipline, animal appetites, in short whatever leads a person from a disciplined and wholehearted devotion
to the divine teachings of moderation, self-control, and conformity
to moral teachings. Some texts and traditions even encourage the
self-consciousness that comes with internal conversations with
this lower self, as if it were another person, until it atrophies in
the clear light of reason and right. One important theme that
emerged from these texts on personal formation was their mate-
riality and practicality. There was no effort to begin by converting

the mind, no priority given to either intellectuality, nor, significantly, spiritual insight or faith as such. Instead the notion was
that one ought to behave as if one already had that intellectual
understanding or spiritual realization since it was precisely by
correct actions that the inner self would, with God's grace, be
transformed. The great Arab philosophers, like Ghazali, following
Greek theories, had discussed this formation of *habitus* or, in
Arabic, *malika*, through physical actions that make their moral
imprint just as, to use a modern metaphor, a person learns to create
music by the physical exercise of playing the piano.

My own contribution to this project was based on a Deobandi
text, the *Bihishti Zewar*, which I subsequently translated (thus
fulfilling a much earlier suggestion from Ralph Russell). This text,
whose title translates loosely as 'Heavenly Jewels', was written by
one of the first generation of Deoband graduates, a prolific writer
and a spiritual guide to thousands of followers. His book has often
been part of the dowry of a Muslim bride. What does the title
'Heavenly Jewels' mean? One guess might be that it means precisely that daughters and wives, properly instructed and pious,
would be the pearls, the adornments, of their husband's and
families' lives. We might think that would be a traditional attitude
toward women.

To the contrary, this text implicitly posits a single notion of
the person and of personal capacity for both women and men.
That women are fundamentally different, physically and morally,
from men turns out to be a particularity of the eighteenth century
and particularly of Victorian thought in the West. Women, in this
Victorian view, were subject to different physical processes that
were intimately related to their cognitive and intellectual development. Women who studied too much, for example, would harm
their reproductive powers. Women should study female subjects,
not male subjects. These pseudo-scientific theories were coupled
with what could be seen as equally limiting praise of women,
that they had a higher spirituality, a finer morality than men. The
women were, in the Victorian phrase, meant to be on a pedestal
they were the angels of the home—something like 'heavenly
jewels'. There would be Muslims in the twentieth century who
shared these views.

In this Deobandi book, however, there was no notion of a
distinct nature or morality for the women. They were meant to

practise the same kind of disciplines and self-control and focus on the same kind of self-realization as men. The women also had the same religious obligations as men. They were supposed to read precisely the same books as men, and, the author noted, in contrast to the burgeoning emphasis on 'domestic science' in Europe at the time, far from wasting their time on cooking and sewing, they should take advantage of not having to go out to work to use the time to learn Arabic and become legal scholars—just like men. There was no suggestion that women had higher spirituality. On the contrary in the current age, the author argued, their education had been neglected and they needed to work harder than men. 'Heavenly jewels' would, thus, be the rewards of discipline and piety that would bedeck *all* believers, women and men, in the paradise which they hoped to attain. There is a story that the author of the book, Maulana Thanawi, was asked to write an equivalent guide to behaviour for men once the first work proved such a success. His answer was that there was no need, as men could use the book as well. He ultimately added an appendix on such obligations as the Friday prayer, which were specific to men. What guide for women published in England or America at this time would have that kind of crossover? If one is interested in opportunities for women to become educated and to have access to authority, there are clearly strengths in the Islamic tradition that have been masked in developments of the colonial and post-colonial period.

The project on personal formation included South Asianists who worked in history, literature, anthropology, music, psychology, and religious studies. We students, of what are sometimes called 'the peripheral Islamic lands', found ourselves taking up classical concepts of unquestioned importance that had been significantly neglected in studies of the Muslim heartland. A handful of participants in the conference and subsequent volume that emerged from this project were specialists in the Middle East and Southeast Asia, including William Roff with whom I subsequently worked closely over several years. The perspective of these specialists gave us an opportunity to probe connections and patterns that transcended the arbitrary boundaries of an area defined in the post-World War II era. It also was an occasion to insist that the Islamic 'periphery', even in relation to what could be seen as a classical topic, deserved study in its own right. Peter

Brown, the distinguished scholar of late antiquity, was also a participant. He showed the value of looking at an Islamic topic in the company of non-Islamicists in order to explore what may be specific to the Islamic tradition and what is not.[11]

## The Joint Committee on the Comparative Study of Muslim Societies

In part because of the fruitfulness of working transregionally, glimpsed in the project on *adab*, a new joint committee was subsequently formed, of which I served as the founding chair in 1985, again under the leadership of David Szanton. The purpose of the Committee was to study the networks, shared discourses, and shared historical experiences of Muslim societies including, but not limited to, those in the Middle East. This was an important corrective to the old-fashioned notion I alluded to above, namely that true Islam, authentic Islam, exists only in the Middle East because only the earliest Arabic texts matter. Islam in South Asia is at once distinctive and Islamic. This is as true of Islam in Saudi Arabia as in Bangladesh or Sumatra. Everywhere Islam is realized in some local expression. Moreover, one might add, scholars of hadith and of mysticism, as well as modernist interpreters of Islam, have made the Indian subcontinent a centre for Muslims elsewhere who have sought instruction and models there. Thus, there was good reason to expand the geographic focus of scholarship on Islam. The Committee was also one of the first steps in the direction of re-organizing area studies activities at the Social Science Research Council which increasingly wished to focus on transregional or even global themes or problems, rather than conduct work which was limited to the geographic boundaries of 'area studies' defined in the context of the Cold War. Islam in its social and political contexts, given the Iranian revolution and what seemed a resurgence of religious ideologies generally in the 1980s, obviously required this more encompassing kind of study.

Over the next decade, the committee explored several issues central to the Islamic societies, viewing them transregionally, comparatively, and in historical depth. I myself participated actively in several projects that emerged as edited volumes: on the 'political economy of meaning'; on classic patterns of movement and travel; on the new Muslim diasporas in North America and

Europe; on Islamic legal interpretation, and lastly on the expansive movement of spiritual renewal of Indian origin, Tablighi Jama'at.[12] During this period I also served as the general editor of a series published by the University of California Press, titled 'Comparative Studies on Muslim Societies', intended also to contribute to defining 'Muslim societies' as a distinct field of study.[13]

This approach yielded many advantages, especially in encouraging the study of Muslim populations and Islamic traditions outside the Middle East. The committee projects were rewarding specifically because of their focus on topics that engaged the internal discourses, vocabularies, concepts, and metaphors used by Muslims in educational, legal, moral, and political debates in a range of changing economic and political conditions. The projects also brought together people trained in different area studies approaches, each with their own set of what Arjun Appadurai calls 'gate-keeping' concepts, as well as scholars trained not only in the United States but in other parts of the world in different scholarly traditions.

Nonetheless, there was a cost in studying Muslim Indians primarily in relation to other Muslims, namely the implication that the Muslims of India have a primary allegiance somewhere else.[14] This issue became a matter not of academic interest but of grim reality given the intensity of anti-Muslim violence that escalated in India after the destruction of the sixteenth century Mughal mosque, the Babri Masjid, and the anti-Muslim pogrom that followed in the years 1992–3, and chillingly reappeared in Gujarat in 2002.

The kind of issues I have described for Muslims—of new institutions linked to 'objectification' of religious tradition, of theories of the person, of new notions of gender presented as old, of religion in public life—all call out for study of the Indian population generally, not just of this one religious tradition. It is not at all uncommon however, for example, for students of Indian history to cover a topic called 'social reform' in the colonial period and focus only on Hinduism, never looking at the Muslim movements that share so much in their basic impulse and agendas, or, in turn, for those writing on Islam to produce histories equally internal to Muslims. Clearly, a pressing agenda for our field is to encourage scholarship that writes Muslims into the shared narrative on Indian history, not outside it. The essays below may, I hope, provide some building blocks for the more inclusive work that needs to be done.

## The Essays

### New Roles, New Contestations, for the 'Ulama

The first section of this volume includes three articles about the Deobandi 'ulama. Chapter 1 describes the critically important transition in this period to popularly supported, formally organized seminaries based on British institutional models.[15] These madrasas were central to the creation of something new in the colonial period: the existence of the 'ulama as a distinct social group with characteristic training and roles. In part their distinction rests on the roles they found to play in the colonial context. In part it rests on the existence of an alternate westernizing educational stream that shaped the status, roles, and accomplishments for the two distinctive groups of educated Muslims—a distinction marked most visibly by the use of the vernacular or the use of English. By contrast, in earlier eras, the educated Islamic elite (or 'Islamicate' to use Hodgson's neologism[16]) had largely shared a common education.

At the time of writing Chapter 1, a quarter century back, as I pointed out above, the dominant scholarly and popular understanding was that religious change in a colonized place like India was largely achieved by those who were engaged with colonial culture and knew at least some degree of English. Even then, however, there was a growing sense of the inadequacy of this interpretation. In that early article I referred to a concern that the study of traditional religious institutions (sufi orders, religious schools, religious endowments) in the colonial period was a seriously neglected field. The same point could have been made about the study of Hinduism. These major lacunae have been richly reduced, if not filled, in recent years as attention has broadened from explicit 'reactions to the West' in movements like the Brahmo Samaj, the Arya Samaj, and the Aligarh movement, important as they all are.[17] Arguably it was instead those Indians who worked in the vernacular languages and within the framework of pre-existing institutions—the Sufi orders, the madrasas, the patshalas, the dharma sabhas—whose influence would prove more far reaching.

The Deobandis are only one of the several groups which sought to reproduce Islamic culture in a colonial period characterized by considerable challenges to the preservation of traditional learning. They turned out to be one of the most influential as their graduates went on to found schools of their own, and they became known not only as a school but as a school of thought. Their geographic range was evident from their earliest years, and even Chapter 1, concentrating on institutional change, mentions a handful of examples of the long ties of Deoband to Afghanistan— a connection that will take on significance at the end of the twentieth century (and discussed in Chapter 11).

The work of the Deobandis was in a variety of roles such as teachers, spiritual guides, writers, debaters, publishers, prayer leaders, and guardians of endowments. Chapter 2 offers an example of a significant dimension of the kind of guidance offered by the 'ulama, namely their granting of advisory opinions, *fatawa*, when requested by their followers.[18] The utilization of inexpensive publication through lithographic presses, so important to the work of the 'ulama over all,[19] was of particular importance in the dissemination of *fatawa*. This chapter analyses two *fatawa* of one of the great scholars and Sufis of Deoband's earliest years, Maulana Rashid Ahmad Gangohi (d. 1905), who will be introduced in Chapter 1. These two *fatawa* are from a chapter on 'hajj' in the published volumes of his *fatawa*. The answers illustrate many points, not least the fact that India, even though ruled by the British, was typically regarded by the 'ulama not as a place where war was incumbent nor even as one where it was illegitimate to remain. They also illustrate the method of the 'reformist' 'ulama, who, far from merely parroting the teachings of the past, at every point, measure current practice against scriptural norms. These *fatawa* are also representative of the Deobandi corpus as a whole since they engage the central concern of the 'ulama, namely correct individual ritual practice and behaviour in everyday life, not, in these years of high colonial rule, issues of larger political or societal concerns.

These *fatawa* also make clear—the main point of the essay—that threaded throughout the opinions is controversy with rival groups of 'ulama, in this case, the Ahl-i Hadis (a school of thought which was always of minute influence within India, although its adherents were frequent interlocutors with other 'ulama and increasingly important in Pakistan at the end of the twentieth century when supported by Saudi extremists). In challenging his rivals, Rashid Ahmad's *fatawa* also give us a glimpse of an individual. In Chapter 1, he is described as a brilliant teacher of prophetic tradition, but one who could reduce his students to peals of laughter (in the course, one might note, of getting the 'bonehead' Afghans to understand an unfamiliar Urdu word). In the *fatawa* as well, he is clearly in his element, as he takes dig after dig at the Ahl-i Hadis with irony, damning understatements, and imputations of expedience instead of principle. The 'ulama were not cardboard figures operating mechanically.

Indeed, the final chapter of this section (Chapter 3) further gives flesh to a specific Deobandi scholar, namely Maulana Muhammad Zakariyya Kandhlawi (d. 1982), through an analysis of his own self-presentation in his multi-volume life story or autobiography. Writing at the end of his life, Zakariyya richly conveys the moral principles, the cherished stories of the elders taken as templates for himself and now offered to others, and many of the specific experiences of his long years as teacher in a major Deobandi madrasa located in Saharanpur. Zakariyya himself identified with no specific movements in the twentieth century, but he wrote the texts that were to become the mainstay of the Tablighi Jama'at movement of spiritual renewal. Centered close to the old fourteenth century shrine of Hazrat Nizamu'd Din, the movement began in the 1930s and became a transnational movement involving millions of Muslims across the world by the end of the twentieth century.

Zakariyya's life makes clear the interaction and shifting loyalties of activist Muslims in the middle decades of the twentieth century. Leaders of the Jamiyyat 'Ulama-i Hind and the Ahrar movement (both supportive of the Indian National Congress) as well as leaders of the emerging Tablighi Jama'at, visited him often, for example, and movements he disapproved of (like the socially radical Khaksar; the heretical, as it was seen, Ahmadiyya movement; and, ultimately, the Muslim League) stimulated lively discussion among him and his followers.

## The Variety of 'Islamic' Cultural and Political Life to 1947

This section includes essays that deal with some, though certainly not all, of the public symbols, ideologies, and movements that engaged Muslims in India in the late nineteenth and twentieth centuries. The first essay, from a volume appropriately entitled *Forging Identities*, takes up the topic of women, a central symbol in reciprocally constituting the identities of colonizer and colonized alike. The essay, again, takes up the issue of variety, teasing out three distinctive strands in Muslim thought about the character and role of women. The strands are associated respectively with the 'ulama, the westernizing elite of Aligarh, and a new Islamist leadership were secularly educated but who sought to speak for the Islamic tradition. The essay also, by focusing on competing texts produced for women, returns to the theme of the importance of vernacular print media, utilizing new genres and expressing new ideas, in the colonial and post-colonial world. The strands discussed are Muslim-specific. There needs to be far more work (beyond anything argued in the essay at hand) in understanding the nature and extent of what might be called the separate public worlds that emerged for religious groups in the colonial period. While Hindus, Muslims, and others who shared the same historical context, typically only spoke to their own co-religionists, however, they also often engaged the same issues, dynamics, and arguments.

Two articles on one of the best known Muslim nationalists, Hakim Ajmal Khan, follow.[20] Study of this humane and creative figure illumines the embrace, typically led by the westernized, of what might be called 'cosmopolitan' Muslim symbols—courtly culture, poetry in Persian and Urdu, music, and, of relevance here, the Greco-Arabic tradition of medicine. These 'worldly' symbols were not for the most part the concern of the 'ulama. To simply focus on such men as Ajmal Khan in terms of their larger political role, important as that is, is to miss the world of the families of physicians of indigenous medicine and their creative reorganizing and rethinking of traditions of the body and healing. It also misses, in his case, his rich spiritual life, and his deep personal bonds forged with both Muslims and non-Muslims even while his primary, at times anguished, concern was with the fate of his fellow Muslims. The second article particularly emphasizes Ajmal Khan's ever-widening circles beyond the city of Delhi, both politically and in relation to his medical work. It tries to ask why, across religious communities, indigenous traditions in such areas as medicine, art, and music have flourished in India, as they have not in many other colonized areas: that is, scholars can study a living tradition of *yunani tibb* in South Asia, for example, but not in the Middle East.

The final essay in this section, like the articles on Ajmal Khan, studies the transformative inter-war decades. The essay, while focusing on one new Islamic movement of that period, the quietist renewal movement of Tablighi Jama'at, illustrates the spread of normative practices, typically linked to upward social mobility, as well as the transition to new kinds of 'lay' leadership—patterns that run across all religions in this period. The social context, I argue, that gave rise to such movements is, broadly speaking, the same as that which gave rise to nationalism. The argument is intended in part to question 'religion' or 'communalism' as the opposite of modernity and nationalism and to see politicized religious identity, rather, as emerging in the same context, and under the same conditions, as nationalism. Another goal of the essay is to provide a historical context for movements like these whose participants insist that their behaviour represents patterns that are timeless. Finally, the essay seeks to show that a movement like Tablighi Jama'at challenges the assumption that all collective religious behaviour can be written, in some way or another, into the narratives of nationalism.

## Islam and Politics post-1947

This section opens with my 1995 presidential address to the Association of Asian Studies, an occasion I used to reflect on the tragic costs of religious nationalism in India, a subject that, alas, as noted above, continues to be all too current. I explore in particular the extent to which historical narratives have in fact been nationalist narratives and, in the case of a previously colonized area like India, ones shaped in what are often destructive ways as minorities are at once made the scapegoat for colonial subjugation and imagined as an 'Other' to an emerging majoritarian nationalist identity. The goal of the essay was to introduce some of the exciting work being done which questions the received narratives and to plead for professional historians to create new stories that, above all, do not treat Muslims as if 'Islam' put them not only outside the national community but also outside intelligible human behaviour and choices, responses, and life experiences.[21]

The next two articles discuss Islamic ideologies and arguments in Pakistan. The first yet again insists on recognizing that 'Islam' is interpreted in multiple ways and that the ideologies of the independent Muslim state have varied widely among Pakistanis and over time. I particularly emphasize in this essay the extent to which Pakistan did not at all come into being as an 'Islamic state' but rather, much like its contemporary Israel which was a product of European Zionist nationalism, as a homeland and refuge for members of a particular religion. Pakistan was conceived in the first instance as a secular state based on British constitutional models. Within twenty years, however, every aspect of the state's activities was called into question—economic, religious, and political. Zulfiqar Ali Bhutto came to power in 1971 on a platform called 'Islamic Socialist', and, with the loss of East Pakistan, this most worldly of leaders oversaw the end of an ideology of 'homeland' in favour of cultivation of a distinctively Islamic ideology that would reach its culmination under the leadership of the general who overthrew him. The meaning of Pakistan as an 'Islamic' state has changed through at least three dramatically different phases.

Chapter 10 addresses the third of these articulations, the Islamizing political ideology of General Ziaul Haq and his supporters in the Islamist movement (discussed briefly in Chapter 4) of the Jama'at-i Islami. I particularly describe the regulations issued during his rule, from 1977 to 1988, concerning women and the responses they provoked within Pakistan. Zia's rule was the period of 'jihad' directed against the Soviet invasion of Afghanistan, and Zia's power and resources were notably enhanced by his being the agent for United States and Saudi funding. Zia's Islamic policy was, understandably, welcomed by the Saudis, as well as, for expedient grounds, by the United States. The resultant vast expansion of madrasas, and the spillover of a 'jihadi' culture within Pakistan bore bitter fruit in the violence and sectarianism that beset the country in the 1990s.

## Islam, Society, and the Imagination of the Self

This final section discusses the writings of authors who have written about their own life experiences and, in the case of the poet Iqbal, explicitly about the nature of the individual self. The first article, dealing with Iqbal, continues, in part, to look at one of the variants of political ideology discussed in the previous section, namely the identification of symbols of 'Islam' with a charismatic community. Among these symbols were ones that pointed to lost worldly glory, here the Cordoba mosque of Andalusian Spain celebrated in one of Iqbal's best-known poems. At the same time, however, this poem represents a radical view of the individual creative self, forged in Iqbal's thought through interaction with German philosophers and Persian metaphysicians, that makes the self, represented in this case by the poet, an analogue to Allah/God as a creative force.

The attachment to symbols outside the geography of the Indian subcontinent, like the Cordoba mosque, was made into an accusation of 'disloyalty' and 'foreignness' against the Muslim minority. These symbols, however, when supported by Gandhi, to protect the Ottoman Caliphate after the First World War were never seen as carrying with them any geopolitical programme or assumption that India's Muslims 'belonged' to other nations. Rather, they fuelled nostalgia for better times, which took many forms in a colonized context, coupled often, in embrace of places like Cordoba, with denunciation of Europeans as conquerors and colonizers. The culminating theme of the Cordoba poem is the one most central to Iqbal: the need to awaken, here through recollection of the mosque, the creative, passionate self, which can recover a past glory of superiority over Europeans in morality as well as in the arts and sciences of civilization.

The next article reviews an under-studied genre of writing, pilgrimage narratives, in this case to the holy city of Mecca. The narratives, I suggest, offer a rare source for seeing the way Muslims over time have represented themselves in relation to the spaces they pass through in travel, the people and sights they encounter, and the symbols of the divine they engage. While obviously limited to those able and choosing to write, the genre seems to attract people from a very wide range of backgrounds. The accounts are constrained, as is all writing, by the conventions of the genre, but, nonetheless, even an initial survey of this literature suggests an increased, more novelistic, attention to the self. Further work is required to look systematically at interactions with other people, for example whether there are shifting patterns of communities (by class and religion, for example) with whom pilgrims interact, or changes in the way peoples outside India are presented.

Chapter 14 focuses on one particular hajj narrative, that of a well-known literary figure, Mumtaz Mufti, who describes himself as 'an unknown, ignorant, but sincere pilgrim' who astonishes himself as well as his secular, leftist friends, by even going to Mecca at all. I wrote the essay in part as a contribution to the controversy surrounding the attacks on Salman Rushdie starting in 1989 after the publication of his novel, *The Satanic Verses*. I wanted to show that in fact Muslims have a rich tradition of writing ironically, even phantasmagorically, about Islamic symbols. Mufti, for example, in a tradition as old as Ibn 'Arabi in the thirteenth century, imagines the Black Stone speaking to him, pictured as nothing less in his case than the radiant face of a *but* or idol of Hindu and Punjabi idolatry. Later he imagines Allah himself departing from the sanctuary in a procession of humble Africans, grief-filled at bringing their pilgrimage to an end. Mufti in his account, runs after them, sinks down, and sees God as a child, holding out his finger and tugging at the skirts of the pilgrims whom he asks to take him along.

In the appendices to this article I added three vignettes of material I had encountered over the years that had percolated in my thoughts as I studied Mufti's text. One described a 'mistake' on my part that brought me smack up against a different way of seeing the world, in this case the interpretation given to dreams. A second is of a conversation, paraphrased here, I had with an academic, a friend of a friend who knew my interest in hajj accounts and arranged the meeting. The conversation opened for me a whole world of longing for a dead father, along with an introduction to the power through meditation of reaching a world of mystic light and openings to the sainted dead. Finally, I include an oft-told anecdote of three great scholars of eighteenth century Delhi who were tested by a notable in order to rank them according to their spiritual greatness. The unexpected denouement of the story gave me a riveting lesson on cultural acceptance of people as they are, justified implicitly in this case by the old humoral theory that each person has a basic character or temperament, a *mizaj*, which is given, not attained.

The final brief chapter is a review essay of three biographies of historical figures: a Mughal queen, a French adventurer in the Mughal successor state of Awadh, and a distinguished Muslim nationalist intellectual. I used the review as the occasion to show that each author shaped the story of its subject's life by uncon-sciously assimilating it to a modern Western biographical notion of the self as autonomous, active in the world, and with charac-teristics developed chronologically. I was struck that the biogra-pher of each of these disparate figures ended the story on a note of poignant melancholy, reflecting in each case on the irony that the subject of the story had miscalculated his or her interests or friends. Identifying the implicit, almost uncannily similar, narra-tives of these authors was a way of suggesting a need for greater self-consciousness about the lenses through which scholars write about other people's lives.

The essays included in this volume represent an attempt to be attentive to Muslim voices. They are intended, however haltingly, to contribute to the study of a population too much neglected in scholarship in the English-speaking world. I am privileged to have worked in this area for many years, and grateful to those, especially in India and Pakistan, who have helped me with patience and generosity.

## Notes

i. I particularly thank my editor at Oxford University Press for her encouragement in putting together this volume and for her astute and constructive advice throughout.

ii. Chapter 8, below.

1. Asad, Talal. 1986. *The Idea of an Anthropology of Islam*. Occasional Paper Series. Washington DC: Georgetown University Center for Contemporary Studies.

2. Metcalf, Barbara Daly, ed. 1984. *Moral Conduct and Authority*. Berkeley: University of California Press.

3. See especially Asad, Talal. 1986. *The Idea of an Anthropology of Islam*. Occasional Paper Series, Washington, DC: Georgetown University Center for Contemporary Arab Studies.

4. Madani, Husain Ahmad. 1370/1953. *Maktubat Shaikhu'l-Islam* (The Correspondence of the Shaikh of Islam), Volume 4. Deoband: Maktaba Diniya. On the subject of Maulana Maududi, to Maulavi 'Abd ul Wahhab Khan, Lahore, see pp. 395–401.

5. Chakrabarty, Dipesh. 2000. *Provincializing Europe: Postcolonial Thought and Historical Difference*. Princeton: Princeton University Press.

6. Lila Abu-Lughod, commenting on this text, writes: 'There is an amazing document from South Asia (*Bihisti Zewar*) that illustrates the way Muslim thinkers can both be working within a separate Muslim tradition, using its

familiar tools and language, and yet be shaped by the colonial encounter.' Lila Abu-Lughod, 1998. 'Feminist Longings and Postcolonial Conditions', in Lila Abu-Lughod, ed., *Remaking Women: Feminism and Modernity in the Middle East*, p. 19. Princeton: Princeton University Press.

7. This is the title of the gem of a memoir written by Mohamed Ali (Lahore, Sh. Muhammad Ashraf, 1942). This section of the introduction draws on my keynote address to the annual meeting of the ASIA Network (St Petersburg Florida, 22 April 1995) called 'Studying Asia: A Personal Perspective'. I am grateful to Greg Gulden for inviting me to give this lecture as one of a series of autobiographical talks by scholars of Asia.

8. I do not mean by this comment that role models must share gender (or race or ethnicity) with those they influence. I include this comment as a kind of shorthand for the cultural norms at the time that did not encourage women to undertake professional studies.

9. These committees were 'joint' in being sponsored both by the Social Science Research Council and the American Council of Learned Societies.

10. Szanton, David. June 1976. 'South and Southeast Asia: New Concerns of the Council', *Items*, 30.2: 13–17.

11. Metcalf, Barbara Daly, ed. 1984. *Moral Conduct and Authority: The Place of Adab in South Asian Islam*. Berkeley: University of California Press.

12. Roff, William R., ed. 1987. *Islam and the Political Economy of Meaning*. Berkeley: University of California Press. See Chapter 10, below. Eickelmann, Dale F. and James Piscalori, eds. 1990. *Muslim Travellers: Pilgrimage, Migration, and Religious Imagination*. Berkeley: University of California Press. See Chapter 13, below. Metcalf, Barbara Daly, ed., 1996. *Making Muslim Space in North America and Europe*. Berkeley: University of California Press. Masud, Muhammad Khalid, Brinkley Messick, and David S. Powers, eds. 1996. *Islamic Legal Interpretation: Muftis and their Fatwas*. Cambridge: Harvard University Press. See Chapter 2, below. Masud, Muhammad Khalid, ed. 2000. *Travellers in Faith: Studies of the Tablighi Jama'at as a Transnational Islamic Movement for Faith Renewal*. Leiden: Brill respectively.

13. A similar impulse has shaped a very successful programme on Muslim societies at Washington University, St Louis, initially funded by the Rockefeller Foundation. I participated in a project organized by John Bowen on vernacular translations of sacred Arabic texts. A selection of the papers was published as a symposium in *The Journal of Asian Studies* 1993, 52, 3, including my contribution on hadith-based Urdu texts written for the Tablighi Jama'at, 'Living Hadith in the Tablighi Jama'at', pp. 584–608.

14. I discuss this subject in Chapter 8 below.

15. This chapter foreshadows my study of the early Deobandis published as Metcalf, Barbara Daly. 1982. *Islamic Revival in British India*. Princeton: Princeton University Press. Second edition, in 2002. New Delhi: Oxford University Press.

16. The term is used by Marshall Hodgson in Hodgson, Marshall. 1975. *The Venture of Islam*. 3 Volumes. Chicago: University of Chicago Press. To make clear that many patterns associated with Muslims may well be shared by non-Muslims and may not be linked to a system of theology, worship, and so forth.

17. Several works have subsequently studied the 'ulama and the madrasas. On the 'Barelvis' (who call themselves Ahlu's-Sunnat wa'l-Jama'at in order to assert that they are true Muslims, not a sect), see Sanyal, Usha. 1996. *Devotional Islam and Politics in British India: Ahmad Riza Khan Barelwi and His Movement, 1870–1920*. New Delhi; New York: Oxford University Press. On the Farangi Mahallis, whose important intellectual contribution is eclipsed in the twentieth century, see Robinson, Francis, 2001. *The 'Ulama of Farangi Mahall and Islamic Culture in South Asia*. London: C. Hurst. On the Ahl-i Hadith, we await the forthcoming dissertation from the University of Erfurt of Jan-Peter Hartung. For the experience of religious institutions in Pakistan, see Malik, Jamal. 1996. *Colonization of Islam: Dissolution of Traditional Institutions in Pakistan*. New Delhi: Manohar. A particularly important study is the recent work of Muhammad Qasim Zaman. *The Ulama in Contemporary Islam: Custodians of Change*, Princeton: Princeton University Press, 2002. See also Dalmia, Vasudha, 1997. *The Nationalization of Hindu Traditions: Bharatendu Harischandra and Nineteenth-Century Banaras*. New Delhi; New York: Oxford University Press.

18. Each article in the volume where this essay appeared includes a fatwa in translation along with analysis that asks questions about the topic, the forms of legal reasoning, the relation of the giver of the fatwa to the state, and so forth. Two articles of particular interest for students of Islam in India are: Masud, Muhammad Khalid. 'Apostasy and Judicial Separation in British India' and Sanyal, Usha. 'Are Wahhabis Kafirs? Ahmad Riza Khan Barelwi and his *Sword of the Haramayn*', in Masud, Muhammad Khalid, Brinkley Messick, and David S. Powers, eds. 1996. *Islamic Legal Interpretation: Muftis and their Fatwas*. Cambridge: Harvard University Press, pp. 193–213.

19. See Robinson, Francis, 2000. 'Islam and the Impact of Print in South Asia', in *Islam and Muslim History in South Asia*, pp. 66–104. New Delhi: Oxford University Press.

20. Although I use the phrase 'nationalist Muslim' in the title of the first article, I must note that scholars increasingly try to problematize this common usage because of its implication that other Muslims are not nationalist; there is no equivalent usage for members of other religious traditions.

21. The issue of the narratives of Indian history within India, and especially in school texts, has only become more pressing since this essay was written. See the many publications of the Safdar Hashmi Memorial Trust (SAHMAT) including 'The Saffron Agenda in Education: An Expose', 2001, 'The Assault on History', 2002, 'Against Communalization of Education', 2002, and, 'Saffronised and Substandard: A Critique of the New NCERT Textbooks', 2002.

# I

# New Roles, New Contestations, for the 'Ulama

I

New Roles, New Contestations,
for the 'Ulama

# 1

## The Madrasa at Deoband
### A Model for Religious Education
### in Modern India

A recent conference of specialists on the study of Muslims in
South Asia identified as one of the neglected areas of the field, the
study of traditional religious institutions in the modern period.
Such institutions as the Sufi orders, the religious schools, and
the system of pious endowments have been treated, if at all, only
in their relation to political developments.[1] Thus the leading
theological academy of modern India, the Dār ul-'Ulūm of Deoband, has been studied because many of its ulama played an
important role in the nationalist politics in India and opposed the
foundation of Pakistan. That motive for study has seriously
distorted the treatment of the nineteenth century history of
the school, endowing it with an anti-British and revolutionary
character when, in fact, the school's concerns were totally apolitical.[2] An investigation of the early history of the school suggests
many other significant historical themes, notably an important
incipient trend toward a formal bureaucratization of the ulama
and their institutions. Studies of religious institutions outside
India such as Gilsenan's study of the Hamidiya Shadhiliya order
in modern Egypt[3] and Roff's study of the Majlis Ugama in
Malaysia[4] suggest that successful functioning in the modern period
has required such a transformation in organizational structure.
This article describes the organization of Deoband in its initial
decades.

## The Organization of Deoband

The madrasa at Deoband began modestly in 1867 in an old mosque, the Chatta Masjid, under a spreading pomegranate tree which still stands. The first teacher and the first pupil, in a coincidence deemed auspicious, were both named Maḥmūd: Mullā Maḥmūd, the teacher, and Maḥmūd Ḥasan, the pupil, who was later to become the school's most famous teacher. Despite the timeless atmosphere surrounding its inauguration, however, the school from its inception was unlike earlier madrasas. The founders emulated the British bureaucratic style for educational institutions instead of the informal familial pattern of schools then prevalent in India. The school was, in fact, so unusual that the annual printed report, itself an innovation, made continuing efforts to explain the organization of the novel system. The school was, notably, a distinct institution, not an adjunct to a mosque or home. As soon as possible, it acquired classrooms and a central library. It was run by a professional staff and its students were admitted for a fixed course of study and required to take examinations for which due prizes were awarded at a yearly public convocation. A series of affiliated colleges was even set up, many ultimately staffed by the school's own graduates and their students examined by visiting Deobandis. Financially, the school was wholly dependent on public contributions, mostly in the form of annual pledges, not on fixed holdings of *waqf*, pious endowments contributed by noble patrons.

In older schools, like the famous Farangī Maḥall in Lucknow, family members taught students in their own homes: there was no central library, no course required of each student, no series of examinations. After a student had read a certain book with his teacher, he would receive a certificate, a *sanad*, testifying to his accomplishment, then seek another teacher or return home. The Farangī Maḥall family depended primarily on revenue from their endowments and on the largesse of princes. The ulama of the school cultivated intellectual interests and trained students to become government servants. The Deobandi 'ulama, in contrast, sought to create a body of religious leaders able to serve the daily legal and spiritual needs of their fellow Muslims apart from government ties.

The structure of the school encouraged the effective pursuit of such a goal and the opportunity for influence over a wide geographic area. The founders had seen the efficiency of a variety of British institutions in pursuing specific goals. Many of them including three Deputy Inspectors of the Education Department, were government servants; some had attended schools like the Delhi College; and now all confronted with concern the influential missionary societies. In dealing with these institutions, they learned their methods and chose to compete with them on equivalent terms. They were familiar as well with a system of formal structure from the days of the Mughals. Then, however, the court had provided a framework of patronage and responsibility for the judicial and educational work of the 'ulama. Now the 'ulama had to create a structure themselves. In doing so successfully, they laid a foundation for effective influence in a modern society. The school produced ulama, recruited from a widespread area, who disseminated a uniform religious ideology to many Muslims who welcomed teachings that emphasized common bonds among Muslims rather than local ones.

In setting up the school on a formal basis, the founders faced two critical problems: the definition of a rationale for relations among members and the establishment of a secure system of financing. One of the leading founders, Maulānā Muḥammad Qāsim, enunciated eight fundamental principles dealing with these issues for the guidance of the initial members of the school. The relations of those associated with the school called for special attention since the school was not in the hands of a single family, subject to the understood and accepted norms of kin behaviour. The personnel consisted of the teaching staff, the administrators, and a consultative council. The staff comprised about a dozen members, ranked by learning with the entire Arabic faculty given precedence over the Persian. There were three administrators: the *sarparast*, the rector, the patron and guide of the institution; the *mohtamim*, the chancellor, the chief administrative officer; and the *ṣadr modarris*, the chief teacher or principal, the person responsible for instruction. In 1892 a fourth administrator, the *muftī*, was added to supervise the dispensation of judicial opinions on behalf of the school. The consultative council was composed of the administrators and seven additional members.[5]

The rules called on all to subordinate personal interests in striving for common goals. Members were to demonstrate openness and tolerance in dealing with each other, engaging in mutual consultation not on the basis of position but on that of the value of their ideas. The principles were as follows:

The councillors of the madrasa should always keep in mind its well-being. There should be no rigidity of views, and for this reason it is important that they never hesitate to express an opinion and that listeners hear it with an open mind. So...if we understand another's idea [to be better], even if it is against us, we will accept it wholly.... For this same reason it is necessary that the *mohtamim* always seek advice of councillors, whether those who are the permanent councillors of the madrasa or others who possess wisdom and understanding and are well-wishers of the school.... Let no individual be unhappy if on a certain occasion he is not asked for advice.... If, however, the *mohtamin* asks no one, all the councillors should object.

It is essential that the teachers of the madrasa be in accord and, unlike the worldly ulama, not be selfish and intolerant of others.

Instruction should be that already agreed on, or later agreed on by consultation.[6]

The last principle was particularly significant, asking the teachers to forego individual inclinations in the interest of a common programme.

Rafī 'ud-Dīn, *mohtamim* from 1872 to 1889, further formalized Muḥammad Qāsim's guidelines for the institution by giving precedence to the council over staff and administration. He insisted that grievances be presented to the council directly. Moreover, he urged that the power of the *mohtamim* be limited by curtailing the amount of money available for use at his discretion. In 1887 he wrote: 'All decisions are made by the consultative council. Even I, though the *mohtamim*, present here in the school for twenty years, will be removed if they see fit.'[7] By having the council so central, the school was freed of both instability and personal whim. No one person either by virtue of his administrative position or by his seniority within the family, was to dominate the school.

A second cluster of principles dealt with the new system of financing. The system arose in part because the founders had no option but to find an alternative to the increasingly insecure princely grants. Muslim princes of states like Hyderabad, Bhopal, and Rampur did, to be sure, patronise learning and extend their bounty across the border to their fellows in British India. Large landlords in an area like the United Provinces did dispense some of their wealth for religious causes. But such contributions could never be as substantial as those of the days of Mughal rule, nor could they be as certain in a period of economic, social, and administrative flux. Nor were the ulama willing to accept British grants-in-aid, for such help was precarious and carried as well the taint of its non-Muslim source. Therefore, the Deobandis solicited annual pledges from their supporters, a method learned from missionary associations. The system was complex, requiring careful records and dependent on the new facilities of postal service, money orders, and even the printing press. Thanks to the last, the annual proceedings were able to publish widely the list of donors who thus received recognition for their generosity. The donors were listed in the order of the size of their gift, but even the humblest contributor was included. The Deobandis also encouraged single gifts in both cash and kind. Especially in the early days of the school people donated books, food for the students, and household items to furnish the school. Groups of people also organized collections of hides of animals left from the 'Id sacrifice, selling them and sending the proceeds to the school. People were encouraged to designate their contributions as *zakāt*, the obligatory alms which in other eras was collected by the state. The resultant network of donors formed a base not only for financial support but for dissemination of Deobandi teachings.

Five of Muḥammad Qāsim's eight principles dealt with this new financial arrangement. They stressed the obligation of all associated with the school to encourage donations of cash and food. They also pointed out the spiritual advantage of poverty in fostering unity by drawing the personnel of the school together.

First, the workers of the madrasa should, as best they can, keep in view the increase of donations; and should encourage others to share this same concern....

The well-wishers of the madrasa should always make efforts to secure the provision of food for the students, indeed, they should try to increase the food.

As long as the madrasa has no fixed sources of income, it will, God willing, operate as desired. And if it gain any fixed income, like *jāgīr* holdings, factories, trading interests or pledges from nobles, then the madrasa will lose the fear and hope which inspire submission to God and will lose His hidden help. Disputes will begin among the workers. In matters of income and buildings...let there be a sort of deprivation.

The participation of government and wealthy is harmful.

The contributions of those who expect no fame from their gifts is a source of blessing. The honesty of such contributors is a source of stability.[8]

In fact, many wealthy people were among the donors and many, no doubt, did expect and receive recognition in return. Still, the system of popular support was effective, both financially and symbolically, and became a model for new religious schools. Other schools, like Farangī Maḥall, which clung to support from landed wealth, have in part for this reason disappeared.

The formal organization of the school was supplemented by associational ties of origin, family, and educational experience. Such ties were not incompatible with a formal system, for in India informal patronage and apprenticeship were characteristic of both the Mughal and the British bureaucracy at least until the end of the nineteenth century. The formal organization of posts does not wholly reveal the lines of influence of Deoband.

The two dominant figures in the school's first decades were Muḥammad Qāsim and Rashīd Aḥmad, both of leading *shaikh* families of the area,[9] sometime students together in Delhi, and common disciples of Ḥājjī Imādullāh in the Chishti order. Muḥammad Qāsim was *sarparast* until his death in 1879, but shunned an active administrative role for fear of tainting the school's reputation because of his participation in the Mutiny.[10] For the first three years of the school, he did not even come to Deoband but stayed at his printing work in Meerut. Nonetheless his influence was central. Rafī' ud-Dīn, the *mohtamim*, said: 'There was such closeness between Muḥammad Qāsim and myself that whatever was in his heart, I knew.... I did what was revealed to him.'[11] Rashīd Aḥmad did not initially hold any formal post but was absent in Gangoh, occupied as Sufi *shaikh*, teacher of hadith, and jurist. However, he, too, was a great force in organizing and shaping the school.

A special bond existed between many because of common allegiance to a Sufi order, particularly so for the many who were disciples of Imādullāh. In general, allegiance to the Chishti order predominated at the school. Moreover, most were *shaikh* in family and many closely related to each other. Muḥammad Ya'qūb Nanautawī, the first principal (1867–96) and Zu'lfaqār 'Ali, Deputy Inspector in the Education Department and a member of the council for forty years, were brothers and cousins of Muḥammad

Qāsim. Muḥammad Munīr Nanautawī, who served as *mohtamim* for one year, 1894–5, was also a cousin of this family, as was Mahtāb 'Alī, a resident of Deoband and a member of the council. Shaikh Nihāl Aḥmad, a ra'is and scholar of Deoband descended from the Mughal diwan Shaikh Luṭfullāh, was also a member of the council. His sister was married to Muḥammad Qāsim and he himself married Qāsim's elder sister in order to set an example of widow remarriage.[12] Fazl-i Ḥaqq, a member of the council and briefly *mohtamim*, was a cousin of Saiyid 'Ābid Ḥusain, a revered elder of Deoband and the first *mohtamim.* In a society where family and clan were so important, such relationships among members of a common enterprise were typical. At Deoband, however, they were to give way to greater diversity in geographic and social origin and to ties based not on kin but on personal achievement and interest. Such a development was implicit in the organization of the school.

## The System of Instruction

The goal of the school was to train well-educated 'ulama dedicated to scriptural Islam. Such 'ulama would become prayer leaders, writers, preachers, and teachers and thus disseminate their learning in turn. To this end the school set formal requirements for admission and matriculation. Local students were admitted to study Persian or Qur'ān, but the Arabic students, roughly three-quarters of the whole, were required to have already studied Persian to the level of the *Gulistān*, to have completed the Qur'ān, and to pass an examination.[13] Only half of those examined were admitted. There were seventy-eight students in the first year, rapidly increasing to a constant two to three hundred for the rest of the century.

Students were expected to study a fixed and comprehensive body of learning in the course of a programme of studies originally scheduled for ten years, later reduced to six. They were not to come informally, sit at the feet of a particular teacher, then move on to another master and another centre of learning. Rather, in this one place, the school claimed, students would be trained in the specialites of the three great intellectual centres of north India: *manqūlāt*, the revealed studies of hadith or tradition and Qur'an associated with Delhi; and *ma'qūlāt*, the rational studies of *fiqh* or law, logic, and philosophy associated with the two eastern cities of Lucknow and Khairabad.[14] Basically, the school taught the *dars-i niẓāmī*, the curriculum evolved at Farangī Maḥall in the eighteenth century that spread throughout India. They made, however, important modifications, particularly in their emphasis on the two subjects of hadith and *fiqh*. These were to be the basis of their popular teaching. In law they stressed not jurisprudence but correct performance of ritual and ceremonial duties. In hadith they greatly expanded the offerings of the Niẓāmī curriculum. Instead of requiring only a summary (the *Mishkāt ul-Masābīh* of al-Ghazālī), they included in their entirety the six classical collections of the precedents of the Prophet. They deemed hadith, the basis of correct practice and belief, the crowning subject. The most influential teacher was the *shaikh ul-hadith* at the school, and only good students were encouraged to study the subject: 'Once a follower asked Rashīd Aḥmad to inaugurate a student's study of Tirmiẓī... for the student's understanding was deficient. Rashīd Aḥmad answered: "When that is the case, teach a student *fiqh* or Urdu or Persian [but not hadith]"'.[15] Moreover, the school de-emphasized the so-called rational sciences, logic and philosophy, that had been the chief distinction of the Niẓāmī teaching.

There was actual opposition led by Rashīd Aḥmad to teaching these rational sciences at all. He felt that the subjects were a waste of time and that the only merit in studying them was preparation for their refutation.[16] Muḥammad Qāsim, in sympathy with this position, felt that students should study, if anything, the 'new philosophy' of the West, not that derived from the Greeks. Rashīd Aḥmad even argued that philosophy was opposed to the sharī'a, but he primarily emphasized that such study was trivial in contrast to study embodying the revealed truth of religion. Many of the staff and council were cautious, however, and wanted students to read the books of logic and philosophy to ensure their getting jobs. Despite Rashīd Aḥmad's indignant response—'Would you clean latrines to get a job?'—the books that had initially been eliminated from the curriculum did gradually creep back.[17]

There were no spokesmen for including English or Western subjects. Muḥammad Qāsim insisted that the school was not opposed to such study, but simply wanted to avoid duplication of government efforts.[18] Students could, he insisted, continue in government schools after completing their studies at Deoband, but

even when the curriculum was reduced to six years, few continued
beyond that long course. Thus, with no new subjects and philosophy gradually restored, the curriculum was not dramatically
innovative. It was, however, to become famous for its emphasis
on hadith, a subject that provided material for popular teaching
and influence.

In technique of instruction there were modifications. Indeed,
many thought the school to be a continuation of the old Delhi
College, not only because of the continuity of personnel and the
modern organization of the school, but also because of the style
of teaching.[19] The technique of Arabic instruction, for example,
was the British one of translation into Urdu and from Urdu into
Arabic. Later, the exercise of monthly compositions written in
Arabic was added in order to improve fluency and command of
the language.[20] Most important, the school continued the use of
Urdu, not Persian, as a medium of instruction and thus shared in
the general trend of the times toward the development of the
modern vernaculars. Students came, even within the first years of
the school's existence, from places as distant as Afghanistan and
Chittagong, Patna, and Madras, but all were to return with a
common language in Urdu.[21] Even those who were of north India
often spoke a dialect in their homes and now acquired a standard
form of the language. Like the westernizing college at Aligarh,
Deoband was instrumental in establishing Urdu as a language of
communication among the Muslims of India. Such a change was
obviously central to enhanced bonds among the ulama and
between them and their followers.

An abortive innovation on the part of the school was the
inclusion of training in crafts and trades. There was hope that
students, thus trained, could support themselves in villages and
small towns and, simultaneously, share the benefits of their
religious training with their neighbours. This would, no doubt,
have furthered the influence of the 'ulama, but the plan came to
nought because the students deemed such work unsuitable. There
was also talk of teaching surveying and cartography in order to
provide students with skills for jobs with the expanded public
works department of the government.[22] But even this plan did
not materialize. The preference for intellectual work and its
concomitant status was too strong. Only two kinds of vocational
training had any place at the school: calligraphy and *ṭibb* or *yūnānī*

medicine. Both were considered suitable activities for the 'ulama, related to the religious activities of copying manuscripts and healing their followers. In 1873 a skilled calligrapher joined the staff to train students for work at the increasingly important lithographic presses.[23] As for *ṭibb*, some, like Rashīd Aḥmad, opposed its inclusion, for they saw it, like philosophy, as distraction from more important matters.[24] However, the school did make *ṭibb* a part of its curriculum at the end of the century. It was the religious sciences, unchanged in substance, which the school primarily taught.

Students were tested on the results of their study. The examinations were an innovation in Arabic madrasas and hence extensively described in the school's annual reports. During a student's first two years, they were simply oral; in the subsequent four years, they were written. The staff took pride in the difficulty of the exams, for there were no optional questions, only five required ones on each book with each answer accorded twenty points. The students were supervised to prevent cheating and identified their examination by number only to ensure objectivity on the part of the examiners. The school was not organized by classes, but by books, so that if a student failed one book he would repeat that but not the others. The students, in fact, did well in their exams and few failed.[25]

At an annual convocation, prizes were awarded to those with the highest grades. *Sanad*s were also distributed, describing the books each student had completed during the year, and commenting on the character, capacity, and skill of the student as well. Those who had completed the entire course and were considered truly outstanding were sometimes awarded a *dastār*, a turban, which was wound on their head by the *sarparast*. The granting of turbans took place on only four occasions, at irregular intervals, and was finally given up after 1909. Those who received turbans were considered to possess both brilliance and exemplary personal qualities, including mastery of cultured language.[26]

As the criteria for distinction indicate, the school sought to shape the character as well as the intellect of the students. A regimen was instituted for their personal lives. They were required to promise that they would be devoted to their studies and obedient to their teachers. Should they nonetheless miss classes, they were deprived of food and if they generally failed to work, they

were simply expelled.[27] John Palmer, a government official who
toured the school in 1875, reported that teachers treated their
students with severity but was impressed by the explanation that
the staff deemed it beneficial to train students while young to have
a sense of work.[28] Except for the Friday holiday and one month
each year, the students did indeed work continually.

They were expected to live respectably but modestly. The school
provided not only books and instruction free of charge but a
collection of necessities for each boy as well: four suits of clothes
each year, two pairs of shoes, a cotton quilt, money for laundry,
oil and matches for light, and medicine and care when sick. At the
end of the century the school established a boarding house. Previously, students had lodged in homes and mosques and received
food from individuals or from the residents of a *mohalla* jointly.
In the boarding house, modelled on those newly established at
Aligarh and the government schools, their daily life was put under
the close supervision of the staff. In that setting, moreover, the
students formed close bonds with each other. Such bonds transcended those of kin and locality and prepared the students for
mutual cooperation and participation not only in religious activities but in government, voluntary associations, and politics.[29]

The faculty was, of course, the chief influence on the students.
They were as a group dedicated to their work. Almost all of the
leading teachers were offered positions in princely states or
government service, but stayed at the school in return for small
salaries of ten or fifteen rupees each month. In 1872, a year of few
contributions, the teachers simply reduced their salaries and
advanced students voluntarily and took on the burden of aiding
them with lessons.[30] Not all the teachers were of equal skill, and
those entrusted with the rational sciences—not surprisingly, given
the emphasis of the school—tended to be less distinguished. Logic
was taught for many years by an Afghan, Maulānā Ghulām Rasūl,
whom the students claimed to be unable to understand.[31] However, there were always a few outstanding teachers. Among them
in the early years was Rashīd Aḥmad who taught hadith to students
in Gangoh.

He was the true successor of Shāh Walīullāh and people came from places
like Bengal, Madras, and Punjab to study from him. He would begin his
teaching of hadith with Tirmiẕī and impress on each student the
interpretation and meaning of the work in simple words. He was very

patient, and often repeated his explanations. For example, he would take a simple word like 'aṭṭārah, perfumer's wife, which I recall him defining three times for an Afghan student, each time in simpler language. He always taught after ablution and required the same of his students. If they got tired he would amuse them with jokes and anecdotes until their stomachs hurt. Then, refreshed, they would be able to go on. He would tell a story so seriously that others laughed the more. Then he would become formal again, maintaining that respect and awe necessary for a teacher. His teaching was unique in that he spoke in accordance with each student's capacity.... His memory was so extraordinary that he could cite the page of a relevant hadith in the saḥīḥ collection.... His students became his lovers, but he considered himself nothing.[32]

After Muḥammad Qāsim's death, Rashīd Aḥmad became *sarparast* of both Deoband and its sister school, the Maẓāhir ul-ʿUlūm in Saharanpur. Like the other great elders of the school, despite his eminence, he was known for his kindness to the students and was not above chiding those he felt did not treat the students generously.

A second great teacher long associated with the school was Maulānā Maḥmūd Ḥasan. He had sought out Muḥammad Qāsim in the printing houses of Meerut and Delhi in order to be one of the few to undergo his demanding teaching of hadith.[33] When Maḥmūd Ḥasan completed his education in 1873 he joined the staff of the school and for the next forty years was a dominating influence in its teaching and administration. He was a man of extraordinary energy, teaching ten lessons each day, writing, caring for Muḥammad Qāsim in his final illness. He was devoted to the school and resisted all invitations to leave it. His fame was especially great in hadith; and, his biographer notes, in the course of his career he taught over a thousand students from such distant places as Kabul, Qandahar, Balkh, Bukhara, Mecca, Medina, and Yeman.[34] Among them were Anwar Shāh Kashmīrī, Shabīr Aḥmad Osmānī, and Ḥāfiz Muḥammad Aḥmad, the leaders of the third generation of ulama at the school.

For the students the years at the school were intensive and formative, providing them not only with intellectual skills, but shaping their personalities and relationships. Ḥusain Aḥmad Madanī, a student at the school at the end of the century, wrote a description of his experiences:

I took up residence with my brothers in a room near the home of Maulānā Maḥmūd Ḥasan. My brothers asked him to initiate my studies as a blessing; and he, assembling a group of ulama, directed Maulānā Khalīl Ahmad to begin my instruction. I was then in my twelfth year, but I was very small. Because a boy so small, from such a distance, was unusual, I was treated with great kindness. I would go to my teachers' houses to help with writing and accounts and received great kindness from the wife of Mahmūd Hasan in particular.

But whatever small freedom I had at home was now gone. My eldest brother beat me often, and never showed me even the occasional kindness my father had. My brother taught me Persian and I also studied from Maulānā Mahmūd Hasan after hours.

I rapidly advanced beyond those in my classes. During the years from 1890 to 1898 I studied from Maulānās Zu'lfaqār 'Alī, 'Abd ul-'Alī, Khalīl Ahmad, Mahmūd Hasan, Muftī 'Azīz ur-Rahmān, Ghulām Rasūl, Manfa 'at 'Ali, and Habīb ur-Rahmān. We studied the books of the *dars-i Nizāmī* ...which was used in the Arabic schools of Hindustan. There were some books of literature, mathematics, and medicine which I could not complete because of our departure for Medina.

I never had much enthusiasm for study and would not review my books. I did well in the beginning books on which there was only an oral exam, but did not do so well in the later written ones.... The night before the exam I would study the whole book, drinking tea, and having snacks whenever I felt sleepy; for I always needed much sleep, and especially felt sleepy when reading. After my first failure, I did better, and I often attained distinguished marks. The exams were very hard in comparison with those of the government schools where there was a choice. Deoband was unique among the Arabic schools in enforcing such a high standard, supervising exams to see that a student had no help.... Unfortunately the education in many of the other schools was defective. When students from here entered other institutions or studied English they were always most distinguished. ˥ ᴅₑₒᵦₐₙ𝒹

˻ Although I never liked work, gradually my intellectual inclination and balance of character grew. At first my interest was logic and philosophy, then literature, and finally hadith.[35] ˺

This account tells much about student life. There appears to have been a closeness between teachers and students, illustrated by the attention of teachers to their students' well-being and, in this case, by the services rendered to the teachers by the students. There was, moreover, a sense of being unique, of being in a school that was better than the others, harder even than the English schools. From this closeness and discipline, Husain Ahmad indicates, he was encouraged to shape his intellectual interests in the direction of those dominant at the school.

At the school, moreover, he received his first spiritual training, taking a member of the staff as a guide. Both he and his eldest brother were disciples of Rashīd Aḥmad; his other brother, of Maḥmūd Ḥasan. In later years all three would return to the school from Medina whenever they came to India in search of brides or in connection with other family business and would always seek advice from their sufi shaikhs and even undertake further study. Ḥusain Aḥmad went on to be a pillar of the school, a distinguished scholar, and a leading figure in nationalist politics. In ulama like him the school fulfilled its goal of preserving the learned tradition and providing a structure of religious leadership for Muslims without the support of the state.

## Two Controversies

Despite such success on the part of the school, there were people who opposed its style of organization. As a result, two major crises arose in the initial decades of the school's existence. The first, in 1876, concerned the issue of erecting separate buildings for the school; the second, in 1895, of opposition to the school's administrative personnel. Both, generally speaking, were resolved in favour of those who supported the original bureaucratic conception of the institution.

At issue in the first quarrel was the question of the school's existence as a distinct institution. At first it did operate in mosques and rented buildings. But the founders, or most of them, held to the idea that the school should have a building of its own. The idea was a new one, and even Muḥammad Qāsim initially felt that a fine building might encourage pride.[36] He was ultimately persuaded of the value of a separate building by the insistence of his teacher, Maulānā Aḥmad 'Alī Sahāranpūrī, that it would be conducive to the independence and efficient running of the school. Muḥammad Qāsim himself recognized the problems of lodging students in mosques when there were hundreds of them, not just an occasional few. The *qaum* of students, he noted, was a free one, and there would be endless complaints of broken vessels, lost lanterns, and other such problems.[37]

Practical considerations aside, there was a symbolic motive in establishing separate buildings for the school. With Mughal decline there were no princes to construct the grand tombs, city mosques, ceremonial gateways, and forts which had been the material statement on the physical landscape of the existence of Muslim culture and society. Rather, through the efforts of the 'ulama and other pious people, madrasas and mosques became not only the loci of the organization of their religious life but also the concrete evidence of the Muslim presence. Separate madrasas had heretofore not been characteristic of Muslim architecture in India, perhaps because the 'ulama and their law schools had not been central in organizing Muslim communal life. Now schools like Deoband served that function and symbolized Muslim culture. The early buildings at Deoband were domed and arched in the style of imperial structures. Early in this century, for example, the school used money donated by the Amir of Afghanistan to construct a grand ceremonial outer gate which particularly evoked an imperial motif.[38]

The leading opponent of constructing the first building was Saiyid 'Ābid Ḥusain, the first *mohtimim* and a man of such great influence that one associate observed that even the sultan of the Turks could not control Deoband without his aid; and another suspected that even the jinn obeyed him.[39] He preferred an informal associational style of education, with no formal buildings. He mainly argued that a separate building would be too expensive and urged instead the building of additional cells, *hujras*, in the new Jāmi' Masjid. In 1871 when he returned from hajj he took up the supervision of the building of that mosque instead of his previous post of *mohtamim*. He used this position to build *hujras*, despite the decision of the council in favour of a proper building.[40] He thus differed with the council not only on a matter of substance but on the legitimacy of their authority to make binding decisions on all associated with the school.

A contemporaneous account claimed that Ḥājjī 'Ābid had the support of the townspeople in this dispute. The nature of this support is difficult to analyse since, the account continued, because of Muḥammad Qāsim's stature 'even though peoples' faces changed, they said nothing.'[41] Presumably Ḥājjī 'Ābid's support was based on his deep personal influence and not on the issue itself. Those active in the dispute, however, were united by a position of principle, not by kin or personal ties. The entire administration supported the cause of a new building. Rafī' ud-Dīn even dreamed of divine indications of the precise spot where it should be built.[42]

Finally, in 1876 Muḥammad Qāsim announced that there would be a new building without indicating whether it would be separate or part of the Jāmiʿ Masjid. He hoped that once the announcement was made Ḥājjī ʿĀbid would accept its being separate. Muḥammad Qāsim set the date for the foundation stone to be laid after a Friday congregational prayer at which he would preach. At the end of his sermon he announced that the school had purchased the *maidān* in front of the *maḥall-i dīwān* and that the new building would be built there.[43] Ḥājjī ʿĀbid cried out in shock. Muḥammad Qāsim, insisting that the decision was a correct one, urged him to join the throng which was then moving to the *maidān* to lay the foundation stone. But Ḥājjī Sāhib left, enraged, and retired to the Chattah Masjid. Muḥammad Qāsim followed him there, touched his feet with his hands, and said to him: 'You are our elder, and we, your younger. You cannot leave us, nor we, you'.[44] Both wept. Reconciled by Muḥammad Qāsim's moving act of personal humility and by the inevitability of the new building, Ḥājjī ʿĀbid agreed to attend the ceremony. Three distinguished elders then laid the foundation stone: Ḥaẓrat Mīyānjī Munē Shāh, a revered *saiyid* and elder; Maulānā Aḥmad ʿAlī, the great hadith scholar of Saharanpur; and Ḥājjī ʿĀbid himself, as representative of the council. The decision made and the work begun, 'everyone's heart felt a strange joy', concluded a historian of the event.[45]

This first building was completed within five years. Like many later buildings, it was financed by a special group of donors, in this case one organized in Hyderabad.[46] The mosque was the special contribution of a wealthy trader, Seṭh Ghulām Muḥammad ʿAzam. The hostel, completed in 1898, was built through the support of the princes of Hyderabad, Chattari, and Bhopal. Ḥājjī ʿĀbid and the people of the town came to accept and take pride in these buildings. There were other occasions when Ḥājjī ʿĀbid differed with other members of the school.[47] The annual reports account for his occasional withdrawal from the school by his preoccupation with his many followers. In fact, he long failed to appreciate the formal, modern format of the school, and its extra-local character.

These issues reappeared in the dispute of 1895, a crisis that lasted longer and was of potentially greater danger to the school. The opponents in this case were leaders of the town whose attempts to gain control of the school were perhaps not unexpected. Muḥammad Qāsim had early set the rule that the councillors should be 'ulama and not 'respectable people', *arbāb-i wijāhat*, in order to ensure that the religious quality of the school would be preserved and that the school itself would not merely be an institution of the town, subject to its local problems and constraints.[48]

Internal problems gave the townsmen an opportunity to criticize the school. In 1892 Ḥājjī 'Ābid Husain, again unwilling to accept a decision of the council, resigned from his post as *mohitimim*. He objected on this occasion to the decision to reduce the pay of a recalcitrant teacher who was felt to compromise the school by resorting to government courts. He also used the occasion to argue in vain that most of the dozen teachers at the school should be fired and only two or three of the very good ones kept. Maḥmūd Ḥasan, who, by this time, was clearly the school's best teacher, supported the continuation of a proper staff and simply insisted that if anyone went it would be he.[49] New crises built on this one.

The council next appointed Maulānā Faẓl-i Ḥaqq Nanautawī, an original member of the council and 'Ābid's sometime aide, as the new *mohitimim*. He was discovered shortly after his appointment to have been guilty of a minor embezzlement of some seventy rupees. Rashīd Aḥmad, as member of the council and *sarparast*, prevailed in his opinion that whatever the repercussions, he be asked to resign. The campaign of the dissidents then began with letters to Rashīd Aḥmad objecting to Faẓl-i Ḥaqq's removal. Rashīd Aḥmad answered them by explaining that he was answerable only to the contributors, an assertion of the non-local character of the school.[50]

Once Faẓl-i Ḥaqq had resigned, the council appointed the venerable Maulānā Munīr Nanautawī, of Muḥammad Qāsim's family, to take his place. They also added two new members to the council: Muḥammad Aḥsan Nanautawī, the teacher and publisher who was also a member of the family, and Ḥājjī Shaikh Ẓahūr ud-Dīn Deōbandī, a favoured disciple of Muḥammad Qāsim. They joined two others who had been appointed during the previous decade, Maulānā Ziyā 'ud-Dīn Rāmpūrī, a revered shaikh, and Ḥakīm Mushtāq Aḥmad of Deoband.[51] Despite the presence of such distinguished elders, the dissidents continued to speak of the school's decline and bad management. Not surprisingly, active among the critics were relatives of Faẓl-i Ḥaqq, prominent citizens of the town who chafed at his disgrace.

The opposition crystallized in the formation of 'The Reform Committee of the Arabic Madrasa of Deoband' which sent out five hundred copies of a complaint against the school which invited supporters to be present at a meeting.[52] It charged that the 'waqf' of Deoband had become the private property of the council members who included two brothers as members and four of their sons as teachers at the school.[53] The pamphlet argued that by the standard of either the shari'a or of the government, such nepotism was inappropriate. They reminded their readers of the importance Muhammad Qāsim had attached to the cooperation of the people of the town, for whom they claimed to be the spokesmen, and insisted that they had no personal antagonism to the school. The statement had twenty-six signatures, headed by three members of the 'municipality', that is, men who had attained influence through the new local government institutions inaugurated by the British. Two were wakils, one a former revenue official, another a ziladar. One identified himself as a maulavi, three as ḥāfiẓ who had memorized the Qur'ān, and four as hajji. Eight began their names with shaikh. The group was thus, presumably, drawn from the most influential of the town's residents, led by men who filled the local councils set up by the British.

Among those who attended the meeting were a dozen men from Delhi, Meerut, and Muzaffarnagar, who were staunch defenders of the school; and they, in the end, dominated the meeting. They accused the critics of seeking their own personal goals against the welfare of the school and of engaging in such despicable tactics as going from mohalla to mohalla to encourage the townsmen to stop their contributions for the students. They also accused them of spreading reports against the school in the newspapers as, indeed, one extant item in the Tūtī-yi Hind of Meerut confirms. In it was reported a sermon given in the Jāmi' Masjid by Munshī 'Abd ur-Razzāq, a member of the municipality and signatory of the circular, who claimed that Ḥājjī 'Ābid had severed his connection with the school and asked that the government intervene in the interests of reform.[54] The defenders also accused the critics of circulating a false announcement in Saharanpur that Rashīd Aḥmad had resigned and that contributions should now be sent to 'Abd ur-Razzāq as the new mohtamim. When this failed, the critics had distributed an announcement entitled 'For the Attention of the Government', a scurrilous attack which claimed that the school educated students for religious warfare and drew students from the frontier particularly for this purpose.

The school's defenders answered these charges of resignations, nepotism, and disloyalty. They were quick to emphasize the influence of Rashīd Aḥmad and said of 'Ābid Ḥusain, as Muhammad Qāsim had said twenty years earlier, 'he cannot leave us, nor we him'.[55] Mohī ud-Dīn Morādābādi, an important supporter of the school, argued that the familial links among the school's members were a virtue and stressed that members were 'united and the same sort of people'. He emphasized that appointments were made by the whole council and that the qualifications of a teachers like Mahmūd Ḥasan, the son of a council member, were outstanding. He cited the important precedent of the Prophet who did not hesitate to appoint his own relatives.

Maulānā Zu'lfaqār 'Alī in particular addressed himself to the charge of disloyalty. He declared that as a 'salt-eater' of the government, he personally took responsibility for the school's loyalty. The district collector, Mr Irwin, was invited to the school to confirm its integrity. He did come, and offered an Urdu speech in its praise.[56] Janāb Bābū Rājā Lāl, a former tahsildar, was asked to investigate the school and subsequently worked for several months, making inquiries in Nanauta, Rampur, and elsewhere. In conclusion he denied the critics' claims and in particular praised the fine students and Zu'lfaqār 'Alī, a man who had been honoured at the Queen's durbar with chair and robe of honour.

Local newspapers reported these two investigations and concluded that the charges of the 'malcontents' had been finally laid to rest.[57]

Meanwhile, supporters of the school hastened to testify to their confidence in the school's administration. Their letters reveal the wide range of support the school now had. The association formed in Hyderabad to raise funds consisting of princely employees, a publisher of religious books, and a religious teacher, used this occasion to declare its opposition to the residents and to send an additional contribution. Fifteen contributors from Bijnur sent a petition of support. A head maulavi in a government school in Banda in the east wrote an appreciation of the school. High officials from the state of Bhopal, including a wakil at the high court and the city munsif, who was from Deoband, added their support. Forty-seven contributors wrote from the qasba of Tandah, in

Oudh, where most of them were posted in connection with government service.[58] Other letters came from a wakil in Jaunpur and the Deputy Collector of Eta.

So serious a dispute could not be resolved by a simple personal act like that of Muḥammad Qāsim's in 1875. The council did not, however, propose arbitration or compromise with their opponents, but rather, unilaterally, rallied support for themselves. In addition to the testimonials from presumably impartial Hindu and British officials and from the loyal donors, they summoned four of the most influential figures associated with the school to render a final opinion. They were Rashīd Aḥmad, *sarparast*; the Nawwāb of Chattari, the philanthropist; Shaikh Bashārat 'Alī, a former deputy collector; and Maulavī Muḥammad Ismā'īl, the successor of the revered Maulānā Muzaffar Ḥusain Kāndhlāvī. The great *sarparast*, the influential landholder and benefactor, and the representatives of the government bureaucracy, and sufi piety respectively, together inspected the school's finances and records and asserted emphatically that all was in excellent order. Then Rashīd Aḥmad, with the agreement of the council, expanded its membership. The six new members were all from outside Deoband and all known for their learning. The 'respectable people' of the city who had sought places were thus defeated.

The council then appointed a new *mohtamim* to replace Maulānā Munīr Nanautawī. The proceedings reported that he had resigned because of his brother Aḥsan's death, but, in fact, he had never been a strong administrator. Maulānā Ḥāfiẓ Muḥammad Aḥmad, Muḥammad Qāsim's son, took his place, there to remain for forty years. He was, at times, a figure of controversy because of his willingness to jeopardize the school's well-being by political involvement, but he was, unquestionably, a strong and effective administrator. Moreover, his position as the son of the founder of the school was of great importance in establishing his claim to authority.

The controversy resolved, the school held its annual prize distribution and convocation, meeting for the first time not in the Jāmi' Masjid of the town but, significantly, in the school itself. The people of the town were invited on the day before the ceremonies for special speeches. Zu'lfaqār 'Alī and Ḥājjī 'Ābid himself presided. And the ceremonies closed with prayers for the wealth and spiritual well-being of the people of the town of Deoband.[59]

The dispute had been more ideological than personal. There were, to be sure, a cluster of relatives on each side. And personal ties certainly played a part in shaping the loyalties of some. One supporter of the administration, for example, simply wrote, 'what can I say, he [Rashīd Aḥmad] is my *murshid* [sufi preceptor] and guide'.[60] But the kin did not wholly account for people's allegiances and some participants explicitly denied its importance. An official from Bhopal mocked the dissidents for sending their announcement to Faẓl-i Ḥaqq's brother 'because they assumed that he would be in opposition.... He is not such a man'.[61] Place of origin did not define the two sides, since many residents of the town supported the administration. Nor did social differences, since both groups were composed of respectable people, largely *shaikh*, many of them associated with government and educated in religious studies.

The sides were, however, united by different positions. The opponents were not committed to the bureaucratic organization of the school and its concomitant broad network of support. Ironically, they, who accused the administration of nepotism, in fact wanted to make the school parochial by putting its control in the hands of townsmen instead of in those of the far-flung contributors and councillors. Most wanted a share in a successful enterprise without understanding the basis of its success.[62] Some few, like Ḥājjī 'Ābid with his proposal to eliminate most of the staff, felt a modest, old-fashioned school sufficient for the town.

The dissidents, moreover, seem not to have subscribed to the scripturalist reform that defined the teachings of the school.[63] A former revenue official, sometime tahsildar in Deoband wrote:

I got the announcement [of the meeting], I suppose, because I am of their *qaum*. I am; and I am well acquainted with all the gentlemen and *shaikh*s of Deoband. And I don't know who the people are who signed it. Look at them—'Deputy', 'Babu', 'Municipality',—not such as are involved in the work of God and his Prophet. Let them give their age, occupation, and whether they fast and pray. I recognized the first two names. I think one of them is some relation of mine. The other carried a *ta'ziya* [Shi'a effigy] in the Muharram celebration.[64]

Even Ḥājjī 'Ābid, however beloved, was less committed to reform than the other Deobandis. Although he had been influenced by Imdādullāh to give up practices of extreme mortification and to be faithful to his religious duties,[65] he never took the active stance of some of the others. His resignation on this occasion, for example, suggests his lack of interest in the reformist cause of adherence to the judicial opinions of the 'ulama instead of the use of government courts.

Those who supported the administration favoured a form of organization that de-emphasized purely local ties in favour of the separate unity and identity of the whole group of Deobandis, whatever their geographic origin. At the same time, they fostered a style of Islam that preferred universal practices and beliefs to local cults and customs. They were inspired by a belief in continuing divine sanction to their work[66] and felt that sanction confirmed by their record of training some six hundred ulama by the time of the dispute.[67] Against such success the opposition could make little headway.

## The Spread of Deobandi Madrasas

The success of the school was measured not only by events at the mother school but by the spread of Deobandi teachings through similar schools. The ulama of Deoband early tried to establish a system of branch schools which were to follow the pattern of British universities with their affiliating colleges and be subject to control of both curriculum and administration. The 'ulama were familiar with examples of such institutions, set up in India pursuant to the Wood Dispatch of 1854; and they, in turn, set up a somewhat similar system of education. They founded many schools, particularly in the Doab and Rohilkhund, which had much the same goals as the mother school: the propagation of reformed religious knowledge and the training of young men for professional religious careers. The schools often submitted their records to Deoband for inspection, sought its approval of major decisions, and received its 'ulama as both external examiners and distinguished visitors. But they were never formally and fully integrated into a single educational system, largely because personal ties were so effective in maintaining contacts. A proposal to appoint an inspector of schools in the British style was considered from time to time but simply deemed unnecessary.

In their first dozen or so years, the Deobandi proceedings included discussions of many of these schools, ranging in administration from one at Thana Bhawan, whose staff for a time was even paid from Deoband, to one at Lucknow which was 'like Deoband'.[68] Many of these smaller schools were the work of a single patron in cooperation with a Deoband graduate while others had complex administrations modelled on the mother school. Among the latter was the large and successful Maẓāhir-i 'Ulūm in Saharanpur. There was never any claim that it was a branch of Deoband, for in size and influence, it was to be second only to Deoband itself in the entire subcontinent. Founded only six months after Deoband, it explicitly modelled itself on the nearby school. Leading Deobandis contributed to the school, presided at prize distributions, and gave examinations. Rashīd Aḥmad was *sarparast* of both institutions at the end of the century and many of the staff moved from one school to the other. The school was more locally based than Deoband. In a dispute similar to the one over the control of Deoband, the city leaders of Saharanpur received some recognition of their responsibility for general administrative decisions and fund raising. The role of people of the city in financing the school was also more marked than at Deoband. The school also adhered longer and more consistently to family connections in making appointments. In part because of its more parochial style, its 'ulama in this century have not played the role in politics that the Deobandis have.[69] Whatever differences of emphasis, the Maẓāhir-i 'Ulūm called itself Deobandi.

Increasingly, the name of Deoband came to represent a distinct style, a *maslak*, of Indian Islam that emphasized the diffusion of scripturalist practices and the cultivation of an inner spiritual life. By roughly 1880 there were over a dozen Deobandi schools; by the end of the century, at least three times that many, some in places as distant as Chittagong, Madras, and Peshawar. Deoband had pioneered a non-governmental style of formal organization for madrasa education in India. Thanks to that structure, the school succeeded in training a large number of 'ulama in its reformist ideology and in establishing a network of ancillary schools further disseminating that teaching. Deoband thus offers a striking and successful example of the bureaucratization of traditional religious institutions that has made them effective in the modern world.

## 52 ISLAMIC CONTESTATIONS

*Notes*

1. William R. Roff, 'Islamization, "Communitas", Symbols, and Institutional Structures'. In Dietmar Rothermund, ed. *Islam in Southern Asia: A Survey of Current Research*, pp. 1–4. Wiesbaden. Gilsenan, Michael. 1973. *Saint and Sufi*. Oxford, 1975.

2. See, for example, Faruqi, Ziya ul-Ḥasan. *The Deoband School and the Demand for Pakistan*. Bombay. 1963.

3. Gilsenan, Michael. *Saint and Sufi in Modern Egypt: An Essay in the Sociology of Religion*. Oxford. 1973.

4. Roff, William R. 1974. 'The Origins and Early Years of the *Majlis Ugama*'. In Roff, ed. *Kelanten: Religion, Society, and Politics in a Malay State*, pp. 101–52. Oxford.

5. Rizvī, Maḥbūb. n.d. *Tārīkh-i Deoband*, p. 116. Deoband.

6. Qāsimī, Muḥammad Ṭaiyib. 1968. *Dār ul- 'Ulūm Deoband kī Ṣad Sāla Zindagī*, pp. 16–17. Deoband.

7. Ibid., p. 19.

8. Ibid., pp. 17–18.

9. At least from the eighteenth century, Indian Muslims distinguished between the well-born or respectable, the *ashrāf*, and all others. The former category was further divided into four ranked grades, each claiming non-Indian descent: the *saiyid*s, the descendants of the Prophet; the *shaikh*s, the descendants of his companions; the Mughals, who entered India with the Timurid rulers; and the Pathans or Afghans, who entered either as rulers or settlers.

10. Gīlānī, Manāẓir Aḥsan. 1955. *Sawāniḥ Qāsimī*. Vol. I, p. 266. Deoband.

11. Kasōlī, Ẓahūr ul-Ḥasan. 1950. *Arwāh-i Ṣulāṣa*, pp. 239–40. Saharanpur.

12. Mīyān, Muḥammad. *'Ulamā-yi Ḥaqq*, pp. 67–8. Delhi.

13. Qādirī, Muḥammad Āyūb. 1966. *Maulānā Muḥammad Aḥsan*, pp. 200–202. Karachi.

14. Rizvī, Maḥbūb. n.d. *Deoband kī Ta 'līmī Khaṣūṣiyāt*, p. 24. Deoband.

15. Mīrathī, Muḥammad 'Āshiq Ilāhī. n.d. *Tazkirāt ur-Rashīd*, pp. 94–5. Meerut.

16. Ibid., p. 153.

17. Gīlānī. 1955. *Sawāniḥ Qāsimī*, Vol. I, pp. 291–8.

18. Dār ul-'Ulūm Deoband. 1873–4. *Rū dād-i Sālānah 1290*, p. 16. Deoband.

19. Nevill, H. R. 1903. *Saharanpur: A Gazetteer*, p. 214. Allahabad.

20. Dār ul-'Ulūm Deoband, 1894–5. *Naql-i Kitāb Tahrīrī-yi Jalshah-yi Ahl-Mashwara*, p. 132. Deoband Mss, and Gīlānī. 1955. *Sawāniḥ Qāsimī*, Vol. I, p. 290.

21. Rizvī, Maḥbūb. *Deoband kī Ta 'līmī Khuṣūṣiyāt*, p. 10.

22. Ikrām, Muḥammad. 1968, 4th edn. *Mauj-i-Kauṣar*, p. 209. Lahore.

23. Gīlānī. 1955. *Sawāniḥ Qāsimī*, Vol. I, pp. 321–4.

24. Deoband, *Rū dād 1313*. 1895–6, and *Tahirīrī Kitāb 1301*. 1883–4, p. 66.

25. Rizvī, Maḥbūb. *Tārīkh-i Deoband*, p. 116, and *Deoband kī Ta 'līmī*

*Khuṣūṣīyāt*, p. 12. Also Dēōband, *Rū dād 1285.* 1868–9, p. 8. *Rū dād 1305.* 1887–8 reports that 88 per cent passed their exams.

26. Dēōband, *Rū dād 1290*, 1873–4, pp. 15–23.

27. Dēōband, *Rū dād 1287*. 1871–2, pp. 6–7.

28. Rizvī, Maḥbūb. *Tārīkh-i Dēōband*, p. 113.

29. For a contemporaneous example of the influence of school organization on forging new social bonds, see Dàvid S. Lelyveld, 'Aligarh's First Generation: Muslim Solidarity and English Education in North India, 1875–1900'. 1974. Unpublished Ph.D. dissertation, University of Chicago. [See also 2nd edn, New Delhi: Oxford University Press, 2003]

30. Dēōband, *Rū dād 1289*. 1872–3.

31. Abd. ul-Hayy, 1958 reprint. *Delhī aur us kē Aṭrāf: Ēk Safarnāma aur Rōznāma 'Īswīn Ṣadī ke Akhir Mēn*, pp. 142–3. Lucknow, records the complaints about the teaching of *ma'qūlāt* made by Maulānā Mashīyatullāh Bijnūrī, then a student, later a member of the council.

32. Ilāhi, Muḥammad 'Āshiq. *Tazkirat ur-Rashīd*, pp. 85–93, paraphrased.

33. Ḥusain, Asghar. 1920, 2nd edn. *Ḥayāt-i Shaikh ul Hind*, pp. 11–13. Deoband.

34. Ibid., p. 22.

35. Madanī, Ḥusain Aḥmad. 1953. *Naqsh-i Ḥayāt*, Vol. II, pp. 44–8, paraphrased. Deoband.

36. Ṭaiyib, Muḥammad. *Dēōband kī Ṣad Sālah Zindagī*, p. 92.

37. Kasōlī, Ẕahūr ul-Ḥasan, ed. *Arwāh-i Ṣulāsa*, pp. 248–52.

38. I am indebted to Renata Holod of the University of Pennsylvania for comments on Mughal architecture that prompted this interpretation.

39. Gilānī, *Sawāniḥ Qāsimī*, Vol. II, p. 253.

40. Ibid., Vol. I, pp. 32–4.

41. Ṭaiyib, Muḥammad. *Dēōband kī Ṣad Sāla Zindagī*, p. 92.

42. Hāshīmī, Anwar ul-Ḥasan. 1955. *Mubashshirāt-i Dār ul-'Ulūm*, p. 23. Deoband.

43. Fākhrī, Ibrahīm. June 1969. 'Dār ul-'Ulūm Dēōband'. *Āj Kal*, p. 40. Delhi.

44. Gilānī, *Sawāniḥ Qāsimī*, Vol. I, p. 228.

45. Kasōlī, Ẕahūr ul-Ḥasan, ed. *Arwāh-i Ṣulāsa*, p. 252.

46. Gilānī, *Sawāniḥ Qāsimī*, Vol. I, p. 326.

47. Kasōlī, Ẕahūr ul-Ḥasan, ed. *Arwāh-i Ṣulāsa*, p. 380. Here is noted yet another occasion when 'Ābid Ḥusain had withdrawn from the school but its personnel maintained affable relations with him.

48. ul-Hayy, Abd. *Delhī aur us kē Aṭrāf*, pp. 98–9.

49. Ibid., p. 144.

50. Ibid., pp. 101–2.

51. See Ṭaiyib, Muḥammad. *Dēōband kī Ṣad Sāla Zindagī*, for the tenure of members of all administrative and teaching positions at the school.

52. The fullest report on the meeting is Morādābādi. 1894–5. *Tazkirat-i 1312: Waqā'i Ḥālāt-i Madrasa-yi Islāmiya-yi Dēōband*. Delhi. The volume

included the statements of both sides. The compiler, a ra'is of Moradabad, entitled himself 'the servant of the ulama', and offered the volume for the benefit of his fellow Muslims. He called Deoband 'the mother of madrasas' and praised it for spreading religious knowledge throughout Hindustan. A companion of Muḥammad Qāsim, he also had a son enrolled at the school at the time of the dispute. He was appointed to the council at the conclusion of the quarrels.

53. Ibid., p. 15. The brothers were Zu'lfaqār 'Alī and Fazl ur-Raḥmān who were khālazād bhā'i or cousins. Maḥmūd Ḥasan was the former's son and his brother taught briefly at Deoband at a different time. The brother of 'Azīz ur-Raḥmān, the school's first mufti, taught at the school on a voluntary basis.

54. Selections from the Vernacular Newspapers Published in the Punjab, North Western Provinces, Oudh, and the Central Provinces, 1894, p. 513. Government of India.

55. Mohi ud-Din, Tazkirat, pp. 36–7 and p. 11. They pointed to two issues that particularly revealed Rashīd Aḥmad's influence: his opposition to the appointment of an official to supervise the collection of pledges and of an inspector of the branch madrasas; and the opposition to the introduction of medical studies.

56. Ibid., p. 43.

57. Selections from the Vernacular Newspapers. 1895. The Mihr-i Nimrūz of Bijnur on 21 February 1895. pp. 113–14, and the Akbar-i 'Alam of Meerut on 5 March 1895, p. 138; both were enthusiastic in their defence of the school.

58. Mohī ud-Dīn, Tazkirat, p. 31.

59. Ṭaiyib, Muḥammad. Dēōband kī Ṣad Sāla Zindagī, pp. 102–3.

60. Mohī ud-Dīn, Tazkirat, p. 22.

61. Ibid., p. 24.

62. Ibid., p. 12. According to Mohī ud-Dīn, the council had restored the salary of the recalcitrant teacher in 1892. The townsmen then concluded that the council was susceptible to pressure. At that point, fifty of them had made requests for membership.

63. One supporter claimed that they actually subscribed to the rival religious orientations of the day. He wrote a 'Mahabharata,' whose highlight was this Urdu verse:

> One will call following the four imams ill
> Another toward the leaders of bid'at incline will
> Another imitates nēcharī heart and soul
> Another thinks that worldly things are all. (Ibid., pp. 36–7.)

64. Ibid., p. 28.

65. Gilānī, Sawāniḥ Qāsimī, Vol. I, p. 239.

66. Thus, at the time of the crisis of 1895, Rashīd Aḥmad reported that he had three times received the same illumination that the madrasa would prosper in the hands of Ḥāfiẓ Aḥmad. Moreover, during a meeting to discuss

the crisis, Rashīd Aḥmad had been inspired with the knowledge that the opponents would fail. Anwar ul-Ḥasan, *Mubashshirāt*, p. 18. Similarly, when Nawwāb Maḥmūd 'Alī Khān of Chattari was leaving Mecca, he was instructed by Ḥājjī Imdādullāh not to oppose Rashīd Aḥmad. He was astonished since at that point there was no thought of his going to Deoband, let alone of any controversy. Shortly thereafter, the great dispute in which he was to play an important role did indeed break out. Thānvī, Ashraf 'Ali. n.d. *Karāmāt-i Imdādiya*, p. 72. Deoband.

67. Ṭaiyib, Muḥammad. *Dēōband kī Ṣad Sāla Zindagī*, p. 25.

68. Dēōband. 1879-80. *Rū dād-i Sālāna 1297*, p. 64.

69. Sources for the history of the Saharanpur school include its own printed proceedings. Available to me at the school were those for the years 1286-8 (1869-72); 1293-6 (1876-9); 1298-9 (1880-2); 1317 (1899-1900); 1318 (1900-1) and 1320 (1902-3). Also Zakariyya, Muḥammad. 1973 reprint. *Tārīkh-i Maẓāhir*. Saharanpur reprint, and *al-Balāgh*. Bombay, December-January 1374/1954-5, pp. 234-7. I visited the school in April 1970 and interviewed the school's venerable director, Maulānā Asadullāh, and a teacher, Maulānā 'Abd ul-Mālik, a B.Sc. in chemistry. The latter particularly stressed the similarity among Deobandi schools: 'Deoband is the elder brother and we are the younger'.

# 2

# Two Fatwas on Hajj in British India

The following two fatwas are translated from Urdu:

*Query*   What of a person who goes to Noble Mecca on hajj and does not go to Medina the Radiant, thinking, 'To go to Noble Medina is not a required duty (*farz-i wājib*) but rather a worthy act (*kār-i khayr*). Moreover, why should I needlessly take such a dangerous route where there are marauding tribes from place to place and risk to property and life. A great deal of money would be spent as well—so what is the point?' Is such a person sinful or not?

*Answer*   Not to go to Medina because of such apprehension is a mark of lack of love for the Pride of the World, on whom be peace. No one abandons a worldly task out of such apprehension, so why abandon this pilgrimage? The road is not plundered every day; (safety) is a matter of chance—so that is no argument. Certainly, to go is not obligatory. Some people, at any rate, think this pilgrimage is a greater source of reward and blessing than lifting the hands in prayer and saying 'āmīn' out loud. Do not give up going out of fear of controversy or concern for your reputation. Should you abandon this pilgrimage from such apprehension and supposition, or put it off, consider, then, which portion is that of full faith. It is a joy to spend money on good acts. To go from Mecca to Medina, travelling first class, costs only fifty rupees. Whoever takes account of fifty rupees and does not take account of the blessed sepulchre of the lord is a person of undoubtedly defective faith and love. Even if not a sinner, this person lacks faith in his basic nature. The end. Almighty Allah knows better. Rashid Ahmad, may he be forgiven.

*Query*   A person is such that he brings many religious benefits, for example, he teaches the Word of Allah, hadith, commentary, etc.

Thanks to him, any mosque he is in is full. Is it better for him to undertake *hijrat* (migration) to the Noble Holy Places, or is his current occupation better? (Marginal note: from 'Azizuddin Sahib, Moradabadi, 1311/1893.)

*Answer*   If there is no harm to the religion of this learned person, and the populace receives religious benefit from him, it is better for him to stay than to undertake *hijrat* to Arabia. But Almighty Allah knows better. Rashid Ahmad, may be forgiven.[1]

These two fatwas were issued in the late nineteenth century in reply to questions posed in 1893.[2] 'Azizuddin, the questioner, is from nearby Moradabad; Maulana Rashid Ahmad, the mufti, is based in Gangoh. Both are country towns in the Upper Doab area, one hundred miles or so from Delhi. 'Azizuddin is the person most frequently noted as the source of questions to Rashid Ahmad in the published collection of his fatwas. Maulana Rashid Ahmad Gangohi (1829–1905) was one of the founders of the reformist madrasa at Deoband (1867). Known primarily as a scholar of hadith and Hanafi fiqh, he also served as a spiritual guide in the Chishti Sabiri lineage, which combined initiation and practices of other lineages, particularly the Naqshbandi Mujaddidi. He held no official position.[3]

## Subject

The two fatwas comprise the entirety of the 'Book of Hajj' in the first of three volumes of the 1943 edition of the fatwas.[4] A marginal notation to the second fatwa in the Deoband edition indicates that this is 'A rule on *hijrat*'.[5]

The choice of these two fatwas from the collection is arbitrary: virtually any fatwa could have been used to illustrate the same points. A rough count of the approximately three hundred fatwas in the first volume of the Delhi edition shows that they deal primarily with *'aqā'id* (beliefs) and *'ibādāt* (acts of worship), in itself a telling comment on the domains central to religious guidance at the height of colonial rule. These two fatwas therefore are typical.[6]

A major concern of the fatwas in this volume (and, in fact, in the other volumes as well) was to evaluate customs and beliefs related to Sufism, examining them to identify reprehensible innovation. Approximately one-third of the fatwas deal with issues related to Sufism: its importance, the primacy of the shari'a, the role of the shaykh, the legitimacy of such practices as saying *zikr* aloud (repeating certain words and formulas in praise of God), conceiving of the image of the shaykh, pilgrimages to saints' graves, the celebration of the death anniversaries of the saints, and the customary recitation of the Fatiha. Roughly one-fifth are devoted to the correct performance of the canonical prayer, reviewing such issues as the correct time, the manner of ablution, procedures, the location of the funeral prayer, ceremonies of fixed days after death, and the character of the imam. Others deal with fasting, reading the Quran, and—the two discussed here—the pilgrimage to Mecca. The fatwa thus served as a central tool for holding up everyday religious practices to the scrutiny of normative principles.

Several fatwas deal explicitly with relations to other Muslim groups, including the Ahl-i Hadith, the Shi'a, and those who adhere to customary practices, later known as Barelvi; to a far lesser degree, they are concerned with Hindus and with the British (*pace* widespread scholarly assumption to the contrary). In fact, as is the case with the two fatwas under consideration, concerns with these Islamic groups, defined by religious orientation, underlay perhaps the majority of the questions answered.

In this regard, the fatwas implicitly resonate with two important themes. Just as fatwas on hajj are typical—in that the fatwas as a whole deal with issues of belief and obligations to Allah—,typical, too, is the first fatwa's particular concern with the definition of correct practice and a correct spiritual disposition in contrast to the stance of other Muslims. The late nineteenth century was a time of intense proliferation of institutions and schools of thought among the "ulama', who used new forms of organization, financial support, and communication to build Muslim communities in the context of colonial rule.

Thus the subject of the first fatwa is, implicitly, the teachings of the Ahl-i Hadith, whose reformist teachings also took shape among a group of "ulama' in late nineteenth century north India. The Ahl-i Hadith, influenced by certain strands of Arab reform, went against the predominant practice of Muslims in the subcontinent, who for the most part were Hanafi, to insist that the learned should consult Quran and hadith directly and not follow the rulings and commentaries of the various schools of law. Their opponents called them *ghayr muqallid*, those who do not follow taqlid, or guidance that has been historically given. They were most notorious for their particular practices in prayer, the lifting of hands and saying *āmīn*, which were not Hanafi practices. Observers often marvelled at the fact that Muslims came to blows over seemingly trivial matters, not realizing that issues of textual and personal authority were in fact at stake in the forms of prayer that were followed.

The members of Ahl-i Hadith were on the whole more extreme than the Deobandis in their zeal to set a single standard of piety and behaviour and in their relentless quest to eliminate all those customary practices that could be construed as reprehensible innovation. Placing the personality and teachings of the Prophet at the centre of what they did, in the fashion of all the movements of this period, they stressed their proximity to him because of their devotion to hadith, from which they derived their name. Despite this devotion, they opposed pilgrimage (ziyārat) to the Prophet's tomb in Medina, as they opposed pilgrimage to all tombs. Thus Nawwab Siddiq Hasan Khan (1832–90), perhaps the best known leader of the Ahl-i Hadith in the late nineteenth century, insisted that no one should make a specific journey to visit the Prophet's tomb, perhaps leaving open the possibility of a visit should one have other reasons to be in Medina.[7] In discouraging pilgrimage, the Ahl-i Hadith shared the orientation of contemporaneous reformers in the Hijaz influenced by Muhammad ibn 'Abdul'l-Wahhab (1703–87) and others who earlier had gone so far as to destroy the tomb of the Prophet. Like the Wahhabis, they valued the work of Ibn Taimiyya (1263–1328) and eschewed virtually all practices associated with Sufism.[8] But the members of Ahl-i Hadith tried to distance themselves from the Wahhabis, disclaiming their violence and their jurisprudential stance (as Hanbali). That Maulana Rashid Ahmad was particularly concerned to challenge and distance himself from the Ahl-i Hadith is also suggested by the introduction to the Deoband edition of the fatwas, where the editor notes that the ṣāḥib-i fatāwā shows respect for all four schools of law (mazāhib).[9]

The second fatwa carries a second implicit theme, namely, that in the context of British India one could be of great service to religion, sustain one's own religion unharmed while staying there, and, under these circumstances, feel no obligation to undertake migration to a Muslim-ruled land. The fatwa thus reflects the stance of the majority of Deobandis toward the colonial power (at least through the First World War): avoidance of any direct confrontation. Other fatwas suggest a moral superiority over British culture, permitting one to lie, since the basis of government was contrary to shari'a; justifying an escape by someone unfairly imprisoned; denouncing missionaries for using bribery; and so forth.[10] Well into the twentieth century, however, Deobandis did not measure British practices or technologies as illegitimate in themselves but condemned them only if some aspect specifically countered shari'a.[11] In a brief, one sentence reply in another fatwa in this volume, Maulana Rashid Ahmad himself, noting that the majority of "ulama' considered 'Hindustan' to be *dāru'l-islām*, chose not to take a position on this point at all.[12] Overall, it was less with the British than with other Muslims that the "ulama' were concerned, as the first fatwa indicates.

## Rhetoric and Sources

The tone of these two fatwas is typical of Deobandi rhetoric as a whole, with its goal to utilize a straightforward, simple language, ideally accessible to anyone. The fact that the "ulama' at this period wrote in Urdu is significant and should not be taken for granted. In fact, some of the fatwas in this volume are received, answered, and reproduced in Persian, which had long been the language of the governing and cosmopolitan classes. At Deoband, however, Persian was no longer taught as part of the education of the learned. The move to Urdu as the vernacular—and increasingly, by the end of the century, a specifically Muslim vernacular—was a result of the colonial framework of both formal decisions and implicit practice interacting with indigenous strategies of cultural reproduction.[13] It was precisely the deployment of Urdu in texts like this that was crucial in creating community and in identifying Urdu as a cultural symbol.

The accessible style of the fatwas is particularly evident in those that are in fact actual exchanges of letters. There is no effort to put all the questions and answers into a single format. Thus a letter will be reproduced with a marginal note that it was sent, '*mursala*', by so-and-so, and the conventional greetings and conclusions are reproduced. Maulana Rashid Ahmad may be addressed as *makhdūm-i zamān, ḥaẓrat, maulānā*—lord of the age (a term often used in a Sufi context), the presence, the master—and he, in turn, signs himself *banda*—servant or slave.

In addition to their simplicity, the writings of the "ulama' not infrequently take on a mocking or ironic tone. Thus, here,

Maulana Rashid Ahmad gently mocks those who would compare the merit of (inappropriate and divisive) practices in prayer with the merit of visiting 'the blessed sepulchre of the lord'. The terms of this comparison are what give us the conclusive clue that the fatwa is fundamentally 'about' the Ahl-i Hadith, whose followers were identified precisely by this public behaviour at prayer. Having asserted the relative value of the pilgrimage, Maulana Rashid Ahmad goes on to dismiss the whole rationale for not going. In so doing, he uses yet another typical strategy: imputing to those who do not go mere expediency instead of principle. Much of the debate of this period operated precisely in this style of (consciously) ignoring the premises of one's opponents.[14] Imagine how infuriating it would be to be accused of caring about fifty rupees when you believed yourself driven by passion for prophetic example itself in not going to Medina—to say nothing of the same motivation for raising of hands and saying *āmīn* in prayer.

The tone of the answer, moreover, was also light-handed in judging those who differed. Here, Rashid Ahmad did not judge a person sinful who did not go to Medina; the Deobandis did not rush to call anyone deviant, let alone kafir, or infidel. Given the competition among the varying schools of thought in this period, each of which insisted that it came closer to the pattern of the Prophet and loved him most, the suggestion that the wrongdoer 'only' showed 'defective faith' and lack of 'love for the Pride of the World' was damning enough: the very understatement makes the accusation more wounding. Maulana Rashid Ahmad's triumphant parry is framed, of course, by conventional modesty: God knows better; may the sins of the mufti be forgiven. Thus, behind the apparent simplicity lay a nuanced and pointed mode of argument valued in a culture that delighted in polished and clever language.

No sources are quoted to bolster the argument, suggesting (as does the simplicity of the language) an effort to gain a wide audience and, perhaps, an awareness of the extent to which people had fallen from a laudable standard of religious learning: in another fatwa in this volume, Maulana Rashid Ahmad explains that he does not cite arguments of hadith and fiqh because the knowledge of both the ordinary and the learned, *'awāmm* and *khawāṣṣ*, is defective.[15] Although some fatwas in the collection mention a Qur'anic verse or hadith, most do not.

A further reason that only a simple answer was given was the emphasis of the Deobandis on the position known as *taqlīd-i shakhṣī*, that each Muslim should follow a single scholar as a definitive guide to correct belief and practice. Parallel to this was the notion that each person should follow a single spiritual guide (*murshid*, or shaykh). These injunctions were intended to bolster the authority of individual "ulama'.

At times, however, Maulana Rashid Ahmad did turn to other scholars to bolster his opinion with testimonials, frequently with seals showing the date. On several occasions in these volumes, opinions are supported by the signatures of a dozen or more additional scholars, who often added a rhyming phrase in Arabic (for example, '*al-jawāb ṣaḥīḥ wa-munkiruhu faẓīh*', the answer is correct and the denier disgraceful) or a sentence in support. This was the case, for example, with a fatwa forbidding the customary celebration of the Prophet's birthday, a contended practice that was spreading, in part because it was espoused by a rival group of "ulama'. The editor, similarly, footnotes on occasion such significant elders of the Deobandis as Shaykh 'Abdul-'aziz Dihlawi (d. 1824) to Hajji Imdadu'llah (1817–99) to render support.

The Deobandis took for granted that their arguments were based on Hanafi fiqh. Occasionally Maulana Rashid Ahmad would make a reference to another law school, for example on a minor matter like saying the *bismillāh* before reading each chapter of the Quran, when he was prepared to accept the practice of another school. He also stretched a point to make acceptable the Shafi'i opinion allowing teachers to accept recompense for teaching Quran and hadith, an issue of importance to the "ulama' at a time when they did not enjoy official patronage: he called the Shafi'i position fatwa, in the sense of what was decreed; the Hanafi, more difficult to practice, he termed piety, or *taqwā*. In general, however, the Deobandis condemned inter-scholastic eclecticism, for fear that it would encourage one to choose the easiest path and prevent the establishment of a single standard. Such discussion, or discussion of such points as the Hanafi emphasis on ascertaining the *ḥaqīqa* (truth, essence) of a problem to identify its correct analogue, rarely entered into the fatwas themselves. Generally speaking, the early Deobandis did not feel any need to lay bare the framework of their analysis.[16]

## Institutional Context and Dissemination

The "ulama' of the late nineteenth century, in the wake of the decisive establishment of British rule following the Mutiny of 1857, turned away from any governing or political role and established themselves as guides to personal behaviour and morality, defined by Islamic authority. Their teachings disseminated a self-conscious identification with Islamic symbols and built new communities, both among subgroups of Muslims (often defined by the various schools of thought, like the Deobandi, Barelvi, and Ahl-i Hadith, that were taking shape in the late nineteenth century) and among Muslims generally. Published fatwas, moreover, were central in defining appropriate codes of behaviour at a hitherto unknown level of detail. The fatwas thus had no support from political powers, nor did those providing them have the authority of any official office. Muftis had only the authority of their learning and moral qualities, coupled with their identification with one or another school of thought.

Popularly supported schools to train 'ulama, who themselves would become learned in hadith and fiqh and in turn be able to offer fatwas, were the institutional foundation and base of Deobandi 'ulama like Maulana Rashid Ahmad. The madrasa at Deoband, founded in 1867, spawned some two dozen schools of similar orientation across India by the end of the century and, in its first hundred years, gave rise to several hundred more schools identified as Deobandi. Individuals not only consulted respected 'ulama associated with the school to secure fatwas but also began to solicit fatwas with the imprimatur of 'Deoband' as well. In 1892 a formal *dāru'l-iftā'* was established at the school, and an *'ālim* was appointed as the school's mufti.[17] This did not mean that others at the school did not offer fatwas, but only that the burden was now particularly focused on one person who had ifta' as his primary responsibility. Beginning in 1911, a register was established into which each question, along with its answer, was recorded. At the time of its centennial, the school counted a total of 269,215 fatwas that had been issued, proudly claiming to have provided answers to most of the questions on the very day they were received.[18]

The dissemination of fatwas by means of lithographed books, along with religious publications generally, was critical to the creation of communities linked by religious style. The importance

of publications in creating 'imagined communities'—imagined in
the sense that they are communities whose members are imagined
rather than known on a face-to-face basis—has been argued by
Benedict Anderson in relation to the emergence of nation-states.[19]
Printed works have been critical as well, however, in creating
ethnically and religiously defined communities. As David Gilmartin
has suggested, there emerged in British India what might be called
a 'particular' space, neither private nor public (in the sense of being
open to all inhabitants of the geographic area), that defined group
commonalities and group interests through what were at the time
new modalities of communication and new institutional forms.[20]
Some of these 'particular' communities, or variations of them,
ultimately competed in a shared public space.[21] 'Indian Muslim'
represents one significant community that occupied that space in
the twentieth century. There was no direct link between the
communities defined by the 'ulama and those that took on explicit
political significance later, but to the extent that the 'ulama and
their publications, disseminated Islamic teachings and entered, as
they did, into debates with non-Muslims, they surely made some
contribution to what became politicized religious identities.

While a great deal is not known about the publishing histories
of fatwa collections, Maulana Rashid Ahmad's fatwas were published at least by 1906, the year following his death, and were
frequently reprinted thereafter. The Delhi edition published in the
1940s carried an announcement on the last page explaining that
despite frequent reprintings, the volumes had been continuously
snatched up and were therefore unavailable; the rights had been
purchased by the Maktaba Rahimiyya, which intended to keep the
volumes in print—and asked that no one pirate the text. A later
edition by the Deoband branch of the company reorganized the
three-volume format into one volume in order to make all fatwas
relevant to a single subject available in one place.

The fatwas of the late nineteenth century, along with those of
Shah 'Abdul-'aziz from earlier in the century,[22] appear to have
taken on the character of 'classics' and continue to be available in
reprints in shops that deal in Urdu books. Important collections
include those of Maulana 'Abdu'l-Hayy Farangi Mahalli (d. 1304/
1886-7; *Fatāwā 'Abdu'l Ḥayy Lakhnawī*), whose decisions were,
broadly speaking, identified as Deobandi; Maulana Ashraf 'Ali
Thanawi (1864-1943; *Fatāwā Imdādiyya*), a disciple of Maulana

Rashid Ahmad; Nawwab Siddiq Hasan Khan (*Majmūʻa Fatāwā*), the Ahl-i Hadith leader; and Maulana Ahmad Riza Khan Barelvi (1856–1921; inter alia, *Fatāwā Rizwiyya*). The last named, an opponent of the Deobandis and a proponent of a more custom-laden religious style, was known for using fatwas against his opponents and for his great efforts to solicit support from scholars in the Hijaz to bolster his opinions. He did not, moreover, follow the pattern of offering a simple opinion, but made what were in fact his primary claims to authority with massive citations of Quran and hadith: his published fatwas fill a dozen volumes, each running to a thousand pages, with a single answer on occasion taking a hundred pages.[23] The fatwas issued by the successive muftis at Deoband also have been published, running now into many volumes. A bibliography of religious works in Urdu lists some ninety-three collections of printed fatwas that were available in Urdu bookshops thirty years ago.[24]

The durability of these fatwas is not unrelated to their domain. As Masud has suggested,[25] the fatwas of this period represent both a narrowing away from issues related to rulership and the state, and a broadening, toward issues not only of religious obligation but also of moral opinion regarding a wide range of customary practices, relevant to the attempt of the ʻulama to define a purified and authoritative personal standard of faith and practice as the foundation of individual and communal life. To the extent that attention to correct individual practice remains at the heart of Muslim religious style, these fatwas continue to have relevance for the Urdu-speaking Muslims of the subcontinent.

## Notes

1. Gangohi Maulana Rashid Ahmad 1362/1943. *Fatāwā-yi Rashidiyya*, vol. I, pp. 43–4. Delhi: Kutbkhana Rahimiyya.

2. The marginal identification of the questioner as ʻAzizuʻd-din is placed next to the second query, but since there is no attribution for the preceding query, both may have emanated from him.

3. Metcalf, Barbara D. 1982. *Islamic Revival in British India: Deoband, 1860–1900*, pp. 76, 78–80. Princeton: Princeton University Press.

4. Subsequent references, unless noted, are to this volume, that is, volume I.

5. Gangohi, Maulana Rashid Ahmad n.d. (post-1960s). *Fatawa-yi Rashidiyya Kamil Mubawwab*, p. 375. Deoband: Kutbkhana Rahimiyya. I am grateful to Gail Minault, whose copy of this edition I was able to consult in the course of surveying her excellent collection of Urdu publications.

66 ISLAMIC CONTESTATIONS

6. Although there was discussion at the time of using the mufti to circumvent the British courts with their hybrid Anglo-Muhammadan law, the published collections deal with issues that were not handled by the courts. Although Deobandis have spoken even of independent courts to handle issues among Muslims, I have not seen sources to document these courts, let alone their extent. See Metcalf, op. cit. *Islamic Revival in British India: Deoband, 1860–1900*. Princeton: Princeton University Press.

7. Saeedullah. 1973. *Life and Works of Nawab Siddiq Hasan Khan of Bhopal*, p. 139. Lahore: Ashraf Publications.

8. Metcalf. 1982. *Islamic Revival*, pp. 264–96.

9. Gangohi Rashid Ahmad. op. cit.

10. Metcalf. 1982. *Islamic Revival*, p. 153.

11. Masud, M. Khalid. 1969. 'Trends in the Interpretation of Islamic Law as Reflected in the Fatawa Literature of the Deoband School: A Study of the Attitude of the 'Ulama of Deoband toward Certain Social Problems and Inventions'. M.A. thesis, Montreal: Institute of Islamic Studies, McGill University.

12. Gangohi Rashid Ahmad. n.d. *Fatāwā-yi*, p. 7. Deoband.

13. Fabian, Johannes. 1991 (1989). *Language and Colonial Power: The Appropriation of Swahili in the Former Belgian Congo, 1880–1938*. Berkeley: University of California Press; Hardy, Peter. 1972. *The Muslims of British India*. Cambridge: Cambridge University Press; Metcalf. 1982. *Islamic Revival*, pp. 198, 206–10.

14. Metcalf. 1982. *Islamic Revival*, pp. 215–34.

15. Gangohi Rashid Ahmad. n.d. *Fatāwā-yi*, pp. 88–9. Deoband.

16. Metcalf. 1982. *Islamic Revival*, pp. 141–3.

17. Tayyib Muhammad. 1965. *Daru'l-'culum Deoband ki Sad Salah Zindagi*, p. 99. Deoband: Daftar Daru'l-'culum.

18. Metcalf. 1982. *Islamic Revival*, p. 146.

19. Anderson, Benedict. 1983 (revised edition 1990). *Imagined Communities: Reflections on the Origin and Spread of Nationalism*. London: Verso.

20. Gilmartin, David. 1991. 'Democracy, Nationalism, and the Public: A Speculation on Colonial Muslim Politics'. *South Asia* 14(1): 141–54.

21. Hardy, Peter. 1971. *Partners in Freedom—and True Muslims: The Political Thought of Some Muslim Scholars in British India*. Lund, Sweden.

22. Metcalf. 1982. *Islamic Revival*, p. 46–52.

23. Metcalf. 1982 *Islamic Revival*, p. 308.

24. Anjuman-i Taraqqi-yi Urdu. 1961. *Qamusu'l-kutub urdu*, Vol. I. *Mazhabiyaat*, pp. 382–90, ed. Dr Maulawi 'Abdu'l-Haqq. Karachi.

25. Masud. 1969. 'Trends in the Interpretation of Islamic Law as Reflected on the Fatawa Literature of the Deoband School', p. 1.

# 3

## The Past in the Present
### Instruction, Pleasure, and Blessing in
### Maulana Muhammad Zakariyya's *Aap Biitii*

Between 1970 and 1981, near the end of his long life, the scion of a family of pre-eminent Islamic scholars and holy men wrote and published, ultimately in some seven volumes of well over two thousand pages, a work he simply entitled *Aap Biitii*, an ordinary Hindi word for one's own life story, whether written or oral. The book is a rich source for the history of the reformist, quietest Islam that has been so pervasive in Muslim religious life in the Indian colonial and post-colonial periods.[1] Above all, it is an intimate and detailed record of what one influential religious scholar wanted himself to be remembered for and the teachings he wanted others to remember. The work at the same time illuminates long-standing traditions of modelling morally exemplary lives and telling stories about them, even while it also yields glimpses of one particular iron-willed, passionate scholar whose active life spanned half a dozen decades before and after Partition.

Maulana Muhammad Zakariyya Kandhlawi (1897–1982) chose to call his work an *Aap Biitii*, preferring this word over more elevated terms commonly used for a biography or autobiography—although one edition at least added in parenthesis a Persianate translation of his title as *Khud-nawisht Sawaanih*.[2] The original title is, however, particularly apt. Muhammad Zakariyya was, in fact, as the English idiom has it, simply 'having his own say', and much of the work was an actual transcript of his speech. He himself was clear that this was a modest, incomplete, sometimes repetitive document. The work was produced piecemeal, responding to specific stimuli or occasions. Indeed, the power of the work in part derives from its production in painful and challenging circumstance, to which the author responded by exuberantly marshalling what, in the end, seemed nothing less than the totality of his life's experiences.

Despite its episodic and disjointed production, the work continues in print, and several volumes have even been translated into English, primarily for the benefit of those beyond the subcontinent who do not know Urdu.[3] The appearance of the book belies its casual production. It is typically published to look like a holy and special book. My own two-volume edition, recently printed in Karachi, is covered in padded, marbled green plastic, embossed in gold, with the title in a sunburst of arabesques.[4] A ribbon bound in the spine serves as bookmark. The author is celebrated on the cover as the 'Shaikh of Hadith', the title by which he is best known. It was bestowed on him by his own Sufi master to acknowledge his role as the chief teacher of prophetic tradition (hadith) at an eminent theological seminary. The cover also describes him as 'The Blessing of the Age', 'The Pillar of the World', and 'The Sojourner in Medina'. The book is special, and its subject is clearly special. The titles taken together identify him as a scholar, as a devotee of the Prophet Muhammad (and, in his last days, resident of the Prophet's city of Medina), and as a Sufi of the highest rank.

Muhammad Zakariyya may have written the book at the end of his life, but in some ways he had been preparing for it all his life. He, and his father before him, were great story-tellers and lived in a milieu where stories of the elders were a focus of scholarly work, instruction, and everyday conversation. By the time he was a young man, there had been several decades of printed Urdu biographies, and he himself was an avid reader of these biographies, many of which he cites in his own life story. He was, in fact, inspired at one point in his account to recall his long-term love for biographies going back to childhood. Always a night owl, he explained that he would read biographies after the night prayer, staying awake the whole night on the occasions, for example, when he waited up for his elder, Maulana Husain Ahmad Madani (1879–1957), who often arrived on a night train. The subjects of biographies he remembered enjoying are those of his elders in the reformist Deobandi tradition, and the names that flowed from his pen, all well known in those circles. The biographies he noted as his favourites were of Hazrat (Rashid Ahmad) Gangohi, Hazrat (Khalil Ahmad) Saharanpuri, Hazrat (Mahmudu'l-Hasan) Shaikhu'l-hind, Hazrat (Ashraf 'Ali) Thanawi, Hazrat (Husain Ahmad) Madani, and Chacha Sahib Marhum (Maulana Muhammad Ilyas). These are all of figures who lived into or in the twentieth century and who were central to the Deoband movement of 'scripturalist' reform centered around a theological academy founded some ninety miles north-east of Delhi in 1867.[5] 'All my life', Muhammad Zakariyya wrote, 'I have loved reading the lives of the elders (*sawaanih-i akaabir*)'.[6] These stories had shaped the way he lived his life and now shaped the way he retold his own. In writing his own life story, moreover, he included anecdotes about many of those he knew or knew of. His explicit goal in writing was to influence the lives of those who read, just as he himself had been influenced.

It rapidly became, as well, a way to have a good time. Early on in his account, at the point when he was about to launch into his stories of childhood chastening (no less), he invited the reader 'to listen to a few incidents', 'whether you enjoy them or not', he continued, 'I will enjoy writing them!'[7]

This text was intended for the specific audience of participants in the reformist tradition, the intimacy of its audience suggested, for example, by the shorthand way of referring to those discussed. The English translation recently published in South Africa therefore had to include a glossary of names as a key to those otherwise only called 'Hazrat Saharanpuri', 'the honoured one from Saharanpur', or 'Chacha Sahib Marhum', 'my late Uncle'. The emergence of the Deoband 'ulama, with the foundation of their major madrasa in 1867, had coincided precisely with what one scholar has identified as the third of three periods in the early history of print in India, the 'post-incunabula'. This was the period in the second half of the nineteenth century when the printed book began to penetrate deeply into Indian society.[8] Across Indian society, not only were there more books, but texts continued to serve as a spur to reading aloud and they were used as much that way as for private reading.[9] Muhammad Zakariyya's hesitance to continue writing was put aside, for example, when he learned from letters from other madrasa teachers that they were using his *Aap Biitii* in their lessons to the great benefit of their students—the very target he had hoped to reach in the first place.[10] The text was also interactive in another way. At one point, for example, Maulana Zakariyya broke his narrative to address readers directly, asking them to make intercessory prayer, and transfer of merit, to those three dozen or so people in his life who were initially opposed to him but then turned their enmity to devotion. It would be, he says, a kind service (*ihsaan*) to him to do so.[11] An autobiography could thus become an extension of the person himself and, in this case, a tool in creating the kind of relational bonds that defined his life.

## Lives as Lessons

It is difficult to exaggerate how important the writing of life histories became for the 'ulama from the late nineteenth century on. In embracing that genre, they drew on a very old tradition of emphasis on the embodiment of Islamic teachings in the life of the Prophet and subsequently his heirs: the Companions, the Sufis, and the 'ulama. The lives of the holy are meant to be reproduced in written life histories and in the lived patterns of their followers, much as the life of every Muslim is meant to be a reproduction of the 'narrations', hadith, of the Prophet himself. Indeed, the goal of Muhammad Zakariyya's own popular writings was clearly intended to make it possible for ordinary Muslims to fashion themselves as 'living hadith'.[12] For all its resonance with enduring Islamic patterns, however, it is notable that an emphasis on exemplary human models, whether of gods, or prophets, or their past and present holy exemplars, cut across religious traditions in the colonial period. In the Muslim case, this meant in the nineteenth century a centrality from among all the Islamic sciences given to hadith.

The privileged place of religious biography is often explicitly discussed in these texts themselves, for example in a preface taken almost at random, the biography of one of Muhammad Zakariyya's elders, Maulana Ashraf 'Ali Thanawi.[13] The preface explains that while the key teachings of faith are to be found laid out in books, it is impossible to understand them without a long-term practical example before one's eyes. For this reason, a living prophet, whether Moses and the Torah, Jesus and the Gospels, or Muhammad and the Qur'an, conveyed every divine book in order to make its teachings visible. Now, in the era after prophethood, one must seek a guide who exemplifies prophetic behaviour, or seek out the reports of such a guide. The author of the preface was disciple of the author, Dr 'Abdu'l-hayy, whose *shaikh*, in turn, was the subject of the biography. He called Dr 'Abdu'l-hayy 'a *mujassam tazkira*', that is, 'a memory rendered corporeal', of his *shaikh*.[14] '*Tazkira*', whose root meaning is memory or aid to memory, is the common term for a biographical memoir. Thus the person and the biography are, at some level, the same since both are triggers to recollection. These texts were explicitly didactic. For example, one recent collection of five biographies, each a 'tazkira' of a holy man, is entitled *Dars-i hayaat*, 'Lessons from life'. The title page explained that it was 'a complete curriculum (*nisab*) of an enlightened lesson (*sabaq*) in dying for Allah and in living for Allah'.[15] For Muhammad Zakariyya the pedagogic potential of life stories was central.

In telling stories about himself and others, Muhammad Zakariyya deployed the conventional rhetorical strategies of the Persianate tradition for this genre, a rhetoric whose contours can perhaps most easily be seen by contrasting it to persistent themes in Anglo-American biographical writing.[16] In the latter, put simply, accounts focus on some singular figure, proceed chronologically, with the life presented as an unfolding, linear story, the fruit of 'development' and 'influences', in which the protagonist independently takes action and where the subject is distinguished by what makes him or her distinctive.[17]

Muhammad Zakariyya presents *his* story with an approach that contrasts with this meta-narrative in at least three striking ways, in each drawing on a long heritage of Indo-Persian life story. First, his material is presented with no concern for chronological development, and, hence, for the presumed notion that a life makes sense in terms of the development that sequentially creates a particular personality and character. Rather the focus is on a person whose essential character is a given and whose life story is best told by recounting episodes—anecdotes—which yield lessons for moral understanding.

Second, the episodes do not show an actor identifying goals, making plans, overcoming obstacles, and progressively moving toward some kind of success—the cluster of activities that might be summed up as his demonstrating his 'agency'. Indeed, the rhetoric of the text suggests the opposite: a life fundamentally shaped by forces larger than one's self, above all by divine power evident in the charisma of elders to whom one owes allegiance, both living and dead.

Finally, and related to this, the material is not presented as Muhammad Zakariyya's exclusive story at all, but, throughout, as the story of his relations with other people. He counts as part of *his* life, stories of the elders he has interacted with or whom he, in turn, knows from stories recounted by others. Indeed, one might say that the 'autobiography' is not much about Muhammad Zakariyya at all. His own life gains significance not by individuality but by devotion to a particular pattern exemplified in specific anecdotal evidence about model figures both living and dead.

The strength of such a genre for didactic ends is clear. No specific set of circumstances, no crucial stages in development, no particular sociological or historical conjuncture is deemed necessary to live as one should. In Indo-Muslim culture, or perhaps Islamic or Indic cultures generally, a particularly pervasive way of thinking about the person is an assumption of the givenness of personal qualities. In this model, which resonates with old Eurasian humoral theories, a person is endowed with certain qualities that persist throughout life. Since character does not develop over time, there is no need for chronology or for dwelling particularly on childhood as autobiographers informed by Romantic individualism and subjectivism unfailingly do. Each person has a temperament but, whatever it is, in the logic espoused by Muhammad Zakariyya, it can be used constructively to seek out and respect those who follow Prophetic examples, both to receive their blessing and to aspire to live as they do. Disrespectful and undisciplined students, whose actions spurred Muhammad Zakariyya to write in the first place, had no excuse.

## Aap Biitii yaa Yaad-i Ayyaam

These characteristics of life stories—the goal of instruction, the passivity of the subject, the inclusion of stories of other people— all made Zakariyya's autobiographical venture less an act of hubris than, arguably, one of humility. The *Aap Biitii*, moreover, was initiated under duress. In 1963, Muhammad Zakariyya had been denounced in print when his seminary was torn by student unrest. The first volume includes a reply from the principal, Muhammad Zakariyya's own reply, and a section he subsequently compiled of anecdotes about the dedication and abstemiousness of the elders of the school. In 1968, Muhammad Zakariyya added to these three documents yet another response to work written about him, this time, surprisingly, by one of his admirers. Neither of the 'offending' documents was included in the volume.

Then, in 1970, while recovering from eye surgery in Aligarh and unable to undertake his scholarly work, Muhammad Zakariyya, by now a man in his eighth decade, in a compressed period of only eighteen days began dictating stories about his life which would ultimately comprise Volumes Two through Five of his *Aap Biitii*. When he came to publish these writings in response to many requests, he began the compendium with the original *Aap Biitii*, now labelled 'Volume One', and called the first of the new volumes, '*Yaad-i Ayyaam*, Memories of Days [past], Volume One, *yaa* [or] *Aap Biitii* Volume Two'. The work is typically known, however, as the 'Aap Biitii', and it is that title and numbering used here.

He began Volume Two with a discussion of the centrality of right intention (*niyat*), an abiding theme in Sufi guidance. This triggered off the memory of a conversation he had had on this subject with a political leader who ultimately became his disciple. This in turn stimulated a section on the restrictions he had placed on student involvement in political activities, which he saw as part of what had undermined student behaviour in his day. He then wrote at length on his own studies, his daily routines, his teaching practices, and a list of his eighty-three writings with notes on the context of their production. Implicitly, he offered a testimonial to a life of extraordinary discipline and devotion. In Volume Three, he retold stories of his 'bad habits', followed by accounts of his 'sorrows and joy', an organizing strategy that recalls the oral genre of women's life stories as reported in ethnographic accounts of this geographic area.[18]

In Volume Four, Muhammad Zakariyya returned to stories of the elders he was privileged to know over four eras, presented successively in terms of the 'favours of Allah' directed toward the author through them. He also included a collection of letters these elders had written to him and a travel account of five of his own visits to the holy places of Mecca and Medina. In Volume Five, Muhammad Zakariyya wrote of his own heart-rending experience of Partition, primarily of Delhi, followed by exemplary stories, once again, of elders he had known and of others known through the Islamic tradition.

Volume Six, well over a thousand pages, represents the longest volume of the work. Muhammad Zakariyya explained that he thought that he had ended the *Aap Biitii* but that between the imploring of his friends, and the stories reverberating in his head, he had decided to continue with more stories about the elders beyond those he personally knew. He organized these stories not by individuals, as he had done earlier, but by moral qualities illustrative of the ideals of a holy life. Finally, in Volume Seven, completed the year before he died, he provided virtually a journal of his final years set in India, Pakistan, and the Holy Places. Overall, the *Aap Biitii* is an overflowing and heterogeneous approach to talking about one's 'own life' and could hardly be more different from the linear, developmentally organized, representation of individual lives in conventional biographies and autobiographies written in the modern West.

Maulana Abu'l Hasan 'Ali Nadwi, his biographer, identified three subjects that Muhammad Zakariyya had sought to report, 'the episodes of his life that offered instruction (*sabak amooz haalaat*); the perfections (*kamaalaat*) and conduct of life (*tarz-i zindagii*) of his teachers and shaikhs; and, finally, episodes of 'sincerity and sacrifice' (*ikhlaas aur isaar*)'. 'Ali Miyan continued that the end product was 'a speaking picture, and a living, breathing image' of an age now past.[19] This last comment reminds us why a reformist like Muhammad Zakariyya, for whom it was so problematic to have texts or representations focused on their own person or lives, wrote at all. He wrote about the past in order to shore up the present, writing about 'days gone by' not with nostalgia but with ramrod conviction to transform the present.

Muhammad Zakariyya lived in a dense network of learned and holy men, dead and alive, whose teachings, charisma, and interactions formed the texture of his world. He was closely related to leading political figures of the day, among them Maulana Husain Ahmad Madani, the leader of the Jamiyyat Ulama-i Hind allied with the Indian National Congress, and Sayyid 'Ata'u'llah Shah Bukhari, leader of the Ahrar. But their political world was on the margins of what was important to him, and he focused on what he took to be eternal models of behaviour that looked primarily within. He wrote about his life not to talk about himself but because he thought the kind of life he represented was at risk, not least from the new generation of students who, he believed, should have been its guardians but instead gave way to worldly tastes and political distractions.

## The 'Strike' and the Defence of Proper Relationships

The beginnings of the *Aap Biitii* merit careful attention because they are profoundly revealing about what Muhammad Zakariyya took to be central to his life. As 'Ali Miyan concluded, what was central to him was the seminary itself. It was the site of his own 'education and training, his intellectual and ethical development, and his acquisition of knowledge and excellence'. It was, moreover, the only means, in his opinion, 'for preservation of religious knowledge, true guidance for Muslims, and prevention of corruption of belief and action'. The madrasa was 'the focus of his thought and attention, the site of his imaginings and hopes, and the refuge of his soul'. And from the seminary stemmed the relationships that 'were dearer than his own life and family'.[20] Nothing made Muhammad Zakariyya angrier than a student 'strike' (the English word was always used) which risked what to him held value over any worldly or political institution or gain. Muhammad Zakariyya's overriding goal in the *Aap Biitii* was to recall students to a time when students obeyed their teachers with fidelity and love.

The seminary mattered because of the kind of people who were there and the kind of people who had gone before. Both the strikers and their opponents focused on personal behaviour. The strikers' polemical attacks singled out Muhammad Zakariyya himself. The then principal, Maulana Muhammad As'adu'llah had been reluctant to dignify the attack with a response, in part because he had assumed the author to be using a pseudonym and claiming a non-existent organization. 'When the attack was first published', As'adu'llah wrote, 'I ignored it because of its frivolity and shallowness, and I assumed that all those who knew the school and the Shaikh would too. Indeed, I assumed that such an attack would, if anything, increase people's bonds (*ta'aluq*) [to the Shaikh]'.[21] But then when the report came to be widely circulated,

As'adu'llah felt he had to make a public statement, although he knew 'it would be a burden to the Shaikh', whose forgiveness for writing he therefore sought.

The strikers apparently made four devastating accusations against Muhammad Zakariyya: imperiousness, [greed for] wealth, [quest for] absolute power, and favouring his own people. The strikers, in short, denied him the qualities that defined model religious leadership: humility, self-denial in worldly goods, withdrawal from worldly power, and openness toward all without discrimination. Maulana As'adu'llah cut to the heart of the matter in his answer. Muhammad Zakariyya, he flatly stated, reproduced in his life the pattern of the great figures of old: As'adu'llah called him *baqiyu's-salaf*, a 'reminder' or 'remnant' of the ancestors. Far from materialist in his goals, he listed his disciplined and sacrificial services to the *shari'a*: his scholarly works on hadith known throughout the world, and his teaching at the Mazahir coupled with his dedication as 'spiritual patron' to the members of the biggest and most far reaching religious movement among Muslims in the world, 'known as Tabligh', whose leading figures, because of him, support and bring their blessed presence to the Mazahir.[22] He provided explicit details of Muhammad Zakariyya's financial arrangements with the school and his gifts to it. He described how Muhammad Zakariyya interrupted his scholarly work for no one. He invoked his very 'personality' (*tabii'at*) and 'nature' (*mizaaj*) to refute the accusations that he was a person who sought power.

As'adu'llah turned the final charge on its head. The attack claimed that Muhammad Zakariyya favoured his own people. In fact, it was a blessing that all the trustees of the school had been in a relation of 'belief' in him and 'love' for him. As it happened, As'adu'llah continued, they had chosen him, not he, them. As for the teachers and employees, they shared in his circle and he was nothing less than 'the entry way to the very grace (*maurid-i fazl-i khaas*) of Allah himself'. The strikers had missed the point. Muhammad Zakariyya was a link in great chains of spiritual blessing of his elders and teachers, a recipient of their blessing and a channel of blessing to those who in turn looked to them. His disciplined labour and his relation to material wealth was, moreover, not motivated by acquisition. Whatever he happened to have flowed through him to others. This is a recurrent image of the Sufi pir, who is a font of material largesse with no obvious source of income of his own.

When Muhammad Zakariyya replied, he limited himself to two incidental statements in the pamphlet, points which As'adu'llah had not even taken into account, one of fact and one of interpretation, that clearly troubled Muhammad Zakariyya greatly. The first was the charge that he had forbidden the madrasa to provide the striking students with food. The second was that he had severed the bond of Sufi initiation (bai'at) with supporters of the strike. As for the first, he made an absolute denial that he had intervened to deny the students food, and, to show how far that accusation was from the truth, he pointed out that he himself had fed the strikers at his own table. As for the second complaint of severing Sufi initiation, he embraced the charge with enthusiasm as 'completely true'.[23]

Muhammad Zakariyya justified his response by invoking the reaction of two great elders, Maulana Husain Ahmad Madani and Maulana Ashraf 'Ali Thanawi (1864–1943), who had recommended expulsion of striking students in earlier strikes at the 'mother' madrasa of Deoband going back four decades. To explain further, however, he reports Hazrat Madani's emotional reaction, during one of the earlier strikes, to seeing Muhammad Zakariyya with one of the strikers from Deoband (whom he did not in fact know to have been involved). Just as Madani was upset then, Muhammad Zakariyya describes himself as filled with hatred now when he sees the very faces of the strikers.[24] Under these circumstances, what benefit could there be to initiation and why should these people stop their own spiritual progress? Muhammad Zakariyya cites hadith that describe the Prophet's great love for his wife A'isha, on the one hand, and his hatred for Hazrat Wahshi, on the other: hate and love are beyond control, he points out, even for the Prophet, and dependent on one's temperament which in this tradition, as noted above, is a given and not a product of experience or environment.[25] To use such capacity for hatred, or any other innate personality characteristic, to a legitimate end is to live as one ought—and here, from Muhammad Zakariyya's own perspective, his rage was being used to the good.

The students, 'guests of the Prophet' as he ironically calls them, were the ones, Muhammad Zakariyya implies, who were motivated by a quest for materialism and worldly power. They wanted,

he writes, fancier diplomas, a different kind of light in the courtyard, better food, courses in literature so they could sprinkle their
discourses with fancy allusions, a 'degree' so they could get employment! *This* is a student (*taalib-i 'ilm* or 'seeker of knowledge'),
he asks? He could not believe that his students, those whom he
himself had taught from the hadith 'the position, dignity, religious
standing, and responsibility attendant on their position', could
abandon their studies for such purposes.[26] Muhammad Zakariyya
had told the students under his influence that it was not legitimate
for them to read newspapers: he had also opposed the formation
of voluntary organizations in the madrasa. Such distractions, he
felt, had cost students focus in their work. In a publication on an
earlier strike quoted by Muhammad Zakariyya, Ashraf 'Ali had
written that religious education itself was worship, '*ibaadat.*

At the end of his statement, Muhammad Zakariyya summed up
his argument, implicitly fitting himself into the Sufi model of
openness and tolerance on the one hand, disciplined relations of
submission and obedience on the other. His *table*, like the
bountiful *langar* of the Sufi shrine, was open, even to non-
Muslims.[27] *Bai'at* was not. On this he quoted one of the student
strikers who reportedly had said in words unthinkable for a
disciple: 'There's no shortage of *pirs* in the world', and, lest that
seem bitter, he modestly added that he was not worthy of such
rank in any case, despite the opinion and kindness of the elders.
But, then, in a chilling finale, he categorized sin as being of two
kinds, *shaitaanii* and *haiwanii*. The latter are sins of instinct and
he had always, he said, for his forty years at the school, insisted
that students who committed such sins be forgiven and reinstated.
But the former sins, the sins of *Iblis*—par excellence those of pride,
rebellion, and exaltation of the self—merited complete separation
from the perpetrators. Maulana Thanawi, writing about an earlier
strike had identified its essence (*haqiiqat*, used as a technical term
in Hanafi jurisprudence) as 'a breaking of relationships' (*qat'-i
ta'aluqaat*). Maulana Muhammad Zakariyya was ratifying what had
already happened. Nothing in Muhammad Zakariyya's life mattered more to him than *ta'aluqaat*—to humans, to the Prophet, and
to Allah—and for him these relationships were mediated through
the Arabic madrasa. The striking students, in his view, were guilty
not of rudeness to him, but of sundering their relation to the
Prophet and Allah himself.

THE PAST IN THE PRESENT

## The Guidance of the Elders and the Temptations of Materialism and Pride

When Maulana Muhammad Zakariyya again wrote about himself, it was in response to someone widely regarded as the pre-eminent Muslim religious figure in India of the late twentieth century, Maulana Abu'l Hasan 'Ali Nadwi ("Ali Miyan', 1914–2000), who, ironically, after Muhammad Zakariyya's death, would write his 'official' biography.[28] 'Ali Miyan, 'ghost wrote'[29] an introductory chapter dealing with Muhammad Zakariyya at the request of the biographer of the second amir of the Tablighi Jama'at (who had died in 1965), Maulana Muhammad Yusuf Kandhalawi, Muhammad Zakariyya's beloved cousin and colleague.[30] Such a chapter was part of the conventional introduction to a biography in the Arabo-Persian tradition, which typically situates the subject in the context of his genealogy and family members.[31]

In large part, 'Ali Miyan's account resonates with the broad themes sketched above, which are characteristic of Indo-Persian biography in terms of seeing Muhammad Zakariyya's character as innately given, the key moments of his life as the product of divine intervention, and his life as a whole the model, the memorial, of the great figures of the past. 'Ali Miyan emphasizes not only his evident services to religious learning, but he also reports many marks of Allah's favour communicated through divine signs. Muhammad Zakariyya was born in the holy month of Ramazan at the very time of the night prayer and thus received the blessings of the family and villagers gathered at an auspicious moment. His paternal grandfather, a great 'aalim and saint, proclaimed that the new baby was his 'replacement', and indeed he was to die that very month. He writes that Muhammad Zakariyya was the recipient of divine dreams and visions, and even underwent physical trans-formations when absorbed in teaching the hadith of the Prophet and when hearing of him or being in Medina. Something like a bolt of lightning would come on all present, especially when he finished teaching a book and prayed.[32] Maulana Muhammad Zakariyya himself, in his hundreds and hundreds of pages, de-scribed almost none of this.

Yet 'Ali Miyan, the cosmopolitan intellectual, also drew on Western theories of development and psychology. His presentation was largely chronological, and as he would do more extensively in the full biography, he tried to analyse his subject's personality over his life course. Albeit only in footnotes, he raised the issue of upbringing, crediting Muhammad Zakariyya's father 'with methods which would drive today's psychologists and educationists, who indulge a child's every whim and preach complete licence, to distraction'.[33] 'Ali Miyan stressed the importance of the influence of environment on a child, in Muhammad Zakariyya's case the opportunity to live amidst holy and learned men in childhood. He identified Muhammad Zakariyya's 'power of observation', evident in his stories of those days, with shaping his own life story, *aap biitii*, and his tastes. Indeed, 'Ali Miyan described Maulana Muhammad Zakariyya with several characteristics that were not the conventional paradigmatic virtues of a holy and learned person: among them, 'courage', 'capacity', and 'breadth', by which he meant an ability to deal with multiple and conflicting demands on his energy and time. But he also characterized him by the trait which was that of the Sufi, par excellence, namely passion in his devotion to the Prophet.

What was there not to like? Muhammad Zakariyya did not mince words: the chapter about him was like a drop of urine in a bottle of rose water that pollutes the rest. First of all, if anyone was going to tell his story, he was the one who would do it, and he invoked an Urdu couplet that he would speak 'his own reproach'—there is no need to listen to anyone else. 'In the end, they will say: "What more is there to say?"' And indeed in this section and throughout he emphasizes his flaws of temper, stubbornness, and unsociability as if to show the students, and others, that anyone could aspire to model behaviour. Second, although more obscurely, he insisted that 'Ali Miyan had written 'those matters which ought not to have been written about and left out those which should have been included'.[34] Presumably by the reference to what should have been excluded he meant the marks of divine favour since the reformists generally saw such signs either as a distraction from moral behaviour for oneself or a motive for undue veneration of someone else. Perhaps he also disliked the very idea of his life presented in such an appreciative, chronologically unfolding form. All he said, however, was that 'Ali Miyan '[had] written about Iran, Turan, and other foolish things which will not benefit anyone, whereas [what he now would include] were the things that were to be written about'.[35]

As in his response to the striking students, Muhammad Zakariyya ignored most of the offending document and chose only two seemingly random points to respond to, in this case a four-page section occurring early in the chapter entitled 'two delicate tests and divine grace', and, second, two footnotes on the subject of his father's 'nurture'.[36] Muhammad Zakariyya expressed dismay that 'Ali Miyan, despite being informed about other trials and episodes of his upbringing, did not include them. Muhammad Zakariyya's response consisted of a retelling of five 'tests', from his period of maturity, and their resolution, as well as eleven stories of his childhood upbringing (*tarbiyat*). In short, he shifts the focus and the framework of his life by focusing on his own weaknesses and the importance of the love and blessing of Allah, his father, and other elders in shaping his life.

Muhammad Zakariyya followed convention in making chronological movement or development irrelevant. The episodes were not organized from the earliest to the latest. Muhammad Zakariyya, as in the narratives of 'sorrows' noted above, identified the first set of episodes, in fact, explicitly as 'trials' (*imtihaan*), or 'afflictions' (*ibtilaa*). Moreover, Muhammad Zakariyya did not suggest that he ever improved.[37] Throughout, he displayed his flawed character, the instinctual reactions he had that he could not control. Only through Allah's grace, and the love and blessing of his father and other elders, were temptations resisted. Thanks to them, he had 'begun to be counted among humans', but nothing had changed his character—any more, he says, than putting a dog's tail in a pipe makes it straight.[38] This is not a story of Muhammad Zakariyya's own agency or development.

Muhammad Zakariyya first recounted an episode which occurred three days after his father's death when he declined an opportunity presented to him by his father's great shaikh and mentor, Maulana 'Abdu'r-rahim Raipuri (d. 1919–20), who transmitted to him an offer to move his father's bookshop to a situation where he would have had expert advice and help. His father had died leaving a substantial debt, and now Muhammad Zakariyya had not only that burden to deal with, but also the responsibility of maintenance for his mother and sister. Hearing this proposal, Muhammad Zakariyya said, he felt the very earth sink beneath him. He rejected the proposal on the grounds that he could not move to a place distant from his own spiritual guide.

In fact, Hazrat Raipuri was pleased with this answer and blessed him, explaining that he had spoken only because of the insistence of yet another elder who had made that offer, someone who could indeed help, but who also wished Muhammad Zakariyya close by. At this, Muhammad Zakariyya was enraged, and this reaction, he saw as his fault, repaying kindness with anger.

Three other episodes involved his turning down generous offers of employment. To an offer from Hyderabad that would have given him perhaps thirty-fold his salary at the Mazahir, he wrote only one line, 'It is not for me to be dependent on favours'.[39] To an offer from Bengal, shortly before Partition, he again wrote back a curt one line. He regretted his emotional make-up that produced such responses but attributed his refusals as an escape from temptation owed only to Allah, who, like his elders, showed him kindness, *karm* and *ihsaan*.

In turning to trials earlier in his life, he reported his response to an offer of marriage into a rich family when he was still a child:

The name of Mirza Surya Jaah is often mentioned in the life stories of Muhammad Ilyas and Muhammad Yusuf. He had great affection for my grandfather, Maulana Muhammad Isma'il, and he wanted his daughter, Qaisar Jahan Begum, to marry my father. My grandfather, in fact, did not want this marriage, and my father concurred. Nonetheless, my father and uncle kept up very close relations with Qaisar Jahan Begum and visited her house often. When I went there as a child, she would wrap me up carefully and put me to sleep with her. She would say to my father, 'You turned me down, but he is my child and he should marry my daughter.' My father retorted, 'How can I choose for him what I turned down for myself?' She still persisted. As a test, my father asked me my opinion. I blurted out that it would be beyond me to walk around serving a *paandan*!

The story behind this was that Qaisar Jahan's husband loved her devotedly, and he did, indeed, prepare and offer her *paan*. This was a shocking sight to Muhammad Zakariyya, as he explained, since in his family the women did the serving. His father was not pleased with the answer and said it had a whiff of arrogance (*takabbur*) about it. When he himself had been asked about marrying into the family, he had answered more appropriately, 'If I marry that princess, I will not be able to sleep on a rough mat', that is that he wanted a humble life. Muhammad Zakariyya concluded that his father was right.[40]

Muhammad Zakariyya continued with the stories of his up-bringing, stories that presumably sprang readily to his pen since, he explained, he loved telling them and would recount them while teaching. These were, moreover, only a selection: he could, he declared, in a reference that evoked his pleasure in storytelling, write an entire *Arabian Nights* of such stories! These stories, like the earlier episode, invariably showed Muhammad Zakariyya in the context of relationships of protection and blessing, and, like them, they parade his flaws of anger, distractions in pleasure, and pride. Again, however, thanks to Allah and his elders he claims to have escaped temptation, which like employment and the wrong kind of marriage, for the most part revolved around material lures.

In the stories, Muhammad Yahya, Muhammad Zakariyya's father, slapped a toddler who offered him his cherished embroi-dered pillow but called it 'mine'. He mercilessly beat an eight-year old who caused a disruption to prayer by resisting help. He beat him again for praying when he should have been studying. He prohibited him from keeping any money, or accepting any food or drink. He investigated any matter involving money or potential lying. He withdrew the promise of an excursion because the boy was too excited at the prospect. Muhammad Zakariyya learned to 're-gift' any beautiful clothes that came his way after his father's fury at his being dressed extravagantly by the family's womenfolk.

The whole account was permeated with court-like rhetoric, with behaviour referred to as 'crimes', the matter that led to a beating being staged as a 'trial' until the truth came out, the father's rules for behaviour termed '*qaanuun*'. The judicial rhetoric was mutual. When Muhammad Yahya accepted an invitation to visit a friend, he wrote—with Muhammad Zakariyya's own pen, Muhammad Zakariyya adds—that now the leg irons of Muhammad Zakariyya, a chain that had held him in place, had finally been lifted. By this, he later explained to Muhammad Zakariyya, who had written of how he missed him and feared harm to himself in his absence, his presence was no longer necessary since now Muhammad Zakariyya had established his own close communication with Allah. Muhammad Zakariyya humbly prayed in response that Allah make this opinion true.[41]

In the final section of this volume Muhammad Zakariyya provided a document written for the teachers and leaders of the school, consisting of fifteen episodes, given as examples, relating to the elders of the Mazaahiru'l-'Uluum.[42] These were stories, he said, that he feared would no longer be remembered as the older generation passed away. It was his *aap biitii* in the sense that it included 'whatever [he] had seen or heard about the elders during [his] sixty years at the school, from the time he was a student at the age of thirteen to the present'.[43] It was meant to offer lessons in the 'strictness' and 'punctiliousness' of the elders: above all, their extraordinary scrupulosity in the use of the madrasa's resources, their punctuality, high standards of teaching, and penury. The document surely served to strengthen the side of the current leadership as they associated themselves with such worthy exemplars of the school's elders. Indeed, Muhammad Zakariyya himself, though he could never counter his attackers directly by citing his own virtues, by writing about the virtues of those he personally knew, could indirectly identify himself with their distinctions. As for the image he presented of himself, he succeeded in both showing how even he, flawed as he was, escaped the damning lures of materialism and worldly ambitions, thanks to accepting the blessing and guidance of Allah and his elders.

## A 'Sufi' in the Modern World

In the classic categorization of Muslim religious leadership as either Sufi or scholar/'*aalim*, Muhammad Zakariyya would likely be assigned the status of an '*aalim*. He was, after all, a formidably learned scholar of Prophetic tradition and an eminent teacher in a major seminary for most of the twentieth century. But, as I have argued elsewhere, if this dichotomy of types of leadership holds in some contexts, it does not for many schools of 'ulama in modern India where a 'composite' type of leadership, albeit tilting in one direction or the other, is common.[44] The face that Muhammad Zakariyya explicitly and implicitly presents of himself in this extraordinary work, so lengthy and presumably so unstudied, is, perhaps surprisingly, in fact one that resonates deeply with paradigmatic models of the world renouncing Sufi that are familiar across Muslim societies, but not necessarily associated, as they were in the India of this period, with 'ulama.[45]

Muhammad Zakariyya in fact was well-known for his opposition to students' becoming Sufi disciples and engaging in the time-consuming disciplines of *zikr* and *shugl* because he feared that would interface with their studies. Moreover, like other Deobandis, he did not participate in the customary 'urs celebrations or encourage pilgrimage to the graves of holy men. He was not well-known as a channel of miracles or healing. He claimed to have no liking for amulets.[46] Yet, for all that, in other ways his life seems to have had Sufi experiences and teachings at its heart. The long pages of his autobiography are filled, line upon line, with references to his relationships to elders whose light and blessing he sought and lived in. Those associated with the madrasa at Saharanpur, among countless others, were particularly devoted to two great Sufis, Hazrat Maulana 'Abdu'r-rahim Raipuri and his son, Hazrat Maulana 'Abdu'l-qadir Raipuri (d. 1955) with whom both Zakariyya and his father had profound and enduring bonds. Muhammad Zakariyya's own shaikh and guide was Hazrat Maulana Khalil Ahmad Saharanpuri. At several points in the Aap Biitii he wrote at length on technical issues in the relationships of saints and their disciples, providing dramatic examples he himself had seen, or heard of, among great saints of the past on the transfer of nisbat.[47] His response to the strikers engaged issues, par excellence, of the Sufi: the open table and the initiatory bond.

Of the many stories he included of what he always called his own shaikh's 'favours' to him, one in particular gives a sense of the depth of the relationship coupled with the wit and affection that fill so many of the stories. Muhammad Zakariyya notes that he tells this particular story only because friends pressed him to. Once during a discussion of the elders and paradise, Zakariyya describes himself as unduly bold in asserting to Hazrat Saharanpuri that he had to take him with him when he entered paradise, to which his shaikh immediately agreed. Some time later, Hazrat Saharanpuri arrived at the madrasa while Zakariyya was teaching and went off with someone else for refreshments at a nearby house. Zakariyya protested that the person should have waited for him, whereby Hazrat Saharanpuri said, 'I did not promise to take you everywhere; the place where I promised to take you, there I will take you'. Since that episode, Zakariyya writes, hope for mercy had driven out fear.[48] To accept the blessing of the shaikh meant acceptance of his authority as well, an acceptance Zakariyya embraced, and the current generation of students did not.

The rhetoric of the entire account fosters an interpretation of events characteristic of Sufism that suggests a kind of passivity to events. The very term *aap biitii* has at root the meaning of 'what has happened to one' and particularly 'an account of one's sorrows', that is, a focus on events like deaths that are indeed beyond one's shaping or control.[49] Muhammad Zakariyya reacts to attacks, responds to readers' demands, and, most importantly, claims to shape his life and activities at the direction of the elders. He explicitly worried about predestination and concluded that indeed the end is beyond one's control but the route to it is open. To illustrate he provided several examples, including a pedestrian one along the lines of being a person fated to eat chicken, a food of the rich. This could be the result of becoming rich oneself; becoming a 'hazratji' and being given such gifts—like himself in fact; or simply being someone else's cook. He did 'fieldwork' to reach this conclusion, questioning people who came to him for amulets: they spoke freely about their lives, assuming he needed the answers to help them.[50]

Although the Deobandis were circumspect about visits to graves, Zakariyya, who relished time spent in *zikr*, especially loved recitation at the grave of Hazrat Hafiz Zamin, a saint from the previous century. He also tells of a time when travelling in the Punjab he found himself at the grave of the great reformist saint Shaikh Ahmad Sirhindi (1564–1624). He was travelling with relatives to a wedding. 'After reaching Sirhind Shariif, I remembered nothing. I do not know how I got off the train and how the ticket inspector let me off the platform without a ticket. Soon I found myself at the grave of Hazrat Mujaddid Sahib.... The whole day I remained there at the latticed screen behind the grave.' When he got home all he could do was to explain that he himself did not know how he got there or returned.

Intrinsic to the charisma of the Sufi is belief that he lives a life of discipline and self-denial. Muhammad Zakariyya's discipline focused around his teaching and writing which no worldly goal could disrupt and which was so intense that mealtimes or sleep could be missed unaware; all his elders, he noted, had great bodily control over waking and sleep.[51] During Ramadan his devotional practices were unrelenting. Once a person who came to see him simply gave up. 'Through Allah's grace the month of Ramadan occurs where we live too', he said, 'but for us it doesn't take the form of a fever!' (Muhammad Zakariyya 1993: 86).[52] He lived simply, his one-room house of mud-baked brick explicitly compared to the house of the Prophet Muhammad.[53] He rejoiced in a student so dedicated that he forsook his curry to eat dry bread so that he could continue studying.[54]

A contemporary Sufi might boast that he differed from the 'ulama who were salaried employees, receivers, not givers.[55] But as the episodes of his youth show, Muhammad Zakariyya similarly resisted salaries and financial dependence. Although constrained to accept a salary from the madrasa, he ultimately (through the blessing of the second Hazrat Raipuri, he explains) was able to decline the salary for teaching[56] and in due course rejoiced that he was able to repay whatever had come from the madrasa entirely. Many of his anecdotes showed how scrupulous the elders were in relation to the resources of the school. Muhammad Zakariyya's economy seems to have had as its principal trust in Allah coupled with acceptance of unsolicited gifts and loans, repaid by rolling over more loans.[57] That his father died indebted hardly seems surprising. Muhammad Zakariyya told, as a mark of God's great blessing, how when he and his party were penniless in the Hijaz, a fellow Indian, worried about the Bedouins, asked him to keep his considerable wealth until they returned to India. With this money, Muhammad Zakariyya could meet his party's urgent needs, confident that resources would appear to repay the trust when he got home.[58] Muhammad Zakariyya's scrupulosity in relation to finances was premised on a belief that any dishonesty would reap instant punishment: he claims to have observed in his lifetime, for example, the illnesses, law suits, and thefts experienced by those who had misused the resources of the madrasa.

Zakariyya's approach to finances was not without controversy. He was berated by younger relatives in Kandhla for living off charity when he could have had a salary. Muhammad Zakariyya confessed to having shown some undue pride when later that same relative saw him solve a property issue for the family by his mere presence.[59] He was also the despair of his bookshop manager since he refused to deal with colonial courts and copyright on the one hand, and continued to ruin his budget by feeding all comers on the other.[60] Like the classic Sufi, whatever he had was meant to be given away. He had resources, he was able to feed others, he provided gifts for weddings, and he ate well himself—his self-denial did not always extend to food.[61] Little wonder that the strikers were confused into thinking he was misusing school resources.

More like a Sufi than like the stereotype of the 'aalim were as
well his relations to competing schools of 'ulama and to politics.
The 'ulama are thought to be strident defenders of minute points
of difference, engaging in 'fatawa wars' of mutual denunciation.[62]
Muhammad Zakariyya, in contrast, said that he looked upon
differences among the 'ulama as a mercy[63] and he wrote at length
about his good relations to the rival reformist school, the Ahl-i
Hadith.[64] He approvingly told an apparently well-known story
urging those 'in a high position of academic activity or in Sufism
or in any other religious service' to look down on no one, even
warning against those who out of pride looked down on non-
Muslims.[65] As for politics, he strove to be open to all sides and
spoke of his motivations as being shaped more by his connections
and love than by ideology. He explained wearing the homespun
of the nationalist movement in terms of his devotion to Hazrat
Madani.[66] The quietist 'ulama, like the Sufis, have seen their
interests best served by the pluralist, liberal state, with whom they
cooperate pragmatically. Indeed, Muhammad Zakariyya wrote a
critique of the foremost Islamist of the subcontinent, Maulana
Maududi.[67]

Quetism does not mean being apolitical. Although Muhammad
Zakariyya discouraged students from being involved in political
activities, he pointed out in one case that students at the madrasa
could learn all they needed very quickly once their studies were
over since politics had the place of a maidservant (laundiyaa) 'in
our house'![68] In Zakariyya's account of his relations with the leader
of the Ahrar movement there are hints of the classic Sufi fable of
the political leader who always comes to see the superior power
of the holy man, a further suggestion that political connections are
inevitable yet meant to be kept in their place.[69]

The anthropologist Pnina Werbner in her study of a late
twentieth century Sufi identified her subject's key characteristics
as being 'entertaining, authoritative, capable of fearful anger, and
mischievous'.[70] All of these characteristics readily apply to
Muhammad Zakariyya, including a quite remarkable streak of
'holy foolishness', shared by his companions, that one might
not expect. To take only one account, he describes a visit to the
household of the daughter of Hazrat Maulana Rashid Ahmad
Gangohi (d. 1905) the great Deobandi elder. In the company of
Maulana Ilyas, the founder of Tablighi Jama'at, and Maulana

Madani, the three turned the household upside down. Welcomed into the ladies' section of the house, they playfully ate all the fine dishes brought to them so that each time a family member went to fetch the bread, he would return to find all the food meant to be eaten with it already gone. Finally, Hazrat Rashid Ahmad's daughter, whom they all cherished, appeared herself to tease them that for three worthies addressed by others as 'hazrat' they actually were all still children.[71]

What did it mean that Muhammad Zakariyya in presenting himself, in all these many dimensions, embraced the Indo-Persian rhetoric with its dominant characteristic of passivity? In a recent study Jill Ker Conway identified the Western autobiographical tradition of individualism, achievement, and overcoming obstacles as a primarily male story, with roots in Greek myth. The female story, she points out, rooted in women's medieval spiritual autobiographies, emphasizes passivity, reliance on the will of God, and the importance of enabling relationships with both God and elders. Indeed this 'relational', rather than 'positional' or 'linear' writing is often taken as key to women's self-narratives.[72] In these stories, there is no place for claims to leadership or agency, and the writer is likely to engage in self-deprecation. Conway speculates that the stories may be one thing and 'real' events another, the stories just strategically deployed to make the actions and the life of the narrator acceptable, particularly if the subject is undertaking novel or controversial activities.[73]

It is tempting to explore this perspective in the case of Maulana Zakariyya, particularly since others regard Maulana Zakariyya's life story as one of leadership and success. Maulana As'adul'llah describes, for example, his role in shaping the affairs of the Tabligh movement and expanding the madrasa. Zakariyya himself recounts situations where he is clearly responsible for the outcome, though he presents himself as wholly passive. He attributes the majority of his books to the request of some elder. However, the fact remains that he wrote dozens of books. He defies family conventions, for example in arranging marriage partners. In what sense is all this 'passivity'?

Rather than seeing rhetoric and reality as separate, sometimes rhetoric may actually be the reality. The strong modern European assumption that individuals seek freedom from submission and constraint, for example as imposed by the traditions of religion, colours the assumption that the rhetoric is a cover. In fact, there are other traditions, including the one represented by Zakariyya and by the Islamic tradition he espoused. In this tradition we encounter strong individuals—though not individualism—yet an energetic commitment to, and pleasure, even passion, for disciplined submission (to Allah and to elders) that entails disciplined action. This, too, is 'agency'. And there is pleasure in the life, and the stories of the lives, that result.

This pleasure, even passion—the Sufi concept of '*ishq*—becomes the driving force for the disciplined behaviour and focus that links the believer to his elders, to the Prophet, and to Allah. 'Passion', not 'passivity', may be seen as the key to the disciplined submission that is Zakariyya's goal and his source of purpose in his world.

The substance of his life, as Maulana Zakariyya writes it, is the study of hadith, which ties him to the Prophet and thence to Allah, and the sustaining, remembering, performing, and cherishing of 'enabling relations', to use Conway's term, with his elders both living and dead. He cherishes their kindness; and he longs to be with them during the holy month of Ramazan, on hajj, in scholarly service to them, or at any time of illness or need. He assigns the 'Id sacrifice to their benefit, he seeks their intercessory prayer, he rejoices at their visits, he hopes to be present at the all-important moment of their death, and then he welcomes their posthumous visitation in dreams. His is a life dense with scholarship and dense with (male) relationships. As in the Western male biographies, there is little space given to private life except for a few touching accounts of the deaths of his womenfolk intended for the moral lessons they yield as examples of a blessed and auspicious death that confirms *their* relations to Allah and his Prophet. An aunt, for example, dies joyous as she sees the Prophet approach.[74]

What emerges from the account is the life of a person of extraordinary discipline and dedication, for whom every moment was a precious opportunity for worship, service to learning, and devotion to his elders. His life moved between intense concentration on his scholarly work and life in the midst of networks of the holy and learned. He insisted on his many flaws, a way of counterbalancing what might otherwise seem undue pride at writing at all, and, of course, he said nothing of the signs of divine favour or a pattern of God-given excellences that made him the 'reminder of the ancestors'. Nor did he give anything like the picture, so evocatively drawn by 'Ali Miyan, of his role in the lives of thousands of disciples, devotees, and participants in the pietist movement of 'internal conversion', Tablighi Jama'at, for which he served as a pivotal figure, a source of guidance and blessing.

Not only Maulana Zakariyya, but his autobiography, like other life histories of the holy, was considered by his followers to be a source of blessing, *baraka*, the very words on the page a source of charisma. In this logo-centric tradition, words always have power. The texts are interactive, most obviously when read aloud. Not only does *baraka* flow to the reader, the reader in return may be stimulated to good actions that rebound to the credit of the author or are explicitly requested by the author.

The autobiography is an invitation to its readers to confirm, or make an empowering choice to voluntarily accept, rules more stringent that those of any bureaucracy or state they may be embedded in. This kind of life is sanctioned by the precedent of the great elders of the past, and holds out the promise of relationships with them and with those who continue their tradition. Readers—whether in India or beyond—are enjoined to find transcendent meaning in the routines of everyday life, the presence of a moral community, and the promise of future rewards, their own lives shaped by, and shaping, the kind of relationships whose stories Maulana Zakariyya loved to tell.

## Notes

1. For background on Deoband, see Metcalf, Barbara D. 1982. *Islamic Revival in British India: Deoband, 1860–1900*. Princeton: Princeton University Press, 1982 and Faruqui, Ziya-ul-Hasan. 1963. *The Deoband School and the Demand for Pakistan*. Bombay: Asia Publishing House.

2. Kandhalawi, Muhammad Zakariyya. n.d. *Aap Biitii (Yaad-i ayyam)*. Volume 2 (*Aap Biitii* 6–17). Karachi: Ma'hadu'l khaliilu'l islaamii.

3. Kandhalawi, Muhammad Zakariyya. 1993. *Aap Biitii*. Volumes 1, 2, 3 (English trans.). New Delhi: Idara Isha'at-e-Diniyat; and Kandhalawi. 1996. *Aap Biitii*. Volumes 4 and 5 [English trans.]. New Delhi: Idara Isha'at-e-Diniyat.

4. Kandhalawi, Mohammad Zakariyya. n.d. *Aap Biitii (Yaad-i ayyam)*. Volume 1 (*Aap Biitii* 1–5). Karachi: Ma'hadu'l khaliilu'l islaamii.

5. These may have included Muhammad 'Aashiq Ilaahi Miiratii (n.d.) (a) and (b); Manaazir Ahsan Giilaanii (1955–6); Husain Ahmad Madani (1953); Abu'l-hasan 'Ali Nadwii (1944); and Asghar Husain (1920–1).

6. Kandhalawi, Muhammad Zakariyya. 1969. *Hazrat Shaikh aur un kii aap biitii*, p. 25. New Delhi: Idaara-yi ishha't-i diinyaat.

7. Ibid., p. 35.

8. Priolkar, A. K. 1973. 'Indian Incunabula', in Marshall, D. N. and N. N. Gidwani, *Comparative Librarianship: Essays in Honour of Professor D. N. Marshall*, pp. 129–35. New Delhi, cited in Darnton, Robert. 2001. 'Literary Surveillance in the British Raj: The Contradictions of Liberal Imperialism'. *Book History*, 4: pp. 133–76. Priolkar dates this period of expansion in the use of print from 1868 to 1900.

9. William Lawler described popular readings in his 'Report on the Bengal Library for the Year 1878', V/23/24, 'Frequently in this very town of Calcutta an observant passerby sees a large number of natives collected round a tailor or native grocer's shop to hear a man…reading a tale in Musulmani-Bengali, in which the auditors appear to take the most lively interest….' Quoted in Darnton, op. cit. The popular Deobandi text for women, *Bihishti Zewar*, included instructions in the text itself for readers to gather other women to whom it should be read out loud. See Metcalf, Barbara D. 1990. *Perfecting Women: Maulana Ashraf 'Ali Thanawi's Bihishti Zewar*. Translation, annotation, and introduction. Berkeley: University of California Press.

10. Kandhalawai, Muhammad Zakariyya. op. cit. Volume 6, p. 817.

11. Kandhalawi, Muhammad Zakariyya. 1970. *Aap Biitii nambar 2 yaa yaad-i ayaam nambar 1*, p. 81. Saharanpur: Kutbkhaana Yahyawii.

12. Metcalf, Barbara D. 1994. 'Remaking Ourselves': Islamic Self-Fashioning in a Global Movement of Spiritual Renewal'. In Marty, Martin and Scott Appleby, eds. *Accounting for Fundamentalisms*. Chicago: University of Chicago Press.

13. 'Abdu'l-hayy, Muhammad. 1972. *Maasir-i hakiimu'l-ummat*. Gaya: Daaru'l-kutab imdaadiyya.

14. Ibid., *daal*.

15. Fakhru'd-diin, Muhammad. 1972. *Dars-i hayaat*. Gaya: Madani kutub khaana.

16. Lewis, Bernard. 1991. 'First-Person Narrative in the Middle East'. *Middle Eastern Lives: The Practice of Biography and Self-Narrative*. In Kramer, Martin, ed. Syracuse: Syracuse University Press, and Hermansen, Marcia K. 1988. 'Interdisciplinary Approaches to Islamic Biographical Materials'. *Religion* 18: 163–82.

17. Metcalf, Barbara D. 1993. 'Remembering Mecca: Mumtaz Mufti's *Labbaik*'. In Folkenflik, Robert, ed. *Autobiography and Self-Representation*, pp. 149–67. Stanford: Stanford University Press (Chapter 14 below); and Metcalf. 1995. 'Narrating Lives: A Mughal Empress, A French Nabob, A Nationalist Muslim Intellectual', *The Journal of Asian Studies* 54, 2: 474–80 (Chapter 15 below).

18. Grima, Benedicte. 1992. *The Performance of Emotion among Paxtun Women: 'The Misfortunes which have Befallen Me'*. Austin: University of Texas

Press; and Narayan, Kirin. 2000.' 'Unspeakable Lives: Silences in the Life Stories of Women in Kangra, Northwest India'. University of Wisconsin: Tyescript.

19. Abul' Hasan, 'Ali Nadwi. 1982. *Hazrat Shaikhu'l-Hadiis Maulaana Muhammad Zakariyya*, p. 106. Lucknow.

20. Ibid., p. 226.

21. Kandhalawi, Muhammad Zakariyya. 1969. *Hazrat Shaikh*, p. 4.

22. For background on Tablighi Jama'at, see Abu'l-Hasan, 'Ali Nadwi, ed. 1944. *Hazrat Maulana*; Haq, M. Anwarul. 1972. *The Faith Movement of Maulana Muhammad Ilyas*. London: George Allen and Unwin; Masud, Muhammad Khalid, ed. 1999. *Travellers in Faith: Studies of Tablighi Jam'at as a Transnational Movement*. Leiden: Brill; Metcalf, Barbara D. August 1993. 'Living *Hadith* in the Tablighi Jama'at', *Journal of Asian Studies* 52: 3, pp. 584–608; Metcalf. 1994. "Remaking Ourselves": Islamic Self-Fashioning in a Global Movement of Spiritual Renewal'. In Marty, Martin and Scott Appleby, eds. *Accounting for Fundamentalisms*. Chicago: Chicago University Press; Mayaram, Shail. 1997. *Resisting Regimes: Myth, Memory, and the Shaping of Muslim Identity*. Delhi: Oxford University Press; and Sikand, Yoginder. 2002. *The Origins and Development of the Tablighi-Jam'at at (1920–2000): A Cross-Country Comparative Study*. New Delhi: Orient Longman.

23. Kandhalawi, 1969. *Hazrat Shaikh*, p. 73.

24. Ibid., pp. 73–5.

25. Ibid., pp. 105–7.

26. Ibid., p. 78.

27. Ibid., pp. 104–5. Werbner, Pnina. *Pilgrims of Love: The Anthropology of a Global Sufi Cult*. Bloomington: Indiana University Press, 2003, for a convincing argument that scholars have missed the implications of the *langar* for understanding the paradigmatic pattern of the 'world-renouncing. Sufi.'

28. Abul' Hasan 'Ali Nadwi. 1982. *Hazrat Shaikhu'l-Hadiis*.

29. Kandhalawi. 1969. *Hazrat Shaikh*, p. 24.

30. Hasani, Muhammad Sani. n.d. (1967?). *Sawaanih-i Hazrat Maulaana Muhammad Yuusuf Kandhlawii*. Lucknow: Nadwatu'l-'ulama.

31. Kandhalawi. 1969. *Hazrat Shaikh*, p. 24.

32. Hasani, Muhammad Sani. 1967. *Sawaanih-i Hazrat*, p. 115.

33. Ibid., p. 78.

34. Kandhalawi. 1969. *Hazrat Shaikh*, p. 24.

35. Ibid., p. 35.

36. Hasani, Muhammad Sani. 1967. *Sawaanih-i Hazrat*, pp. 95–9; fn. 78 and fn. 83.

37. Kandhalawi. 1969. *Hazrat Shaikh*, p. 31.

38. Ibid., pp. 33, 50, 52.

39. Ibid., p. 30.

40. Ibid., pp. 31–3, paraphrased.

41. Ibid., p. 53.
42. Ibid., pp. 54–71.
43. Ibid., p. 53.
44. Metcalf, Barbara D. 1982. *Islamic Revival*; and Sanyal, Usha. 1996. *Devotional Islam and Politics in British India: Ahmad Riza Khan Barelwi and his Movement*, 1870–1920. Delhi: Oxford University Press.
45. See Werbner, Pnina. op. cit. This study of a contemporary Sufi saint, Zindapir (d. 1999) sets up significant contrasts—above all in his focus on disciples and not scholarship—but also some striking similarities in personal discipline, economic dealings, and political attitudes to a scholar like Zakariyya.
46. Kandhalawi, Muhammad Zakariyya. 1996. *Aap Biitii*, Volume 5, p. 315.
47. Kandhalawi, Mohammad Zakariyya. 1993. *Aap Biitii*, Volume 4, p. 156 and Kandhalawi, 1996. *Aap Biitii*, pp. 419–36.
48. Kandhalawi, Mohammad Zakariyya. n.d. *Aap Biitii* (Yaad-i ayyam) [Volume 1 (*Aap Biitii* 1–5)], Volume 4, p. 92.
49. Dihlawi, Sayyid Ahmad. 1896 (1974 edn). *Farhang-i asafiiya*. 4 vols. Delhi: National Academy; and Fallon, S. W. 1879 (1986 edn). *A New Hindustani-English Dictionary*. Lucknow: Uttar Pradesh Urdu Academy.
50. Kandhalawi, Muhammad Zakariyya. 1970. *Aap Biitii nambar 2*, pp. 150–1.
51. Kandhalawi, Muhammad Zakariyya. 1996. *Aap Biitii*, p. 89
52. Kandhalawi, Muhammad Zakariyya. 1993. *Aap Biitii*, p. 86.
53. Kandhalawi, Muhammad Zakariyya. 1996. *Aap Biitii*, p. 52.
54. Ibid., p. 131.
55. Werbner, Pnina. op. cit.
56. Kandhalawi, Muhammad Zakariyya. 1996. *Aap Biitii*, p. 29.
57. Ibid., p. 106.
58. Ibid., p. 205.
59. Kandhalawi, Muhammad Zakariyya. 1993. *Aap Biitii*, pp. 137–40.
60. Ibid., p. 339.
61. Kandhalawi, Muhammad Zakariyya. 1996. *Aap Biitii*, p. 62.
62. Werbner, Pnina, op. cit.
63. Kandhalawi, Muhammad Zakariyya. 1996. *Aap Biitii*, p. 119.
64. Ibid., pp. 323–7.
65. Ibid., p. 444.
66. Ibid., p. 77; 1993, p. 363.
67. Kandhalawi, Muhammad Zakariyya. 1970. *Aap Biitii nambar 2*, pp. 159–60.
68. Kandhalawi, Muhammad Zakariyya. 1993. *Aap Biitii*, p. 73.
69. Ibid., pp. 59–63.
70. Werbner, Pnina, op. cit.
71. Kandhalawi, Muhammad Zakariyya. 1993. *Aap Biitii*, pp. 24–6.

72. Peterson, Linda H. 1993. 'Institutionalizing Women's Autobiography: Nineteenth Century Editors and the Shaping of an Autobiographical Tradition'. In Folkenflik, Robert, ed. *Autobiography and Self-Representation*, pp. 80–103. Stanford: Stanford University Press.

73. Conway, Jill Ker. 1998. *When Memory Speaks: Reflections on Autobiography*. New York: Alfred A. Knopf; and Margzadant, Jo Burr, ed. 2000. *The New Biography: Reforming Femininity in Nineteenth Century France*. Berkeley: University of California Press.

74. Kandhalawi, Muhammad Zakarriya. 1971. *Aap Biitii nambar 3 yaa yaad-i ayaam nambar 2*. Saharanpur: Kutbkhaana Yahyawii.

# II

# The Variety of 'Islamic' Cultural and Political Life to 1947

# 4

# Reading and Writing about Muslim Women in British India

Many Indian writers and activists in nineteenth-century British India made the subject of women a central topic in their programmes of cultural reform and redefinition, expressing this concern, above all, through the newly available medium of print. Hence the story of reformist movements related to women is, in a fundamental sense, a story of the writing and circulation of vernacular pamphlets and books. The network of those who shared reading materials comes to constitute distinctive groups, defined in part by the very act of what they read. This process was true for all kinds of groups, but was particularly striking in the case of women among whom many, for example, did not go to public meetings or schools. The emphasis on reading also suggests the extent to which these were primarily movements of the elite.

Why did issues related to women become so important? Recently scholars have insisted that the emphasis on women cannot be explained simply as the old colonial historical narrative would suggest. That story goes like this: the British came; they recognized the depravity of purdah, widow burning, child marriage, and female infanticide; sensible Indians immediately recognized a superior culture when they saw one, and, thanks to British tutelage, they began the 'regeneration' their society needed. Historians like Lata Mani, looking closely at the key issue of sati among Hindus in Bengal—where the colonial narrative was primarily forged—have convincingly demonstrated that the British used certain customs (including sati which involved only the tiniest fraction of the population) as the site to at once legitimize their rule and also to identify an Indian 'tradition' that was in fact of limited provenance and importance.[1]

An emphasis on issues related to women established, at least to themselves, British moral authority on gender roles. Moreover it allowed Britons to characterize Indians as effeminate on the very grounds that their men failed to 'protect' and 'respect' women as they should. Such emphases had far-reaching effects on fundamental British conceptions and institutions. By this argument, issues related to gender in Victorian England itself cannot be understood apart from the colonial context. Although I can only allude to these issues here, they are suggestive of a broad trend in the study of the colonial period today that insists on a model not of 'impact' and 'response' but of mutual change in both societies.

As for Indians, excluded from many aspects of political life, it was only in creating domains of 'religion' and 'community' that they could find permissible arenas of power. Those wishing to establish themselves as 'leaders' with access to official power, of necessity interacted with, even as they transformed, the concerns of their rulers. Indians, not just Britons, were active participants in shaping the colonial experience.

The content of Bengali Hindu social reform was to have far reaching implications. The social reformers ultimately identified the middle class, educated housewife with nothing less than the preservation of 'Hindu' religion and culture, and even with India itself as Bharat Mata.[2] The 'New Hindu woman' was at once different from the unreformed, poor, and uneducated women; from English women, who were both a model and a threat; and from non-Hindu, above all Muslim women. To the extent that such an image was at the heart of Hindu cultural nationalism, it helps explain the failure of political nationalism to engage the imagination and commitment of large segments of the population. The new Hindu woman in the nineteenth century, as now, represented a minority. The historian Partha Chatterjee, sensitive to the alienation of large segments of the population from contemporary political structures on the one hand and to the latter day manifestations of Hindu 'fundamentalism' on the other, has seen in these reform movements a negative legacy that the conventional narrative ignores. That the shaping of the 'particular' or 'communal'—in which issues of gender were so important—was to be fundamentally political is only too obvious today.

When we turn to the subject of Muslim women, certain themes clearly overlap with these. First, the colonial context is critical. That context, however, worked in a variety of ways and was evident not only in ideas and policies as such, but in the very structure of colonial rule. Some Muslims engaged with the official British discourse on women, much as Bengali Hindu reformers did, but others, although still responding to the colonial context, forged a more autonomous agenda. Secondly, while claiming to offer universal messages based on an enduring 'tradition', different reformers spoke to different groups. 'Tradition' turns out to be both variable and recent, although the very quest for an 'authentic' tradition is itself a characteristic of this period of colonial rule. A third theme that runs through these reformist movements is the critical importance of print media and of restricted literacy, noted above. Scholars now recognize the importance of print capitalism in the spread of nationalism,[3] but vernacular publications have been critical in creating more narrowly limited solidarities as well. The remainder of this paper reviews three different reformist movements related to Muslim women in British India, and in so doing suggests new solidarities, both among Muslims and, implicitly, between 'Muslims' as a putative whole and other communities, divisions where women have been a pre-eminent symbol.

Listening to the many voices raised concerning the behaviour of Muslim women in the half century or so before Independence, it is notable, first of all, that we can distinguish different styles of argument. Near contemporaries in a common cultural area, all of whom base their position on shared scriptural sources,[4] offer a variety of interpretations. Those seeking change today can thus query how far positions that are presented as having absolute authority and historic depth in fact do so.

Most striking of all is the very fact that, while the protection and control of women has been an important theme historically, the notion of women as themselves repositories of normative tradition and moral exemplars was not. In Brahmanic priestly texts, after all women, like 'low-born' sudras, were threatened with molten lead in their ears if they heard the Vedas.[5] Public symbols of Muslim identity, the mosque, and the *khanaqa*, have been pre-eminently associated with men. Men learned Arabic and conventionally carried distinctive Islamic names; women knew the regional languages and their names often evoked only beautiful qualities or flowers. Today, in contrast, in many contexts women are expected to be the public signs of Islam, by their dress and deportment and, beyond that, to master and practise distinctive Muslim teachings. This suggests a shift in the boundaries of public and private from an ideal long held in Islamic societies: women are, ironically, now part of public life. It is talk about women that fills public space.

As a partial baseline against which to measure these changes, we can place the model of women that pervades much of Muslim letters, notably the advice books for aristocratic men, that present women as *fitna*, as a source of potential disorder and, essentially, as adherents to a pagan past.[6] Women are potentially out of control. Persian ethical guides that were part of the education of generations of privileged men, like the *Qabus nama* or the *Akhlaq-i nasiri* or Yusuf Gada's *Tuhfah-yi nasa'ih*, confirm what can only be called a conventional misogyny in relation to women. These texts certainly do not encourage education for women.[7]

They are particularly detailed on the choice of brides who should, for example, be 'lower' than the husband 'in years, height, rank, and wealth'. Yusuf Gada's verse continues:

> You should never marry a short fat woman or a tall thin one:
> You should never marry an older woman; she will bear a worse son.
> You should never marry a woman who weeps, nor one with hairy legs;
> Avoid a demanding one who is an ugly deceiver.
> The woman who causes trouble, with prancing legs and feet.

A woman should speak softly, not complain, not go out without permission, not eat before her husband. Yusuf Gada, reviewing the problems of wives, recommends a concubine 'for ease in this world'.[8]

The reformers of the late nineteenth century associated this picture of women with what came to be seen as the decadence of a nawabi lifestyle, summed up by the female figure of the courtesan.[9] When turn-of-the-century Hindi playwrights took up the controversy over Hindi and Urdu as official languages in a debate that helped undermine the old shared Persianate culture of the elite derived from Mughal days, it is significant that they represented the two 'languages' as women: Hindi (written in a script derived from Sanskrit) was a respectable cow-and-Brahmin-nurturing matron, while Urdu (written in Perso-Arabic script) was nothing less than a heartless aristocratic strumpet. Queen Devanagri was, in fact, as much the image of the new middle class Hindu housewife as of any queen; Begum Urdu was the unreformed and uncontrolled woman, projected, one might suggest, onto a Muslim from outside.[10] Ironically, Muslim reformers disavowed such an image no less than did Hindus.

Muslims did not only question the old cosmopolitan tradition; they also challenged local traditions where, also far from guarding normative Islam, women came to be seen as engaging in regionally shared life stage ceremonies and 'superstitions'. The regional culture and its language are identified in some contexts with the *nafs*, the faculty within the person that opts for the self-indulgent, in contrast to *aql*, the good sense that adheres to discipline and self-control, as elaborated in texts of ethics and moral formation. Some traditions explicitly link women to the impulsive and childlike qualities of *nafs*, so that in women's association with regional traditions these two themes are powerfully joined.[11]

Clearly, while this 'baseline' image draws on two different streams of tradition, one cosmopolitan, the other local, both posit women as, above all, disorderly and a stimulus to disorder; they are far from being the guardians of Islamic morality and truth. Similarly, the Shariat tradition, formulated in legal thought and guarded by scholars from the earliest centuries of Islam, focused not so much on women's own moral and intellectual life as much as on control of their sexuality. The jurists demanded that women be secluded; their contact with men of marriageable degree; highly regulated; and their presence in public space, even the mosque, discouraged. The Shariat is of course realized in different ways in different contexts, but these have been persistent themes.

In contrast to all those models that focus on the need to impose external controls, the reformers invariably turned to other themes in the Shariat. Despite their differences, all were united by an interest in shaping women's character and knowledge, not merely in defining external controls. In doing so, moreover, the reformers were also alike in speaking to the 'particular' community—'Indian Muslim'—defined by the colonial culture.[12] The movements varied, however, to the extent to which they engaged with the actual critique of Indian women articulated by Europeans. They also varied in what they emphasized as an Other or an 'enemy', on the one hand, and models, or female ideals, on the other.

## The Ulama: A Single Standard

The late nineteenth century saw far-ranging attempts to preserve Muslim education and standards through networks of popularly supported ulama, new formally organized schools, and an extensive programme of publication and translation into the vernacular.[13] While clearly both stimulated and made possible by the colonial presence, the ulama at the heart of these movements did not know English or speak to the content of European norms about women. They extended their instruction to women in part because they sought a popular audience of Muslims who were not merely Muslim in name but who demonstrated a high level of commitment to Islamic rituals and practice, a goal that urgently required female participation, as the target of religious teaching focused not on rulers and worldly elites but on families and individuals. The desire to include women in normative standards was charged with anxiety, given the complex range of cultural themes noted above: in challenging women's regional practices, for example, the reformers were confronting what was presumably part of the fabric of their own everyday lives.

For the ulama in the late nineteenth century, the model of the European woman or Europeanized Indian woman was ignored; similarly irrelevant was the Hindu woman. It is important to underline this silence since the opposite is often wrongly imputed. What was significant was only the 'enemy within': the unreformed, uneducated woman who did not know Islamic doctrine, was caught up in expensive and corrupting ceremonial practices and handled badly the responsibilities of her everyday life. While the teachings of the ulama implicitly distinguished Muslim women from non-Muslim women, they explicitly drew the line between the proper, well-brought up Muslim woman and the ignorant one whether she was rich and self-indulgent or poor and misguided.

The teachings of the ulama were meant to secure a better moral and material life for women and their families. Some challenges to custom were seen as securing women their rights: marriage customs (that entailed isolation and deprivation before the ceremony) were regarded as a source of privation and suffering; the prohibition on widow remarriage was considered to cause unfair suffering; the disinheriting of women, as both unfair and un-Islamic. The insistence that women should be able to read and write so that they could know religious texts was essential to both worldly and religious welfare. Of course, women were still expected to play their proper role: of deference to their husbands and of fulfilment of a range of household obligations. They were to avoid any public life and even avoid undue outings from their home.

For all that, the teachings of the ulama, grounded in Qur'an and Hadith, were striking in the significant respect that they did not elaborate a difference between women and men. There was of course the crucial difference of role that placed women squarely in the home. But in terms of essential nature and potential, women and men were regarded as one. The assumption that any patriarchal system must posit notions of a distinctive female nature of male-female complementarity and, hence, of 'opposite sexes' is clearly wrong. One of the pre-eminent texts of the ulama, the *Bihishti Zewar* of Maulana Ashraf Ali Thanawi, written in the first decade of this century, has been read to confirm those opinions, but such is not the case.[14]

Thanawi argued that women and men are endowed with the same faculties and that both are responsible for their conduct. Both must contend with the fundamental human condition of the struggle between intelligence or sense, *aql*, and the undisciplined impulses of the lower soul, *nafs*. Looking around him, and heir to a certain 'common sense' in his society, Thanawi believed that women were more likely than men to be troubled by *nafs* but, to use modern language, he found this situation culturally, not genetically, determined. If properly educated, women have every potential of men. At the same time, they are not superior. The home is not (yet) the haven of Islamic life, nor do women have any special spiritual capacity.

Girls, like boys, had to study. Thanawi demonstrated none of the nineteenth century European pseudo-science that suggested that too much study was detrimental to girls; nor did he and his fellow ulama assume that certain subjects—certainly not the novels and poetry deemed appropriate to European girls—were suitable,

less of a strain, for girls' delicate nature. Girls should learn Arabic
and read the same texts as boys:

In a short time, God willing, you will...become a maulvi—that is, a
scholar of Arabic.... You will achieve the rank of a learned person, and
you will be able to give judicial opinions, as learned men do. You will
begin to teach Arabic to girls, just as learned men do.... You will be
granted the reward equal to that bestowed on each person to whom you
have given guidance with your preaching and opinions, teaching and
books (Thanawi, 1906).

Words rarely used of women today—maulvi—are readily used here.
Far from exalting 'domestic science', Thanawi dismissed cooking
and sewing as subjects that could be learned in weeks and should
not be allowed to waste all one's time.

Thanawi included in his book one hundred anecdotes concerning good women. Here again we find unlikely terms: they are
*badshah, hakim, ustad, alim, sardar, buzurg* (emperor, doctor,
teacher, learned, chieftain, elder). The stories are moreover introduced by the story par excellence, that of the character of the
Prophet Muhammad. There is no separate standard for women,
but rather a common model of humanity for both. '[The Prophet
Muhammad] was very gentle.... At night...he would do everything very softly, so that no one's sleep would ever be disturbed....
When he was happy he lowered his gaze. What young girl would
have been as modest as this?'[15] Thanawi included among his
anecdotes stories of the two prototypical women in Christianity,
Eve and Mary: Eve as a model of true repentance, not temptation;
Mary, a model of obedience and piety, virtues not specific to
women.[16] Fatima, a more central figure in Muslim tradition, is also
depicted as an embodiment of core values.[17]

The conclusive evidence that Thanawi enjoined a single standard
of behaviour for women and men was his response when he was
asked to write a companion guide, a *Bihishti Zewar* directed to men.
He replied that the existing book would serve perfectly well—he
simply added an appendix describing practices such as the community prayer specific to men. Indeed, the English translations of the
work in use today (which leave out the sections pertaining to
practical domestic life) give no indication that the book was once
meant solely for women.[18] It is hard to imagine a guidebook for
women written around 1900 in Europe or America that could also
be recommended as a proper guide for men.

What distinguished the proper Muslim woman? Thanawi provided the answer to this question with a list of characteristics, all the fruit of proper education. Literate in Urdu, a good woman revealed herself when she opened her mouth, for her language was clear and correct. Second, she fulfilled her religious obligations correctly. Third, she kept her house in perfect order. Fourth, she raised her children to be of good character. Fifth, knowing each person's rights and obligations, she sustained proper hierarchic relations with all. Finally, because she could write letters, she could handle intimate matters without divulging them to intermediaries. Since all these achievements were increasingly seen as marks of respectable status, Thanawi's readers should have concurred that education was worthwhile—as well as being religiously correct.

The teachings of these 'ulama were not revolutionary, but they are notable in two ways in particular. First, they arose largely independent of any engagement with European critiques of Indian women and they did not define themselves by either emulating or opposing a European pattern. That only familiarity with European critiques and models of women stimulated reform is not the case. Second, they spared women what can be seen as the burden of being idealized as especially gifted for domestic life and endowed with purity and moral sensitivity: there is no Victorian elaboration of a female specificity, placing woman on a pedestal or proclaiming the apotheosis of woman as the 'angel of the house'.

## The Social Reformers and Apologia

Another group of thinkers who also flourished from the turn of the century, adopted a stance in some ways similar to that of the ulama. Those, whom we might call social reformers, also challenged the behaviour of the uneducated woman, given over to customary practices and unfamiliar with Islamic teachings. At the same time, however, their work was charged with interaction with an interlocutor, implicit or explicit, in the models of European women and the critique Europeans levelled against the treatment of women in Islam. This influenced the very issues they chose to address as well as the interpretations they put upon them.

The reformers accepted the educational agenda of the ulama, but made it at once more European and more agenda specific. They shared a commitment to 'restoring' some Islamic legal rights, but focused less on those that challenged vested interests (like female rights to inheritance). Responding to European criticism, they denied (or redefined) the Islamic tradition of polygamy, a subject to which Thanawi, for example, gave no notice, and they tried to modify purdah.

Recent scholarship has gained some distance on the so-called social reformers—the category of Hindu spokesmen discussed above—who were once exclusively praised as heralds of 'renaissance' and reform. Whether Hindu or Muslim, they are now seen at least in part as colonial collaborators, people who basically accepted the overall framework of British rule and sought to identify with its core values. These are, above all, people who internalized the Orientalist argument that Indic traditions had fallen into decay and stagnation, and argued that they could, perhaps, regain vitality through education and reform. Their agenda formed a bond between them and the British.

Sayyid Mumtaz Ali (1860–1935), for example, who with his wife founded a newspaper for women, took up an agenda largely set by the English: polygamy, the age of marriage and the girl's right to approve of the marriage, the role of the wife in the marriage, purdah, and the need for education. In every case he claimed to be following true Islamic practice. Like the ulama, he was keen to see girls educated, but he favoured a more cosmopolitan approach to education, allowing them, for example, to read the old Persianate tales and epics (that the ulama judged decadent), as well as history, geography, and science.

Mumtaz Ali argued that men and women were equal, insisting that physical strength was a trivial measure of superiority and that in all important aspects, including intelligence, all humans were the same. If the Quran discounts a woman's testimony, he insisted, that was because of social conditions that deprived her of experience: it did not suggest any inherent defect. He circumscribed the husband's right to polygamy (suggesting that the sanction was for serial wives or at least that it required the wife's permission). He accepted purdah as natural to human nature, but sought to modify its limitations so that women could visit public places or attend meetings in their husband's company. Men remained the actors: it was they who granted women education; they who were called upon to be generous to women.[19]

Mumtaz Ali's ideas were shared by many of those associated with the westernizing movement at Aligarh. Sayyid Ahmad Khan himself had focused attention on education for women when, on his trip to England (1869–70), he had written home in despair after finding scullery maids, unlike aristocratic women at home, able to read and write. Nonetheless, he himself had little interest in encouraging girls' schooling, preferring to let education for boys filter down. Others of his associates, Shaikh Abdullah, Hali, and Nazir Ahmad, however, were, like Mumtaz Ali determined to seek change directly. Hali, as early as his *Majalis un-Nissa* had urged a basic vernacular education for girls, imparted in their own homes.[20] Nazir Ahmad's novels held out living examples of the fruit of education and behaviour along the lines encouraged by Mumtaz Ali. Nazir explicitly depicted models of happy English homes and introduced a competent English lady doctor among his characters, as he tried to persuade his readers that educated women could best perform their domestic and religious duties to the benefit of all.

In 1906, after years of discussion in the Mohammadan Educational Conference, Shaikh Abdullah collaborated with his wife in founding a separate school for girls in Aligarh itself. The school was supported by aristocratic and government subventions, and sufficiently committed to supervision and purdah to win the support of the elite.[21] By the time a proper building opened in 1914, the school had a European woman principal and English was taught one hour a day; by 1937 it offered degree classes. The school inculcated an ambivalent attitude to Western models of female behaviour which were regarded as at once exemplary yet less noble than those sanctioned by Islam at its best. Less ambivalently, it imparted the message of social reform as a characteristic of an aristocratic (*sharif*) life, thus fostering a distinctive elite cultural style for women that contrasted with that of the vast majority of the population.

In this regard, the work of a female advocate of social reform, the Bengali woman, Rokeya Sakhawat Hossain (b. 1880), is notable. She lobbied endlessly for education for girls and for an end to the excessive absurdities of seclusion.[22] During the first decades of the century, she too wrote widely for the *sharif* classes like her own, typically people with landed wealth and ties to the British government and educational institutions. As the wife of a civil servant, Rokeya was able to see the advantages reformed Hindu women had in gaining access to the new culture of their husbands. She argued that women, admittedly weaker and appropriately dependent on their husbands, needed education to fulfil their domestic role properly. Above all she insisted that the extremes of purdah which she chronicled in her *Avarodhbasini* as both 'comic' and 'excit[ing] pity', must be ended.[23]

Rokeya added a woman's perspective to these teachings, arguing that the current situation created an unbalanced cultural development (as she said on one occasion), as if a single body were five feet on one side and four feet on the other.[24] Beyond that, she added a pointed edge to the discussion, nowhere more strikingly than in her *Sultana's Dream*, written in 1905, a fantasy of a utopia where men were kept in seclusion and women ran the country. She pointed out that if women were secluded to protect them, that end could be more effectively met by containing the potential aggressors. Would you, she asks, 'imprison the sane people of a country if a lunatic escaped?'

Equally striking, in contrast to the main thrust of early social reform, Rokeya recognized the needs of poor women. She organized a voluntary association of Muslim women to attempt to spread literacy to slum women, coupled with simple instruction in health and childcare.

Two themes in her writing were to become increasingly prominent as the century wore on. First, she saw not only the advantages that accrued to European women because of their education and relative freedom, she also identified what she felt to be the victimization of women by Western men and their laws.[25] One writer has called this kind of mixed judgement 'the two sides of Occidentalism'.[26] The first was the idealization of educated European women who serve as a model; the second, the ever stronger identification of Western women and their westernized imitators as the powerful Other against which, in principle, one defines oneself. This was not sufficient, however, to secure Rokeya from popular criticism that she was mouthing the critique of foreign observers about her own people. Second, albeit in her fantasy, she struck a note of spiritual and moral superiority on the part of women. In her dream the Queen explained how she allowed trade: 'No trade was possible with countries where the women were kept in the *zanana*s and so unable to come and trade with us. Men, we find, are rather of lower morals and so we do not like dealing with them.'[27]

A second Bengali, Ameer Ali, the enormously erudite and sophisticated lawyer and writer, further developed these two last themes. His celebrated work, *The Spirit of Islam*, was written in English and first published in 1921 in London. Usually character-ized as apologetic, the work was meant to be 'the history of the evolution of Islam as a world religion' and it ranged over the whole of human history, typically contrasting the shortcomings of other religions in comparison to Islam.[28] Ameer Ali avoided discussion of contemporary problems and the need for reform, preferring instead to demonstrate the superiority of Islam as properly known. His concern with meeting the prejudices of non-Muslims gave shape to his argument. Thus in his treatment of women, he focused most on the criticism of Islam as supporting polygamy. One recalls that Lutfullah, an early nineteenth century traveller to London, commented on European monogamy only in terms of its advan-tages for securing household order, a persistent theme in the Persianate *adab* literature described above.[29] In this period he did not need to confront the European critique that engaged Ameer Ali some hundred years later.

Ameer Ali, in contrast, insisted that polygamy was 'an unen-durable evil', the result of a particular situation of warfare. He showed its prevalence throughout all traditions. He insisted that in Islam there was effectively monogamy because of the require-ment that a husband take only one wife unless he could show impartiality, a patent impossibility. He freely quoted Europeans who supported his views and cited as well those he felt he had to refute. The very choice of this issue, on his own account relevant only to a miniscule proportion of the population, indicates that his concern was not current behaviour, as it was with other reformers, but rather an assertion of cultural pride and a refutation of what he judged were biased critiques. His insistence on the cultural superiority of Islam to the West was to be an ever more important theme in later Islamic movements.

Similarly, Ameer Ali for the first time developed the theme of difference between women and men that identified women as spiritual and moral. As noted above, this had not been a classic theme either in Islam or in European thought. For Ameer Ali, for example, the Prophet's daughter Fatima was 'the embodiment of all that (was) pure and true and holy in her sex—the noblest ideal of human conception'.[30] 'The idealization of womankind', he wrote, 'is a natural characteristic of all the highest natures.'[31] More specifically he identified chivalry toward women as more intimately associated with Islam than with any other faith or institution: a gift to Europe via Andalusia. His vision of domestic relationships suggests a modern pattern of nuclear families, not that of a multiple extended household in a tribal society. With Khadija, he wrote, the Prophet enjoyed 'an uninterrupted sunshine of faithfulness and happiness...[she was] his sole companion and helper'. The idealization of women and the idealization of domesticity went hand in hand, its inspiration more European than Quranic.

## The Islamist Movement: Opposite Cultures and the Opposite Sex

By the 1930s a further voice was added to the discussion on women, that of the 'Islamists' who purported to challenge the existing structure of social and political organization in favour of a new Islamic order. Most notable in the Indian subcontinent was Abul-ala Maududi (1903–79), whose Urdu journal, the *Tarjuman-ul-Quran*, and frequent publications set the issues for his society, the Jamaat-i Islami. Maududi, like many who were to be active in this movement, was not trained in the classic religious disciplines of the madrasa; on the contrary, much of the leadership came from the secularly educated who independently gained expertise in religious texts. The movement as conceived in the 1930s has been compared to fascist and communist movements both in its emphasis on the importance of creating cells of committed followers and in its ultimate goal to control the institution of the modern state.[32]

Maududi, unlike the social reformers, denounced European women. Typically his work dwelt at length on the horrors that followed upon the freedom of Western women. Against this he set not the actual life of women in Muslim societies but an ideal of social life, accessible if at all only to the more privileged classes, he found in Islam. Compare this to Rokeya who retold the comic-tragedies that befell women trapped in houses or swathed in burqas, or to Maulana Thanawi who deplored the frustrations of female illiteracy or the pointlessness of 'sitting *maiyun*' for a bride before her wedding.[33]

In 1935 Maududi published a series of articles in his *Tarjuman-ul-Quran*, subsequently published in many editions as *Purdah and the Status of Woman in Islam*.[34] At first blush Maududi's work seems like Ameer Ali's in taking up broad historical themes and in looking at issues related to women in a number of historical settings, only to find that Islamic doctrines defined a superior status for women than did any of the others. Unlike Ali, however, Maududi was particularly concerned to show contemporary abuses of women in the West. His works, like the works of others in his movement, drew not on Western legal or religious texts, but on newspaper accounts, investigation of abuses, conservative socio-logical critiques, and medical accounts written by Europeans them-selves. His successors, ironically, read feminist journals like *Signs*. Maududi found three pernicious doctrines that subverted what he presented as the very order of nature: the equality of women, the economic independence of women, and the free intermingling of the sexes. For him they were the source of the entire decay of society, a reversion to animal passions instead of control, and the undermining of all mental and moral capacities.

As part of the colonial experience, however, he argued that these ideas had taken hold among Muslims, or so-called Muslims, as well. Maududi's intended audience, unlike Ameer Ali's, was not westerners at all (or at least not primarily); instead it was the westernized, those he called the 'Oriental Occidentals' who mim-icked and parroted the West without knowing the implications of what they were doing. He challenged them by what he called the very laws of nature that define sexual and marital relations, and set out the Islamic teachings on women that form the basis of a correct social order. The teachings of all the social reformers implicitly drew sociological lines, above all a line that excluded poor and uneducated women. The reformist ulama also excluded the women of nawabi culture with their cosmopolitan tastes. Now another line was being drawn, in this case to exclude the new cosmopolitanism of the westernized, typically those with access to a European style of everyday life.[35]

Maududi was clear that Islam recognized the 'natural superiority' of husband over wife. He spoke in terms of rights for women: the right to receive provisions from husbands; the right to inheritance and to control their own money; the right to refuse marriage against their will (but not to choose against the will of their families). A woman's duty is to run the house. She is severely curtailed in leaving the house and in undertaking any kind of journey. Maududi insisted that women's education was as important as men's, but that 'the right sort of education for woman is that which prepares her to become a good wife, good mother and good housekeeper... she should be trained primarily in those branches of knowledge which make her more useful in that sphere'.[36] The contrast with Maulana Thanawi is marked. While Thanawi shared the opinion that women should stay at home, he dismissed household lore as something that could be learned in a few weeks, and encouraged women to undertake precisely the same serious studies as did men. Women, Maududi repeatedly says, are the 'queen' of the home, but the society that would give them public authority is doomed.

Maududi's elevation of domestic knowledge and skills went hand in hand with a new elaboration of women's difference. Women were not merely different from men in role and hierarchy. We now find women as essentially different in kind: they are opposite to men. Woman is 'by nature emotional and sensitive and inclined to extremes.' Critical to Maududi's argument is the use of the modern medical differentiation of women from men that posits an essential physiological difference between them.[37] He exuberantly cites European specialists on menstruation and pregnancy, adducing descriptions of mental imbalance, derangement and, at best, lack of concentration to prove scientifically the importance of secluding women. It thwarts nature, he says, for women to follow the same careers as men:

Since biologically woman has been created to bring forth and rear children, psychologically also she has been endowed with such abilities as suit her natural duties. This explains why she has been endowed with tender feelings of love, sympathy, compassion, clemency, pity and sensitiveness in an unusual measure. And since in the sexual life man has been made active and woman passive, she has been endowed with those very qualities alone which help and prepare her for the passive role in life only.... That is why she is soft and pliable, submissive and impressionable, yielding and timid by nature.[38]

Writing in pre-Independence India, Maududi deplored the intrusiveness of the political and cultural life that thwarted this vision of a proper society of which women were the key. 'The principles of un-Islamic morality and the ideas of un-Islamic civilization have spread like germs of plague and cholera', he wrote. Films, music, un-Islamic dress, education that diffused the 'moral ideas of the West', the replacement of the Islamic Penal Code by British law, all made for continuous assault on proper values.

With lines drawn against the westernized elite, and secondarily against the poor and uneducated, Maududi and his fellow Islamists planned an Islamic social order but in fact retreated to focus on the arena opened to them, that of the home and, above all, that of women in the home. They argued that restrictions on women, above all those associated with purdah, be strictly adhered to in the interests of the social and moral order as a whole. Their idealization of domestic space and of women as queens of that space, endowed with unique personal qualities, at once idealized women and made them subject to male control, in a pattern familiar in modern Europe as well. This pattern has proven remarkably enduring in the contexts of religiously defined cultural resistance, characteristic initially among Muslims in British India and then subsequently in ideologies widespread in the independent successor states.

## Conclusion

The three distinctive positions in relation to women outlined above all assume that women will play a (primary or exclusive) domestic role. All speak moreover, to the relatively privileged in society where women do not need to work in the fields, clean other people's houses, or engage in petty trade: this is, after all, a story of written texts and of people who read them. This reinforces and redraws hierarchies. The ulama and the Islamists not only stand apart from the poor but also criticize the cosmopolitan classes caught up in what are seen as either nawabi or Western social practices, thus placing the respectable middle classes as the (potential) model of correct behaviour for all. Those evaluating various reformist positions must disentangle the sociological implications of ostensibly universal arguments. In this regard, Rokeya, with her attention to poor women, however limited, reminds one of alternatives. In contrast, Akbari, Nazir Ahmad's quintessential unreformed woman, is marked negatively from the opening words of his celebrated didactic novel, the *Miratu-l Arus*, because she shares the company of poor, uneducated women.[39]

A second area of difference is in the attitudes about the essential nature of women. The glorification of women's special qualities, argued by Maududi, turns out not to be 'traditional'. Here, perhaps surprisingly, 'ulama like Thanawi, far less caught up in European models and critiques, strike a distinctive note. He insisted that women were in the end essentially like men, some good, some bad, with the same moral and mental make-up and the same intellectual potential. Humans vary, he says, quoting a Persian couplet that 'God did not make identical the five fingers of a hand'.

A final difference is in the attitude to Western women: they are ignored by the ulama, considered a positive model for many of the reformers, and excoriated by the Islamists, particularly in what is seen as their derivative manifestation as 'Oriental Occidentals'. In assessing arguments about women today, one would do well to ask what implicit or explicit 'Other' various thinkers are caught up with and how such a target constrains and shapes what they do. The ambivalent charged image of 'the West' has been allowed to play too large a role, one might think, in living out Islam in the context of today's world, and nowhere more than in relation to women. Taking these three points together, the reformist movements thus vary in relation to what we might almost call class, gender, and race.

The variety of the movements reminds us that 'tradition' in the cultural contestations of this past century has been defined and redefined and made new. In the colonial context, Indians gave new importance to articulating cultural values: they emphasized ethnic or 'particular' domains defined by social and cultural life when many dimensions of public life were beyond their control. The shaping of the 'particular' or 'communal' proved to have profound implications not only for gender but for ethnicity and class. Changes interpreted both then and now as 'social' or 'religious'—among them the movements of social reform—were, we now know, to be fundamentally political, their legacy only too obvious today.

## Notes

1. Mani, Lata. 1989. 'Contentions Traditions: The Debate on Sati in Colonial India', in Sangari, Kumkum and Sudesh Vaid, eds, *Recasting Women: Essays in Colonial History*. Delhi: Kali for Women. pp. 88–126.

2. Borthwick, Meredith. 1984. *The Changing Role of Women in Bengal 1849–1905*. Princeton: Princeton University Press; Mani, Lata, op. cit.; Chatterji, Partha. 1989. 'Colonialism, Nationalism and Colonized Women: The Contest in India', *American Ethnologist* 16: 4, pp. 623–34; Tagore,

Rabindranath 1915. *The Home and the World*, trans., Surendranath Tagore. Hardmonsworth: Penguin Books. [1985 edn]

3. Anderson, Benedict. 1991. *Imagined Communities: Reflections on the Origin and Spread of Nationalism*. London, New York: Verso.

4. Talal Asad argues the importance of seeing Islam (or any religion) as a 'discursive tradition' not as an immutable body of unchanging attitudes and understanding. Asad, T. 1986. 'The Idea of an Anthropology of Islam'. Washington: Georgetown University, Center for Contemporary Arab Studies, Occasional Paper Series.

5. Leslie, Julia I. 1989. *The Perfect Wife: The Orthodox Hindu Woman according to the Stridharmapaddhati of Tryambakayajyan*. New Delhi: Oxford University Press.

6. Devji, Faisal Fatehali. 'Gender and the Politics of Space: The Movement for Women's Reform in Muslim India, 1857–1900'. In Zoya Hasan, ed., 1994. *Forging Identities: Gender, Communities, and the State in India*, pp. 22–37. Delhi: Kali for Women.

7. Naim, C. M. 1984. Prize-winning *Adab*: A Study of Five Urdu Books Written in Response to the Allahabad Government Gazette Notification'. In Metcalf, Barbara, ed., *Moral Conduct and Authority: The Place of Adab in South Asian Islam*. Berkeley: University of California Press.

8. Digby, Simon. 1984. 'The Tuhfa-i-nasa'ih of Yusuf Gada: An Ethical Treatise in Verse from the Late Fourteenth Century Delhi Sultanate'. In Metcalf, ibid.

9. Ruswa, Mirza Muhammad Hadi. 1899 [1961]. *Umrao Jan Ada* (Courtesan of Lucknow), trans., Khushwant Singh and M. A. Husain. Bombay: Orient Longman Ltd.

10. King, Christopher. 1992. 'Images of Virtue and Vice: The Hindi-Urdu Controversy in Two Nineteenth Century Hindi Plays'. In Jones Kenneth W. ed., *Religious Controversy in British India: Dialogues in South Asian Languages*, pp. 123–50. Albany: State University of New York Press.

11. Kurin, Richard. 1988. 'The Culture of Ethnicity in Pakistan'. In Ewing, Katherine P., ed., *Shariat and Ambiguity in South Asian Islam*, pp. 132–59. Berkeley: University of California Press.

12. Gilmartin, David. 1991. 'Democracy, Nationalism, and the Public: A Speculation on Colonial Muslim Politics'. *South Asia* 14: 1, pp. 123–40.

13. I am speaking here primarily of the Deobandi 'ulama, but these activities were undertaken by other 'ulama as well. See Metcalf, Barbara D. 1982. *Islamic Revival in British India: Deoband, 1860–1900*. Princeton: Princeton University Press, Second edition, New Delhi: Oxford University Press, 2002.

14. Thanawi, Ashraf Ali. 1982. *Perfecting Women: Maulana Ashraf Ali Thanawi's Bihishti Zewar*, Metcalf Barbara trans. and ed. Berkeley: University of California Press.

15. Ibid., p. 256.

16. Ibid., pp. 258, 271.

17. Ibid., pp. 267–78.

18. Ibid.

19. This section draws substantially on the publications of Minault, Gail. 1983. 'Shaikh Abdullah, Begum Abdullah, and Sharif Education for Girls at Aligarh'. In Ahmad, Imtiaz., ed., *Modernization and Social Change among Muslims in India*, pp. 207–36. Delhi: Manohar.

20. Hali, Khwaja Altaf Husain. 1874; 1905 [1986 edn]. *Voices of Silence* (English translation of Hali's *Majalis un-Nissa* and *Chup Ki Dad*), Minault, Gail, ed. and trans. Delhi: Chanakya Publications.

21. Minault, op. cit.

22. Hossain, Rokeya Sakhawat. 1927 [1987 edn]. *Inside Seclusion: The Avarodhbasini of Rokeya Sakhawat Hossain*, Jahan, Roushan, ed. and trans. Dhaka: Women for Women.

23. Ibid.

24. Jahan, Roushan. 'Introduction', to Hossain: 15.

25. Her translation of an English novel of Marie Correlli told the story of the marriage and abandonment of an heiress by a ruthless fortune-hunter. Roushan Jahan, 'Introduction' to Hossain, Rokeya. 1905 [1988]. *Sultana's Dream and Selections from the Secluded Ones*, p. 18. Jahan Roushan, ed. and trans. New York: The Feminist Press.

26. See the forthcoming work on the European woman in Iranian imagination by Mohammad Tavakoli-Targhi, who uses this expression.

27. Hossain, ibid.

28. Ali, Syed Ameer. 1922 [1961 edn] vii. *The Spirit of Islam: A History of the Evo-lution and Ideals of Islam with a Life of the Prophet*. London: Christophers.

29. Lutfullah. 1863. *Autobiography of Lutfullah, A Mohamedan Gentleman: and his Transactions with his Fellow Creatures: Interspersed with Remarks on the Habits, Customs and Character of the People with whom he had to Deal*. London: Smith Elder and Company. I owe this astute comment to Faisal Devji (oral communication).

30. Ali, op. cit.

31. Ibid.

32. Adams, Charles J. 1966. 'The Ideology of Maulana Maududi'. In Smith, Donald Eugene, ed. *South Asian Politics and Religions*. Princeton: Princeton University Press.

33. In this custom, the girl is confined to the corner of a room before her wedding, seated on a low stool, and anointed with ointments while various customs are carried out. Thanawi (1906), p. 116.

34. Maududi, S. Abulala. 1939 [1972 edn]. *Purdah and the Status of Woman in Islam*. Lahore: Islamic Publications Ltd.

35. See for example the denunciation of '*apwaaeen*', participants in the All Pakistan Women's Association, an organization of westernized women devoted to philanthropic social work, discussed in Metcalf (1988).

36. Maududi, op. cit., p. 156.

37. For a path-breaking study of this post-Enlightenment, not 'traditional' view, see Laquer, Thomas. 1990. *Making Sex: Body and Gender from the Greeks to Freud*. Cambridge: Harvard University Press.

38. Maududi, op. cit., pp. 120–1.

39. Ahmad. 1869. In the published English translation, Akbari's husband begins the book by explaining to his new wife what she had done wrong: 'Whatever people there are of the commonest sort living in the mohalla, you treat *their* daughters as if they were your sisters. Chuniya—the daughter of Bhondu the sutler, and Zulfan—the daughter of Bakhshu the tinker, and Rahmat—the daughter of Kimmu the water-carrier, and Sulmati—the daughter of Maulan the greengrocer, are received by you with open arms.... The whole mohalla is talking about it and saying, "What sort of a bride has come here now? Whenever you see her, only girls of *that* sort are sitting with her".' The names themselves conjure up the lowly. Ward, G. E. trs. 1903. *The Bride's Mirror: A Tale of Domestic Life in Delhi Forty Years Ago*, p. 19. London: Henry Frowde. [Reprinted, New Delhi: Permanent Black, 2001].

# 5

# Nationalist Muslims in British India
## The Case of Hakim Ajmal Khan

Islamic political rhetoric has had a wide variety of meanings in twentieth century South Asia. This variety has often been obscured by observers who assume Islamic political symbols to have a single set of meanings as well as by contemporary political figures who attribute to earlier figures their own particular views. In Pakistan, for example, all national heroes of the past are assumed to have used Islamic symbols exactly as does the current regime. At the height of General Ziaul Haq's rule, for example, prizes were offered for portraits depicting Muhammad 'Ali Jinnah, the urbane, westernized lawyer, in Islamic dress. Such reinterpretation can force resort to explanations of expedience to reconcile apparent inconsistencies, arguing, for example, that political figures spoke differently to different audiences. What else could one make of a Jinnah if he is clothed as a fundamentalist? But desire for legitimacy—here as everywhere—outweighs accurate history.

The purpose of this essay is to look at one label used to describe Muslim political figures and to try to understand its meaning in particular contexts. This term, 'Nationalist Muslim', is among those subject to misconstrual, in this case by assuming the 'Muslim' element to be minimal and the 'Nationalist' element to be secularist and constitutionalist. Such an interpretation is understandable, given the desire of Western observers to link political behaviour to patterns familiar to them from their own cultures; it is also understandable that contemporary Indian politicians would want to find precedents for positions valued today. The term was first used in the 1920s to identify Muslim political figures who supported the Indian National Congress and eschewed communal organizations. The term in fact reflects alliance more than the content of the participants' programme. Recent research, for example, describes the support given by Maulana Azad—one of the best known Nationalist Muslims, Gandhi's ally, and India's first Education Minister—to Muslim terrorist movements in Calcutta.[1] It clearly is inappropriate to equate the term 'nationalist' with liberal constitutionalism and secular abandonment of religious identities. Above all, it is necessary to see the extent to which the political action of both Muslim separatists and nationalists was stimulated by the interests of their religious community.

Hakim Ajmal Khan (1863–1928), the figure whose political views form the subject of this paper, is remembered as a 'nationalist' and a 'modernist'. His public life, extending over three decades, illumines three successive political strategies of the Muslim well-born in this period, drawing on different symbols of Muslim life and forging different alliances with non-Muslim groups. His political activities provide a contrast to a fourth strategy of Muslim political action, that of the religious leadership, which is also discussed below. These strategies together provide examples of the variety of implications carried by the term Muslim in differing political contexts. Throughout, the approach to politics was one which was defined by religious community.

Hakim Ajmal Khan was among the most influential of Muslim political leaders in the first decades of this century. He has been little studied, in part, perhaps, because his activities are not easy to categorize. Yet in the judgement of one historian 'he was the nearest the Muslims had to Gandhi in terms of breadth of political appeal: he was highly regarded by government, respected in the Congress, and amongst Hindus generally, and was one of the few Muslims who could feel equally at home among ulama, Nawabs and [westernized] Aligarh graduates.'[2] Humane, intensely committed, and articulate, he is an arresting figure in himself and a representative of important themes in recent Muslim history.

Ajmal Khan was the scion of a family of physicians who had long served the Mughal court and, after their decline, the courts of regional princes. Like his father before him, Ajmal Khan was an influential figure in the city of Delhi, respected for his aristocratic standing and behaviour and renowned for seemingly miraculous cures. The members of his family were men of refinement and cultivated tastes who participated in the cosmopolitan Persianate culture of the old capital. In the late nineteenth century they were drawn to the Aligarh Movement of Sir Sayyid Ahmad Khan in both its political and educational dimensions. Politically, the movement represented the attempt of the well-born of the Muslim community to create a special relationship with the British rulers on the basis of their history as previous rulers and of their shared monotheistic faith. Educationally, it represented the attempt to assimilate to European learning and styles of behaviour. It was welcomed by the British whose whole idiom of rule was cast in terms of religious community.[3] Under the influence of the Aligarh movement, Hakim Ajmal Khan's elder brother, Hakim 'Abdu'l-Majid Khan, began the formal institutionalization of the indigenous medical teaching and the reform of its content that his brother was to bring to fruition. The revival of traditional medicine may seem alien to a movement often described as modernist, but in fact it fits logically into its overall concerns.

## The Aligarh Style and the Revival of Medicine

The Aligarh definition of politics had two prongs. Most basically, it focused on the protection of the interests of the Muslim well-born including princes, courtiers, landlords, and professional men.[4] Its causes were those of adequate representation, education to make representation possible, and protection of Urdu as official language for both cultural and political reasons. Secondly, aside from the protection of these interests, participants in the Aligarh movement celebrated Muslim culture as a focus of self-esteem. In part they recalled the historical glories of the Muslim past; in part, they cherished the hallmarks of elite Persianate urban culture as it had evolved in India. Urdu language and poetry and the customs of aristocratic gatherings were central in this latter focus; the revival of indigenous medicine belongs here too.

It is worth underlining one important characteristic of this programme. Neither the focus on interests nor the concern for Muslim culture is in a narrow sense 'religious' except in so far as they ensure the status and self-confidence of the old Muslim elite. The cultural symbols to whose elaboration Ajmal Khan and his family made their contribution are what might be called cosmopolitan or Islamicate symbols, that is symbols derived from those aspects of civilization associated with Islam in which non-Muslims played significant roles.[5] They are, quite literally, worldly symbols in that they are linked to historical romanticism and look to restoration of worldly glory. They contrast with the very different kind of religious symbols that became prominent later on.

Hakim Ajmal Khan's most original contribution was in almost single-handedly making traditional Muslim medicine, *yūnānī ṭibb*, part of the repertoire of Muslim (and later nationalist) political symbols. Like the poet Hali and others associated with Aligarh, Ajmal Khan was convinced of the greatness of the Muslim cultural past, of the vicissitudes in the fortunes of all cultures, and of the possibility of restoration of Muslim greatness in the present. He assimilated, as did many colonialized intellectuals, the Orientalist dichotomy of East and West in assessing the cultural and political context of his times.[6] In 1891 he expressed this view in the introduction he had prepared to a catalogue of Arabic and Persian manuscripts:

Although the sun of Eastern arts and sciences kept rising in its own time, and many nations drew benefits from its light, now that sun has declined and the age, as is its habit, has given birth to a new sun that fulfils the needs of the people of the age.... The result of this reversal, which previous nations have already endured, will happen to us: we will see our former greatness and glory in the land of oblivion if we do not take thought to preserve it.[7]

Ajmal Khan's first efforts were devoted to reversing the tide of cultural decline in medicine; his political activities were an inevitable outgrowth of them.

The strategies for reform of medicine were like those employed in the reform of other branches of indigenous knowledge, particularly religious education.[8] There was the same attempt to gain institutional equivalence to the British schools by creating formal schools with paid staff and fixed requirements to replace the personalistic informal settings of family homes and apprenticeship. There was also the same shift to the use of the vernacular language of Urdu in order to make knowledge more widely available. In 1897, for example, Ajmal Khan wrote a booklet on plague, prefaced by a defence of his writing in the *mulkī zabān* (territorial language) instead of in Arabic; he expected, he said, that this use of Urdu would be regarded as a *bid'a* (the terminology used in the religious law to define a reprehensible innovation).[9] In terms of content, the medical reformers made the same attempt as the religious scholars to find systematic, generalizable principles, in this case scientific principles that were analogous to the systems available in the West. These were to replace popular practices that were seen as outside the scientific system. In some ways the technique for creating this intellectual equivalence was the same in all subjects, namely the return to texts of the literate culture at the expense of customary or local practice. Thus the adversaries of the reformers were practitioners of unsystematic folk medicine, often midwives and other women and poorly trained *yūnānī* practitioners. As in the case of religious education, this is scripturalist reform, but here reform by the cosmopolitan, not the shari'a-minded.[10] An important difference from other areas of reform, however, was that at no point did the reformers attempt to identify Indic or Hindu elements in medicine as distinct from a fundamentally Islamic core.

The modern revival of Islamic medicine was thus more communal, even secular, than religious in the sense that it was linked not to Islamic practice but to pride in Muslim culture and to Muslim social identity. The medical system is inherently plural in its origin and continuing openness. It is called *yūnānī tibb*, Greek medicine, and came into Muslim culture in the period of 'Abbasid rule in Baghdad when a common culture was being forged out of the disparate elements embraced in a great empire. Islamic medicine is the medicine of Galen and Hippocrates translated into Arabic, enriched even in its early centuries by contact with Indian specialists in Ayurveda who shared the humoral theories common to the whole of the old world.[11] The period of the Mughal empire saw a second important occasion of interaction between medical traditions when both pharmacopoeia and therapeutics were modified on both sides.[12] In principle such adaptations could not be seen as accretions because the theory of Islamic medicine is holistic and demands adjustments in accordance with the local context. In the same way Ajmal Khan argued that there were new diseases in the modern world and that for them one ought to learn from the West. Although in some cases he recommended learning techniques from Western medicine, notably in surgery, he insisted that this was necessary only because of neglect of *yūnānī*'s own texts.

Other techniques, like the uses of hot and cold baths he observed in Germany, fit well into *yūnānī* theory. Influence from Western medicine was thus limited and did not extend to basic principles. *Yūnānī* was seen as a scientific system of its own, deduced from a coherent set of principles, confirmed by empirical evidence, and able—in theory—to encounter the Western system as an equal.

Central to the movement for medical reform was what one might call the biomedical paradigm of illness argued on the basis of empiricism and rational therapeutics in contrast to a metaphysical, psychological, or social paradigm whose adepts would be less technicians than holy men.[13] Thus, the famous blind hakim of Nizamu'd-Din in Delhi today scoffs at those who talk of possession by demons: 'Some people's imagination becomes overheated and operates beyond all rational bounds. What has happened in these cases is that certain nerves in their brains have become stretched, and I can generally treat these patients successfully with medicines.'[14] He is in the tradition of Ajmal Khan in being personally pious but scientific. Modern Indians and westerners who dismiss all indigenous systems as 'faith healing' thus miss an important distinction. As science, medicine became a political symbol of Muslim cultural pride and, linked with Ayurvedic medicine and its revival, a national symbol as well. This has been called the 'resecularization' of medicine to suggest that the system was originally developed as a scientific system; it was later made part of religious systems; and now in the recent period it has been re-formulated as scientific.[15]

Some continued to understand *yūnānī* medicine in an Islamic religious framework, and the reformist ulama in particular took part in its revival. Practitioners ran the gamut from those who focused primarily on scientific principles to those who stressed divine intervention. At Deoband, the centre of scripturalist religious reform, many of the ulama were also hakims. There was some opposition to including *ṭibb* in the curriculum, in part because it was a distraction from the more important studies of the fundamental texts, in part because some felt the pious ought only trust in God and see illness as a visitation offering an opportunity for spiritual growth. But *ṭibb* was ultimately included in the curriculum and many of the ulama, always recognizing God as the ultimate healer, disseminated scientific medicine. Hakim Mansur Ahmad Khan, a Deoband graduate and chief physician at the court of Hyderabad early in this century, wrote a compendium of proofs of the existence of God, many of them drawn from the beneficial principles enshrined in scientific Greek medicine.[16] The most important Deobandi text for women included a basic primer of *ṭibb* as part of the attempt to include women in the general movement for reform.[17] But as far as the overall revival of *ṭibb* went and the creation of separate schools for its instruction, the emphasis was wholly secular.

In the revival of medicine, both institutional changes in teaching and intellectual changes in content were inextricably linked to the political context in which they were made. The professionalization of medicine thrust its authors into a public arena, as issues taken up, for example, by the reformist ulama did not. The scholars could quietly create formally organized seminaries, publish and write on religious responsibilities in Urdu, and generally instruct Muslims in individual responsibility for the fulfilment of the religious law. Public debates aside, they could pursue their interests without encounters with the government. Hakims by contrast needed official recognition, both for psychological reasons and for their very survival. This was particularly true as Western and Western-trained doctors (in India called allopaths), moved to make the same claims to a monopoly of legitimacy in India as had their counter-parts in Europe. At mid-nineteenth century, the British had been inclined to use hakims for programmes of medical relief and to establish courses for their training, but that had given way under pressure just a few decades later. The major assault, as it was seen, on the indigenous systems came with the attempt by British and Indian allopathic physicians to secure registration acts in each province so that no doctor of indigenous medicine could be legally recognized to give testimony in legal disputes, to certify illness for workers, or to perform any other legally required function. Between 1912 and 1916 medical registration acts were passed in Madras, Bombay, Bengal, the United Provinces, Punjab, Burma, Bihar and Orissa.[18] The reformers, moreover, fought to claim a monopoly of legitimacy for those indigenous practitioners who were educated in their new institutions, and periodically called on government to help them, for example, in hiring only their graduates for government positions.[19] Given such concerns, politi-cal organization and activity were inevitable. *Yūnāni* medicine, both scientific and Muslim, could not easily be dismissed.

Even before the decade of intensive activity stimulated by the attempts to pass registration acts, Ajmal Khan had sought a constituency for his programme of medical reform. In the initial period of his public activities, he directed his attention primarily to the princely elite, the theoretically autonomous rulers of one-third of the subcontinent. They were in fact the creatures of the British who nurtured them in return for loyalty and whatever sanction for imperial rule they could provide. In this situation there were many among the princes who chose to use their resources to patronize indigenous culture as a source of their own and their people's self-esteem. The flourishing of indigenous art, music, and learning in general in the colonial period derives in part from the structure of British rule that supported the princes and others of the old elites. Of the groups whom Ajmal Khan found to support his schemes, the princes more than any other group valued medicine intrinsically as well as for its symbolic value. The Muslim nawab of Rampur cherished Ajmal Khan personally and supported the medical and political institutions he espoused. The ruler of Bhopal had a state-wide organization of medical care staffed by *yūnānī*-trained doctors. The rulers of the princely states almost single-handedly provided the capital for the college that Ajmal Khan founded for indigenous medicine following the First World War.

From the very beginning of his career, Ajmal Khan also attempted to gain the respect of the British for his endeavours. In this his concerns were like those of the Aligarh modernists and other apologists who required validation of their efforts by the British. In his newspaper published in the 1880s and 1890s, or at meetings held at the Delhi town hall with British officials present, he presented himself to officials as someone who shared their values and was open to change. In a speech in 1889, for example, he implied—without ever saying—that Western medicine was superior by stressing the need for training indigenous practitioners when Western-trained doctors were so few. He ventured that indigenous medicine was more suited to the local temperament but at the same time acknowledged the superiority of Western doctors in a limited range of anatomical and surgical skills, pointing out that these were now taught in his school. In this way he conveyed an impression of openness and rationality. Later he was to add a note of threat by alluding to the possibility of Muslim disaffection if British authorities denied them respect.

The British were ambivalent about Ajmal Khan's efforts on behalf of indigenous medicine. What support they gave was politically inspired, given to secure the loyalty of a person understood to be at the centre of an influential network based on family and education. British officials graced almost every important occasion associated with the reforms his family initiated: the opening of their school in 1889, the opening of the women's branch of the school in 1909, the laying of the cornerstone of the college in 1916, and the opening of the research institute in 1930. Given his reservations about indigenous medicine, however, it was with great reluctance that the viceroy, Lord Hardinge, laid the foundation stone of the college in 1916; it was only his personal respect of Ajmal Khan and a promise that instruction in some aspects of Western medicine would be included that persuaded him to attend.[20] Ajmal Khan's hope of serious official respect, even preference, for the *yūnānī* system was never even a possibility. Respect for him and for his associates was more readily granted on the basis of their political influence.

## Ajmal Khan and the Muslim League Style of Politics

Shortly after the turn of the century, Muslims in north India moved from the darbar model of Sayyid Ahmad—seeking roles as trusted and loyal advisors to their ruler patrons—to a more assertive political position. Disappointments in the special relationship, above all over the issue of giving Hindi equal place with Urdu as the official language, coupled with the prospect of constitutional reform, stimulated efforts to organize that culminated in the first delegation of the Muslim League to the viceroy in 1906. Ajmal Khan was part of that delegation to press Muslim interests, and he continued active in the League until the non-cooperation movement following the war. The League became the chief actor in the arena created for political activity by the Indian Councils Act of 1909 that provided, however narrowly, for some popular influence on the workings of government. It made the relationship to the British more adversarial, but the basic programme of the Muslim elite remained the same. They continued to define the community as that of the landed and professional elites and their programme as one of securing the political interests and the cultural respect owed that elite. Ajmal Khan's own relation to individual Englishmen and his political position convey the ambivalence and contradictions of seeking a special relationship with the rulers.

Ajmal Khan's relation to the British was predicated on a quest for respect, for '*izzat* and *wiqār*, a problematic goal in a relationship between colonial ruler and colonized subject. He sought this respect for himself, for his family, and—as in the registration act controversy—for his art. He accepted the family title of *ḥaziqu'l-mulk* ('the skilled one of the kingdom') from the British in 1908 and he was honoured by being consulted as a respected source of native opinion. Hailey, the chief commissioner, wrote to the viceroy in 1913: 'He is a man whose opinion...is of great value as he comes across all classes of men and has a very sound judgement in all such matters.'[21] When Ajmal Khan found individual Englishmen who accorded him respect, he was capable of forming with them the intense and passionate friendship cherished by his culture, friendships which were typically reserved for fellow Muslims. Among his English friends were C. F. Andrews, the Anglican missionary who identified himself personally with Tagore and Gandhi and politically with the interests of nationalists and of Indians overseas. Andrews spoke of 'an ever deepening friendship' with Ajmal Khan and revered him for his integrity and dedication.[22] Ajmal Khan deeply respected the viceroy, Lord Hardinge (1910–16), and valued his relationship with him and with his wife beyond any question of mere expediency. Theodore Morison, on the staff at Aligarh, facilitated Ajmal Khan's trip to Europe. But even in these friendships and even when most single-mindedly asserting his loyalty to the British crown and his conviction of British beneficence, Ajmal Khan, like all Indians, knew himself at perpetual risk of insult in any encounter. His friend C. F. Andrews sensed an important element in his attitude to the rulers. Andrews often saw the hakim at parties of the deputy commissioner that both were expected to attend. 'It was easy to find the Hakim Sahib on such occasions, for he would sit apart and would do nothing to court favour or to gain recognition'.[23] The whole situation, Andrews explained, must have irked a person who had once been honoured by the Mughals.

Ajmal Khan, too, had his share of railroad experiences, the single most telling locus of class encounters. To give only one example, faithfully recalled by a disciple, he once 'during the period when he was particularly close to the rulers' entered a first-class carriage and spread out his bedding. An Englishman came in and ordered him to move to the other side of the compartment. Ajmal Khan's servant pointed out to the Englishman who this was, whereupon the Englishman apologized, withdrew his order, and gave an elaborate explanation of why he had acted as he had. Ajmal Khan refused to accept his apology or accommodate his wishes on the grounds that the Englishman had acted as he had out of racism.[24] Later, when political events had begun to alienate Ajmal Khan from loyalty to the British, a second personal experience effectively moved him to break with his previous stance. This was the internment and accusation of subversion laid against his nephew, Hakim Muhammad Ahmad Khan, in 1918 when he had travelled to the frontier. 'It is against my expectations of the government', Ajmal Khan wired to the Chief Commissioner of Delhi, '[and] I need hardly say that the order not only casts a slur on Mohamed Khan but also on all the members of the family.'[25] Once again this was a matter of '*izzat* and *wiqār*. One recalls Sayyid Ahmad Khan's bitterness in his later years when the living embodiment of his belief in cultural assimilation, his Cambridge-returned son, was still only treated as 'a native'.

Through the First World War, however, Ajmal Khan and people like him adhered to the policy of loyalty as the best guarantee of their interests. In 1910 Ajmal Khan delivered a welcome address to the third annual session of the Muslim League. The speech is virtually a textbook example of the salient points of this period of Muslim politics. Ajmal Khan denounced terrorism, recalled Sayyid Ahmad Khan's aloofness from the Indian National Congress, and reiterated the special relationship possible between Muslims and their rulers—and the motive for fostering it:

Loyalty to his rulers is engrained in the Muslim's nature and is inculcated by his religion. The Quran expressly lays down that the Musalman and the Christian are nearer each other than the followers of any other two faiths. We also realize that the presence of the British in India is the best guarantee for the preservation of peace and order in the country and the equitable protection of Muslim interests.[26]

He also lauded the political relation of the British to their subjects: 'British statesmanship, ever characterized by generosity and beneficence, is exerting itself to lead the peoples of this Eastern land, step by step, along the path of political progress on Western lines.'[27] These attitudes would not outlive the decade.

More long-lived was Ajmal Khan's conviction that political
activity had to be understood in terms of community membership
and mediated through communal organization. At this point he
emphasized the theme of Muslim backwardness: 'Our share in the
public service of the land is yet absolutely inadequate. In education
we are still very backward. We have only lately entered political
life.'[28] He reviewed the particular arenas in which Muslim interests
needed to be safeguarded and pointed to the importance of representation in universities, on municipal and district boards, on
legislative councils, and on the viceroy's council, citing the principle 'of having a Musalman...to represent the Muslim point of
view'. He concurred with the League policy of favouring separate
electorates (in which each community elected its own representatives) rather than general electorates. On all this, he would later
modify his position, either in principle or in emphasis, but most
enduring was his insistence on the legitimacy of separate organizations to press for communal interests:

Those, however, who take exception to the existence of bodies established
for safeguarding communal interests, forget that in advancing the cause
of one section of the population you advance, indirectly the cause of the
whole, and that a network of Hindu associations and *sabhas* is already
striving for the promotion of sectional interests. So long as such sectional
interests, whether of the Hindus or the Mohammedans, do not jeopardize
the larger interests of the country or community, we should welcome
them....[29]

In all this, Ajmal Khan was one with the early leadership of the
League.

Unlike them, however, his commitment to the preservation and
development of indigenous medicine had required him to ally with
non-Muslims for political action in their area of common interest.
These were defenders of the other major indigenous system, the
Ayurvedic. In terms of reform of content of *yūnānī*, there is no
evidence that Ajmal Khan had ever hoped for collaboration. He
believed that both systems, the Ayurvedic and the *yūnānī*, had
entered a period of decline: indeed that of the former was far the
greater and he ventured that it had seen no development for
eighteen hundred years whereas *tibb* had only stagnated for four
to five hundred![30] For reform of content, he turned to Western
medicine to learn some techniques and some approaches to new

illnesses, but primarily to recover areas like surgery and an underlying belief in progress that had been forgotten. It was to Western
medicine that Ajmal Khan wanted a reformed *tibb* to answer. Only
the threat of the Registration Acts forced cooperation with the
other indigenous system; and in 1910 Ajmal Khan organized the
All-India Ayurvedic and Tibbia Conference. Thereafter, it met
annually and virtually all petitions and representations to the
government were couched in terms of the two traditions. When
Ajmal Khan moved on to raise funds and plan for the foundation
of a college, it was to be a college that taught both *yūnānī* and
Ayurvedic. When Ajmal Khan moved away from his position of
loyalism during the war, this experience of communal collaboration was influential in shaping his political stance.

## Ajmal Khan and Religious Reform

Ajmal Khan, in his espousal of the interests of the Muslim well-
born and his commitment to Muslim cultural symbols, stood apart
from and indeed opposed an alternative definition of Muslim
community and politics held by some of his Muslim contemporaries. The reformist ulama had, particularly after the Mutiny of
1857 and the evident display of British superiority, turned inward
in their teachings and focused on creating a community defined not
by Muslim political structure and symbols, but by individual
adherence to Islamic norms of conduct and belief. Their definition
of community extended beyond elites to ordinary Muslims, men
and women, of every background. To train religious scholars, they
had organized new schools with formal, bureaucratic characteristics that had been learned from British examples. They created a
vernacular religious literature meant for ordinary Muslims. They
undertook public preaching and debates. The content of their
teaching was primarily personal legal obligations and the techniques of personal spiritual development. Underlying all their
efforts was a belief that Muslims had strayed in their understanding
of Islam and in their commitment to religious obedience. It was
necessary to return to the basic texts and to eliminate from current
practice all false accretions and deviations that the passage of time
and the local environment had produced. They offered a perfunc-
tory loyalty to the British (while regarding them as unclean and
their rule as illegitimate) until after the World War.

There were two main groups of reformers in this period in north India shared similar institutional and methodological orientations. They differed over their attitude to the historic schools of law: the Deobandis continued to follow the Hanafi school which was widespread among Sunni Muslims (and hence they were known as *muqallid* or conformers); and the Ahl-i Hadith discounted the historic schools in favour of direct use of Qur'an and hadith (and hence they were known as *ghair-muqallid*). Disputes between these two groups were particularly intense. Both were, moreover, challenged and were challenged by those who objected to any change at all, a group known as the Barelwis. In the course of their debates, the Barelwis became ever more like their opponents in organization and in a concern with codification of legal norms. The reformers chose as their particular targets, as had Sunni Muslims from the time of Ibn Taymayya, the accretions they attributed to false Sufism and to the Shi'a, both of whom they felt compromised the unique position of God by the powers they ascribed to saints and imams. They rejected what they understood to represent a more dependent religion in which the believer looked to intermediaries for mediation instead of to his own responsibility for fulfilling the Law and developing his own personal qualities. Reform religion was well suited to a period of alien rule since the locus of authority was not the state; and it was also suited to a period of greater geographic mobility since the believer was no longer tied to local customary practices on fixed occasions.

From his earliest public statements, Ajmal Khan deplored the reformist orientation of the ulama. Indeed there was a family tradition of opposition to reform since Ajmal Khan's grandfather, Hakim Muhammad Sadiq 'Ali (d. 1264/1847–8), had written the *Taqwiyatu'l-aqā'id* as a refutation of the first great reformist tract of the nineteenth century, Maulana Isma'il Shahid's *Taqwiyatu'l-īmān*.[31] Above all else, Ajmal Khan abhorred the divisiveness and public controversy that seemed intrinsic to the efforts at reform. He used the columns of the family newspaper to denounce the rivalries of the *muqallid* and *ghair-muqallid* in Delhi in the 1890s.[32] At a meeting in 1909 he declared that there had been more mutual denunciations of infidelity (*fatāwa-yi takfīr*) in India since 1857 than there had been previously in the whole history of Islam. Moreover, he regarded the apolitical efforts of the reformers as inconsequential. For him community long continued to be defined as the community of the well-born landed and professional classes and the goal of political action to be a place for them and their culture in the courts and councils of the rulers.

Ajmal Khan's whole style of behaviour and belief was unlike that of the ulama and was indeed characteristic of many of those who were to go on to play a role in nationalist politics. His was an aristocratic style. He was a patron and a host, invariably in the company of poets and literati, landlords and government servants; one anecdote has him in the company of two women singers.[33] Under the nom de plume of Shaida Dihlawi he wrote his own Urdu and Persian poems.[34] As he grew older his sporting activities shifted from the traditional *akhāra* (wrestling pit) to billiards and shikar.[35] During most of his adult life he wore the sherwani and fez of Aligarh, the former an adaptation of the Western coat and the latter a symbol of admiration for Ottoman social change; both garments were regarded as unacceptable by most of the ulama.

Ajmal Khan's own religious style was not that of the reformist ulama. Although a Sunni, in direct contrast to the reformers he cherished precisely the two orientations they opposed, an inclination toward Shi'i beliefs and reverence for the shrine-based Sufis. After his first heart attack in 1905, he chose to make his trip abroad for recuperation to the Shi'i shrines of Iraq. There he set out from Kufa to the shrine of Hazarat 'Ali and finding himself alone at one point continued on foot. At the shrine, he later wrote, he experienced an emotion of deep happiness that was to last his entire life.[36] The Shi'i nawab of Rampur, his patron, said after Ajmal Khan's death that had he had a Sufi master, it would have been him.[37]

Ajmal Khan is said to have loved to be in the company of Sufis, and he and other members of his family were buried at the shrine of the seventeenth century saint, Hazarat Khwaja Sayyid Hasan Rasul Numa.[38] Ajmal Khan probably had initiation at the hand of Miyan Munawwar 'Ali Shah of the Chishti Nizami order whom he admired—in a conventional form of praise for holy men—for being learned without having studied. Through Nawab Mushtaq Hussain, Wiqaru'l-Mulk, a leading administrator at Aligarh and his close associate in Muslim League politics, he was put in touch with a second influential *pīr*, Maulana Sayyid Sikandar Shah. He is known to have held him to be a great 'source of peace and comfort'; and is alleged to have been able to practise the Sufi discipline of holding the picture of the master in his memory, remarkable in this case because the master and disciple had never met. As a mark of respect, Ajmal Khan taught *ṭibb* personally to Sikandar Shah's chief disciple. Ajmal Khan contrasted the Sufis with the ulama, arguing that they did not raise disorder (*fasād*), but 'with one glance could bring a message of healing to the ills of the heart.'[39]

Unlike the reformist ulama who made ritual practice central to their lives, Ajmal Khan is said to have been careless of keeping the prayers and the fast.[40] Yet he was personally pious. His peshkar (deputy) of many years recalled Ajmal Khan's dismissal of his hesitation to begin a *yūnānī* education because of lack of resources. 'A student must begin his education by trusting in God. The Lord is the Provider.'[41] Moreover, as a boy and young man he had himself pursued the classical learning tradition seriously and was teased for being a 'mulla' in his youth. Opposition to the reformist ulama did not mean that one was worldly and irreligious, but rather, perhaps, that one was religious in a different way.

Yet Ajmal Khan, for all his marked differences with the ulama, shared certain of their orientations that were increasingly common among all shades of Muslim opinion, whether reformist or not. Like the reformers, he disapproved of excessive spending on rituals and life cycle ceremonies. Like them, too, he urged study of the fundamental scriptural sources of the faith, even for those associated with the shrines. In 1916 he presided over the annual meeting of the Madrasa Mu'iniyya 'Usmaniyya at the great Chishti shrine of Shaikh Mu'inu'd-Din in Ajmer. The school had been founded shortly before at the instigation of the head of religious affairs for the princely state of Hyderabad who continued as its patron. Meant to educate the sons of the descendants of the shaikh who controlled the shrine, at its height it had some 150–200 students and twenty-five teachers.[42] On the occasion of his visit, Ajmal Khan declared that this was the first school to teach Sufism properly. He diffidently urged that each branch of knowledge be taught by a specialist and that those more learned than he revise the curriculum in such a way that the books of the great thinkers of the past be once more studied.[43] The school was also visited during the Khilafat movement by such figures as the 'Ali Brothers and Maulana 'Abdu'l-Bari, a relationship suggestive of the political utility of an open attitude toward the influential shrines, parallel in fact to the utility of an open attitude to the often influential Shi'a.

Ajmal Khan's opposition to the reformers coupled with his desire for unity and learning was reflected in his support of two religious institutions that were founded in these years. The first was the Nadwatu'l-'Ulama in Lucknow, an institution meant to unite the ulama of all schools on the basis of serious scholarship and to offer them a political platform. Ajmal Khan was a member of their Board of Management for many years, presided over their annual meeting in 1909, and was part of a committee to reconcile conflicts at the school in 1914. He was sympathetic to the school's emphasis on Arabic and to its inclusion of literature and history in its teaching. He also supported the Nazaratu'l-Ma'arif founded by a graduate of Deoband, Maulana 'Ubaidullah Sindhi, in the hopes of uniting those with traditional learning and those with Western learning in an institution that focused on study of the Qur'an.

Again like the reformist ulama, he placed enormous value on a disciplined and controlled life. He exemplified 'control of the lower self', as it was called; and the testimonials about him collected from his associates after his death are largely couched in the technical terminology, mostly from the Sufi tradition, that is used to discuss a disciplined and well-formed life characterized by complete self-control, unselfishness, and truthfulness.[44] His deputy identified his most singular characteristic quality as *quwwat-i taskhīr*, the power of subduing, and said it resulted in each person's feeling uniquely loved by him.[45] In every educational institution with which he was involved, Ajmal Khan insisted on the necessity of teachers who personally embodied the lessons they attempted to teach. Ajmal Khan thus shared the commitment of the reformers to certain personal values, to abandonment of elaborate ceremonials, and to education in the Islamic classics. But he stood decisively apart from their passionate concern with establishing correct belief and practice among all Muslims, defined in part by opposition to shrines and Shi'is, as well as from their attempt to operate outside the political structure.

## Nationalist Muslims: Communal Symbols and Non-Communal Cooperation

In the decade that began in 1912, both Ajmal Khan and a segment of the reformist ulama were to move to a political paradigm that represented neither the interest-oriented community-focused programme associated with Aligarh nor the politically aloof programme that defined community by individual adherence to religious norms associated with the reformist ulama. In that period, Muslim political leaders felt betrayed by the British by a series of policies that were carried out both inside and outside India. Within India there was anger over the revocation of the partition of Bengal that had given the Muslim majority of that province the eastern section under its own control. There was acute disappointment over the government's unwillingness to encourage the development of Aligarh as a Muslim university. There was concern that the constitutional reforms would not offer enough to Muslims and a feeling that Muslims had to organize to bring continuous political pressure. Outside India there seemed to be unending pressure on the Muslim world and in particular an undermining of the Ottomans in their central and symbolically significant area of authority. The Balkan Wars particularly focused Muslim opinion on the Middle East and the larger Muslim world; and the subsequent years were to see Muslim causes outside India as the central focus of Indian Muslim political organization and mobilization. Many of these discontents were focused on the Kanpur Mosque incident of 1913, the first occasion when influential political figures and religious leaders from outside took up an essentially local issue. By 1913 the Muslim League was calling for self-government. In the same year, Ajmal Khan emerged as a major figure in the organization of a medical delegation to the Balkans.

In these years the rhetoric of Muslim political language moved from an emphasis on the preservation of elite interests and cosmopolitan cultural symbols to more emotive, populist, public symbols of Muslim corporate identity. Politicians did not take up the programme of the ulama directed toward individual education and moral reform; the symbols were not religious in that sense. Rather they focused on Muslims as a special community, the best community, a community to be reckoned with seriously. This was a community to be defended by all Muslims as a sacred duty. At the same time as developing this religious rhetoric, Muslim political leaders moved to cooperate with non-Muslims in their common cause of opposition to the British. The landmark of this cooperation was the Lucknow Pact of the Muslim League and the Indian National Congress in 1916 in which a common platform of political demands was obtained. Sections of the ulama, drawn by the religious issues and by the opportunity to oppose the British, organized as a political group to cooperate with the others. Leadership increasingly passed to Gandhi who took up the cause of preservation of the Ottoman Khilafat; and in 1921 both Hindus and Muslims followed him into non-cooperation. Ajmal Khan was centrally involved in the development of these organizations and programmes. It was Ajmal Khan (and Dr Ansari) who first invited religious leaders to the Muslim League; and Ajmal Khan was perhaps the Muslim closest to Gandhi.

At the same time he continued to be deeply involved in his defence of the indigenous medical system and to seek the cooperation of hakims and *vaids* as essential to its success. The All India Unani and Ayurvedic Tibbia Conference continued to hold annual meetings and to lobby for protection against discriminatory laws. In 1916 Ajmal Khan succeeded in having the issue of the protection of the indigenous systems raised in the legislative council and a resolution was successfully passed that attempts would be made to place 'the ancient and indigenous systems of medicine on a scientific basis.'[46] At a meeting with Madan Mohan Malaviya present, Ajmal Khan argued the necessity of founding tibbia colleges throughout the country, all under the control of a central tibbia university.[47] Writing in the annual report of the Tibbia College in 1920, Ajmal Khan insisted on the identity between indigenous medicine and self-government, using the swadeshi argument (although not the term) associated with Gandhi: 'If we want to take the administration of government into our own hands, we must right all national things, including the indigenous method of healing. Our real progress depends on these things. We fail in serving our country if we are dependent on outside things.'[48] National leaders regularly presided over the annual functions of the conference and the college. In 1921, Gandhi himself dedicated the newly completed buildings of the college. With the passing of the Montagu-Chelmsford constitutional reforms of 1919, health was made a provincial subject under the control of elected officials. From that time on, fear of discrimination largely ended and the policy of governments, continuing to the present, has been, in varying degrees, the patronage of the indigenous systems.

For Ajmal Khan the support of non-Muslim political leaders was essential both to provide a united front against government discrimination or neglect and, as the nationalist movement grew, to gain the support of those who were increasingly powerful. The support that was given to medicine by these leaders was in part based on genuine commitment to the value of the old systems but in part it was based on political motivation, just as British support had been. The most dramatic example of this ambivalence was in Gandhi's address at the laying of the foundation stone of the Tibbia College in 1921. At the height of the non-cooperation movement with all the hopes and anxieties that the attempt at Hindu–Muslim cooperation entailed, Hakim Ajmal Khan and his college represented a symbol of genuine open-mindedness and cooperation that Gandhi felt had to be recognized. On the other hand, he opposed all systems of medicine and regarded, he frankly said, all hospitals as a sign of failure. *Tibb* in its current form, he continued, was nothing more than black magic and one ought in any case to concentrate on nourishing the soul rather than on wrongly ministering to the body.[49] His rather astonishing remarks aside, it was nonetheless significant that Gandhi had chosen—and been chosen— to preside over this occasion since only a few months earlier it had been expected that the viceroy would play this role.[50] On the left side of the main entrance to the college is the stone laid by the viceroy in 1916, on the right hand side is the stone commemorating the inauguration of the building by Gandhi—a dramatic picture of the rapidity with which Muslim political orientations had changed in those years.

Three aspects of Muslim cosmopolitan culture became associated with nationalist symbols in these years and continue so to the present; these are Sufism, music, and medicine, all regarded as part of a shared culture that can be valued by both Muslims and non-Muslims. In Delhi in the 1980s, for example, the Muslims most likely to appear on public political and cultural platforms were the city's leading hakim and a distinguished descendant of the family of the Sufi, Hazrat Nizamu'd-Din.[51] Thus medicine, early in Ajmal Khan's life, was a symbol of the cultural pride of the Muslim cosmopolitan elite; more enduringly it became a symbol of cultural integration.

Ajmal Khan's complete commitment to Hindu–Muslim cooperation was shaped by this long and deep experience of the value of cooperation in the field of medicine. This is not to say that others without such experience were not also committed, only that in his case the experience in medicine, and indeed his whole predisposition toward the more cosmopolitan aspects of his culture, was of formative importance. Although active in the Muslim League from the beginning, he, unlike many in the tradition of Sayyid Ahmad Khan, had not seen the Indian National Congress as necessarily antagonistic to Muslim interests. He, moreover, was convinced that one could further Muslim interests and at the same time move increasingly toward a common national culture; few of the Muslim leaders at this period shared his commitment to this latter goal.

For many of the Muslims, cooperation with non-Muslims was merely expedient as, indeed, was the acceptance of Gandhi's policies; they joined him out of desire to present a common platform of opposition to the rulers. This was largely true of the charismatic journalist and politician Muhammad 'Ali. The ulama, moreover, cherished a plan for a wholly autonomous social and political life, linked to non-Muslims in the loosest of federations once Independence was attained.[52] Although in 1919 Ajmal Khan had been instrumental in organizing the association of the ulama, the Jami'atu'l-ulama-yi Hind, joining with the leading Deobandi of Delhi, Mufti Kifayatu'llah,[53] he strongly opposed the Jami'at scheme to create a separate system of law courts under an organization of the ulama as the beginning of what might be called the 'mental partition of India' that they envisaged.[54] Ajmal Khan believed fully in communal cooperation and at the same time shared in the increasing focus on emotive, public, religious symbols of Muslim corporate identity. In significant ways these symbols derived more from the cosmopolitan complex of values cherished by those associated, however loosely, with Aligarh, than from the complex of symbols articulated by the reformist ulama. It had been those who wrote in English or had interacted with the British and their views of Muslim culture who created the romantic and apologetic writings of the late nineteenth and earlier twentieth centuries—writers like Ameer Ali, Chiragh Ali, Shibli No'mani, the novelist Sharar and the poet Hali. They had responded to Orientalist criticisms of their religion and culture and had directed attention to the larger historic and geographic world of Islam. Among the ulama, it was Nadwa, most the product of those interacting with the British, that focused most on the larger Muslim world. As Muslim countries seemed increasingly threatened, journalists and polemicists like Muhammad 'Ali and Maulana Azad created an ideology of Indian Muslim identity with the fate of Muslims elsewhere. The reformist ulama to be sure were also conscious of Muslim interests outside India; indeed, they had been involved in collecting money on such occasions as the Russo-Turkish war of 1878. As others took the lead, some among them entered active political life for the first time, most notably some leading figures from Deoband and from Farangi Mahall who thus, it has recently been shown, were able simultaneously to enhance their own positions within their institutions.[55] Once involved, the ulama were a determining force in the shape of the national movement, pushing for extreme action and often succeeding.

Ajmal Khan's own views in these years are evident in many of the speeches he delivered at the numerous organizations of which he was a part. In 1918, for example, he was part of a group of Muslim barristers, wakils, and traders, along with his beloved associate, Dr Ansari, the publisher Maulana 'Abdu'l-Ahad, and the imam of the Jami Masjid, in attempting to establish an Islamiyya College in Delhi. In his statement he talked much as he had in earlier years of the decline of Muslim culture, blaming the sorry state of education for the under-representation of Muslims in what he called the *sharīf* professions: barristers, doctors, engineers, wakils, and teachers. But he now broadened his earlier focus and looked also at the low numbers of Muslims in industry, crafts, and trade, and lamented the condition of ordinary education. He spoke overall of the decline of Muslim dignity and honour (*qaumī wiqār aur 'izzat*), and of the decline in Delhi especially. He recalled the great scholars and Sufis of the city 'whose messianic breath breathed new souls into the dead body of the nation.' 'Now look,' he added, 'at the autumn of the city whose spring was this.' He continued to enjoin Muslims to act on the basis of their religious obligations and drew heavily on words charged with meaning in Muslim religious life.

Our children who were once educated in madrasas and households now play in the streets. Who can go into any Muslim neighbourhood and return dry-eyed? Our children are not responsible for this. God has given us the power of discrimination [*tamīz*] and we are responsible for their education, nurture, and Islamic culture and deportment. What answer will we give in the afterlife [*ākhirat*]? Shall we answer that we took loans for ceremonies for them, ceremonies that were against the *sharī'a*, and left them free in the streets to add to their hearts and minds the accretions that darken the skirt of Islam and humanity?... They are the victims of their poverty and our forgetfulness [*ghaflat*]. Every delay in creating a school increases the sin [*gunāh*] which is on the neck of every Muslim of Delhi. It is the duty [*farz*] of every Muslim of Delhi to lay the foundation of an Islamic college. And when a Muslim undertakes a work, he does it with the enthusiasm of Islam and the emotions of the faith [*islāmī jōsh aur īmānī jazbāt*].... We must put our trust in that God whose kind glance falls on every lowly servant and rescues every faltering work, then place our hope in our Islamic brothers, confident that all will unite in putting this on their weak shoulders with dependence [*tawakkul*] on God.[56]

The speech reflects both the more inclusive corporate identity and the use of religious symbols characteristic of Muslim political life in this period.

These themes reappear in speech after speech. As chairman of the Khilafat Committee in 1921, Ajmal Khan called on Muslims to sacrifice, for example in such matters as using homespun. 'You must say *labbaik* ["I am present," as one says most dramatically at the Meccan pilgrimage] to a voice inviting you to protect Islam and stop injustice.... If we are not ready for this, we have no right to mouth Islamic injunctions or to hope for God's mercy.'[57] In appealing for contributions to the Angora Fund he said, 'If you fall short in any way in helping...now, consider this to be an unforgivable sin.... Prove that in your veins, by the grace and generosity of God, even now Islamic blood flows. This is a sacred duty [*muqaddas farz*].'[58] Emboldened by the knowledge that they were part of a larger world and not merely a minority in a single country, political leaders asserted a picture of Islam as a special community, unique by virtue of its revelation. Instead of distinguishing certain Muslims as the well-born—*sharīf*—Ajmal Khan would enjoin all Muslims to certain actions because as a whole they were well-born—a *sharīf qaum*.[59]

In his speech as president of the Muslim League at Amritsar in 1919, Ajmal Khan, speaking as well to the Congress leaders who were present, made clear how far he had come from his position of a decade earlier. Over half of his speech was given to a precise analysis and denunciation of government repression.[60] He then continued on the theme of Hindu–Muslim relations:

The secret of the success, not merely of the Reform Scheme, but of all the work which is being done by Indians in India and abroad, lies in

Hindu–Muslim unity. Hindu–Muslim relations...appear to be infinitely more satisfactory than they have been in past years. The question of Government appointments is no longer capable of engaging our attention to any appreciable degree.[61]

He called on Muslims to give up sacrifice of cows as a response to the generosity of Hindu support for their cause of the preservation of the Khilafat. To encourage this, he argued in fundamentalist, legal terms by citing precedents of the Prophet to show that sacrifice of other animals was preferred. Such an argument, of course, had little impact on a practice that now often had less to do with religion than with communal self-assertion. Two years later he made the same argument to the Hindu communal organization, the Hindu Mahasabha, whose annual meeting he chaired in keeping with the view of the complementarity of religiously-defined and territorially-defined institutions.[62]

A second major theme, directed more to the British than to other Indians, was his insistence on the power of Muslims and the extent to which their loyalty depended on the nature of British activity in the Muslim world. His underlining of the importance of a pan-Islamic identity was not meant, he explained, to raise questions in anyone's mind of Muslim loyalty to their own homeland.

I am aware that the exceptional nature of events now happening in the Muslim world has led me to dwell at length on topics of exclusively Muslim interest, but I have done so advisedly and in the confident hope that it cannot, at this time of day, lead any one to doubt the Musalmans' vivid consciousness of the solemn duty they owe to their motherland. As children of the soil, they know and fervently desire to fulfil their duty to the country of which they, in common with Hindus, Christians, Parsis and other communities are the proud inheritors.... For India the unseen future holds a magnificence and splendour compared with which the most glorious grandeur of her past will be but small. Let all hands of men as well as of women join to unveil that vision.[63]

Ajmal Khan's final comment was more than a stirring conclusion, for he worked ceaselessly for that kind of unity.

He had a vision of Hindus and Muslims not only living side by side but of knowing each other's cultures and interacting with each other in common institutions. During the final years of his life, he worked tirelessly for the foundation of a nationalist Muslim university, the Jami'a Millia Islamia, a school founded for Aligarh students who wanted to join the non-cooperation movement;

it was later established in Delhi. As first *amir* of the institution, he expected the students to know each other's culture: 'The firm foundation of a united Indian nationhood depends on this mutual understanding'.[64] Along with Maulana Azad, Dr Ansari, and Muhammad Kichlu, he was one of the prominent Muslims who continued Congress membership during the 1920s. He supported C. R. Das in the proposal to participate in the government's councils in order to work for further change from within. As perhaps his final political effort before his death, he was one with the nationalist Muslims who accepted the Nehru Report of 1928, a proposal meant to reconcile Muslim and Hindu constitutional demands; it included, among other proposals, the acceptance of joint electorates in the hope that candidates would then be forced to a moderation acceptable to members of the other community.

Against the background of these educational and political efforts, India, in the final years of Ajmal Khan's life, witnessed intensified communal bitterness and experienced many violent communal incidents. A series of riots began after the calling off of the non-cooperation movement when it appeared to Gandhi that control could not be maintained. In Delhi Ajmal Khan had been able, in 1919 for example, almost single-handedly to maintain control and organize a shadow government to police disorder. In the Multan riot of 1923, by contrast, he met complete failure and could only tell the Punjab Congress Committee in his parting words that their communalism would undo everything: 'You will always be slaves'.[65] In 1924, as the list of troubled cities grew, a peace conference met in Delhi, working mostly at his house. The calling off of non-cooperation, the bursting of the pan-Islamic bubble with the Turkish abolition of the Khilafat in 1924, the intensification of communal rivalry with the implementation of the provincial reforms, the deteriorating economic situation—all this contributed to an ever-worsening situation. As the situation deteriorated, so too did the hakim's health and in 1925 he left for Europe.

Ajmal Khan died a relatively young man, utterly exhausted and utterly defeated in the vision of 'glorious grandeur' he had expected Hindus and Muslims jointly to unveil. He left behind him two institutions of considerable promise: the Tibbia College and Jami'a Millia—one the child of his youth, the other of his old age, as Muhammad 'Ali said.[66] His hopes for a common nationalism were belied by events on every side. His expectation of the possibilities of a plural nationalism in which emotive religious identities existed concurrently with a national culture ended in disappointment. His experience hauntingly echoes that of Sayyid Ahmad Khan a generation earlier whose vision similarly faltered, in his case in his expectation that the special relationship of the Muslim elite with the rulers meant that they could relate to each other with dignity and respect.

The Khilafat leaders and nationalist Muslims generally believed that a religious-based identity focused on public symbols of the faith could exist as a complement to a composite nationalism. Ajmal Khan justified religiously-defined associations and identities throughout his entire life. A position like his was evidently sincere; it was also theoretically possible that the kind of society he envisaged based on religious community could have worked out in India as it had elsewhere.[67] In the situation of British India, however, the encouragement of separate organizations and identities only served to exacerbate competition and communal tension—however little that may have been intended.

Ajmal Khan had no experience to understand the local tensions and rivalries that lay at the base of communal riots; he stood before them dumbfounded. His own career in both medicine and politics had been built on forging alliances among the elite—with the princes, with the British, with professional allies, and with political leaders—and not with building up local constituencies where such tensions were a reality. He created in indigenous medicine an area of accomplishment and a symbol of both communal and national pride. He expected in vain the same kinds of accomplishments in forging a unified political life, but this goal failed in a context where other demands and priorities outweighed his.

Ajmal Khan is remembered as a nationalist Muslim. The many meanings of that term must be peeled away to do justice to the content of his career. Two broadly separate stages must be identified, first that of an Aligarh (and later a Muslim League) orientation in the defence of the interests of the well-born and the preservation of cosmopolitan Muslim cultured symbols; and second, that of identification with emotive, public symbols of Muslim social identity and collaboration with non-Muslims against British rule. Both stages focus on Muslim corporate identity defined in the first case by a cluster of aristocratic, cosmopolitan symbols, in the second by emotionally charged symbols associated with being part of a larger Muslim world and by the very fact of being Muslim. They contrast with the symbols of the reformist ulama, weighted toward personal fulfilment of the religious law. In each stage, Ajmal Khan, again in contrast to the early reformists, sought collaboration with non-Muslims, first with the British and then with the largely Hindu Congress; and he insisted on an active political life. The initial stance of Muslims like Ajmal Khan was predicated on many of the same assumptions that had characterized princely political life, but the vision of well-born Muslims as privileged participants in rule was doomed both by the colonial situation and the reality of a plural society. The subsequent expectation of intense communal identity in harmony with a unified nationalist programme was similarly to give way after Ajmal Khan's lifetime toward the ideal of a more secular nation-alism on the one hand and the demand for a separate Muslim state on the other.

Throughout, religious identity remained the fundamental build-ing block of most political positions for Muslims; and the language of political discourse in shifting contexts drew on the repertoire provided by Islam. Islam offered a wide range of orientations, not one single stance, a range whose symbols shifted from the cosmo-politan; to those of personal religious responsibility; to symbols of a charismatic community; to those of a shared national culture. Ajmal Khan in his life knew this entire range. This variety, as well as the evident crisis in social and political life that the riots dis-played, suggest the anguish of trying to find a satisfactory definition of Muslim political identity in the long period of colonial rule in India.

## Notes

1. See 'Revolutionaries, Pan-Islamists and Bolsheviks: Maulana Abul Kalam Azad and the Political Underworld in Calcutta, 1905-1925.' In Hasan, Mushirul, ed. 1981. *Communal and Pan-Islamic Trends in Colonial India*, pp. 85-108. Delhi.

2. Robinson, Francis. 1974. *Separatism among Indian Muslims: The Politics of the United Provinces Muslims, 1860-1923*, p. 377. Cambridge.

3. Hardy, P. 1972. *The Muslims of British India*, esp. Ch. V. Cambridge.

4. See Lelyveld, David. 1978. *Aligarh's First Generation: Muslim Solidarity in British India*. Princeton.

5. The term 'Islamicate' is from Hodgson, Marshall G. S. 1974. *The Venture of Islam: Conscience and History in a World Civilization*, I: 57–60. Chicago.

6. For a discussion of the Orientalist mentality, see Said, Edward W. 1978. *Orientalism*. New York.

7. Excerpted in Ḳẖāṅ Ḥakīm Jamīl, n.d. *Sirat-i Ajmal*, p. 11. Delhi.

8. For a discussion of changes in religious education in the late nineteenth century see Metcalf, Barbara D. 1982. *Islamic Revival in British India: Deoband, 1860–1900*. Princeton. [2nd edn., New Delhi: Oxford University Press, 2002].

9. Dihlawī, Muḥammad Ajmal [Ḥakīm Ajmal Ḳẖāṅ]. 1897. *al-Ṭāʿūn*, pp. 2–3. Delhi. One assumes that a legal term like this is used because the legal paradigm informs every approach to knowledge. Examples are many. More serious than the imputation of *bidʿa*, opponents to Ajmal Khan's medical conference in 1892 are said to have called those who attended non-Muslim—*kāfir* and *murtad* (Abdu'l-Ḡẖaffār, Muḥammad. *Ḥayāt-i Ajmal*, p. 24). In contrast, a supporter spoke of Ajmal Khan as a *mujtahid* (one able to exercise legal judgement) in an era of *taqlīd* (legal conformity) (Muḥammad Ḥasan Qarshī, Zubdatu'l-Ḥukma, ed. November–December 1928. *Mashīru'l-aṭṭiba: Masīḥu'l-mulk nambar*, p. 12). Dr Zakir Husain after Ajmal Khan's death spoke of him as a *mujtahid* and *muqallid* as well ('Abdu'l-Ḡẖaffār, Muḥammad. *Ḥayāt-i Ajmal*, p. 529).

10. The terms are again from Hodgson, cited above, note 5.

11. See Ullman, Manfred. 1978. *Islamic Medicine*, esp. ch. II. Edinburgh.

12. Thus Hakim Sharif Khan, Ajmal Khan's early eighteenth century ancestor, had, for example, made changes in the mixtures known as *kushta* under the influence of the Indic system. See Hamadānī, Muḥammad Kamālu'd-Dīn Ḥusain. 1976. *Maṭab-i Masīḥ*, p. 12. Aligarh, and Qarshi, Muḥammad Ḥasan, ed. November–December 1928. *Mashīru'l-aṭṭiba*, p. 11.

13. This distinction is paraphrased from Kakar, Sudhir. 1982. *Shamans, Mystics, and Doctors: A Psychological Inquiry into India and its Healing Traditions*, p. 31. New York.

14. Ibid., p. 30.

15. See Leslie, Charles. 1977. 'The Ambiguities of Medical Revivalism in Modern India'. In Leslie, Charles, ed., *Asian Medical Systems: A Comparative Study*, p. 360. Berkeley.

16. Ḳẖāṅ, Ḥakīm Manṣūr Aḥmad. 1907–8. *Mazhab-i Manṣūr*. Hyderabad.

17. Thānawī, Maulānā Ashraf 'Alī. 1906. *Bihishtī Zēwar*, Book IX. Muradabad.

18. Officiating Deputy Secretary, Government of India, to Chief Commissioner, Delhi, 25 November 1919, in B File #70 of Home, 1920, in Delhi Archives Research Room.

19. See, for example, K. B. Pirzada Mohamad Husain, M.A., to E. R. Abbott, Chief Commissioner, Delhi, 14 February 1925, in B File #5 of Education 1925, Delhi Archives Research Room.

20. B File #5 of 1930, Education, Delhi Archives Research Room.

21. W. M. Hailey to Private Secretary to H. E. the Viceroy, 12 June 1913, in B File #168 of Education 1913, in Delhi Archives Research Room.

22. Andrews, C. F. 1926. 'Hakim Ajmal Khan'. In *Eminent Musalmans*, p. 287. Madras: Natesan.

23. Ibid., p. 293.

24. 'Abdu'l-Ghaffār, Muḥammad. *Ḥayāt-i Ajmal*, pp. 477-8.

25. Telegram posted 14 August 1916 at Mussoorie in Home Confidential File #48 of 1916, Delhi Archives Research Room.

26. Welcome Address at the Third Session of the Muslim League, Delhi, 29-30 January 1910, in Zaidi, A. M. 1975. *Evolution of Muslim Political Thought in India, I: The Emergence of Jinnah*, p. 188. New Delhi.

27. Ibid., p. 181.

28. Ibid., p. 188.

29. Ibid., p. 185.

30. 'Abdu'l-Ghaffār, Muḥammad. 1976. *Ḥayāt-i Ajmal*, p. 64.

31. Hamadānī, Muḥammad Kamālu'd-Dīn Ḥusain. *Maṭab-i Masīh*, p. 12. Aligarh.

32. 'Abdu'l-Ghaffār, Muḥammad. *Ḥayāt-i Ajmal*, p. 38.

33. Ibid., p. 496.

34. Published after his death by Dr Zakir Husain at Jami'a Millia.

35. He went along on the hunt but never actually shot anything, arguing that a hakim ought not take but give life. Amrohawī, Ḥakīm Rashīd Aḥmad Khān. 1938. *Ḥayāt-i Ajmal*, p. 32. Delhi.

36. 'Abdu'l-Ghaffār, Muḥammad. *Ḥayāt-i Ajmal*, p. 55.

37. Ibid., pp. 51-2.

38. The graveyard is now inhabited by squatters and most of the gravestones broken (April 1982).

39. 'Abdu'l-Ghaffār, Muḥammad. *Ḥayāt-i Ajmal*, p. 82.

40. Amrohawī, Ḥakīm Rashīd Aḥmad Khān. Shifā'ul-Mulk. 1938. *Ḥayāt-i Ajmal*, pp. 34-5. Delhi. This last comment is staunchly denied by Mufti Kifayatu'llah's son, Hafiz Rahman Wasif, who knew Ajmal Khan in his later years (In private conversations in Delhi, July 1982). His biographer explained the failure to keep the fast as a concession to his heart condition.

41. Amrohawī, Ḥakīm Rashīd Aḥmad Khān. *Ḥayāt-i Ajmal*, p. 17.

42. The school is now very modest and mostly teaches Qur'an to local boys. The teacher, fittingly, doubles as hakim at the shrine's clinic in the afternoon (Interview with Hakim Muhyi'd-Din, the teacher, 22 December 1981, Ajmer). Information about the school's history is from Maulana Aijaz 'Ali, former accountant for the school, 17 February 1982, Ajmer.

43. Khān. Ḥakīm Jamīl, *Sirat-i Ajmal*, pp. 100-101.

44. These comments are collected in 'Abdu'l-Ghaffār, Muḥammad. *Ḥayāt-i Ajmal*, pp. 467-532. See also Amrohawī, Ḥakīm Rashīd Aḥmad Khān, *Ḥayāt-i Ajmal*, pp. 27-9, the sections headed *kasr-i nafsī* and *ẓabṭ-i nafs aur matānat*.

45. Amrohawī, Ḥakīm Rashīd Aḥmad, *Ḥayāt-i Ajmal*, p. 30.

46. Quoted in B File #179 of 1919, Home, Delhi Administration Research Room.

47. Khāṅ Ḥakīm Jamīl, *Sirat-i Ajmal*, p. 119.

48. Ibid., pp. '132–3'. This edition is defective; quotation marks indicate the second set of pages.

49. Ibid., p. '134'.

50. Government of India, Legislative Department, Proceedings of the Indian Legislative Council, Delhi, 10 March 1920, Delhi Administration Research Room.

51. Medicine, music, and Sufism cluster in the programmes of the Indian Institute of Islamic Studies, an institution supported by the Hamdard Foundation (which markets *yūnānī* medicines, now a part of Jamia Hamdard). At an event, for example, they offered ghazals sung by Muslim members of the Rampur gharana and by a Hindu woman who had studied at Shantiniketan, each presenting, among other numbers, works by Ghalib; this was for an audience of archivists from the whole subcontinent (15 October 1981). On the occasion of an international conference on the great philosopher and contributor to *yūnānī* medicine, Ibn Sina, they presented the devotional singers (*qawwāl*) of the shrine of Hazrat Nizamu'd-Din, thus combining medicine, music, and Sufism (4 November 1981).

52. Hardy, Peter. 1971. *Partner in Freedom—And True Muslims: The Political Thought of Some Muslim Scholars in British India 1912–1947.* Lund.

53. Minault, Gail. 1982. *The Khilafat Movement: Religious Symbolism and Political Mobilization in India*, p. 82. New York. He also apparently encouraged the formation of a parallel association among Hindu religious leaders, a Jami'at-i Panditan. Noted in Chandra, Bipan, 'Communalism and the National Movement'. In Hasan, Mushirul. *Communal and Pan-Islamic Trends*. p. 196n.

54. The phrase is Peter Hardy's in *The Muslims of British India*. p. 195.

55. This argument has been developed by Minault, Gail, *The Khilafat Movement*.

56. Khāṅ Ḥakīm Jamīl, *Sīrat-i Ajmal*, pp. 108–9.

57. Ibid., pp. 161–2.

58. Ibid., p. 169.

59. In his speech as president of the Muslim League, Amritsar, 1919, ibid., p. 137.

60. The proportion is based on the thirty-five-page extract given in Zaidi, A. M., *Evolution of Muslim Political Thought in India, II: Sectarian Nationalism and Khilafat*, pp. 173–214.

61. Ibid., p. 192.

62. 'Abdu'l-Ghaffār, Muḥammad, *Ḥayāt-i Ajmal*, p. 251.

63. Ibid., p. 214.

64. In his speech at the first graduation ceremony of the school, held in 1922. Madhūlī 'Abdu'l-Ghaffār, 1965. *Jāmi'a kī kahānī*, p. 38. New Delhi.

65. 'Abdu'l-Ghaffār, Muḥammad. *Ḥayāt-i Ajmal*, p. 287.

66. Madhūlī , 'Abdu'l-Ghaffār. *Jāmi'a kī kahānī*, p. 73. The Tibbia College was torn with dissensions, many surrounding Ajmal Khan's son and successor, from the beginning. After Partition it was closed for five years. Currently administered by the Delhi Municipality, few are hopeful of its future as it struggles on in the buildings and with the equipment it had at its inception. Jami'a Millia, now a national university, has had many distinguished faculty and distinctive achievements.

67. N. C. Saxena has reviewed the historiography of writing on India to argue the extent to which religiously-defined community action has always been regarded as wrong; the word 'communal' is invariably pejorative whereas culturally plural societies have and can exist on such a basis. 'Historiography of Communalism in India'. In Hasan, Mushirul, ed. *Communal and Pan-Islamic Trends in Colonial India*, pp. 302–25.

# 6

## Hakim Ajmal Khan
### *Rais* of Delhi and Muslim 'Leader'

The learned let flow the river of learning, then went on;
The preachers of our race awoke the sleeping, then went on;
Some spoke well, showed their magic, then went on;
Some were messiahs, raised the dead, then went on;
   One plank of your broken boat remained to you;
   The flood of death, *O Delhi*, took it off too.
*O City*, it seems from you has gone the greatness of the race;
Departed now long since is the honour of the race;
But wait—Mahmud Khan's strength was an honour to our race.
But he, too, left the world. Alas, the fortune of our race!
   What will you show now to recall the former times? Well?
   In whom will you take pride now, *O Jahanabad*? Well?

Altaf Husain Hali, on the death of
Hakim Mahmud Khan, 1900[1]

Physicians of indigenous medicine have long brought distinction to
the city of Delhi. Hakim Ajmal Khan (1863-1927) pictured in his
prime in Figure 1, was the son of the Mahmud Khan celebrated
above. He is known to students of modern India for his efforts to
professionalize Islamic medicine (*yunani tibb*) and for his involvement in nationalist politics, particularly in the years immediately
following World War I when he worked closely with Gandhi
and others committed to Hindu–Muslim unity in the nationalist
movement. Ajmal Khan's life exemplifies qualities characteristic of
the notables—the *rais*—of Delhi of his times. Social leadership like

FIGURE 1: Hakim Ajmal Khan, Masih ul Mulk and Rais Azam, Delhi.

his was based on professional skills and, above all, on personal
qualities that together provided a standing quite apart from any
formal office or political position. It is thus wholly apt that toward
the end of his life Ajmal Khan was spoken of as 'a king without
a crown'.

Both Ajmal Khan and his father were towering figures in the city
of Delhi. Professionally, both were considered unrivalled in their
ability to effect seemingly miraculous cures. Socially, they were
part of the cosmopolitan Persianate culture of the old Mughal
capital, men of refinement, cultivated tastes, and accomplishments.
Ajmal Khan, as a poet, was known as Shahid Dihlawi ('the possessed
lover from Delhi') and was the author of a substantial *diwan*.[2] Most
of Ajmal Khan's friends were Muslim, but true to the ethos of this
world, his circle included Hindus, too, and even a few British, men
like C. F. Andrews and Lord Hardinge, who valued the culture of
Delhi's élite and were at least on its fringe.[3] On religious matters,
Ajmal Khan outspokenly deplored the reformist religious movements of his time; he saw them as sectarian and divisive.[4] The father,
and even more the son, participated in the changing political
structures of their times. The British officials of Delhi long regarded
both as men of good sense and modern inclination.

Ajmal Khan's public career evenly spanned the four decades at
the turn of the century. In this period, effectiveness as a local
notable was increasingly enhanced by effectiveness in a larger
arena. Ajmal Khan in this period moved to create central institutions for indigenous medicine and its practitioners, and became
himself a national figure. His widening circles of influence point
to significant developments in the history of Delhi and of India
in general. In part the institutions Ajmal Khan was associated with
represent developments within pre-existing structures, like the
family; and in part they represent the creation of new, formally
organized institutions based on shared interests rather than origin,
and organized for a wide variety of political, educational, and social
ends. These institutions were made both possible and necessary by
new developments in communication and transportation on the
one hand and a new structure of political life on the other.

Ajmal Khan was motivated in his endeavours by the view of
Muslim decline that inspired Hali's verses above. His concern for
the preservation of his art was closely linked to his concern for
Muslim status and welfare. This did not conflict with his close

relations with non-Muslims and his desire to work closely with them for shared purposes. His measures for the preservation and encouragement of indigenous Muslim medicine were not an isolated endeavour, but one of many movements for cultural self-esteem in this period of alien rule. The revival of medicine was notable among the many movements of this period because it involved a great deal of interaction with its Western counterpart and because medicine was not a religious but a communal symbol of Muslim society. The institutional and intellectual developments in medicine in this period reflect these two characteristics.

Part of Ajmal Khan's effectiveness derived from his belonging to a distinguished and respected family. Although perceived as an unchanging institution, the family in fact took on new importance for those engaged in cultural activities like music and medicine at this time. The great scholars and artists, particularly those in Delhi, had depended on patronage from the royal court and from nobles associated with it. With the end of this patronage, they adopted new strategies to sustain themselves, of which one was to place far greater emphasis on the family as an institution and focus of identity. Exactly when the title 'sharifi' to identify Ajmal Khan's family came into common usage, for example, is not clear. It harks back, however, only to the great *hakim*, Sharif Khan (d. 1790) who flourished in the eighteenth century; built the family mansion and mosque in Ballimaran, the street of poets and *hakim*s; and wrote widely on a range of scholarly subjects.[5] In the second half of the nineteenth century, at exactly the same time and for the same reasons that the *gharana*s of musicians became important, physicians focused more centrally on their lineage and their past, in this case producing memoranda and biographies to help shape a sense of their corporate identity.[6] Hakim Mahmud Khan's *Dar hal-i bazurgan-i khandani wa sar guzasht-i khud*, written in Persian, established the arrival of the family in the subcontinent at the time of the emperor Babar; and his sons, including Ajmal Khan, investigated such questions as the places where later members of the family settled. Biographies of Ajmal Khan inevitably begin with a survey of his lineage and can claim, as at least one does, that for three hundred years there was an unbroken succession of distinguished doctors.[7]

The advantages of a family identity were clear. It provided a focus for reputation and recognition, particularly important as *hakim*s came to travel more widely in a new era of transportation and foreign rule, in search of patrons instead of staying in Delhi. It also provided for control of education, 'quality control' in locating instruction within a single family of repute: a scion of the *sharifi khandan* could expect recognition for superior training. The family focus could also keep professional secrets private since in both medicine and music it had come to be understood that the great families had esoteric techniques to create the magic that both arts sometimes seemed to possess.[8]

In medicine, however, far more vulnerable to the competition of a Western system, the institution of the family came to be perceived as insufficient. In the case of medicine and music both, in fact, the late nineteenth century saw the foundation of formally organized schools. But these were to go much farther in medicine than in music in becoming the most significant arena of education.[9] Nonetheless, respect for family accomplishment and heritage continued to be of great importance; and for a *hakim* to be known as part of one of the great Delhi families—the families not only of Sharif Khan but of Hakim Baqaullah, Hakim Talib Ahmad, and Hakim Ghulam Najf Khan—was an important claim to recognition even as schools and organizations developed.[10] The British, for example, thought of Ajmal Khan at the centre of an influential family network. When in 1916 he submitted, at their request, a list of the distinguished *hakims* of Delhi, the Chief Commissioner immediately tallied up that over a sixth of the forty-two names were of the family and another third of people trained in their school.[11] Figure 2 shows a family gathering at Sharif Manzil on the occasion of a wedding in 1904, and Figure 3 shows family and friends at leisure on *shikar*.

Reform in medicine, as in religious education, involved new institutions. In 1889, inspired by the new college at Aligarh, Ajmal Khan's elder brother, Hakim Abdul Majid, opened a new school in an attempt to make the family-base of instruction more formal and coherent.[12] The teachers were the family and the school remained in Ballimaran. Even then there was opposition directed primarily toward the family's insistence that *yunani* medicine must be open to Western techniques, notably in surgery and anatomy. Characteristic of Islam, where a legal idiom permeates all realms, this was judged a reprehensible innovation, *bida'*, and the *sharifi* family was denounced as *kafir* and *murtid*. The family launched yet another tool of more extensive influence, the newspaper

FIGURE 2: The wedding of the son of Hakim Abdul Majid, 1904. Ajmal Khan is third from left in the middle row.

FIGURE 3: Hakim Ajmal Khan, lounging third from left with his son Jamil. The children wear old style courtly dress, but most of the adults have adopted the Western influenced coat or jacket and the Turkish fez popularized at Aligarh.

*Akmal ul-akhbar* managed by a Hindu disciple of the poet Ghalib. It was meant to defend reform in medicine and to survey political and cultural issues generally. In 1902 Ajmal Khan began a second publication, the *Mujalla-yi tibbiya*, a monthly with news of the school and essays on *tibb*.[13]

From the beginning there was concern over financial support for the school. The brothers moved to found a pharmacy, a *dawakhana*, that would provide both *yunani* and *ayurvedic* medications. At first a joint stock company, it was later made a pious endowment vested in the madrasa. It was significant in two ways. First, it meant the end of family secrets since all the family remedies were given over to the *dawakhana*. Second, it anticipated a standardization of medicines instead of the highly particularized compounding of remedies for each patient on the basis of his constitution and environment. The *hakims* of course continued to prescribe for each patient, but the existence of a separate manufactory was a first step toward the patent medicine available now. Known as the Hindustani Dawakhana, its elegant building in Ballimaran was opened by Raja Kishan Kumar in 1910.[14] It had branches all over India.[15]

In 1901 Ajmal Khan's eldest brother died; the middle brother died three years later. At that point, Ajmal Khan took the central role in the school and its related activities. In that same year he made an appeal for funds for the school at the Delhi town hall, with the deputy commissioner present, citing proudly the number of graduates (some sixty-five) and pointing out the service to the *watn*, the homeland, such education provided. In 1906, he founded a Tibbi Conference to tie physicians together and to disseminate his arguments on the need to reform medicine: to know the classic books; to be open to new problems and solutions; to develop the indigenous pharmacopia; and to join with *vaids* (doctors of *ayurvedic* medicine) in common concerns.

Ajmal Khan and his fellow reformers directed their efforts toward other Indians in order to deny other practitioners legitimacy, and toward the British in order to gain recognition from them. They strongly opposed the practitioners of unsystematic folk medicine, often midwives and other women. The ninth book of the reformist *Bihishti Zewar*, an encyclopaedic work directed toward women, sets out the principles of scientific medicine precisely for this reason. Because of this concern, it is not as surprising as it might seem that in 1908 a department for women was opened at the school. It was never well attended, but it set the precedent that still continues of educating women in high culture medicine. A second internal target was little-educated *hakims* and *vaids* who claimed learning and recognition. The Tibbi Conference and later organizations fought to claim a monopoly of legitimacy for those educated in their institutions. They were not only concerned about out-and-out quacks, but about those who attended second-rate institutions. They periodically called on the government for help in what proved an intractable problem. In 1925, for example, there was a protest against the indiscriminate hiring of indigenous practitioners by the Delhi municipality and a complaint of lack of differentiation 'between the Hakims and Vaids who have not qualified themselves in any recognized and regular institutions and those who have done so, and among the latter between the diploma holders of those institutions whose course of study extends over *four* years [and those of two].'[16] Ajmal Khan had little patience with those who did not educate themselves well: 'The class referred to [as incompetent] have only themselves to blame if they have failed to raise the standard of their attainments.'[17]

The reformers never made out that their target practices originated in the Hindu tradition. This distinguishes them from Muslim reformers in most other areas. In part this was because the challenge to the *yunani* system was perceived not as *ayurvedic* but Western medicine. To answer that, not only were techniques to be borrowed from Western doctors, but equivalence was to be created, both theoretical equivalence by emphasizing *yunani* theory, and institutional equivalence through professionalization. For that to be possible, at least minimal recognition was necessary from the government.

For over a decade, beginning in 1908, Western medicine challenged a specific issue, the attempt by British and Indian allopathic physicians (as they were called) to secure registration acts in each province, so that no doctor of indigenous medicine could be legally recognized to give testimony in legal disputes, to certify illness for workers, or to perform any other legally required function.[18] Ajmal Khan saw this attempt at establishing a monopoly in legitimacy as the death-knell to his profession. He lobbied extensively against the acts, and in 1910 he created the All-India Ayurvedic and Unani Tibbia Conference, an outgrowth of the earlier Tibbi Conference, to enlarge the organization of *hakims* beyond family units and to offer a united voice to the government. That voice, joined later by the Trustees of the College, insisted on the legitimacy of indigenous systems and set standards for indigenous practitioners to make them worthy, as they understood it, of recognition.

As Ajmal Khan's institutional base grew stronger and encompassed a wider geographical area, opposition to him increased, particularly from the *hakims* of Lucknow. Although they objected to cooperation with *vaids* as potentially damaging to their system, this was not matched by any effort to expunge the elements that had evolved in *tibb* in the Indian environment. The real issue appears to have been geographic rivalry. The Lucknow physicians felt that these new institutions threatened their prestige to the benefit of the Delhi doctors—a rivalry, as one writer noted, well known to poets of the two cities, but hardly to physicians![19] In 1911 the annual meeting of the new conference was held in Lucknow itself and Ajmal Khan drew on medical metaphors to make his points: As in the body each part is dependent on the other, so now all must work together—the League, the Congress, the *vaid* and the *tabib*. Ajmal Khan insisted that the conference was not an organization limited to Delhi, but a nationwide one; and it continued to meet outside Delhi in places that included Amritsar, Lucknow again, Patna, Rampur, and Karachi.

Ajmal Khan continued to be concerned with the *madrasa* in Delhi whose status he wanted to raise to that to a national college teaching both *yunani* and *ayurvedic* medicine. A trip to Europe in 1911 convinced him of the importance of institutions like the ones he saw there. The decision to move the capital to Delhi, a move he interpreted as a favour to a backward area, was the occasion to request land, which he successfully did, in Karol Bagh to the north-west of the new buildings. The funding came largely from princes, with a sprinkling of merchants and others of the well-to-do joining in. The buildings themselves recall Aligarh, and are much closer to the traditionalist Indo-Saracenic than to the classical style the British had come to prefer, and included a large square for an experimental garden in front of the main buildings, and playing fields behind.[20] The buildings were meant to recall past splendour, not present empire: 'If you see the buildings from afar', wrote an associate of Ajmal Khan, 'they seem like a broad expanse of the splendid buildings of the Mughals.'[21] Figure 4 shows a side wing of the central building.

offer a united voice to the government. That voice, joined later by the Trustees of the College, insisted on the legitimacy of indigenous systems and set standards for indigenous practitioners to reach

FIGURE 4: The Rampur lecture rooms, Ayurvedic and Unani Tibbia College, Delhi.

and buildings of the Mughals. Figure 3 shows 3 side wing of the central building.

The foundation stone of the Ayurvedic and Unani Tibbiya College was laid by Lord Hardinge, the Viceroy, in March 1916, and the college was formally opened by Gandhi in 1921. Gandhi on this occasion frankly acknowledged his scepticism about the school. He called the medical systems black magic and said he held all medicine a sign of failure to lead a well-ordered life. His motive in attending was political—to show his respect for this joint Hindu–Muslim venture and for the non-communal stance of Ajmal Khan.[22] Despite such scepticism and the pressing political activities of those years, Ajmal Khan continued to press for the foundation of more *tibbiya* colleges and departments in universities throughout the country.

It is striking how quickly the transition to formal education for medicine was made. A memorandum to the Delhi government in 1916 showed that almost all doctors were educated in schools, with only two distinguished *hakim*s still educating pupils privately. Outside Delhi there were now schools in Lucknow, Hyderabad, Lahore, Amritsar, and Bhopal.[23] In part, medicine had traditionally been considered accessible through books, without the personal presence of a teacher and guide who embodied the teachings, the more usual form of education.[24] In part the push to professionalize in this context of British rule and of a competing system of medicine was very great.

By the early 1920s, Ajmal Khan had created three lasting institutions: the central college in Delhi; the pharmacy or manufactory of indigenous medicines; and the Tibbi Conference, later the All-India Ayurvedic and Unani Tibbia Conference. Following the passage of the Montagu-Chelmsford reforms of 1919, medicine was made a provincial subject under the control of elected ministries. From that time on, the issue of official discrimination against indigenous practitioners was dropped and governments to varying degrees supported the indigenous systems, a practice that has continued to the present.

In the course of creating formally organized, all-India institutions, Ajmal Khan succeeded in winning the support successively of three significant groups of elite patrons. An important strategy for the *hakim*s from the nineteenth century on had been to cultivate the patronage of the princes whose courts flourished when that of the Mughal emperor did not. The pattern of seeking close ties with princes for both financial support and often residential base, continued as British rule became firmly established from the late nineteenth century. The particular structure of imperial rule in India preserved and enhanced the position of segments of the old elite who had both means, and, in their dependent situation, motive, to patronize those who enhanced their status and their sense of cultural worth—precisely in such areas as traditional art, music, and indigenous medicine. This accounts in part for the continuity of these traditions here in contrast to their eclipse in the Middle East.[25]

Mahmud Khan was particularly tied to the Raja of Jind; his brothers to the Maharaja of Patiala. These ties protected the family in the revolt of 1857 when their house in Ballimaran became a storehouse for the valuables of others who fled and Mahmud Khan intervened on behalf of those accused.[26] Ajmal Khan himself was the protégé of the Nawab of Rampur. As a young man he spent nine years at the Nawab's court and developed with him the kind of passionate bond of friendship that was so cherished by men who were part of this cultural world. When Ajmal Khan died, the Nawab said, 'I am a Shi'i in religion and do not accept the relationship of spiritual guide and disciple (piri-muridi), but I know that if I were anyone's disciple in this world, I would have been Ajmal Khan's. What things I found in him cannot be found in the greatest saint.'[27] After he gave up residence at the court, Ajmal Khan continued to receive a pension from the Nawab and hastened to him when any of the family needed care or when the Nawab wanted him to be there.

Particularly in the twentieth century, the hakims, again like the musicians, travelled to the courts of the princes, the former when summoned for illness, the latter for scheduled engagements. The biography of Ajmal Khan, written by a man who was briefly his 'private secretary' in fact chronicles his visits: Rampur, Kashmir, Patiala, Jaipur, Bahawalpur, Bundlekhand, Balrampur, Baroda, Kutch, and so on.[28] Even for princes, the rule held that they paid no fees if they themselves came to Delhi. If summoned to a court, however, Ajmal Khan charged an astonishing one thousand rupees a day. When a young man of the sharifi family was accused after World War I of travelling to the frontier for subversive activities, his defence was not only his integrity and the honour of a distinguished family, but the inordinate financial handicap of being confined to Delhi where, by long established custom, the hakims of his family charged no fees.[29] Princely patronage was not limited to largesse to the great *hakims*, but involved the employment of doctors on a regular basis, for example in Bhopal where each *tahsil* had a *yunani* dispensary.[30] For Ajmal Khan, the continued support of princes was essential to his success, as he moved into new political and educational endeavours far different from the activities one would earlier have expected from a traditionally-learned man with noble patrons.

Ajmal Khan's ever-widening activities in medicine and politics were inextricably intertwined. His motive in both was to secure the cultural heritage and the position of well-born Muslims. A generation younger than Sir Sayyid Ahmad Khan, he shared much of his view of the perilous state of Muslim fortunes, and of the need to redress those fortunes by assimilating to British modes of behaviour; by acquiring some of their technical skills; and by cultivating a special relationship with them. Ajmal Khan was not alone among *hakims* in continuing as an influential figure in Delhi, and, indeed, the *hakims* were unusual among Muslims in continuing their civic role after the eclipse of Muslim fortunes in the city after the Mutiny. From the beginning of the Delhi municipality in 1863 up to 1921, three *hakims* served substantial terms and played an active role in local politics.[31]

Ajmal Khan, like Sayyid Ahmad, moved successfully to establish himself as a credible and influential figure in the eyes of the British. C. F. Andrews, who came to Delhi as a missionary but soon became absorbed in Indian religion and nationalist politics, described 'an ever closer friendship' with him over some twenty years and saw him as a Christ-like figure, ministering to the sick and oblivious of his own narrow interests. Sir Theodore Morison, at Aligarh, helped facilitate his trip to visit hospitals and medical libraries in Europe in 1911 as did Lord Hardinge himself. His relations with these Englishmen were not merely expedient; he admired and valued them, as he did Lady Hardinge, for their commitment to India and to Indians.[32] Figure 5 shows Ajmal Khan as host to British guests and fellow Indians, both Muslim and non-Muslim.

Government records reveal both explicit comments about Ajmal Khan and implicit actions based on the respect he enjoyed. When opinions were sought on current issues, his were taken seriously and others' brushed aside. His behaviour was taken as a measure of others' opinion. Hailey, the Chief Commissioner,

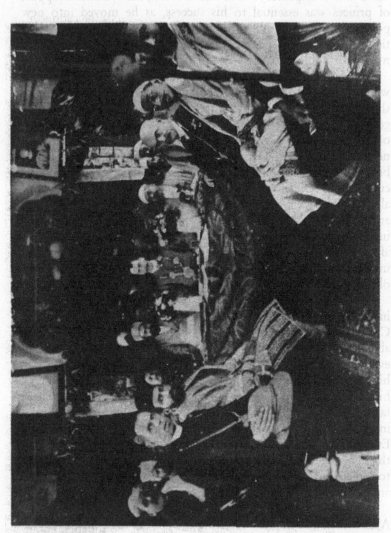

FIGURE 5: A civic function at Sharif Manzil. Ajmal Khan is third from left.

wrote to the viceroy in 1913, 'He is a man whose opinion [on Muslim feelings generally] is of great value as he comes across all classes of men and has a very sound judgement in all such matters.'[33] And when he was moved to action, officials were truly worried: 'A somewhat disquieting symptom is the fact that...Ajmal Khan departed from his previous policy of keeping aloof from such gatherings and was not only present but is reported to have approved of a virulent speech.... If the really influential men are to be goaded into a more active line, the situation will require still more careful watching.'[34]

The officials formed a second group, after the princes, from whom Ajmal Khan could expect protection and support. Their attitude toward his work in indigenous medicine and his insistence on governmental recognition of its importance was ambivalent (as was Gandhi's). But Ajmal Khan found arguments that implied that he shared their respect for Western systems and appreciated, as they did, the importance of politic action. He pointed out that the people of India could not for generations have adequately trained allopathic physicians and that the indigenous doctors were in fact learning from areas where Western medicine was superior. And he reminded the British that measures that denied legitimacy to indigenous practitioners would wound nationalist pride and create public disaffection. Support for Ajmal Khan rested in large part on official belief that he and his cause were politically important. In this regard it is particularly striking to see a long letter, prepared in 1916 by one of the *hakims* of Delhi, arguing the futility of trying to develop the research side of the indigenous systems. He made a quite modern assessment that the pressing need was for more practitioners of all systems trained in basic health care as well as for the kind of public health measures the government had already identified as chiefly responsible for controlling cholera, smallpox, and plague. The letter was filed with the comment that Ajmal Khan alone had been consulted.[35] Official action was based as much on politics as on medical science.

In 1927, the then Chief Commissioner of Delhi presided over an occasion at the Ayurvedic and Unani Tibbia College and recalled the association of earlier officials with late *hakim*'s endeavours:

Though this great institution is not in any sense a Government institution it has often looked to Government for help and friendly countenance. The land on which these buildings stand was provided by Government and interesting stages in the career of the institution have been marked by the presence of Government officers. The Deputy Commissioner opened this school in 1889. Twenty years later the Lieutenant-Governor opened the Zenana Madrasa. In 1916 you had the signal honour of having the foundation stone of the college laid by His Excellency Lord Hardinge and now that you are making another big stride forward, you have done your Chief Commissioner the honour of asking him to declare your Research Institute open.[36]

He did not note that when the college was opened it was not the viceroy—as had been predicted even five months earlier[37]—but Gandhi who presided. But then the nationalist histories do not recall that even on that occasion life-sized portraits of Lord and Lady Hardinge were unveiled.[38]

By the post-war period Ajmal Khan had added, as we have seen, a third group of powerful partons to aid his endeavours, namely that of the nationalist 'leaders'—the English word was always used. And he continued to have the impressive ability to attract new elements of support without completely losing the old. He himself was a member of the Simla delegation in 1906, active in Muslim League politics until 1918, and a strong supporter of Aligarh. He strongly believed in what he considered to be the non-sectarian stance of Nadwa, an institution that hoped to create a united front for Muslim religious leaders throughout India, and was active in that organization from 1910 until shortly before his death. He played an active role in Kanpur at the time of the mosque incident of 1913, a landmark in creating a non-local Muslim leadership, and shared the concern for Muslim interests in the Ottoman empire that stimulated Muslim political emotions and solidarity. It was his role in launching a medical delegation to the Balkans in 1913 that made him, as one biographer wrote, not only a *tabib-i haziq* and a *rais* of Delhi, but a great 'leader' of the Muslims.[39] In World War I, he became alienated from the British because of their repressive policies and because of such personal experiences as the imprison-ment of his nephew noted above. He became active in Congress and insisted that Muslim interests were best served in that organization. He supported non-cooperation and returned the title that had been awarded to him by the British in 1907. In 1918 he was chairman of the Congress Reception Committee and in 1921 he was elected president of Congress. He was active in the creation of the nationalist Muslim school and university, Jamia Millia.

In all these activities, Ajmal Khan was able to further his concern with the development of medicine by his political involvements. He persuaded other political figures of the importance of his projects. In 1917, for example, Madan Mohan Malaviya presided over the annual meeting of the Tibbi Conference and Sir Sankaran Nair at the annual convocation of the new college. Protection of indigenous medicine became part of the Congress platform. In 1920, in the annual report of the Tibbia College, Ajmal Khan insisted on the identity of indigenous medicine and self-government, 'If we want to take the administration of government into our own hands, we must right all national things, including the indigenous method of healing. Our real progress depends on these things. We fail in serving our country if we are dependent on outside things.'[40]

Ajmal Khan's life thus saw the development of new institutions, ever more formally organized and ever larger in scope, that became the basis of the *yunani* system; and he embedded these institutions in networks not only of like-minded physicians but of influential groups of patrons as well. Throughout he was aided by a political environment in which Muslims sought to revive their cultural heritage; in which the idiom of British rule and the interests of some officials contributed to a fostering of much in the traditional culture; and in which nationalists focused on some aspects of the shared culture as a source of indigenous pride.

Indian art and music were particularly important in this last regard, but medicine, through the linking of *yunani* and *ayurvedic*, was too. *Yunani* medicine itself, moreover, had always been part of cosmopolitan Muslim culture, drawing on varied traditions and open to Muslims and non-Muslims both.[41] As medicine underwent revival in the modern period, it was increasingly secularized, at least in the colleges and conferences, and emphasis given to the scientific principles that underlay it. The religious superstructure that sanctioned medicine and the use of amulets and prayers to accompany it had no formal place. This made it the easier to argue for British support and then nationalist support successively. Theory aside, medicine was available to all. 'My first visit to the waiting room', wrote C. F. Andrews, 'brought home a shock to the opinion I carried from England that Hindus and Muslims could not mix. [Ajmal Khan] treated all alike, Hindu and Muslim, rich and poor.'[42]

While medicine was not an expression of religion in the narrow sense, it was an expression of Muslim culture and a source of

Muslim pride. The verses cited at the opening of this chapter reflect what might be called the Aligarh view of the situation of Muslims, with its emphasis on the decline of the community from the glory of the historic past. Ajmal Khan himself, in the introduction to the catalogue he prepared for the Nawab of Rampur's library in 1901, identified himself with what might be called this 'Orientalist' view.[43]

The remains of world civilization and progress are found in many forms. Sometimes an old city appears by chance… similarly the writings of each *qaum* point the way to the thought of that *qaum* for future generations. Although the sun of Eastern arts and sciences kept rising in its own time and many *qaum*s drew benefits from its light, now that sun has declined and the age, as is its habit, has given birth to a new sun that fulfils the needs of the people of the age…. The results of this reversal, which previous nations have already endured, will happen to us: we will see our former greatness and glory in the hand of oblivion if we do not take thought to preserve it.[44]

His life's work was to stem reversal in the area of medicine.

Ajmal Khan's non-communal strategies for his work were shaped in part by the fact that medicine, while a symbol of Muslim pride, was outside the core religious subjects and was open to all. But they were also shaped by his rootedness in Delhi's cosmopolitan culture and his personal experience of being part of a composite élite. One of Ajmal Khan's most effective experiences came in the terrible riots of 1919 when he and Swami Shraddhanand, singlehandedly quieted the city and were at the centre of an informal shadow government. He was 'a king without a crown'. 'It was then', wrote Andrews, 'that I saw the Hakim Sahib in all the true greatness of his character. Night and day he laboured for peace.'[45] Ajmal Khan's role as a privileged Muslim in pre-Lutyens Delhi gave him an aristocratic vision: in some ways he and people like him were the city. This is implicit in Hali's verses above that identify the fortunes of the *qaum* with the fortunes of the city, which he apostrophizes to give the lament its power—Delhi's glory and the glory of the *qaum* are the same. Ajmal Khan's work made the explicit assumption that it was in everyone's interests that Muslim culture be preserved and that the obvious strategy for this was collaboration in common interests, medicine and politics both.

In this, Ajmal Khan moved far beyond Delhi. His base as a physician moved beyond his family to a national college and to an association that included both *ayurvedic* and *yunani* doctors from across India. Dependent on princely largesse, he did not, like his father, stay in Delhi, but was resident at the Rampur court and travelled constantly from state to state. As his ties with the British increased he was ready every summer to go to Simla, and he travelled twice to Europe, in 1911 and 1925—trips that contrasted with his first travel abroad to Shi'i holy places in 1905. As a political leader, he followed the schedule of annual meetings of Muslim League and Congress. Ajmal Khan even changed in style of dress—from the princely embroidered cap and tight coat of his elders, to the sherwani and Turkish fez of Aligarh, to homespun under Gandhi's influence, to a Western suit on his last trip to Europe.[46] In all his widening circles he remained a man of enormous self-discipline, self-sacrifice, and singleness of purpose. He was in no sense the marginal figure this versatility might suggest. His standing in Delhi as a *rais*, distinguished by his aristocratic origin, his cultural breadth, and his medical skills, provided him the base for becoming an influential leader committed to securing Muslim interests in the context of Hindu–Muslim cooperation.

## Notes

1. Quoted in Abdul-Ghaffar, Muhammad. 1950. *Hayat-i Ajmal*, p. 20. Aligarh.

2. Published by Zakir Husain and available in the Jamia Millia library. See Ahmed, Ali. 1973. *Twilight in Delhi*, pp. 117–18. New Delhi, for a description of a *mahfil* in which poetry was discussed and which included the historical figure Nawab Sirajud-din Khan Sail, the son-in-law of the poet Dagh. Sail and his brother Taban were among Ajmal Khan's closest friends. Muhammad Abdul-Ghaffar, *Hayat-i Ajmal*, pp. 498–506, recounts poetic assemblies much like the fictional.

3. His son's biography begins with a list of his father's closest friends. Khan, Hakim Jamil. n.d. *Sirat-i Ajmal*, pages *dal* to *toe*. Delhi.

4. Ajmal Khan in his newspaper, for example, denounced the rivalry of the *muqallid* and *ghair-muqallid*. Abdul-Ghaffar, Muhammad. *Hayat-i Ajmal*, p. 38; and denuciation of divisiveness was a major theme in his addresses to religious leaders.

5. His writings are listed in Hamadani, Muhammad Kamal Husain. 1976. *Matab-i Masih*, beginning at p. 11, Aligarh. They include Quranic commentary, translations of hadith and works on Sufism as well as writings on medicine.

6. Neuman, Daniel M. 1980. *The Life of Music in North India: The Organization of an Artistic Tradition*, especially pp. 104–5, 146, 168. New Delhi.

7. Abdul-Ghaffar, Muhammad. *Hayat-i Ajmal*, p. 27.

8. There was a belief that the *sharifi* family had a special verbal formula (*amal-i taskhir*) and that Ajmal Khan in addition had a special medicine chest whose contents never failed him. 'Hakim Ajmal Khan: A Champion of Indian Medicine', Studies in History of Medicine. 4: 3, September 1980, p. 159. New Delhi. Also, Amrohawi, Hakim Ahmad Riza Khan. 1938. *Hayat-i Ajmal*, p. 30. Delhi.

9. 'No student trained primarily in a music school has ever become recognized.' Neuman, *The Life of Music in North India*, p. 199. Music cultivated the relationship between teacher and disciple as an essential part of training, as medicine did not. By the second decade of this century, virtually all Delhi *hakims* were trained in schools.

10. For descriptions of other families, see Sabiri, Imdad 1972. *Dihli ki yadgar hastiyan*, pp. 189–92, 292–6, 348–52. Delhi.

11. In B file 68 of Home, 1916, in Delhi Archives Research Room ([formerly at] Interstate Bus Terminal, Kashmiri Gate). Hereafter, DARR.

12. The director was Bihari Lal Mushtaq. Abdul-Ghaffar, Muhammad. *Hayat-i Ajmal*, pp. 34–40, including quotations from Ajmal Khan's writings for the paper.

13. Qarshi, Muhammad Hasan, ed. November–December 1928. *Mashirul-attiba: Masihul-Mulk Nambar*, p. 22.

14. Khan, Jamil, *Sirat-i Ajmal*, p. 44.

15. Hamadani, Muhammad Kamalud-Din Husain. 1976. *Matab-i Masih*, p. 14. Aligarh.

16. K. B. Pirzada Mohamad Husain, M.A. to E. R. Abbott, Chief Commissioner. Delhi, 14 February 1925 (in B file 5 of Education, 1925, DARR). The two-year colleges intended were the Islamia College and DAV College, Lahore. The letter continues by listing the texts, with page numbers, that were used for Western subjects in the college.

17. Hakim Ajmal Khan to Personal Assistant, Chief Commissioner of Delhi, 25 July 1911 in ibid.

18. Between 1912 and 1916 acts were passed in Madras, Bombay, Bengal, UP, Punjab, Burma, Bihar, and Orissa. (Officiating Deputy Secretary, Government of India, to Chief Commissioner Delhi, 25 November 1919 in B File 70 of Home, 1920 DARR.)

19. Abdul-Ghaffar, Muhammad. *Hayat-i Ajmal*, p. 92.

20. Issues related to the building are in the files of the DARR. See Off. B file 115 of 1915; B File 94 of Education, 1916; B File 44 of Education, 1920; and B File 3(60) of Education, 1920. The Secretary, Imperial Delhi Commission, wrote to the Secretary of Government, GOI, on 14 February 1916 concerning the building plans: 'These would not have been approved of by the Imperial Delhi Commission had the buildings been situated in or near to the New City.' The issue may have been the Indo-Saracenic style was now deprecated in favour of the classical.

21. Qarshi, Muhammad Hasan, ed., *Mashirul-attiba*, p. 58.

22. His speech, the fortnightly report drily noted 'contained several remarks depreciatory of the indigenous as well as any other system of medicine, and must have been galling to Ajmal Khan and the other organizers of the event.' (Fortnightly reports on the internal political situation in the Delhi Province, Confidential Home, B File of 1921. DARR.)

23. In B File 68 of Home, 1916, DARR.

24. The method of self-instruction was even argued to be superior by Ibn Ridwan. Gary Leiser, 'Islamicate Medical Education from Muhammad to the Ottomans', a paper presented at the colloquium 'Biology, Society, and History in Islam', September 1977, University of Pennsylvania.

25. See, for example, Nancy Gallagher and Peter Gran, 'Medical Conflicts in the Early Modern Middle East', a paper presented at the colloquium 'Biology, Society, and History in Islam'.

26. 'Some of [the favoured servants of the Maharaja of Patiala] were distinguished noblemen of Delhi, holding high rank at his court, and among them were Hakim Mahmud Khan, Hakim Murtaza Khan, and Hakim Ghulamullah Khan, all sons of that Hakim Sharif Khan who dwells in Paradise: and they lived in our lane. Their houses stretch in a long line, threshold to threshold, roof to roof, on both sides of the lane, and the writer of these words had been for years the neighbour of one of these beneficent men. The first of the three, with his wife and children, lived in the capital, in accordance with the tradition of the family, while the other two lived in Patiala, privileged to be companions to the Maharaja. Foreseeing the retaking of the city, the Maharaja in his gracious kindness to his servants, had secured from the mighty warrior-lords...a promise that when the flowing tide of time should bring them victory, protectors should take their stand at the gate of this lane.' Russell, Ralph and Khurshidul Islam. 1969. *Ghalib, 1797–1869*, vol. I, *Life and Letters*, p. 142, London. In fact, Sharif Khan was their grandfather. For discussion of an illness attended by Hakim Mahmud Khan, see pp. 268–70.

27. Abdul-Ghaffar, Muhammad. *Hayat-i Ajmal*, pp. 51–2.

28. Gopamaui, Muhammad AbrarHusain Faruqi Naqshbandi. 1972. *Masirul-Masih*, Hardoi, UP. See also the work of Ajmal Khan's *peshkar*, Hakim Rashid Khan, Ahmad 1938. *Hayat-i Ajmal*, covering 1910–18. Delhi.

29. Home Confidential File 48 of 1916 in DARR.

30. Chief Commissioner, Delhi, to Secretary to Government of India, Home 1.13.16 (in B File 68 of Home, 1916, DARR).

31. See Sabiri, Imdad, *Dihli ki yadgar hastiyan*, pp. 252–3 for an account of Hakim Zahirud-din Khan who was a member of the Delhi municipality for twenty nine years. Three *hakims* served substantial terms up to 1921: see Parshad, Rai Sahib Madho 1921. *History of the Delhi Municipality, 1863–1921*. Allahabad. For the context of this civic activity, see Gupta, Narayani. 1981. *Delhi between Two Empires, 1803–1931*, Delhi.

32. Andrews C. F. 1926. 'Hakim Ajmal Khan'. In *Eminent Musalmans*, pp. 287, 294, 295. Madras. The College Sub-Committee of the Tibbi Conference proposed to name the 'female college' after Lady Hardinge 'in commemoration of the sad and untimely death of that good Lady, which all of us lament…as an irreparable loss to the women of India.' This was not permitted since there was already a Lady Hardinge Medical College, but the Chief Commissioner suggested the female portion be named the 'Lady Hardinge Wing'. (B File 75 of Education, 1914, DARR.)

33. W. M. Hailey to Private Secretary of H. E. the Viceroy, 12 June 1913 (in B File 168 of Education, 1913, DARR).

34. Fortnightly reports on the internal political situation in the Delhi Province, 16 April 1920, Home Confidential B File 3 of 1920 DARR.

35. Hakim Raziuddin Ahmad Khan, Khan Bahadur, Shifa ul Mulk, to Chief Commissioner, Delhi, 1 July 1916, and hand-written note, 6 July 1916 (in B File 68 of 1916, Home, DARR).

36. B File 5(25) of 1930, Education. In fact, the *zanana madrasa* was opened by his wife, Lady Dean.

37. When discussing a grant of five lakhs of rupees to the College (Government of India Legislative Department. Proceedings of the Indian Legislative Council, Delhi, 10 March 1920 in B File 179 of 1919, Home, DARR).

38. Noted in 'Fortnightly reports on the internal political situation in the Delhi Province', 17 January 1921 (in Confidential Home B File 3 of 1921, DARR).

39. Abdul-Ghaffar, Muhammad. *Hayat-i Ajmal*, p. 123.

40. Khan, Jamil. *Sirat-i Ajmal*, pp. '132–3' (pagination defective; the quotation marks refer to the second time these numbers appear).

41. It is interesting that when Ajmal Khan prepared lists of distinguished physicians in Delhi for government in 1916, all the *yunani* physicians were Muslim and all the *ayurvedic* physicians Hindu although two of the latter were identified as *hakim* not *vaid*: the implication is that the doctors were categorized by religion, not their actual learning. In the early 1980s, at the two leading *yunani* colleges in Delhi, substantial percentages of students and faculty were non-Muslim.

42. Andrew, 'Hakim Ajmal Khan', pp. 290–1.

43. The 'Orientalist view', which Third World intellectuals often assimilated, meant acceptance of an 'East' and 'West' dichotomy as well as of the view of Eastern decline evident here. See Said, Edward. 1979. *Orientalism*. New York. It became standard to speak of *yunani* as 'Eastern medicine'. Thus the college talked of itself as 'one of the unique Institutions wherein East and West are mingled'. (Jt Secretary, Board of Trustees of Tibbia College to Chief Commissioner, Delhi, 20 May 1937 in B File 5 [90] of 1937, Education, in DARR).

44. Khan, Jamil. *Sirat-i Ajmal*, p. 10.

45. Andrews, C. F. 'Hakim Ajmal Khan', p. 298.

46. Amrohawi, Rashid Ahmad Khan, *Hayat-i Ajmal*, p. 32.

# 7

## Nationalism, Modernity, and Muslim Identity in India before 1947

> If there is one other sin with which I charge Great Britain, in addition to the charge of emasculating India, it is the making of wrong histories about India and teaching them to us in our schools.
>
> *Mohammad Ali,* addressing the Plenary Session of the
> First Round Table Conference in London, 19 November 1930

The study of nationalism as a phenomenon has changed profoundly in recent years, in part because of a focus on world history that not only encompasses multiple areas but also looks afresh at the processes and interrelations among those areas. In the case of nationalism, the conventional assumption has been that metropolitan developments flowed from a centre to a periphery: thus, that nationalism arose in Europe and was transplanted elsewhere. Instead, recent work by Benedict Anderson and others has placed metropolitan and colonized areas into a single historical space where many processes, in fact, have turned out to be simultaneous and the product of complex interactions.[1] The most fundamental institutions of society and economy, even the very concept of the nation, along with gender, class, and caste, prove to have been constituted as part of these interactions. One dimension of this is that terms that have been used as scientific categories, not least *modernity* and *secularism* on one side, and *tradition* and *religion* on the other, are increasingly studied as political categories dependent on each other.

I want to illustrate this by some comments on Muslims in northern India in the 1920s and 1930s, focusing on a pietist movement called Tablighi Jama'at that has typically been taken—and indeed takes itself—as 'traditional' and 'apolitical'. This is an oblique perspective from which to raise issues related to nationalism in contrast to a focus on the Indian National Congress or the Muslim League, which were centrally involved in the nationalist movement.

But Tablighi Jama'at, in fact, participates in characteristics shared by both these movements as well as by other movements typically glossed as 'modern' or 'social reform'. Calling Tablighi Jama'at traditional, however, served its participants to confirm their authenticity, much as nationalism, however modern, must always seem timeless.[2] And calling Tablighi Jama'at traditional or fundamentalist or reactionary—allows opponents to constitute themselves as modern and, indeed, nationalist—adherents of a nationalism that sees itself justified in implicitly excluding certain categories of people from true citizenship, among them those relegated to the category of traditional or obscurantist. We need therefore to question the meaning of binaries like traditional and modern, yet, simultaneously we need to recognize the necessity of the dichotomy for creating the very categories they purport to describe.

Mohammad Ali's comment at the beginning of this essay is an invitation to rethink the place of movements like Tablighi Jama'at in our telling of twentieth century Indian history. The sections that follow attempt, first, to open up the description of the activities of a movement like Tablighi Jama'at in order to appreciate its complexity; second, to recognize Tablighi Jama'at's own implicit contestation with the narratives into which it is placed; and then, in the final section, to tease out dimensions of the intimate and interdependent relationship between movements and approaches that are not the dichotomies they purport to be.

## Tablighi Jama'at: Social Reform, Political Silence

The Tablighi Jama'at movement enters most historical narratives as part of a mutually aggressive communal reaction to the failure of the Khilafat and Non-cooperation movements of the early 1920s. Alliterative pairs are often counterposed: Tabligh and Tanzeem of the Muslims, Shuddhi and Sangathan of the Hindus.

The area of Mewat associated with the early period of the Tablighi Jama'at movement was, in the 1920s and 1930s, in fact rife with competing proselytizing movements both Hindu, including the Arya Samaj,[3] and other Muslim movements (among them others named 'Tabligh').[4] This was where the mass contact movement of the Congress, with the enrolling of '4 anna' members from 1920 on, took place. These movements were clearly not all the same. Thus, in the case of the Tablighi Jama'at, rather than see it as simply competitive with external groups, one can equally see it as a vehicle for social mobility and community, geared not at all to external confrontation but to internal issues very much like those of concern to the reform movements glossed as modern.

Here is an excerpt from an Urdu history of the movement, describing one of its founding moments:

Thanks to the deep relations Maulana Muhammad Ilyas (d. 1944) had with the people of Mewat, in August 1934 a *panchayat* was held under his chairmanship in the qasba of Nuh. In it were gathered *chaudhuri, miyan ji, zaildar, in'amdar, nambardar, subahdar, munshi, safeed poosh*, and other forward-looking (*sarbarawarda*) people of the region of Mewat [those listed are government functionaries, hereditary headmen, individuals with claims to some book learning and piety]. Their number was approximately one hundred and seven. First of all at this meeting, the importance of Islam was discussed and then a compact (*ahd*) was made of total adherence to the pillars of Islam, of collective work for spreading religion, and of creating *panchayat* for furthering this work. The pact entered into was for the matters noted below:

1. Correct recollection of the *kalima* [the attestation of faith].

2. Adherence to the canonical prayer.

3. Attainment and spread of education.

4. Islamic appearance and demeanour (*shakl o surat*).

5. Adoption of Islamic customs and elimination of unfaithful customs (*rusum-i shirkiyya*).

6. Adherence to modesty (*parda*) among women.

7. Performance of marriages in an Islamic style.

8. The custom of Islamic dress among women.

9. No abandonment of any Islamic belief and no acceptance of any non-canonical conduct (*ghair mazhab*).

10. Protection and safeguarding of mutual rights (*bahami huquq*).

11. Inclusion of responsible dignitaries in every meeting and gathering.

12. No provision to children of worldly education without religious education.

13. Effort and work for *tabligh* (preaching, proselytizing) of religion.

14. Consideration of purity.

15. Protection of each other's dignity and honour.

It was also decided in this *panchayat* that *tabligh* was not only the work of the religious scholars but a duty of all Muslims and, so that we all should undertake it, all that was decided was written down. The *panchayat nama* was compiled and the participants all affixed their signature... the message of faith was to be spread to all classes of the *millat*... temporarily leaving one's homeland was deemed necessary for this.... [Among the injunctions was to] act towards ordinary Muslims with extreme consideration and kindness; speak to them gently and adopt a kindly manner. Look at no Muslim with contempt or hatred and especially do not stint in respect and honour for the scholars of religion.... On one occasion Maulana Ilyas proclaimed, 'The real purpose of this movement is that the *ummat* be shaped by the full intellectual and practical system (*nizam*) of Islam'. [5]

In describing the modus operandi of the Tablighis, the author further explains that 'Maulana Ilyas had prepared maps of all the *tahsil* subdivisions of Mewat as well as of the whole district of Gurgaon, set directions and routes, wrote out guidance for the preachers, as well as population of the villages, and the distance and the names of the *nambardar*s; he thus established a proper system for *tabligh*'.[6]

The vignette of this meeting recalls nothing more than the caste-uplift movements that proliferated across India in these decades. Groups of barbers or petty traders, led by their *panchayat*, the traditional 'five' who adjudicated disputes and led activities, would meet and pledge a range of behaviours that would bring them into conformity with the respectable in a process sometimes called 'sanskritization' or 'ashrafization'. The targeted behaviours invariably included greater control over women, since the presence of women in public space was regarded as typical of the lower orders, and restrictions on their dress. Also, as here, there was typically a move to rationalization of expenses on such events as marriage that came to be seen as 'extravagance' once social relations were constituted on new grounds. These are movements that discourage custom in favour of more universally held norms; and they respond to broader social networks defined by behaviour and achievement, not only by birth.

Not only were compacts signed but they were often reproduced on lithograph presses, a brittle, yellowed copy still occasionally to be found. Injunctions, as evident here, ranged from fidelity to the holiest practices of the faith to everyday domestic practices. Thus women, who were encouraged from the beginning to go out in groups for *tabligh*, were, for example, to stay in houses with indoor toilets, a custom then unknown in Mewat but now common, as one history writes, 'through the blessing of *tabligh*',[7] thus replacing the rural custom of night-time trips to the fields with the interior toilets of the urban and respectable.

Tablighi Jama'at is notable for its generalization of leadership to lay participants,[8] a transition shared by many South Asian movements in the twentieth century. This characteristic is evident even in this early list above, not only in the guidelines for inclusiveness in relation to all potential participants but in the respect accorded to the most humble. The authority attributed to single elders now is diffused into the charismatic body of the group acting in concert. This movement provides a particularly far-reaching example of the larger move in religious organization from a 'vertical' to a 'horizontal' structure with the new emphasis on lay leadership.

Thus what is presented in the larger Tablighi Jama'at literature as a timeless reappropriation of pristine behaviour clearly has the push to shared, respectable norms of behaviour in an increasingly integrated and mobile society as one of its building blocks. The notion of *panchayat* with its lineage and village connotations soon gave way to the term *jama'at* or association, which, like the *anjuman* that proliferated in this era, meant a voluntary association, albeit in this case notably loose in its organization.

Like the other revival and self-help movements of the day, Tabligh Jama'at drew on new modalities of communication, not least print;[9] note here the reference to maps, statistics, and local officials, all of course intrinsic to colonial culture. Tablighi Jama'at leadership has often been drawn from the bureaucracy and the army, the latter in particular credited in recent years with the careful organization of the hundreds of thousands, even millions, who attend annual meetings.

Two further characteristics of this movement resonate deeply with fundamental shifts evident in other settings in this period, both deeply affecting individual behaviour and consciousness. One is the central focus on time, on managing time, measuring time—not wasting time—setting aside time for what is valued. A second is the interiorization and individualization of religious practice, for although participation in the group is central, participants also abjure the local customs of shrines and life-cycle ceremonies, minimize the role of the hierarchy as mediators, and have no expectations that social and political institutions will foster a moral life. That is left to the individual in such a way that—like speaking prose unaware—the Tablighi, living his everyday life in society, can be constructed as truly 'secular'. In all these ways, a movement seen as 'traditional' is strikingly new: new in its reach, new in its lay organization, new in its intensity, new in its modes of communication and organization, new in its self-consciousness as it deliberately strikes a 'counterculture' relationship to economic and political life. Tablighi Jama'at takes hold in profoundly different local settings and means different things at different times, but the themes emphasized here have been pervasive throughout.

## Politics between Khilafat and Partition: Competing Historical Narratives

The absorptions of Tablighi Jama'at in fostering individual Islamic self-fashioning, and eschewing participation in public life, are more remarkable in the context of north India in this period. The 1920s ushered in an unprecedented period of religious violence, competition for leadership, and the decisive emergence of mass politics. This was specifically when competing historical genealogies of Muslim history gained currency, usually summarized as the 'nationalist' and the 'communalist' interpretation of Muslim identities, histories that increasingly legitimated divergent ideologies. Tablighi Jama'at leadership simply ignored these issues despite the fact of being led by the same kind of people who joined the association of 'ulama (Jamiyat Ulama-i Hind) allied with the Indian National Congress, and, in the 1930s, supported the state-oriented Islamist movement of Maulana Maududi (1903–79).

All the movements of this era, including, notably, the Gandhian movement, included a spectrum of activities from what can be called the 'guidance-oriented' at the one end, with its focus on individual moral improvement, to the state-focused, political end, concerned with shaping and controlling public life, on the other.[10]

Widespread assumptions about Islam suggest that Muslim movements invariably seek that kind of political control. In fact, there are long and pervasive orientations within Islam that have precisely focused on the individual end of the spectrum, not least those associated with Sufism. Although in the quotation above about the purpose of Tablighi Jama'at, Maulana Ilyas speaks of an Islamic *nizam*, a word that takes on new meaning in the twentieth century with the Islamist movements of Hasan al-Banna (1906–49) in Egypt and Maulana Maududi in India, Tablighi Jama'at ideology has not even posited a staged programme with a focus on individual regeneration as a prelude to a changed society. The reorganization of society was simply left to some unknown future.

There was, moreover, a significant stream of thought, even among those engaged in the negotiations and competition of public life, to propose a vision of identity without territory. As Peter Hardy's study of the ideology of the Khilafat movement, and the subsequent proposals of the Jamiyat Ulama-i Hind have shown, the 'ulama who were engaged with Congress favoured a kind of community federalism far more concerned with legal guidance and education than with state institutions. Joined to the Congress leadership by a common desire to remove the British from power, they envisaged an independent India comprised of religious communities whose own leaders would provide a framework for justice, education, and welfare—a kind of 'jurisprudential apartheid'. In basic ways this was reminiscent of earlier polities, like the Ottoman *millat* system, whose leaders served as intermediaries in regimes defined by relationships of loyalty and protection, not universal citizenship and land.[11] Thus the apoliticism of the Tablighi Jama'at—far from being peculiar to itself—is in fact not all that unlike the high politics of Muslim activists on the national stage.

When we turn to one critical dimension of defining community, that of constructing a historical genealogy, we also find a way of reconfiguring what are often taken as opposites. The usual binary has been drawn between those who, like Muhammad Ali Jinnah (1876–1948), pursued separate Muslim political interest and those who cooperated with the Congress, 'from Azad to Rafi Ahmad Kidwai', about whom, Mushirul Hasan, for example, has written 'there was no trace of "Muslimness" in their public life, except during the Khilafat movement'.[12] On the contrary, I would argue, virtually all participants in public life worked from the assumption that 'India' was a natural entity, inhabited by communities defined above all by religion. This perspective puts Jinnah and Congress on one side, the Tablighi Jama'at which opts out of a territorially based, national response, on the other.

The shared discourse is evident throughout the writings and speeches of the two great exemplars of what are, I suggest, wrongly taken as antithetical perspectives. Thus in a speech choosen almost at random given in 1941, Jinnah recounted the narrative of Muslims as a nation, once great and now fallen:

[A] nation must have a territory.... Nation does not live in the air. It lives on the land, it must govern land, and must have territorial state.... It is the biggest job... since the fall of the Moghal Empire.... We come under the category of the fall. We have seen the worst days.... Our demand is not from Hindus because the Hindus never took the whole of India. It was the Muslims who took India and ruled for 700 years. It was the British who took India from the Musalmans.... Our demand is made to the British, who are in possession. It is an utter nonsense to say that Hindustan belongs to the Hindus.[13]

Maulana Abu'l Kalam Azad (1888–1958), in his celebrated address as Congress president at Ramgarh in 1940, assumed the same narrative line of India, invaders, and Hindus and Muslims, albeit to a different conclusion:

It was India's historic destiny that many human faces and cultures and religions should flow to her, finding a home in her hospitable soil.... One of the last of these caravans... was that of the followers of Islam.... This led to a meeting of the culture-currents of two different races.... We brought our treasures with us, and India too was full of the riches of her own precious heritage.... We gave her, what she needed most, the most precious of gifts from Islam's treasury, the message of democracy and human equality.[14]

This assumption of separate communities as the fundamental building blocks of Indian society is equally evident in the language of Gandhi and even of Nehru. It continues in Pakistan, not surprisingly. It continues unquestioned, despite a constitution based on universal individualism, in what might be called the official discourse of the government of India. Considerable recent scholarship has problematized this narrative, locating its origin in British histories and practice, and demonstrating the anachronism of reified religious communities in the pre-colonial period.[15]

The Tablighi Jama'at ideology is in this regard strikingly distinctive because it puts no gloss on the history of India at all, rather steeping its participants in historical examples drawn from the earliest days of Islam. The emphasis is less on history in the sense of tracing change over time than in historical exemplar, the lives of the Prophet and his companions as models in behaviour and morality for Muslims living today. This is mythic history in which there are overlays, replications, of the past. Thus Tablighis tell the story of their efforts for the 'internal conversion' (to use Geertz's term)[16] of Mewat as nothing less than that of the conversion of the Arab Bedouins from the ignorance of the pre-Islamic period toward the truth of Islam, for example, in writings of Maulana Maududi (who initially admired the Tablighi Jama'at) in his description of the Mewatis with their ignorance of prayer, idols, and tufts of hair.[17] Little matter that later Mewatis have countered with a history of Islamic learning and spirituality in their area[18] or that sociologists have offered a much later timetable for change.[19]

A variation of the shared linear history dwells on imagined places outside India. Faisal Devji, for example, has described the new *marsiya* of the nineteenth century, the mourning elegies of the Shi'a, which develop a presentation of unfolding dramatic scenes, depicting the moral drama of Karbala as a story of a people's political loss.[20] Later in the century, novelists like Sharar turned to historical novels, nostalgically re-creating past settings of Muslim worldly glory.[21] Similarly, the poet Muhammad Iqbal (1876–1938), returning home from one of the Round Table Conferences, stopped at the mosque of Cordoba and wrote one of his greatest poems, a meditation on the flow of time, interrupted, as it was there, by creative genius, now lost.[22] These writings 'straddle' the imagination of a linear narrative of India and the imagination of a recurrent mythological moment of Islam. Yet, I would suggest, they are fundamentally about the British and about the experience of loss, even though that transition is played out in a non-Indian setting.

It is tempting to write the historical imaginings set outside the subcontinent into a teleology that culminates in Pakistan. But they are not fundamentally about geopolitics; they are not irredentist statements. They are in the end about the colonial predicament. Gandhi could embrace the Khilafat cause not only out of expediency but because imagining Istanbul as a site of British perfidy was another way of imagining India.

These various histories, the secular, the communal, and the pan-Islamic, thus share fundamental characteristics as nationalist and territorial. Both before and after Partition, the single story, with its competing variants, has dominated public debate. Histories like that of the Tablighis have operated in a different sphere. The Tablighi Jama'at itself, a minor movement until the post-independence periods, in India in particular, has simply been assimilated to evidence of Muslim difference.

In retrospect, however, it is useful to show that there were and are alternatives to the pervasive framework of history and nation that is taken as natural, among them identity constituted without reference to territory, as in Tablighi Jama'at. Even here, however, the Tablighi Jama'at typological history takes as a given the shared question of all twentieth century Muslim leaders: what is the cause of Muslim degeneracy and its cure?[23] The answer from the Tablighi Jama'at was not that of the Muslim 'leaders' concerned with negotiating representation in electorates, councils, education, and so forth. Yet their historical imaginings too, even though the issue is often represented by silence, were responses to the colonial situation and thus part of a shared modernity. The Tablighi Jama'at is not an anachronistic fossil; it, with other Islamic movements, is grounded in the context of Indian nationalism and modernity.

## Islam, Identity, and Nationalism

British nationalism and identity are inextricably linked to the encounter with what are considered non-British lands and ways of living. Britain is a 'green and pleasant land' only because there are jungles and wilderness out there; Britain is enlightened and modern only because other societies are constructed as benighted and like Britain's own past.[24] As in Britain itself, however, Indian nationalism has its own internal foils for identity, among them in some contexts Muslims, including the kind of Muslims represented by the Tablighi Jama'at.

Muslims are, in this imagination, the limiting case of 'religion'. Religions, Nehru writes, have 'tried to imprison truth in set forms and dogmas...discouraged [man] from trying to understand not only the unknown but what might come in the way of social effort....As knowledge advances, the domain of religion...shrinks.'[25] He continues that India must lessen its 'religiosity' and turn to science, himself implicitly accepting the Orientalist stereotype of India as a place dominated by outdated modes of thinking, hence religion.

The rules and regulations of the kitchen dominate [the Hindu's] social life. The Moslem is fortunately free from these inhibitions, but he has his own narrow codes and ceremonials, a routine which he rigorously follows, forgetting the lesson of brotherhood which his religion taught him. *His view of life is perhaps even more limited and sterile than the Hindu view.*[26]

Such a perspective ignores the relationship between nationalism itself and many dimensions of religion and religious movements in the twentieth century as products of the same historical forces, and implicitly reveals an intimate relationship in which the modernity of nationalism is defined by the presumed archaism of religion. This angle on Muslims was reinforced by the perception of nationalist leaders, like Nehru, that the Muslim leadership, above all the leadership of the Muslim League, represented the 'feudal' landlords who would stand in the way of centralization and socialism in the independent state.[27]

The Muslim League leadership of course insisted equally on the distinctiveness and community identity of Muslims, but with a striking difference. Jinnah argued in his well-known presidential address of 1940 that Islam was *not* a religion, perhaps his own gesture, stemming from the cosmopolitanism and isolation from mainstream religious practice he shared with Nehru, toward self-presentation as 'modern'. Thus the Muslims were a nation, not a religion.

The problem of India is not of an inter-communal character but manifestly of an international one, and it must be treated as such...the only course open to us all is to allow the major nations separate homelands by dividing India into 'autonomous national states'. It is extremely difficult to appreciate why our Hindu friends fail to understand the real nature of Islam and Hinduism. They are not religions in the strict sense of the word.[28]

Despite Jinnah's efforts, the distinctiveness of Muslims was in fact construed internally as well as externally as religion, and the role of key spiritual leaders in areas of Sind and the Punjab was critical to Muslim League success.[29]

There is thus a long genealogy for the current Hindu nationalism of the Bharatiya Janata Party in insisting that they are not a religious movement but a cultural movement; to be 'religious' is to be medieval. 'Islam', as they conceive it, is what they are not. Even Nehru, despite his subtle and informed analysis of historical parallels and background, gave 'purdah' importance 'among the causes of India's decay in recent centuries'—and linked it to the presence of Muslims.[30] Just as for the British the presumed Indian male treatment of women was a central legitimating argument for their rule, so among Hindu nationalists, as debates over the Shah Banu decision and subsequent legislation in 1986 attest, the status of Muslim women is used to bolster their cultural superiority. The displacement of gender issues onto a presumed retrograde Other deflects attention from fundamental issues related to women and simultaneously suggests a contrast between oneself as enlightened and the Other as backward.[31]

Equally critical in this economy of meaning has been the definition of the Muslim as the one irreducibly inassimilable group marked precisely by religion as the essentialist base of all difference. Nehru, again the more interesting for his own cosmopolitanism and subtlety, can only introduce the subject of Muslim dynasties in the subcontinent by entitling that section of his book 'New Problems'.[32] The focus on Muslims in twentieth century India has helped obscure social differences, starting in the 1930s debates on untouchables and continuing in the escalation of the anti-Muslim movement to destroy the mosque at Ayodhya precisely when, in 1990, opposition to the Mandal Report (expanding entitlements for the 'backward') got out of hand. Especially with the creation of Pakistan and the political reality of separate nations, it could be seen—not always or in all contexts but clearly so in the early 1990s—as 'legitimate' to denounce Muslim difference, thus directing attention away from the legally illegitimate but pervasive differences of hierarchy based on birth.

## Muslim Identity before Partition

This sketch thus far suggests at least three arguments concerning modernity, nationalism, and identity, particularly in relation to Muslims.

1. The decades preceding Partition were a remarkably active and transformative period for religious life, above all in terms of institutional change and the spread of normative practices.

Although I have illustrated this process with one Islamic movement, the same kind of process was widely evident. The Tablighi Jama'at illustrates a characteristic transition to lay participation and leadership and a diffusion of normative practices.

The social context that gave rise to such movements is, broadly speaking, the same as that which gave rise to nationalism. Central are the sense of decline and the perceived need for change on one hand and the stimuli of travel and communication on the other. Mines's work on south Indian villagers exemplifies this transition: villagers, indistinguishable as Muslims at home, dress, eat, and identify as Muslims when they go to the city, thus securing a basis for community in a context of physical dislocation.[33]

By stressing movements like this as a kind of social reform, and with the allusion to Mines who grounds the evolution of such new organizations in a functionalist interpretation, I write the Tablighi Jama'at into a narrative of social change. I do this in part to problematize the place of religion as foil in narratives of modernity and nationalism. But my narrative is partial, and meaningless to the participants who would prefer, of course, to see themselves as representing what is timeless and free of social contexts.[34]

2. While many of the *anjuman* and associations like the Tablighi Jama'at conceived of themselves as apolitical, they by their very existence represent political positions. They are often written into the ever present and conceptually 'natural' narrative of nationalism: a kind of cultural 'pre-nationalism' awaiting fulfilment as a Muslim nation or interest group. This is, indeed, how they often are viewed in contemporary India. Politically active or not, the Tablighi Jama'at in India has made Muslims into a more visible and culturally distinct 'ethnicity'. At the least, moreover, a movement like the Tablighi Jama'at delegitimizes nationalist claims that the nation is a natural and inalienable part of identity. Tablighis are widely criticized in contemporary Pakistan for not helping 'build' the nation, even while political leaders in recent years praise their Islamic commitments. Tablighi Jama'at activities may, in fact, in India or Pakistan, be facilitated by political parties or government officials who see its apolitical stance as something to be encouraged. In India, Congress supporters identify Tablighi Jama'at with the politically active Deobandi 'ulama allied with them.

Tablighis' implicit counternarrative to nationalism, above all its marked a-territorialism, has taken on new salience with the Muslim diaspora in North America and Europe. Indeed many of the spatial imaginings of Muslims—of Karbala, of Cordoba, of Mecca and Medina, even of Istanbul—are significant not because they suggest an extraterritorial identity, as nationalism would require—but because they suggest an identity spatially located nowhere. With today's transnationalism and movement, it is easier to see this pervasive impulse in twentieth century Muslim thought as potentiality rather than as failure.

Such a-territorialism was also an element, as noted above, following the work of Peter Hardy, in the participation of 'ulama in the Indian nationalist movement. No spokesman was more articulate on this than Maulana Husain Ahmad Madani, who engaged with Iqbal and others, in pamphlets and letters, on the subject of common nationalism (*muttahidah qaumiyyat*) as distinct from *millat*: the latter he identified as a community based on shared textual tradition, the former on shared residence. Thus the *hindustani qaum*, he argued, bore no reference to religion. He made this latter judgment, he explained on one occasion, on the pragmatic basis of having lived abroad for sixteen years and knowing how the designation was used in the world at large[35]—a reminder that his position came from someone cosmopolitan and well travelled. For him the term *qaum*, far from having religious implications, could be applied either to descent or behaviour; and he listed a variety of uses for the term: language, region (*'arab*, *'ajam* [non-Arab; Irani]), nation (*irani*, *misri* [Egyptian]), descent (*sayyid*, *shaikh*, *mochi* [shoemaker]), colour (*gora* [white], *kala* [black]), even occupation/lifestyle (*sufiyoon ki qaum* [Sufis], *dunyadaroon ki qaum*, [worldly people]). *Qaum*, the nation, was based on territory, *watn*, but since the central issues of everyday concern were to be handled by constituent groups, the *qaum* was little more than an empty space free of intrusive imperial rule.

Madani's impulse mitigates against such concerns as competition for entitlements in voting and employment since the regulation of the *millat* is ultimately internal. Its orientation to imagined spaces beyond geopolitics extends to withdrawal from competition over local place, like Ayodhya, in a later era, as well. In its expression in the Tablighi Jama'at movement, this a-territorialism is as widespread, and as detached from the state, in the so-called

Islamic Republic of Pakistan as it is in the secular state of India. Can one write a narrative that makes Tablighi Jama'at postmodern, transnational, before its time?

3. Current revisionist scholarship on Partition emphasizes far more ambivalence on the part of the Congress leadership in favour of Partition than the nationalist myths of either India or Pakistan allow.[36] Muslims, Asim Roy argues, were taken to be an obstacle to all, a leader like Nehru wished to build in terms of a secular, socialist state, so that separating off a large share of their population and leadership had certain advantages. Muslims and Islam have continued their role in the non-Muslim political imagination in India, not least in the ideology of Hindu nationalist movements like the Rashtriya Swayamsevak Sangh (RSS).[37] One tantalizing probe into the complexity of the place of Muslims in the nationalist imagination—most intimate of relationships—is Roy's study of the film superstar Nargis, whose '(absent, ephemeral, discreet) Muslimness' is intrinsically linked to her classic role in *Mother India*: 'If Mother India is, at least partially, an allegory of the repudiation of Muslim difference, and of becoming a Hindu, then only a Muslim can assume the iconic position of that maternal figure'.[38] The image of a Muslim as Mother India can serve as metaphor for the way Muslim movements have been part of the same modern transitions as other social and political movements in this century, at once integral yet a foil.

## Notes

1. Anderson, Benedict R. 1991. *Imagined Communities: Reflections on the Origin and Spread of Nationalism.* 2nd edn. London: Verso.

2. Ibid.

3. Aggarwal, Partap C. 1971. *Caste, Religion, and Power: An Indian Case Study.* New Delhi: Shri Ram Centre for Industrial Relations.

4. Siddiqi, Majid Hayat. 1986. 'History and Society in a Popular Rebellion: Mewat, 1920–33'. *Comparative Studies in Society and History* 28: 442–67; Minault, Gail. 1982. *The Khilafat Movement: Religious Symbolism and Political Mobilization in India*, 193–8. New York: Columbia University Press. Mayaram, Shail. 1997. *Resisting Regimes: Myth, Memory, and the Shaping of Muslim Identity.* Delhi: Oxford University Press.

5. Qadiri, Muhammmad Ayyub. 1971. *Tablighi Jama'at ka tarikhi ja'iza* (A historical survey of the Tablighi Jama'at), 91–7. Karachi: Maktaba Mu'awiya.

6. Ibid., 99.

7. Firozpuri, Miyanji Muhammad 'Isa. n.d. *Tabligh ka maqami kam* (The local work of Tabligh), p. 105. Delhi: Rabbani Book Depot.

8. Metcalf, Barbara D. 1993. 'Living Hadith in the Tablighi Jama'at'. *Journal of Asian Studies* 52: 584–608.

9. Metcalf, Barbara D. 1994. '"Remaking Ourselves": Islamic Self-Fashioning in a Global Movement of Spiritual Renewal'. In Marty, Martin, and Scott Appleby, eds. *Accounting for Fundamentalisms: The Dynamic Character of Movements*, 706–25. Chicago: University of Chicago Press.

10. Mukarram, Ahmed. 1991. 'The Tabligh Movement and Maulana Abul Hasan Ali Nadwi: Guidance-Oriented Strand of Contemporary Islamic Thought'. Typescript. Oxford University.

11. Hardy, Peter. 1972. *The Muslims of British India*, pp. 190–1. Cambridge: Cambridge University Press. Hardy, Peter. 1971. *Partners in Freedom—And True Muslims: The Political Thought of Some Muslim Scholars in British India, 1912-47.* Lund: Studentlitteratur.

12. Hasan, Mushirul. ed. 1972. *Islam and Indian Nationalism: Reflections on Abul Kalam Azad*, 5. Delhi: Manohar.

13. Jinnah, Muhammad Ali. 1968. *Speeches and Writings of Mr Jinnah*, ed. Jamil-ud-din Ahmad, 2 vols, 1: 236–9. Lahore: Mohammad Ashraf.

14. Azad, Abu'l Kalam. 1940. 'Presidential Address to the Indian National Congress'. In Hasan, Mushirul, ed. *India's Partition: Process, Strategy, and Mobilisation*, p. 67. New Delhi: Oxford University Press.

15. Barbara D. Metcalf 1995. 'Presidential Address: Too Little and Too Much: Reflections on Muslims in the History of India'. *Journal of Asian Studies* 54 (1995): 1–17 (see Chapter 8 in this volume).

16. Geertz, Clifford. 1973. '"Internal Conversion" in Contemporary Bali'. In *The Interpretation of Cultures: Selected Essays*, pp. 170–89. New York: Basic Books.

17. Abu'l-ala Maududi, Maulana, '*Ihya-i din ki jidd o jahd ka sahih tariqa aur ek qabil-i* taqlid namuna' (The correct means of struggle for the revival of religion and an example worth imitating), in Nu'mani, Muhammad Manzur, ed. 1939. *Tablighi jama'at, jama'at-i islami aur barelwi hazrat* (The Tabligh Jama'at, the Jama'at-i Islami, and the Barelvi Gentlemen), p. 25. Lucknow: Al-Furqan Book Depot.

18. Qadiri, *Tablighi Jama'at ka tarikhi Ja'iza*, 54–63.

19. Aggarwal, *Caste, Religion and Power*, 1971.

20. Devji, Faisal. 1994. 'Muslim Nationalism: Founding Identity in Colonial India', chap. 1. Chicago: University of Chicago, Department of History. Unpublished Ph.D. dissertation.

21. Sadiq, Muhammad. 1984. *A History of Urdu Literature*, 2nd edn, pp. 430–5. New Delhi: Oxford University Press.

22. Metcalf, Barbara D. 1977. 'Reflections on Iqbal's Mosque'. *Journal of South Asian and Middle Eastern Studies*, 1: 68–74 (see Chapter 12 in this volume).

23. Kandhalavi, Maulana Ihtishamu'l-Hasan. 1939. 'Muslim Degeneracy and Its Only Remedy' (*Musalmanon ki maujuda pasti ka wahid 'ilaj*). In Zachariyya, Muhammad, ed. *Teachings of Islam: Tablighi Nisab No. 1*, p. 10. Delhi: n.p.

24. Colley, Linda. 1992. *Britons: Forging the Nation, 1707-1837*. New Haven, Conn.: Yale University Press.

25. Nehru, Jawaharlal. 1956. *The Discovery of India*, p. 389. New York: Anchor Books.

26. Ibid., 393-4, emphasis added.

27. Ibid., 301.

28. Jinnah, *Speeches and Writings*, 1: 168-9.

29. Gilmartin, David. 1988. *Empire and Islam: Punjab and the Making of Pakistan*. Berkeley: University of California Press; Ansari, Sarah F. D. 1992. *Sufi Saints and State Power: The 'Pirs' of Sind, 1843-1947*. Cambridge: Cambridge University Press.

30. Nehru, *The Discovery of India*, 144.

31. Engineer, Asghar Ali, ed. 1987. *The Shah Bano Controversy*. London: Sangam.

32. Nehru, *The Discovery of India*, 129-97.

33. Mines, Mattison. 1975. 'Islamization and Muslim Ethnicity in South India'. In Rothermund, Dietmar, ed. *Islam in Southern Asia: A Survey of Current Research*, pp. 55-7. Wiesbaden: Steiner.

34. Cf. Siddiqu, Majid Hayat. 1986. 'History and Society in a Popular Rebellion: Mewat, 1920-33'. *Comparative Studies in Society and History*, 28: 442-67.

35. Sayyid Husain Ahmad Madani, '*Maslah-yi fitna-yi qaumiyyat: 'Allama iqbal ka i'tiráz aur hazrat maulana madani rahmat allah ka jawab*' (The problem of the dispute over 'qaumiyyat' [nationalism]: The objection of 'Allama Iqbal and the answer of the Hazrat Maulana Madani, on whom be peace), in Ahmad Salim, Ahmad, ed. 1990. *Khutbat-i madani* (Sermons of Madani), pp. 169-77. Lahore: Nigarishat.

36. Jalal, Ayesha. 1985. *The Sole Spokesman: Jinnah, the Muslim League and the Demand for Pakistan*. Cambridge: Cambridge University Press; Roy, Asim. 1990. 'The High Politics of India's Partition: The Revisionist Perspective'. *Modern Asian Studies* 24: 385-415.

37. Bacchetta, Paola. 1994. 'Communal Property/Sexual Property: On Representations of Muslim Women in a Hindu Nationalist Discourse'. In Hasan, Zoya, ed. *Forging Identities: Gender, Communities, and the State in India*, pp. 188-225. Boulder, Col.: Westview Press.

38. Roy, Parama. 1995. 'The Spectral Nargis'. Typescript, p. 17. [See Parama Roy, *Indian Traffic: Identities in Question in Colonial and Post-Colonial India* (1998)]

# III

# Islam and Politics post-1947

# 8

## Too Little and Too Much
### Reflections on Muslims in
### the History of India

I want to begin this evening by recalling my immediate predecessor as AAS president from the South Asian field, Barbara Stoler Miller, whose untimely death in 1992 took from us a distinguished Sanskritist, a gifted teacher, and a generous colleague whose absence we mourn. In my address I continue themes taken up by Barbara Miller four years ago[1] as well as by Stanley Tambiah, as president from the Southeast Asian field,[2] the year before. Then, as now, scholars across the disciplines—whether, like Barbara Miller, a scholar of classical texts; or like Stanley Tambiah, an anthropologist; or myself, a historian of British India—have struggled to understand the religious nationalism of South Asia, one of whose most tragic outcomes has been an accelerating violence against the Muslim minority.

A striking characteristic of recent public life in India has been an intensified use of historical narratives to define the nature of India's people and draw the boundaries of citizenship. A few years back, these histories began swirling around an obscure mosque in Ayodhya, built in 1528. The mosque was physically destroyed in late 1992 by organized Hindu activists, men and women, who tore down the mosque stone by stone. These activists argued that the mosque builders had themselves destroyed an ancient temple, built on the very site of the birthplace of Lord Ram, a god whose drama of exile and perfect kingship, always well-known, had swept India in a televised serial a few years earlier. They insisted that they could not await the decisions of an ordinary court to adjudicate rights to the land: their claim transcended mundane legality. Terrible conflict followed the destruction of the mosque. Most of the victims were Muslims.[3]

The version of history implicit in the destruction of the mosque was one deeply engrained in its basic outline in what we call 'common sense', current not only in India but outside: There was once a Hindu Golden Age; Muslims came as foreign invaders; Muslims were oppressors who ultimately ushered in a period of decline. Versions of this narrative had been current in the independence movement and had justified, for some, the separate state of Pakistan. This history had, moreover, long been a subject of contestation in independent India, as historians like Romila Thapar from the late 1960s on had struggled to make explicit the implications of such narratives for India's public life.[4] What has been new in the past decade has been the revival of this narrative as sanction for an explicit programme of public action, a revival that inter alia called for mosques, especially when presumed to have been built on the sites of earlier temples, to be removed and for Muslims to assimilate—in some sense—or leave. Arguments from history have been taken to transcend other sources of morality and even institutions as basic to civil life as courts.

Historians in India have recently renewed debates about the political implications of their scholarly practice for public life.[5] A new issue has been raised by the work of historians, including some among the so-called 'Subalternists', who have chosen not to work within the old nationalist narrative but to reject the great teleological 'metanarratives', including the nationalist narrative, completely.[6] Critics of this radical approach, in turn, have asked if such work, by destabilizing the conventional narrative, has not opened the field precisely for Hindu nationalists to utilize history for their own 'supremacist' ends.[7] Would it not be better to revitalize a liberal nationalist past? Such issues have engaged politicians, put members of the Indian History Congress on the cover of the Indian equivalent of *Time* or *Newsweek* (*India Today*), and stimulated discussion among diaspora Indians, many of whom have embraced what seems an authentic historical heritage as part of their Hindu identity.[8]

Those of us who study India outside India must also recognize the extent to which our scholarly work has typically reinforced the fundamental assumptions and parameters within which the old nationalist and 'the new Hindu history',[9] alike, operate. It is primarily to us in the American academy that I direct my comments this evening and thus call attention to the politics of knowledge entailed by our own conduct of scholarship. This knowledge is as much a part of American public life as it is of Indian public life, defining by presumed contrast who 'we' are, and, in parallel cases like Bosnia, shaping our responses to international affairs.[10]

## Colonial and Nationalist Narratives

Two major scholarly projects have begun to wrench us from the problematic received narrative of Indian history. The first, and more complete, has been to recognize, in India as everywhere, the extent to which the writing of history since the nineteenth century has been intimately tied to the project of the nation-state. Today's public narrative, we now realize, while new in its emphases and its use, has roots that can be clearly identified as part of colonial practice that forged a powerful outline of the history of India, a history that simultaneously contributed to the construction of Britain's own history of itself.

In that colonial history, India was already a bounded entity inhabited by two religiously defined communities. And in that India, British historians imagined Hindus as the original inhabitants and Muslims rather as they, the British, imagined themselves: as foreign rulers, as imperial rulers, who arrived as successful conquerors. Muslims served as a foil against which the British defined themselves: by saying that Muslims were oppressive, incompetent, lascivious, and given to self-indulgence, the colonial British could define precisely what they imagined themselves to be, namely, enlightened, competent, disciplined, and judicious. At the same time, they imputed to Muslims certain qualities they admired, like qualities of masculinity and vigour, in contrast to the allegedly effeminate Hindus. Such stereotypes shaped policy and legitimated British presence to themselves, and, for a considerable period of time, to many of those they ruled as well.[11]

This was not done subtly. The long standard translations of the Persian histories of the pre-colonial period, *The History of India as Told by its own Historians*, some eight volumes published in the decade from 1867 to 1877, invited the reader to selections purporting to show the 'intolerance' of the Muhammadans, a story 'of idols mutilated, temples razed, of forcible conversions and marriages, of proscriptions and confiscations, of murders and massacres, and of the sensuality and drunkenness of the tyrants who enjoined them'. Lest the point be missed, Elliott, one of the editors, added, '[The translations] will make our native subjects more sensible of the immense advantages accruing to them under the mildness and equity of our rule.'[12] Little wonder that British records, often produced through such lenses, as Gyan Pandey has shown, cannot be taken as a guide to contemporaneous events labelled 'Hindu-Muslim riots',[13] let alone, following Richard Davis's work on Somnath, as an accurate record of events of earlier centuries.[14]

But why did this colonial narrative in its basic outline take hold? In part the explanation rests in a range of colonial practices in British India that systematically institutionalized a nation of communities, above all what were deemed the two great communities of Hindu and Muslim. These practices, embedded in what Peter Hardy has called the very 'idiom' of British rule,[15] included the measurement common to the modern state, including the census and ethnographic surveys, highlighting religion as they did not do in Britain itself. This arithmetic in turn provided grounds for claims to education, employment quotas in the army and in government services, and electoral reservations.[16] How could leaders of the presumed communities not project their existence into the past as they competed among themselves and with each other?[17]

Many Indian nationalist leaders found it useful, specifically, to accept the notion of an Indian Golden Age that ended with the presumed oppression of Muslim rule.[18] This explained the British takeover and the need for regeneration. Such a story enhanced cultural self-pride since there had been, after all, a Golden Age, and its existence offered hope for the future. Like the colonialist history, it revolved around self-conscious communities of 'Hindus' and 'Muslims' as 'the master cleavage', in Susanne Rudoph's term, at the heart of contemporary history and politics.[19] Whether 'secular' or 'communalist', these histories have etched ever deeper the essentialism of an India composed of two eternal groups. Historians of the nationalist movement, moreover, have identified mainstream Indian nationalism as having increasingly espoused cultural Hinduism as a source for common symbols of unity and a way to broaden the base of support beyond the English educated elite.[20]

There are both scholarly grounds and political incentives to insist on the 'construction' of contemporary identities and thus to challenge their claim to being natural and primordial. Nation, caste, language, and above all religion, are, in their politicized and enumerated form, contingent and recent. Indeed, it is the excavation of the contingent nature of such identities as much as anything that distinguishes recent scholarly work from the positions often taken by the older histories or by lay people, whether politicians or journalists or expatriate engineers propounding their version of history in newsgroups on the Internet.

Although substantial and sophisticated scholarship in recent years has shown that the conventional historiography of India is deeply implicated in the political context of British India, the categories and the narratives of that historiography still serve as the implicit framework not only of history but of the humanities and social sciences generally as they deal with India. We teach courses on 'civilization'; we assume that there are enduring continuities to being 'Hindu' or 'Muslim'; we attribute explanatory value to these essences in historical settings; and we extrapolate from them to bounded sociological categories.[21] Even Peter van der Veer, writing on contemporary religious nationalism, admits, despite his intention to avoid 'reifying' the object of his discussion, 'I am certain that parts of this book will have fallen prey to the very essentializations my argument attempts to problematize'.[22]

But most writing evinces no such self-consciousness. Samuel Huntington's much discussed article published two years ago, summed up by its title 'The Coming Clash of Civilizations?' seemed plausible to most people as it predicted a greater awareness of difference, and hence conflict, among contending bounded and coherent civilizations, like 'Islam' and 'Hinduism'.[23] On 'Islam', V. S. Naipaul's *Among the Believers* (1981) discovered precisely what he set out to find. It is these often implicit assumptions in relation to Islam I describe in my title as 'too little and too much'.[24]

One cardinal assumption of the civilizational approach to culture and society is its focus, as Edward Said, above all, has made clear, on pristine texts and presumed 'authenticity'.[25] In the case of the history and culture of Muslims of South Asia, or indeed of Asia generally, that has been an element conducive to scholarly neglect. To be sure, the issue of 'too little' is one which perhaps everyone identifies: Asian topics in general are in fact not given the attention which is their due. I think everyone moreover has at least one graduate school story, often in the mode of the misguided obduracy of the older generation ultimately proven wrong by the younger (at least in the younger's opinion). My story is relevant to the amount of attention given to my subject. Early on I was asked by a senior professor what I planned to specialize in, and I answered that I intended to work on Indian Muslims. His reply—no doubt intended for my welfare—was a splutter: 'Muslims! Why they are no more than 5 percent of the population and they simply do not matter.' I remember the percentage because it was so wrong, but the point was not really the number. The point was the assumption that 'civilization' and 'high culture' mattered, and that to study Muslims outside their area of origin in the Middle East was irrelevant.[26] One sought to study the 'authentic', the 'pure', the 'textual'. This tradition of scholarship, in short, fit India's Muslims perfectly into the narrative of 'foreignness' and 'inauthenticity' outlined above.

But 'too little' can have a second, although related, interpretation. Too often the history of Muslims is reduced to Islam in the sense of taken-for-granted assumptions in which words like 'monolithic', 'militaristic', 'simple', 'fanatic', 'egalitarian' resound. This textually based, narrowly defined Islam 'too little' to describe the complex and varied practices and loyalties of actual Muslims, yet 'Islam' is made into the single most important causal variable for whatever Muslims do. 'Too little' in this interpretation becomes 'too much'.

In colonial history, 'religion' in general is taken as central to defining the fundamental properties of non-European cultures—societies that are backward, irrational, and medieval. By the nineteenth century, the West is meant to be beyond religion in public life: religion is, in these formulations, limited to spiritual matters, to private life, ultimately to something like a lifestyle or hobby; only the marginal or the reactionary would bring religion into public life. In nineteenth century Europe, moreover, 'the economy', 'the society', and 'public opinion' are taken as major forces in history, with 'religion' only one force among many. In a place like India, by contrast, 'religion' is typically taken as the central or the only force. The societies understood to be dominated by religion become, in this account, like the West in an earlier period. The British histories of India, in keeping with this theory, identified three periods of Indian history: the Hindu, the Muslim, and a third not defined by religion at all, the British. Despite critiques of this periodization and approach, a great deal of what is taught on South Asia even today focuses on 'religion', especially as embedded in texts as the defining marker of 'civilization'. This essential religiosity then becomes the speciously plausible explanation for religious politics and ethnicity in the contemporary world, instincts, as it were, that well up without the guiding control of Western or, in Central Asia, Russian colonialism.

## Alternatives

Historians of the colonial period have, thus, shown definitively the limitations and political implications of the history forged in the context of colonialism and nationalism. What then can take its place? The second scholarly approach I alluded to above seeks precisely to offer new approaches to the medieval and early modern period, implicitly offering an alternative to 'religion' or 'Islam' as the pre-eminent explanatory variable in such areas as policy, social allegiance, and creative expression—the use of Islam I have called 'too little' and 'too much'. The following examples are meant to be suggestive of the kind of work being done—and needing to be done.

First, we need to understand better the organization and ideology of Muslim politics, especially given the presumed truism that there is no difference between religion and politics in Islam. What could that possibly mean? The fact that actual Muslims have lived under every conceivable form of polity suggests the limitations of that claim. Stephen Humphreys' well-chosen word to describe the common relationship between Muslim political leaders and religion is *indifference*. In most Muslim ruled polities throughout most of history, the nature of ritual practice, codes of law, spiritual orientation, or whatever has been irrelevant to the state. The religious leadership has lent legitimacy to those polities that maintain a framework of institutions within which Muslims can lead their religious life; they expect patronage to mosques, schools, and shrines but not control of what goes on. But non-Muslim populations expect patronage to their institutions as well.

Use of a term like 'tolerance' or 'secularism' to describe this arrangement on the part of any ruler, Muslim or not, is anachronistic: there were always preferences and hierarchies. But there were assuredly not, in the normal course of events, attempts by Muslim kings and sultans to legislate theology or enforce some 'orthodoxy'.[27] Claims of deviance were levelled at opponents at times of political conflict, while celebrations of ritual and moral conformity were offered as praise, but that is a far cry from any notion of 'an Islamic state'. And rhetoric of heroic feats against the infidels may be no more than a form of panegyric to communicate that a king should be thought of as good.[28]

Indeed, far from kingship or any other political structure being intrinsic to Islam, a theorist like the fourteenth century Delhi-based Barani argued that the sultan put his soul at risk precisely because kingship, in this case, required what was un-Islamic—attitudes like arrogance, for example, and the compromises of political life.[29] 'The Islamic State', let alone the resources to impose it, is typically a variant of nationalism and hence a profoundly modern idea.

Loyalty, not a distinctive Islamic ideology, held the state together. Under the Mughals, a Hindu Rajput who was loyal was praised; a Muslim who was disloyal was subject to jihad. The Mughals initial conquest in the subcontinent was of other Muslims. Loyalty was a Muslim virtue, but it was also a Rajput virtue.[30] Conversion was not required to be part of the Muslim state. 'Islam' does not provide a blueprint for organizing a state; it does not by itself explain political action; it does not predict participation or enmity in relation to the state.

These issues signal the need for precision in calling anything 'Islamic'. We need always to ask what is meant when that term is deployed. Often an institution or practice is indeed regarded by participants as 'Muslim' or 'Islamic', but is nonetheless not specific to Muslims. The case of 'loyalty' as an attitude was just noted. The institutions of the Mughal state were bolstered by an Islamic ideology but were in their basic structures similar to those of early modern agrarian empires in China and elsewhere. A wide range of techniques, crops, and objects in general are often called 'Islamic' simply because they are associated with populations that are predominantly Muslim, but such a use implicitly evokes essentialized religion.[31] In each of these cases, alternative adjectives, and hence categories, would stimulate more contextual, more historical analysis than the overused modifier 'Islamic'.

A second thicket in pre-colonial history is social identity and the deep dead end tracks carved through it by the categories 'Hindu' and 'Muslim'. These are hard routes to avoid; but some recent scholarship is suggestive in showing the significance of ethnicity, rather than religion per se, as a category; the presence of a multiplicity—not a binary opposition—of competing groups; and, in general, the varied shifts and contingencies of alliances among elites.

In the kingdom of Vijayanagara, texts of the fourteenth to sixteenth centuries as Philip Wagoner has shown, do not use the term 'Muslim' at all but rather 'Turk', *turushka*, an ethnic group whose religion is only one of its many characteristics. Turks, Telugu Brahmins, and others, as he puts it, moreover, 'interact in the same social space'.[32] Making a similar argument from Telugu inscriptions, Cynthia Talbot found the Turks identified by such terms as *ashwapati*, the lords of the horses, one of multiple—not binary—competing groups, like the 'lords of the elephants' in Orissa, or the Telugu warriors themselves, 'lords of men'.[33]

Talbot also found, however, that in the period of initial conquest, the Turks were described as *mleccha*, a term often translated as 'foreigner' but in fact also used for hill dwellers or indigenous 'tribes', and as *yavana* ('Ionian'), used since the time of Alexander the Great for those who came from the north-west. These texts described the Turks as creators of chaos who overturned images, destroyed temples, and slaughtered Brahmins, exactly, Talbot argues, as do texts that describe any truimph of the 'lower orders' over Brahmins. Overturning or capturing temple deities was common to all conquerors since temples were so clearly part of claims to sovereignty.[34] Muslims were, in short, assimilated to known categories; they were not the unique foreign category some later ideologies made them out to be.

Vijayanagar's neighbouring and rival state of Bijapur, whose Adil Shahi rulers had strong Persian connections, mirrored Vijayanagar in its political organization and ethos, even sharing a name, 'Bijapur', that like 'Vijayanagar' meant 'city of victory'. Wagoner has identified inscriptions that show Turks serving Vijayanagar and Brahmins serving Bijapur. In these texts, dated over many decades, institutions of whatever provenance appear to be understood as equivalent. Thus, a mosque inscription in Vijayanagar calls the building a *dharmsala*, a charitable rest house, since a mosque would have been a place of rest for travellers; the merit for building it is assigned to the non-Muslim overlord, the Shaivite king.

To be sure, being Muslim mattered in a wide range of ways, fostering networks among different kinds of elites and shaping many aspects of daily personal life. But loyalties were often highly specific. Scholars often emphasize that what we call 'Hinduism' historically had no single organization or doctrine; and, anthropologically, until the twentieth century, the same statement could be made about Muslims, given the affiliations that have existed around Sufi saints or shrines, sectarian groups, law schools, or lineages.[35] As Peter Hardy wrote over twenty years ago, although the British may have thought of Muslims, in the words of Lord Dufferin in 1888, as a nation characterized by 'monotheism...iconoclastic fanaticism...animal sacrifices...social equality and...remembrance of the days when, enthroned at Delhi, they reigned supreme', this image, Hardy insists, 'would have startled the Muslims of (the) earlier, pre-British period'. Those Muslims spoke a variety of languages, excluded the humble from their mosques, and many often owed their primary loyalty to devotional cults at shrines and temples. Muslims were, as Hardy puts it, scarcely 'more monotheistic than their non-Muslim neighbours'.[36]

Two key dimensions of these identities distinguish them sharply from those that have emerged in recent times. One was that they were primarily local, even face to face. Thus, in the book honoured today with the Ananda Coomaraswamy Prize, Richard Eaton dramatically shifts our image of 'conversion', the very word so laden with our Pauline notions of individualism, doctrine, and instantaneous and total change, that the term itself perhaps needs to be dropped.[37] In Bengal and the Punjab, what we call conversion is above all allegiance to Sufi intermediaries. In these settings, Sufi elders often served as agents of agrarian change, entrusted with rights to land as they oversaw its being brought under settled agriculture. They served as intermediaries to regional and central political authorities, mediating between recently sedentarized communities and large scale polities. Similar processes took place in areas of non-Muslim rule with Brahminic caste leaders and, later, under colonial rule with Christian missionaries as intermediaries. In the Bengal case, a closer identification with Islamic symbols did in fact eventually emerge, but that was very gradual and in fact most marked only in the colonial period.[38]

Neither the pull of presumed egalitarianism nor the push of 'the sword'—the usual stereotypical explanations of conversion to Islam in South Asia—produced the new networks of patronage and loyalty, perhaps devotion, that we speak of as 'conversion'.[39] Indeed, a Muslim allegiance was not dramatically visible. As is well known, only with the first British census in 1871 did anyone discover that the majority of the Bengali population was Muslim: up until then numbers did not matter, the concept of 'majority' meant nothing, and no value was placed on those of some shared identity over a large area acting in concert.[40]

A third vexed area in discussion of the pre-colonial period is that of so-called cultural 'syncretism', a term used to describe religious styles and art, for example. The term implies that the categories 'Hindu' and 'Muslim' are fixed, a notion already argued as problematic, and that bits of both in some sense mix. It encourages what one might call the 'vertical fallacy', that it is possible to make lists, even contrasting lists of what is 'Hindu' in one column and 'Muslim' in another. It also tends to call 'Hindu' or 'Muslim' elements in the culture that may be neither or both.[41]

Thus Catherine Asher has argued that architectural styles, labelled as Hindu or Muslim in the colonial period, in fact initially participated in a shared 'taste' with no archaeology of origin ascribed.[42] Or, put differently, the significance was typically not linked to religion in any narrow or exclusive sense. Thus, to use the Vijayanagar example again, a ruler who patronized Shaivite deities also built public buildings with domes and arches, in the style of the northern Muslim rulers, and, even more intriguingly, dressed in public settings as a 'sultan', all this to participate in what was less 'Islamic', than a shared discourse of rulership.[43]

If there is a 'vertical fallacy' associated with 'syncretism', we might also posit a 'horizontal fallacy', following Peter Brown's identification of the post-enlightenment 'two tier' theory of religion. In this theory, rational monotheism is a higher form of religion and therefore maps onto the upper classes and the educated; superstition and 'syncretism' represent more primitive religion and are presumed characteristic of the humble.[44] By this reckoning, the upper classes are 'good Muslims'; the rural and uneducated Muslims, more immersed in local cultures, are taken as deviant. If Islam is considered foreign, the lower orders are, therefore, 'more Indian'.

Indeed, when I mentioned to colleagues at last year's meeting that I was to pick the cover design for this year's annual meeting programme, I was advised to turn to folk art—in a sense to choose something not 'too Islamic'—or to hedge the problem by using an object from the Indus Valley civilization. I was intrigued by this advice but I decided simply to search my memory for something visual I had seen and loved.

I chose Miskin's late sixteenth century Noah's Ark, certainly an example of 'high', not 'folk', culture (Figure 6). Yet this painting at once represents a central Islamic symbol and a work specific to this geographic region. It could not have been done anywhere else but the Mughal court. This is so even though it is impossible to extricate any element and label it 'Hindu'. What is Indic is not limited to folk art. The Mughal paintings have a vitality, an individualizing of animals and humans, a use of colour and in some cases perspective, that set them apart from the Persian miniature tradition from which they derive.[45] (Welch 1978, 56–7; Okada 1992, 125–36; Beach 1981, 124).

Miskin's painting spills over with animal and human energy in a continuum from the water to the ark to the air. In this perfectly balanced composition, aloof from the teeming decks and man overboard around him, sits the Prophet Noah at the centre, transcendently intent on his companion, who holds some holy book. It is perhaps not too fanciful to recall Shiva Nataraj with his perfect balance and tranquillity within a circle of moving flame. Thus a central, normative symbol of Islam, the prophet, takes on new meaning in a new cultural world. The powerful image of the

FIGURE 6: *Noah's Ark*, attributed to Miskin, India, ca. 1590, Mughal, Akbar period. Colours and gold on paper: 28:1 x 15.6 cm. Courtesy of the Freer Gallery of Art, Smithsonian Institution, Washington, DC.

prophet is profoundly enriched in the Indic context by some combination of assimilation and resistance that takes shape in creative expressions like these.

But the story is more complex: the painter is not a Muslim but Miskin, son of Mahesh, and we can only guess at the content of the multiple meanings a painting like this would have had for the many different audiences it delighted in Akbar's court.[46] Not least, Noah is visually an emblem of the king, recalling countless compositions of the haloed ruler seated with advisors, his smaller sons ranged at his side, the pivotal figure in relation not only to humans but to creatures generally. The king is bound to his subjects not by the shared 'identity' of the culturally homogeneous modern state but by ties of protection and obedience—just like Noah with his disparate elephants and cats. The painting thus turns out to be, in part, a subtle representation of the kind of early modern polity sketched out above.

But if one leaves aside architecture and art, what of texts where the labels 'Hindu' and 'Muslim' are actually used? Clearly these terms carry a wide variety of meanings of which one example may suggest the need for specific, contextual studies. Some thirty years ago Aziz Ahmad described a selection of texts he labelled 'epic and counter-epic', arguing that in them we find a genre divided down the middle: 'A Muslim epic of conquest, and a Hindu epic of resistance...planted in two different cultures; in two different languages; in two mutually exclusive religious, cultural and historical attitudes each confronting the other in aggressive hostility'.[47] Before heaving a sigh of relief that we can go back to the simple story we all, so to speak, grew up with, let me call attention to two important recent studies, Richard Davis' of the construction of the Somnath legend and Aditya Behl's study of one of these texts, the *Padmavati*.[48]

This text, written in Awadhi by a Muslim, Malik Muhammad Jayasi, in about 1540, purports to tell the story of the victory over Rajput Chitaur of the evil king Alauddin Khilji, who is driven by desire for the beautiful Padmavati. Ahmad concludes that Jayasi, located as he was some distance from the court, 'in all simplicity' must have accepted the Rajput legends and hoped 'to tell a good story which would appeal to his fellow-villagers, the large majority of whom were Hindus'.[49] Any Muslim using the vernacular (even after centuries) and steeped in local symbols and stories, must, in short, have been a bumpkin—echoes of 'the horizontal fallacy' sketched out above.

And indeed Behl and Davis give us a very different picture. Jayasi's patron was a Hindu, but the dedication of the poem was to the sultan, Sher Shah Sur. The poem, far from simple, is a complex allegory shaped by Nath yogic and Sufi cosmology. The so-called 'epics and counter-epics', as Davis explains, are in fact rhetorically similar and appealed to an elite cosmopolitan audience constituted in part by patronizing, writing, and hearing texts like these. In this poem, the villain, to be sure, is the Muslim king, but 'Islam' conquers. In the poem's brilliant concluding pun, 'Chitaur becomes Islam': the town, Chitaur, is in ashes, but 'chita' (mind) and 'ura' (heart), consumed in the fire of love, reach the annihilation of the Sufis, whose doctrine Jayasi espoused.[50] 'Islam' and 'Hinduism' are, then, not the binary at all but rather true Islam, in the person of the Rajput hero, and false Islam, in the person of the conqueror (helped by a Brahmin advisor and a Rajput assassin), who are all ignorant of the path of asceticism and love. This is a story of resistance to a Turk, a sultan who is an enemy of Islam/truth/the divine. It is not the Hindu-Muslim gap that expresses the void between the divine and the worldly, but the gap between those who seek the spirit/beauty and those who merely conquer and conspire. This was perhaps a story to put Sher Shah Sur in his place—as the Chishti Sufis liked to do. But far more important, it was a story that profoundly enriched Sufi teachings by the utilization of local legends and histories, the deployment of new symbols to describe the quest for the beloved, and a new depth in understanding the ardours of the Sufi path through the sophisticated theories of yogic discipline available in the culture at large. In literature, as in architecture and art, new work, rooted in diverse social and political contexts, points us beyond the static dichotomies that have shaped historical narratives too long.

These brief comments on aspect of state, society, and art enlarge definitions of Islamic practice to include, for example, loyalty, temple patronage, courtly painting, and epics about Rajput heroes. At the same time, they show that Islam, especially when reduced to a narrow list of 'beliefs', cannot be used to explain everything. A stereotypical Islam offers us little guidance to understanding the nature of Muslim polities or the dynamics of their societies, including, perhaps surprisingly, even the process usually labelled 'conversion'.

## Concluding Reflections

Why do these proposed correctives matter? The situation of Muslims in India today can be compared to the situation of African-Americans in the United States. This may seem preposterous: Muslims were once rulers, builders of the Taj Mahal; India is bordered by two states with primarily Muslim populations; India has had presidents of Muslim background. Yet Dipesh Chakrabarty, in part to de-exoticize India, has recently argued that the term 'communalism' to describe ethnic relations in India should in fact be replaced by 'racism'. Chakrabarty points to the everyday behaviour that in Europe or Australia would indicate racism, for example, informal unwillingness to sell property to Muslims[51]— to which one could add references to Muslims as dirty or having too many children, or, as in the American south, the remnant left when the smart ones go north. No analogy is perfect: others have found anti-Semitism a useful parallel. One can also link Indian Muslims, Copts, Ahmadis, and Bahais who are labelled in their respective countries as the cosmopolitans, people of mixed loyalty with links to outsiders, secretly privileged and powerful, in short, the language once used of European Jews.[52] In all these cases minorities are forced to play roles not of their own choosing, not least that of foil against which the unity of others—Hindus, the nation—can be constituted, and injustices of class and wealth obscured. The history that identifies Indian Muslims as aliens, destroyers, and crypto-Pakistanis, with its profound moral and political implications for citizenship and entitlements, is critical in sustaining that role. It presumably cannot be successfully challenged until, as has happened only partially and very recently in the United States in relation to African-Americans, the social and political interests that sustain belief in fundamental difference are changed.

The professional historian may thus, for the moment, have little chance in offering correctives, the more so since the debate within India has been drawn between the 'authentic' on the one hand and the 'deracinated secularist' on the other.[53] Indeed, some of the latter have evinced a grudging admiration for the 'postmodernism' of the

Hindu nationalist response to the devastating critique of their claims about the presumed ancient temples of Ayodhya: that not facts but beliefs about what happened alone matter.[54]

Ayodhya was, in fact, not the site of an ancient temple. A temple was almost certainly not destroyed to build the mosque: the first written reference to that claim comes not in the contemporaneous records where it might be expected but in a nineteenth century colonial gazetteer. Ironically, the inscriptions on the mosque spoke not of conquest and destruction but of Babar's *justice* as a building that reached the heavens and of the mosque as 'a resting place for angels'.[55] Ironically as well, the town developed as a centre of devotion to Ram in the context of Muslim rule and with the patronage of Muslim rulers.[56]

Muslims did destroy temples, even if not in this particular case; Hindu nationalists claim a right to destroy mosques in revenge. But note the difference of the latter claim. The Hindu activists speak for a nationalist ideology that denies diversity. The pre-colonial states, by contrast, incorporated diversity. The difference is summed up by the goal of destroying all mosques,[57] to which end books have been published cataloguing hundreds of targets. Earlier, rulers used destruction in limited and strategic ways or—to use an Indic term—looted religious buildings for their wealth. The meaning of destroying a monument is no longer the same, and we need to counter a history that suggests that it is.

Histories will always be rewritten. One reason is the relatively straightforward one that new material will be unearthed—the scent of untapped source materials that makes historians salivate. But a second reason is that the world changes. History is ultimately a pragmatic science: in a wide variety of ways we write and read history precisely because at some level it is used to make sense of the past for the present.

In the nineteenth century it was useful for colonialists, and, later, nationalists, with their own emphases, to write a history of difference, a pragmatic benefit that continues for religious nationalists today. On the verge of the twenty-first century, in a world of increasing interdependence, others of us need a history of connections among disparate settings,[58] of mobility across space,[59] of analogous institutions that are not 'Western' or 'Eastern',[60] of engagement with other geographic areas in our disciplines that belies Orientalist specificity.[61] Such history is also, of course, produced in a political context. Even so, historians can insist that, in the end, some history is better than others. The postmodernist Hindu nationalist argument that only belief matters is, in this perspective, bad history.

Historians need to tell a new story about South Asian Muslims—for themselves and whoever can hear them. That history has been doubly marginalized by legacies of European Orientalism and Indian politics. More of us need, above all, to take Muslims into account—an end to the neglect I have tagged 'too little'—and all of us need to build a history that does not make 'Islam' prior—the stereotypical thinking I have called 'too much'. We need scholars who, unlike my generation, do not study Muslims alone.[62] And, instead of creating difference, we need to draw boundaries around common human experiences and, above all, around common social and political structures, situating Muslims squarely within the complex world of opportunities and constraints, motivations, and tastes they shared with everyone else.

## Notes

1. Miller, Barbara Stoler. 1991. 'Contending Narratives: The Political Life of the Indian Epics'. *Journal of Asian Studies* 50: 783–92.

2. Tambiah, Stanley. 1990. 'Presidential Address: Reflections on Communal Violence in South Asia'. *Journal of Asian Studies* 49(4): 741–60.

3. For background to the crisis brought on by the destruction of the mosque at Ayodhya, see the important collection edited by S. Gopal (Gopal, Sarvepalli, ed. 1991. *Anatomy of a Confrontation: The Babri Masjid Ramjanmabhumi Issue*. New Delhi: Penguin Books India), and for comments on the situation after the destruction of the mosque, see the special issue of *South Asia*, 'After Ayodhya' (1994). See also two forthcoming edited volumes, one on communalism edited by David Ludden [*Contesting the Nation: Religion, Communism, the Politics of Democracy in India* (Philadelphia: University of Pennsylvania Press, 1996)] and one on the new role of women in religious nationalism edited by Amrita Basu and Patricia Jeffrey [*Resisting the Sacred and the Secular: Women's Activism and Politicized Religion in South Asia* (Delhi: Kali for Women, 1999)].

4. Hoffman, Steven A. 1993. 'Historical Narrative and Nation-State in India'. Skidmore College: Typescript; Rudolph, Susanne and Lloyd Rudolph. 1983. 'Rethinking Secularism: Genesis and Implications of the Textbook Controversy, 1977–9'. *Pacific Affairs* 56.1: 15–37; Thapar, Romila, Harbans Mukhia, and Bipan Chandra. 1968. *Communalism and the Writing of Indian History*. Delhi: People's Publishing House.

5. See Gopal, Sarvepalli. 1991-2. 'History and Politicians: BJP Attack on the History Congress'. *Frontline* 8(26) (21 December 1991-3 January 1992): 91. My focus on India rather than Pakistan in these comments is a response to the use of history in India's public life, a use that has substantially receded in favour of Islamic and other discourses in Pakistan. See Metcalf, Barbara D. 1987. 'Islamic Arguments in Contemporary Pakistan'. In Roff, William R. and Dale F. Eickelman, eds, *Islam and the Political Economy of Meaning: Comparative Studies of Muslim Discourse*, pp. 132-59. Berkeley: University of California Press (Chapter 10 in this volume).

6. Prakash, Gyan. 1994. 'AHR Forum: Subaltern Studies as Postcolonial Criticism'. *American Historical Review* (December): 1475-90.

7. Ghosh, Amitav. 1995. 'The Fundamentalist Challenge'. *The Wilson Quarterly* 19.2: 19-31.

8. The letters to the editor of *India West* have been filled with such historical discussion over the past year. *Hinduism Today* (December 1994; posted on H-ASIA 28 November 1994) produced a new chronology of India which stimulated considerable Internet discussion. The push for a single ethnicity is also evident in discussions over the Aryans who are, conventionally, seen as foreign invaders. The new Hindu historiography identifies the Aryans not as Indo-Europeans but as indigenous Indians who carry culture and language to Europe; this revisionism is the goal of the American Institute of Vedic Studies. See '400 at YUVA Spring Conference' in *India Abroad*, 6 June 1994.

9. Pandey, Gyanendra. 1994. 'The New Hindu History'. *South Asia, Special Issue: After Ayodhya*, 17: 97-112.

10. As I ready this talk for publication, a reporter on National Public Radio's 'All Things Considered' asks a historian to comment on President Clinton's statement that Bosnia-Serb hostilities represent 'intractable' differences going back some 'nine hundred years'—the same kind of essentialist continuities so familiar from the narratives of Indian history. The historian scoffed at the nine hundred years, dismissed the comment as 'nonsense', suggested that events of World War II were the relevant time frame for the current hostilities, and attributed this false historicism to looking for an excuse for inaction (19 July 1995).

11. Metcalf, Thomas R. 1994. *Ideologies of the Raj. New Cambridge History of India*, III, 4, pp. 138-44. Cambridge: Cambridge University Press.

12. Chatterjee, Partha. 1993. *The Nation and its Fragments: Colonial and Postcolonial Histories*, p. 101. Princeton: Princeton University press.

13. Pandey, Gyanendra. 1990. *The Colonial Construction of Communalism in Colonial North India*. New Delhi: Oxford University Press.

14. Davis, Richard H. 1994. 'Somnath Reconstructed: Tracing a Communalised History'. Paper delivered at the 46th Annual Meeting of the Association for Asian Studies, 25 March, Boston [See also Richard H. Davis, *Lives of Indian Images*, Princeton].

15. Hardy, Peter. 1972. *The Muslims of British India*, p. x. Cambridge: Cambridge University Press.

16. Chakrabarty, Dipesh. 1994. 'Modernity and Ethnicity in India'. *South Asia, Special Issue: After Ayodhya* 17: 143–56, Cohn, Bernard S. 1987. 'The Census, Social Structure and Objectification in South Asia'. In *An Anthropologist among the Historians and Other Essays*, pp. 224–56. New Delhi: Oxford University Press; Fox, Richard. 1985. *Lions of the Punjab: Culture in the Making*. Berkeley: University of California Press; Lelyveld, David. 1978. *Aligarh's First Generation: Muslim Solidarity in British India*, chap. 2. Princeton: Princeton University Press.

17. Freitag, Sandria B. 1989. *Collective Action and Community: Public Arenas and the Emergence of Communalism in North India*. Berkeley: University of California Press.

18. Chandra, Sudhir. 1992. *The Oppressive Present: Literature and Social Consciousness in Colonial India*. New Delhi: Oxford University Press.

19. Rudolph, Susanne. 1995. 'Now You See Them, Now You Don't: Historicizing the Salience of Religious Categories'. Paper delivered at conference on Religious Forces in the New World (Dis)Order, 23–5 February, Interdisciplinary Humanities Center, University of California, Santa Barbara.

20. Kaviraj, Sudipta. 1992. 'The Imaginary Institution of India'. In *Subaltern Studies* VII, edited by Partha Chatterjee and Gyanendra Pandey. New Delhi: Oxford University Press; and Chakrabarty, Dipesh. 1994. 'Modernity and Ethnicity', p. 154.

21. Ludden, David. 1994. 'History Outside Civilisation and the Mobility of South Asia'. *South Asia* 17.1: 1–23.

22. Van der Veer, Peter. 1994. *Religious Nationalism: Hindus and Muslims in India*, p. xiv. Berkeley: University of California Press.

23. Huntington, Samuel P. 1993. 'The Clash of Civilizations?', *Foreign Affairs* (June): 22–49.

24. Naipaul, V. S. 1981. *Among the Believers: An Islamic Journey*. London: A. Deutsch.

25. Said, Edward. 1978. *Orientalism*. New York: Pantheon.

26. On the issue of the neglect of Islamic issues in Southeast Asia, see the review essay by Roff, William R. 1985. 'Islam Obscured? Some Reflections on Studies of Islam and Society in Southeast Asia', *Archipel* 29: 7–34. The Joint Committee on the Comparative Study of Muslim Societies of the Social Science Research Council and the American Council on Learned Societies, which worked for about a decade beginning in the early 1980s, took as one of its premises the importance of studying Islamic issues not exclusively in the Middle East but across Muslim societies generally. Among relevant publications are Metcalf, Barbara D., ed. 1982. *Moral Conduct and Authority: The Place of Adab in South Asian Islam*. Berkeley: University of California Press; Roff, William R. and Dale F. Eickelman, eds. 1987. *Islam and the Political Economy of Meaning: Comparative Studies of Muslim Discourse*.

London and Berkeley: University of California Press; and Eickelman, Dale F. and James Piscatori, eds. 1990. *Muslim Travellers: Pilgrimage, Migration and the Religious Imagination*. London: Routledge and Berkeley: University of California Press.

27. Masud, M. Khalid. 1984. '*Adab al-Mufti*: The Muslim Understanding of Values, Characteristics, and Role of a *Mufti*'. In Metcalf Barbara Daly, ed., *Moral Conduct and Authority: The Place of Adab in South Asian Islam*, pp. 124–51. Berkeley: University of California Press. He persuasively argues that misapprehension in part derives from mapping the colonial bureaucracy onto the Mughal. Thus the *mufti* who gives pronouncements on religio-legal guidance was not part of a hierarchy offering binding judgments as often depicted but individuals, sometimes with state patronage, offering advice.

28. Eaton, Richard. 1994. 'Indo-Muslim State Formation, Temple Descecration, and the Historiography of the Holy Warrior'. Paper delivered at the 46th Annual Meeting of the Association for Asian Studies, 25 March, Boston. Thus, Richard Eaton notes, Ibn Battuta, the great traveller of the fourteenth century, described someone with no reference to his military feats as a fighter on the Islamic frontier (a *ghazi*); that quality was imputed to him only in later panegyrics. Similarly, in the defeat of Vijayanagar in 1556, the Qutb Shahi ruler himself claimed that he established a mosque on the remains of a temple. Yet inscriptions show that five years later that same Qutb Shahi was granting villages to support the same temple. [See also *Frontline*, 17, 25 and 17, 26 (2001–2)]. See Talbot, Cynthia. 1994. 'From Mleccha to Asvapati: Representations of Muslims in Medieval Andhra'. Paper delivered at the 46th Annual Meeting of the Association for Asian Studies, 25 March, Boston. [See also *Comparative Studies in Society and History*, 37, 4 (1995), 692–722].

29. Hardy, Peter. 1984. 'Didactic Historical Writing in Indian Islam'. In *Islam in Asia*, Vol. 1, pp. 38–59. Jerusalem: The Magnus Press.

30. This argument is persuasively made in a study of the Rajput *mansabdar* of Aurangzeb, Bhimsen done by Richards, J. F. 1984. 'Norms of Comportment among Imperial Mughal Officers'. In Metcalf Barbara Daly, ed., *Moral Conduct and Authority: The Place of Adab in South Asian Islam*, pp. 255–89. Berkeley: University of California Press.

31. Marshall Hodgson's use of such neologisms as 'Islamicate' or Persianate' signalled this issue very well but never caught on Hodgson, Marshall G. S. 1974. *The Venture of Islam: Conscience and History in a World Civilization*. Chicago: University of Chicago Press.

32. Wagoner, Philip B. 1994. 'Understanding Islam at Vijayanagara'. Paper delivered at the 46th Annual Meeting of the Association for Asian Studies, 25 March, Boston.

33. Talbot, Cynthia, op. cit.

34. A lively debate ensued at the 1994 Boston meeting on this subject. Lloyd Rudolph noted that Aurangzeb, painted as the great destroyer of Hindu temples in the received historiography, in fact built far more temples than he destroyed.

C. M. Naim pointed out that rival Muslim powers destroyed the ritual centres of their opponents, for example, the Mughals destroyed the gate to the Jami' Mosque of the Sharqi dynasty in Jaunpur. Richard Eaton's paper described Shaivite sacking of Jain temples. Eleanor Zelliott suggested that Hindus tended only to take over images of rivals while Muslims destroyed them.

35. Ahmad, Imtiaz, ed. 1981. *Ritual and Religion among Muslims in India*. New Delhi: Manohar; Mujeeb, M. 1967. *The Indian Muslims*. London: Allen and Unwin.

36. Hardy, Peter. 1972. *The Muslims of British India*, pp. 1–2.

37. Eaton, Richard M. 1993. *The Rise of Islam and the Bengal Frontier, 1204–1760*. Berkeley: University of California Press.

38. Ahmed, Rafiuddin. 1981. *The Bengal Muslims, 1871–1906: A Quest for Identity*. New York: Oxford University Press.

39. The other source of the Muslim population is sometimes alleged to be descent from invaders or settlers, an origin indicated by the claim to status as 'saiyyid' or 'shaikh'. Even if dismissed as ahistorical, does this claim indicate a sense of 'foreignness', as is sometimes alleged? The meaning and import no doubt shifted in different contexts, but one hypothesis surely might be that the significance had about as much geopolitical import as did the Rajput claim to descent from the Sun or the Moon.

40. The fluidity of the earlier systems, and the multi-strandedness of identities, should give pause to those who, ignoring the power of the modern nation state, have proposed a revival of Ottoman style self regulating *millets* as the solution to India's current social dilemmas, at considerable cost, however, to individual choice.

41. Compare the arrangement of artifacts in the Freer Gallery in Washington, DC, where in a recent installation, the South Asian gallery was divided into a Muslim and a basically Hindu half. Thus the great courtier 'Abdu'r-Rahim Khan-i Khanan would have found his pen case in the Muslim half, the painting he patronized of the Ramayana hung not with other miniatures of love and separation, but across the boundary in the 'Hindu' half.

42. Asher, Catherine B. 1992. Architecture of Mughal India. *New Cambridge History of India* 1, 4. Cambridge: Cambridge University Press; Metcalf, Thomas R. 1989. *An Imperial Vision: Indian Architecture and Britain's Raj*. Berkeley: University of California Press.

43. Wagoner, Philip B. 1995. 'Sultan of Hindu Kings: Court Dress and the Islamicization of Hindu Culture at Vijayanagara'. Paper delivered at conference on Shaping Indo-Muslim Identity in Pre-modern India,' 20–23 April. Triangle South Asia Consortium, Duke University.

44. Brown, Peter. 1981. *The Cult of the Saints: Its Rise and Function in Latin Christianity*. Chicago: University of Chicago Press.

45. Beach, Milo Cleveland. 1981. *The Imperial Image: Paintings for the Mughal Court*, p. 124. Washington, DC: Freer Gallery of Art, Smithsonian Institution; Okada; Amina. 1992. *Indian Miniatures of the Mughal Court*,

pp. 125–36. New York: H. N. Abrams; Welch, Stuart Cary. 1978. *Imperial Mughal Painting*, pp. 46–7. New York: George Brazilier.

46. Behl, Aditya. 1995. 'The Landscape of Paradise: Malik Muhammad Jayasi and the Embodied City'. Paper delivered to the Ninth Annual South Asia Conference, University of California, Berkeley, 5 March.

47. Ahmad, Aziz. 1963. 'Epic and Counter-Epic in Medieval India'. *Journal of the American Oriental Society* 83. 4: 470–6.

48. Davis, op. cit.; Behl, op. cit.

49. Ahmad, op. cit., pp. 475–6.

50. Behl, op. cit., p. 6.

51. Chakrabarty, Dipesh. 1994, op. cit.

52. Bal Thakeray, leader of the Shiv Sena, is quoted, speaking of Muslims, that if Muslims 'behaved like Jews in Nazi Germany', there would be 'nothing wrong if they were treated as Jews were in Germany'. Sen, Amartya. 1993. 'The Threats to Secular India'. *New York Review of Books* (8 April): 26–32. See also, Kulke, Herman and Dietmar Rothermund. 1986. *A History of India*. Totowa, NJ: Barnes and Noble, a widely used text: 'Like Shylock in *The Merchant of Venice*, Mohammad Ali Jinnah had asked for his pound of flesh.'

53. An especially significant contribution, widely reprinted, was a collective statement by a number of historians at Jawaharlal Nehru University. See Gopal, S., Romilla Thapar, and Bipin Chandra. 1989. 'The Political Abuse of History'. New Delhi: Centre for Historical Studies, Jawaharlal Nehru University.

54. Thus K. R. Malkani: 'Perhaps these ideas about Rama, and his birthplace, are just concepts. It is possible that Rama never existed. The birthplace of Rama reflects the dreams, hopes, and values of Hindus. To the average Hindu, Rama very much existed and Ayodhya is his birthplace. That is what matters', in Sen, Amartya. 1992. 'Storm over Ayodhya'. *New York Review of Books* (14 May): 37–9.

55. Similarly, the inscription at the entrance of the mosque implicitly stressed the insignificance of any worldly building, built after all, 'in the name of that One who'—note the non-sectarian terminology—had created all the worlds and was himself beyond place (*la makani*), and with praise of the 'joy of the prophets of both worlds (*do jahani*)', this world and the next. This building in contrast was merely 'a home in this world' (*khana dar jahan*) in the time of Babar, the *qalander*, not a conqueror or marauder, but a mendicant man of God, who knew good fortune (for the Persian text, though without translation, see Srivastava, Sushil. 1991. *The Disputed Mosque: A Historical Inquiry*. New Delhi: Vistaar Publications).

56. Van der Veer, Peter. 1994. op. cit.

57. Verma, G. L. 1991. *Conversion of Hindu Temples (1000–1800 AD)*. Delhi: Shabad Prakashan.

58. Tilly, Louise. 1994. 'Connections'. *American Historical Review* (February): 1–20.

59. Ghosh, Amitav. 1993. *In an Antique Land*. New York: A. A. Knopf; and Ludden, David. 1994. op. cit.

60. Dale, Stephen Frederick. 1994. *Indian Merchants and Eurasian Trade, 1600–1750*. Cambridge: Cambridge University Press.

61. Khalidi, Rashid. 1995. 'Is There a Future for Middle East Studies?' (1994 MESA Presidential Address). *Middle East Studies Association Bulletin* 29.1: 1–6.

62. Susan Bayly's study of south Indian Christians and Muslims. Bayly, Susan. 1989. *Saints, Goddesses and Kings: Muslims and Christians in South Indian Society*. Cambridge: Cambridge University Press; Ritu Menon's work on abducted women during Partition; and Paula Richman's on Tamil Muslim poetry are outstanding examples of such inclusive work.

# 9

## The Case of Pakistan

In any consideration of nationalism and, in particular, any consideration of the relation between religion and nationalism, the case
of Pakistan is one of great fascination. Here the symbols of
nationalism do not simply have features analogous to the symbols
of religious mythology but are themselves meant to be part of a
religious structure of meaning. Moreover, Pakistan stretches the
classical definition of nationalism set out by Professor Smart to the
extreme of its limits.[1] Third World countries in general, shaped by
the arbitrary boundaries of colonial rule, fit this definition uneasily
at best, their origins often at conflict with ethnic realities. Pakistan
at its birth defied virtually every criterion of nationhood. Its
territory, far from contiguous, was separated into two segments
divided by a thousand miles of alien territory. Its international
border segmented two core regions of the subcontinent, the Punjab
in the West and Bengal in the East, each united by custom and
language and ethnic pride. The case of Bengal was particularly
striking, for it had long been known as an area marked by regional
consciousness and common language, a region whose Hindu and
Muslim population both seemed to have the potential hallmarks
of a modern nation. As for a cherished history shared throughout
the area, much of the population had been unaffected by the
historical interpretation and present policy that the leaders of the
Pakistan movement, themselves from elsewhere in the subcontinent, had finally seen triumph. As for language, it was the mother
tongue of these leaders, Urdu, that was initially set up with English
to be the official language of the new state. Urdu was the first

tongue of a mere 4 per cent of the population; English was the second language of only a handful.

The short history of Pakistan is also absorbing to the Western scholar for the haunting resemblances it bears to that of the other post-war state based on religious nationalism, that of Israel. The size of the two countries is certainly not analogous, nor is the fact that, from a Third World perspective, Pakistan represents a resurgence against colonialism, while Israel is held to be one of the last gasps of European domination of a Third World area. Yet both shared at their inception a vision of themselves as a refuge and a homeland for the persecuted, while tragically and ironically finding themselves subsequently the oppressor of Arabs and Bengalis, respectively. Both were opposed by substantial numbers of their religious leadership who held aloof from the secular goals of the political leadership and even from the concept of a nation.[2] Both countries have groped for self-justification, shifting in their ideological formulations between what in the South Asian case is called communal interests on the one side—the preservation of the lives, interests, and culture of a community—and religious on the other—the creation of a utopian society on religious principles. Both, indeed, have cherished the vision, now tarnished for both, as countries militarily impregnable on the outside and justly and humanely ordered within.[3] Both finally bear, along with Ireland, the heritage of British control that by its idiom of rule and its deliberate policy, exacerbated in all three cases the divisions that have given these areas their shape.

The creation of Pakistan, the movements in its favour, the pressures that in the end seemed to necessitate it, all this together forms a complex story. The role of the British, who had ruled the areas that came to make up the new country as part of the Indian Empire for between a hundred to one hundred and fifty years, was of course central, both because their policies in education, justice, and politics encouraged religious identity and because the social and economic changes that came in the train of imperial rule fostered new forms of horizontal loyalty. In 1947, the British, weary of war and of an increasingly aggressive nationalist movement, justified their transfer of power to two sovereign nations on the grounds that the Hindus and the Muslims were in fact two separate nations defined in religious terms. The focus of this brief essay is not to examine the legitimacy of that claim or the process that made it necessary, but rather the situation afterward when Pakistan found itself in existence.[4] For that, history is only relevant for the construction it is given in the present.

Pakistan has had not only to come to terms with its history but with two of the great tragedies of the twentieth century. The first, 1947, when the country was born in chaos and bloodshed, with a terrified migration of Hindus and Sikhs toward India and Muslims toward Pakistan. Perhaps ten million people moved; an estimated one million died. Barely twenty-five years later, faced with demands for autonomy from Bengal, the central, West Pakistani-dominated government, joined battle with the East. Ten million refugees fled to India, Bengalis were brutally massacred, the Indian army moved in, and Pakistan was humiliated by the capture of 100,000 of its soldiers. Pakistan was reduced to its Western provinces, its claim to be a Muslim homeland undercut by its reduction to the third largest Muslim population of the subcontinent, following those of the new nation of Bangladesh and that of India itself.

Against such an origin and such a history, it is not surprising that Pakistanis have been absorbed in self-justification and that the country has produced a rich variety of nationalist interpretations. The feature celebrated throughout—to use Professor Smart's term—has been Islam. To say this, however, is only to begin, for the socio-political and even spiritual implications of Islamic interpretations have varied substantially. Virtually every political figure has made his proposals in an Islamic framework. Secondly, every figure has implicitly or explicitly set his interpretations in an international context. In the first two decades, which in terms of nationalist symbols forms the first period, that context was opposition to and distinction from India. In the decade of the 1970s after Bangladesh, the second period, the context has been identification with the countries of the Middle East. The passionate, self-conscious identification of Pakistanis with Islam is notable even to other Muslims.

Is it possible to distinguish patterns in the various Islamic ideologies that have been expounded? Much as opponents may do it, one can certainly not distinguish between some authentic statement of Islam on the one hand and the opportunistic use of Islam on the other. One distinction, alluded to as significant in Israel as well, is that between the more communal emphasis on the one hand and the more radically religious on the other. The first has primarily stressed the interests of the Muslim community and the protection of its culture. It has passionately embraced the glories of the high period of Muslim culture and determined to make Muslims powerful again. It has even been called secular. It has often looked to the West, not only for technology but for the radical disjuncture of domains, so that such areas as economics are guided by principles apart from religion. In this sense it is modern; in the context of the subcontinent, it is associated with the 'Aligarh perspective'. Listen to a young Pakistani student speaking at the University of Southern California in April 1948:

I only want to tell you of the Islam that was the burning light of yesterday, the ember that it is today, and the celestial flame of tomorrow, for that is how I envisage the future of Islam. I must also tell you that religiously speaking, I am not a devout Muslim. I do not say my prayers regularly, I do not keep all the fasts, I have not yet been on a pilgrimage to Mecca. Therefore religiously speaking, I am a poor Muslim. However, my interest is soaked in the political, economic, and cultural heritage of Islam.

This was Zulfikar Ali Bhutto, then a student at Berkeley, rejoicing in the creation of Pakistan and looking ahead to a confederation of Muslim peoples.[5] He defined religion in terms of personal piety and the power and protection of Muslim peoples, not as a guide to social and political life. Generally speaking, this 'communal' position has been socially conservative and has been identified with the preservation of vested interests of landowners, businessmen, the army, and politicians. It has dominated Islamic ideology throughout most of the history of Pakistan.

The more radically religious interpretation of Islam looks less to the glorious peaks of Muslim civilization for its inspiration than to the pristine revelation of the Prophet itself. It sees in it social revolution, the overthrow of the oppressive exploitative powers, the end of the contempt and pride of the rich in favour of egalitarian and human social principles. This ideology was a secondary stream in the Pakistan movement, associated with the urban Punjabi movements of the 1930s, notably the Ahrar, and with the grassroots Muslim League support in Bengal organized by Abu'l-Hashim.[6] The radical interpretation was also present in the beloved poetry of Iqbal, a side of him recited but rarely heard. It emerged again in the ideology of the PPP, the Pakistan People's Party, led by no one less than the same Bhutto, whose party, in the wake of skewed economic development and disruptive social change, in the late 1960s embraced a platform of what was called 'Islamic socialism'. It is significant that even at its inception Pakistan was not merely a sanctuary for Muslim landed, merchant, and professional groups in search of their own interests but also was a focus for radical social aspirations, a vision that has had the potential of periodic reassertion.[7]

Keeping in mind that all is set in an Islamic framework, one can distinguish three strands in Pakistani nationalism in the first period. The first represented espousal of the European model of the elements that make up a state, known of course through British example and education. The second, whose form derived from the nature of great power relations and general post-war concerns in the new states, emphasized the symbols and realities of modern technological development, coupled closely in this case with a high valuation of law and order. The third, itself consisting of complex parts, concerned the attempt to shape a cultural consensus through a commonly understood history, a current destiny, and a cultural heritage, summed up above all by the place of the respective languages of diverse populations. Here, as in the second period discussed below, one is struck by the extent to which these symbols do not evolve autonomously, but in the context of a highly integrated world economy and of political rivalries and involvements of the more developed nations.

In the post-colonial states in general, the leaders of the newly liberated states had wholly assimilated the requisites of a state on the European model. A capital, a flag, an anthem, a constitution, parties and elective bodies, army, and bureaucracy were all to be acquired. Jinnah, the nation's founder, indeed took pride in being more cosmopolitan, more constitutionalist, than Gandhi.[8] Pakistan comprised the corners of a previously united polity and initially operated out of provincial offices, but rapidly set about to create the hallmarks of an independent state. Its new capital, set in the beautiful, rolling Margalla foothills of the Himalayas, was to be Islamabad, 'the abode of Islam', its simple and elegant white buildings the work of a Philadelphia architectural firm—a mix of Muslim identity and technical expertise that was perhaps the heart of the ideal of the early leaders. The pride in the institutions of the country was the greater since they seemed to appear from nothing.

The European model of how to create a country is clear in a book that most Pakistanis would have considered eccentric throughout, *Pakistan: The Fatherland of the Pak Nation*, by Choudhary Rahmat Ali.[9] First printed in 1935, it was reprinted in several editions. Rahmat Ali is best known for his coining of the acronym that was to be name of the new country—symbol of a nation par excellence—while a young student in London in the early 1930s.[10] He subsequently committed himself to propaganda in favour of the creation of a number of Muslim homelands throughout the subcontinent with the vision of ultimately winning the whole subcontinent to Islam. How does one control an area? In part, as Edward Said has recently argued for European colonialists, by knowledge, and by presumed mastery of the culture and terrain of an area.[11] Rahmat Ali set out to do the same by cataloguing every detail of the area he hoped to be Muslim: frontiers, coastline, and islands; physical features and climate; flora, fauna, and forests; agriculture and minerals; industry, commerce, and communications. He surveyed the human geography as well—'Provinces, States, Enclaves, and Notable Places' with attention to history and archaeology. He discussed the people, as had the colonial bureaucrats before him, on the basis of racial and ethnic stock. He described and tried to shape the symbols of the nation: faith, flag, calendar, festivals, language (Urdu), laws, 'code of honour', and 'courtesy titles'. He summarized a 'National Story' and (in the third edition) what he saw as betrayal at the time of Partition.

That Pakistan was to have the shape of a nation state in the far reduced area that was to be its, was, in a sense, taken for granted. The ideals of the new state were somewhat less so. If, however, a central vision of the leadership was to be elicited from the early period of the country's history, particularly from the late 1950s to the late 1960s, it would be the celebration of technological and economic development. It was this, rather than any cultural or immediately human concerns, that dominated the actions and goals of the leadership. A corollary to this, in part the legacy of the imperial state that had nurtured them, was an overriding concern with law and order and an impatience with political activities. To be sure, the base for democratic political activities was very weak: a heterogeneous area, much of it never integrated into even the limited political institutions created by the Raj, and no coherent and long-lived political organization like the Indian National

Congress to be a force for stability. The very powerful bureaucracy and the army together grew impatient with the faction ridden, landlord dominated political institutions unsympathetic to central authority and economic change. On 7 October 1958, the army and the president assumed military rule. The subsequent mixture of an emphasis on stability and modernization was helped by the international political alignments of the period, above all by the congeniality found between American political leaders and Pakistani bureaucrats and generals. The Americans, dubious of India's non-alignment and mystified by her culture, found, as had the British before them, the sturdy Muslims of the Northwest far more to their liking.

Helped not only by American foreign policy but by American scholars, Ayub Khan, the Chief Martial Law Administrator and President, joined by generals and elite civil servants, embraced a theory of development that urged rapid growth with no concern whatsoever for distribution either among the regions or the classes. Rapid growth overall was to make the entire pie larger so that all would benefit. This was classic modern Western economic theory, in which economics was wholly divorced from moral considerations and seen instead as subject to its own laws. Mysteriously, the whole enterprise would conduce to the good. The oft-quoted title of a work by one of the American economists summed up the short term implications: 'The Social Utility of Greed'.[12] The result of course was growth, but skewed so much that one could speak of the 'twenty-two families' that controlled virtually all of industry, insurance, and banking. As the civil war was to make clear, there was not only inequality but inequality increasing at an accelerated rate.[13] Ayub Khan, as military dictator from 1958 to 1968, explicitly made economic growth the basis for national unity. He was not unaware of regional disparities and sought to redress them, but his efforts were too few and his political base too exclusive. The very symbolic weight put on development made its failures the greater. An East Pakistani intellectual made the point: 'The elevation of economic goals to the level of symbolic and transcendental ends...*created* conflicts concerning solidarity and identity'.[14]

Although opponents at the time and historians later have criticized Ayub for using Islam as a veneer to protect vested interests and justify authoritarian rule, such a conclusion is only circumstantial. Personally pious and known to rely on the *pir* (spiritual leadership) of Golra Sharif,[15] Ayub justified his system as serving the interests of Muslims and of Islam. His Islam was thus modernist in the sense of not providing a blueprint or guide to policies or actions but by being the ultimate interest served by the policies followed. This had an appeal. But the contradictions of this style of Islamic emphasis, and the scepticism it produced in many, were felt by Ayub himself. He spoke of the urgent need to find a concept to 'weld the people into unity...an answer which is comprehensive, tangible, arouses spontaneous and consistent enthusiasm, and is workable in the light of the requirements of modern life....I have not been able to find an effective answer so far'.[16] Nor would he in the whole of his rule.

The nationalist rhetoric of the regime focused on what we have called Islam in its communal sense: the place of Pakistan as a homeland and a refuge and as a guarantor of the rights of some fifty million Muslims in India. It was fuelled by the continuing sense of being mistreated and misunderstood, above all over the issue of Kashmir. The present plight was made the more poignant by the creation of a Pakistani historiography that read back into the past the self-conscious religious identity of the present: found heroes in the military conquerors and proponents of legalist, uneclectic Islam; and generally painted a picture of a glory that was to be reclaimed. The anger channelled against India and the pride in a Muslim state were expressed in the 1965 war, a defeat both to the hopes of seizing Kashmir and to the belief in military might.

The religious style espoused by the state lacked coherence and popular support. The treatment of Islam by the elite had two significant elements. One was its modernist orientation; the other, more implicit, was its contempt for regional expressions of Islam, a corollary of its economic and governmental policies. The influence of the religious leadership in these formulations and on the government in general was always peripheral. Its strength was felt in the Punjab disturbances of 1953, an outburst of the always simmering antagonism felt toward the highly cohesive and upwardly mobile sect of the Ahmadiyyah. But the involvement of the 'ulama on that occasion and the subsequent judgment of the commission of inquiry that the religious leadership was ignorant even of its own texts, increased the impatience of the elite with the 'traditionalists'. Nonetheless the pressure of the 'ulama was sufficient to bring about a statement in the Constitution of 1956 that no laws would be enacted repugnant to Islam as laid down in the Qur'an and *sunnah* and that existing laws would be revised in conformity with Islam. A commission was to be appointed to carry out these provisions. As a constitutional authority dryly noted, 'Nothing effective appears to have been accomplished in the exercise of these functions'.[17] After the military coup, the new constitution of 1962 continued the repugnancy clause, but deleted the reference to *sunnah*, which was viewed as an effort to introduce modernist reforms and subsequently amended. More significant was the provision that the effective implementation of this principle was assigned to an Advisory Council on Islamic Ideology whose members, appointed by the President, not only were to be scholars of Islam but experts on the 'economic, legal and administrative problems of Pakistan'.[18] This ensured a modernist interpretation of Islam.

For those of the elite committed to Western-style state and technological advancement, religion was to be modern too. True Islam was understood primarily as personal piety; when it intruded on socio-economic issues, it did so in conformity with Western standards of practice and interpretation. One of the most distinguished advisors to the government, Professor Fazlur Rahman, in retrospect, suggests Ayub Khan's instrumental motive for even addressing the Islamic aspects of his policies: that without attention to Islam 'it might become difficult for East Pakistan and West Pakistan to stay together, for apart from their attachment to Islam, linguistically and culturally the two wings had little in common. As time went on Ayub Khan became more and more convinced of the importance of Islam as the basis of the Pakistani nationhood'.[19] In the end, the style of Islam espoused was to be more disruptive than unitive.

The interpretations offered by the advisors to the government represented a jurisprudential position that had its roots in nineteenth-century reform, one that was confirmed by the scholarship of some Western Orientalists. It denied the validity of the recorded sayings of the Prophet, a major source for the historic interpretations of the Law, and even questioned the eternity of the legal injunctions of the Qur'an. Perhaps the issue best known of those they considered was that relating to family law, for in acts passed in 1961 Pakistan moved decisively outside what were considered the legal injunctions of Islam on issues related to polygamy, divorce, and the inheritance of orphaned grandchildren. A related, equally inflammatory attempt to argue the sanction of Islam for family planning was meant to bolster the foreign aid projects of USAID and UNICEF (whose offices, moreover, were to be a focus for political support for the regime).

As well as these attempts to define the content of Islam, certain acts of the government specifically threatened the financial base of the religious leadership. Notable were central government efforts to control pious endowments and the canonical tithe, a sum of money estimated at one point to be potentially twice the income of central government revenues. The centre moreover took over such duties as the sighting of the $^{c}Id$ moon, trading romance and tradition for the scientific accuracy of the Meteorological Department.

Fazlur Rahman himself, again looking back, speculated that the attempt to interpret Islam 'in rational and scientific terms to meet the requirements of a modern progressive society', had three possible effects: the desired one of increasing the interest of the educated in serious attention to Islamic issues, or the effect of driving the educated to secularism and strengthening the 'traditionalists'.[20] It was to be the latter two that happened. A later scholar has judged that the advisors lost all credibility because of their failure to address the principles of the whole system of Islam in favour of piecemeal change based on jurisprudential radicalism, an approach which made them seem only opportunist, the tool of the ruling elite.[21]

The second element in the particular kind of Islam fostered by the regime was its rejection of regional forms of Islam. Both Khalid bin Sayeed and Nasim Jawed have argued in analyses of the separation of Bangladesh that the modernist Islam of the regime was much closer to the scripturalist and legalist Islam current in some circles in the West than to the Islam of Bengal.[22] Bengal, with a population almost one-fourth Hindu, and with a tradition of openness to Bengali literature and folkways, was deemed religiously suspect. This view of Bengali Islam was shared, in fact, not only by the elite but by the organization that most consistently opposed the Islam of the ruling class, the Jama'at-i Islami led by Maulana Abu'l Ala Maududi, a proponent of pervasive Islamicization on the presumed basis of sacred texts.

Besides Islam, the elite attempted to make certain other symbols a focus of national loyalty. Their consistent policy was to downplay the importance of the regional cultures in favour of central symbols, a policy which in retrospect could only bring opposition in such an ethnically and culturally diverse population. Pride of place was given to the elite culture of the North, a culture expressed above all in Urdu and embodied in poetry, art, music, and dance. This not only clashed with the regional languages, which had their own traditions, but also, one might note, at least in part with the puritanic values of the 'traditionalists'.

Urdu, from the late nineteenth century on, had become the symbol par excellence of Muslim communal interests in north India and fears for its place as a government language and language of education were one of the motivating forces for opposition to Congress politics. Used as an official provincial language by the British, it had undergone a literary flowering in new genres of both prose and poetry. It had, moreover, become a major vehicle for disseminating Islamic religious values, especially the tenets of a more informed Islam, as part of the reform movements of the modern period. Knowledge of Urdu defined one as a person worthy of respect, and cultivation of that form of the common language, written in Perso-Arabic script and including large numbers of Persian and Arabic loan words, increasingly defined one as a Muslim, one apart from those who used Hindi written in Devanagari. The importance of language as a symbol of group identity perhaps transcends all others.

To adopt Urdu as the national language seemed only logical. It was the mother tongue of the *muhajir* who had fled from north India and settled in cities, especially the cities in Sind, which underwent a demographic revolution as their majorities became Urdu-speaking.[23] It had as well the most developed tradition of use as a language of government and education. Not only the first language of the migrants, it was the second language of elite groups throughout the new country, among them the upper class, or *ashraf*, of Bengal. Many had attended elite institutions, in what is now India, places like Aligarh University and the theological academy at Deoband, and had mastered standard Urdu. Ayub Khan himself, from the North-West Frontier, described his own experience as a student at Aligarh, sensitive about his rough speech but soon master of a more refined diction. Such hard won accomplishment seemed the more valued.

Decisive in the relative success of Urdu as the national language was its position in Punjab, which was not only the dominant province in the west, comprising about two-thirds of the population, but, as study after study has shown, the region that controlled both the civil service and the army. Urdu had long been the language of education for all communities in the Punjab. Punjab had, moreover, its own tradition of Urdu literature, capped by the triumphs of Iqbal. Urdu was closer to Punjabi than to any other regional language, both in grammar and in a heavily overlapping vocabulary. It was already effectively the second language of most of the province.[24]

Not surprisingly, language proved to be a major source of tension both between the two wings and within the west. Before the first decade was over, Bengali language riots had, at least on paper, assured equal status for Bengali as a national language. Bengali was one of the most developed languages of the subcontinent, with a distinguished literary tradition of its own. That the giants of that tradition were mainly Hindu—and valued nonetheless by Muslim Bengalis—did not make this concession, as it was seen, the more palatable. Despite the accommodation, a legacy of bitterness remained.

The same problem of linguistic self-assertion was evident in the west. In Sind, for example, which had never had the tradition of Urdu as a second language, the new place of Urdu was particularly charged, because it was associated with the now economically dominant new settlers, whose role aroused predictable antagonism. Movements for Sindi provincial autonomy, focused on the place of language, grew as the 1960s progressed. In the Frontier and Baluchistan, the opposition to the domination of the centre was potentially more far reaching than mere demands for language reform, since both had a tradition of looking to their ethnic fellows across the Afghan border and of threatening wholesale separatism. Even in Punjab there were cultural movements in Lahore and elsewhere as early as the 1950s. Held in check by martial law, they again became prominent in the 1970s. In all the provinces proponents of the local language fostered its use by politicians, patronage of literary circles, increased publication, and demands for television broadcasting.

From 1967 civil unrest in Pakistan grew. Every symbol of the regime was called into question. The economic changes of the development policy led to a sense of gross socio-economic injustice on the part of industrial workers and others who felt excluded from adequate returns. Those who had profited, including urban professionals and rural smallholders caught up in the green revolution, felt excluded from the political process. Antagonism to India continued virulent, but Pakistani aims appeared thwarted by military failure in the 1965 war and diplomatic failure at Tashkent. The religious policy of the regime was wholly discredited. Indeed, all discontent was focused, as so often happens, on religious symbols; it was the religious leadership which became the focus for protest in urban areas. The Islamic policies in general and the writings and decisions of Fazlur Rahman in particular were major targets. In Bengal the continued insults to cultural self-esteem and the ever worsening economic disparities led to increased demands for autonomy.

The elections of 1970 saw the decisive victory of Bhutto's Pakistan People's Party in the West and Shaikh Mujibu'r-Rahman's Awami League in the East. The failure to grant Mujib the premiership he had won and to accommodate the six demands for provincial autonomy he requested resulted in the tragic civil war and the end of Pakistan as it had existed. The subsequent decade was one of substantial change in Pakistan, and, not surprisingly, of a dramatic reordering of national symbols.

The PPP, which controlled the government until 1977, was led by a cosmopolitan, personally secular figure, and focused on anti-Indian sentiments and a radical socialist rhetoric. Against India, Bhutto swore a war of a thousand years. Against the propertied and wealthy, he promised a redistribution of economic goods for the common man. Significantly, the party aligned itself with a group led by Hanif Ramay, who called themselves Islamic Socialists; the rhetoric of the party was wholly Islamic. The symbol the party chose summed up the elements of its platform. It was the carved sword or scimitar of 'Ali, the heroic grandson of the Prophet, and hence pointed simultaneously to the party's leader, who was felicitously named Zu'l-faqar. This means literally 'the cleaver of the vertebrae', the name of the sword of a slain unbeliever that passed to Muhammad and thence to 'Ali. It was thus held to be the sword of victory over one's foe and, in the hands of 'Ali, the sword of social justice.[25]

Bhutto rejected the foreign policy of his predecessors, turning dramatically away from Pakistan's long alignment with the United States and calling for bilateral rather than bloc agreements. He established close relations with China and at the same time, aided by the new-felt power of the oil producers in the early 1970s, sought to ally himself with the Muslim states of the Middle East. The web of substantial relationships with Middle Eastern countries grew, with Pakistan seeing itself as a potential source of sophisticated technical training for overseas students and, at the same time, as a seemingly bottomless reservoir of unskilled manpower for the wealthy oil states. Never losing its self-image as a military fortress, it called itself the $qila^c$ or fortress, the Eastern outpost of Islam. The highpoint of Bhutto's turning toward the Middle East came in the Islamic Summit Conference held in Lahore in 1974, when the attention of the population was riveted on the presence of such figures as King Faisal, Colonel Qaddafi, and Idi Amin. A review of Pakistan's relations with the Islamic States, published in 1977, insisted that these links were the true orientation of Pakistan, the legacy of Indian Muslim involvement in the Khilafat movement. Pakistan had been only temporarily diverted by the short-sighted policies of a misguided military regime, which led to such embarrassments as the Pakistani position on Suez:

After the confusions of the past...after the hypocritical separation of the Islamic loyalty from the Islamic imperatives of justice between people and regions which was responsible for the disaster of 1971, Pakistan has now rediscovered its Islamic identity and set its feet firmly on the path ordained for it by its everlasting faith. The path is that of promoting the brotherhood of all Muslim peoples and helping to banish divisive prejudices. It is that of participating with the fellowship of other Muslim countries, in humanity's struggle toward an equitable world order. During the last five years, Pakistan has provided proof that it will suffer no deviation from that path.[26]

Bhutto had in fact turned his back on the subcontinent. No longer was it to be the emotional other against which the country defined itself. At the end of his career, a broken man awaiting execution at the hands of the man who overthrew him, ironically perhaps yet wisely, he saw the greatest accomplishment of his whole career as nothing other than the agreement of June 1976—the restoration of diplomatic relations with India.[27]

In keeping with this, the image of Pakistan as homeland and protector of Muslims was no more. Pakistan was now to be a

Middle Eastern state, its attention toward its West and not its East. One important expression of this new orientation was the attempt to emphasize the regional continuity of Pakistan. As expressed by the distinguished archaeologist Professor A. H. Dani, it took the form of identifying a continuing Indus civilization from a Gangetic pattern. The former was the 'life-blood of Pakistan', the latter, 'the fountainhead of Hinduism'.

Punjabi and Sindhi are part of the Indus system as also are Pashtu and Baluch (i.e. the four provincial languages). Hence all the symbols—whether language, music, dance, decorations, arts and crafts, clothes or dress, pottery and food habits, behaviour patterns, etc.—associated with them belong to Pakistan.... Islam has imbibed the ethno-cultural elements of this land.[28]

Gone were the emphasis on a separate political identity of Muslims throughout Indian history, the attempts of the majority to deny Muslims their culture, and the need for a separate homeland; in its place was the acceptance of a territorially defined nationality. Dani's interpretation is the more significant as an attempt to argue a fundamental union and coherence to what remained of Pakistan, itself internally divided by ethnic loyalties. Regional tensions in fact increased as Bhutto continued the policy of extreme centralization.

For both economic and political reasons Bhutto sought to eliminate all intermediaries between the central government and the people—provincial authorities, tribal chiefs, landlords, powerful industrialists, Sufi pirs. The so-called twenty-two families were to be broken up. Government moved to take over the cotton, insurance, banking, and rice industries. Land reforms were passed in 1972 and 1976 to make real the election slogan, 'land to the tillers'. The powerful shrines—in a coupling of scripturalist reform and political interest—were to be controlled by government officials and the potentially charismatic scions of the saintly families were to be mere caretakers.[29] The ideals of the party soon gave way to deals with bureaucrats, landlords, and the old industrial elite. The result was the same: economic grievances, now fuelled by inflation, public protest, and virtual civil war in the provinces, this time in Baluchistan.

The military coup of Zia'u'l-Haqq on 5 June 1977 was seen as an attempt to restore law and order and, increasingly, as the vanguard of an even more self-consciously Muslim state. Supported by the Jama'at, Zia moved simultaneously to bolster his own position and to implement certain Islamic measures: criminal penalties, special court benches to review very limited segments of law, and government collection of the tithe.[30] As before, Islam was the ideology of vested economic and political interests. It continues to impose a narrow definition of Islam, this time fundamentalist. Pressure in this direction was evident even before the coup in the anti-Ahmadiyyah riots of 1974, which were followed by an unprecedented act in Muslim history: a government declared a sect to be un-Muslim. Women protested against actions that controlled them. Civil protests were raised by a growing Shi'a population against measures they deemed acceptable only to Sunni Islam.[31] The Islamic symbols of the regime, while clearly salient to those associated with and sympathetic to the Jama'at, had little appeal to the sectarian minorities or to those, whether motivated by Islam or by secular ideologies, who were committed to a humane reordering of society. Other symbols of national identity were anti-Americanism, evident in the seizure of the embassy in Islamabad in November 1979, and a decreased role for English as a medium of elite education, coupled with a concern for economic and military power of their own epitomized in the development of a controversial nuclear reactor.

One is tempted to argue that the short history of Pakistan has seen an increasing convergence of 'religious myth and nationalism', but such a conclusion is probably unwarranted. There has not been a 'rebirth' of Islam in Pakistan. A passionate attachment to a Muslim identity has been constant in Pakistan's self-image and in the rhetoric of its politicians. The content given that identity has shifted, particularly in its 'charged story', moving from one that emphasized its subcontinental role as a homeland for the persecuted to one that stressed its geographic place with other Muslim states. At the same time, the interpretation of Islam fostered by the state changed from one that sought to be 'rational and scientific' to one that stressed adherence to what could, cynically but legitimately, be called the cosmetic and highly visible symbols of Islam—for example, certain public punishments and the prohibition of alcohol. Only fleetingly have there been spokesmen for radical Islam who have challenged vested interests and the status quo. The changes in the symbols of national unity have been related above all to shifting international currents. In the first phase, the rivalry of the Americans and the Soviets in the subcontinent led Pakistan to throw in its lot with the Americans, politically, economically, and even ideologically. In the second phase, after Bangladesh, the hegemony of India in the subcontinent led Pakistan to turn away from it as a focus of political activity, and to forge ties to the newly assertive countries of the Middle East. Nationalist symbols have not evolved autonomously. Throughout this, the most central of these symbols for most Pakistanis has been Muslim identity, whether defined primarily as a push away from India or a pull toward the countries of the Middle East. That that symbol is sufficient to sustain Pakistan as it is currently structured is a matter of considerable doubt. Judging from the past, one might argue that de-emphasis on a highly centralized state and its symbols would in fact contribute to the state's coherence. One might further venture that the territorial emphasis (rather than an emphasis on a Muslim homeland) is a promising one, particularly if it leads to an appreciation of Pakistani ties to and common interests with India.

Pakistan, a new nation, has borne the heavy burden of a troubled origin, an intractable ethnic and geographic diversity, and a vulnerable international position, both politically and economically. Its nationalist symbols have often proven incapable of sustaining the loyalty of its people. Its very survival, however, and that it does now have a past and some ideological ferment, do mean that Pakistanis continue to hope that their potential—for it was that and not any existing condition that justified their nation's creation—may yet be realized.

## Notes

1. Smart, Ninian. 1983. 'Religion, Myth and Nationalism'. In Merkl, Peter H. and Ninian Smart, eds. *Religion and Politics in the Modern World*, pp. 15–28. New York: New York University Press.

2. See Friedmann, Yohanan. 1971. 'The Attitude of the Jam'iyyat-i 'Ulama'-i Hind to the Indian National Movement and the Establishment of Pakistan'. In Baer, Gabriel, ed. *The 'Ulama' in Modern History*, pp. 157–83. Jerusalem.

3. Binder, Leonard. 1972. 'Prospects for Pakistan', p. 14. University of Chicago, Muslim Studies Sub-committee Occasional Paper Series.

4. For an excellent account of this history, see Hardy, P. 1972. *The Muslims of British India*. Cambridge.

5. Reprinted in *Pakistan Economist*. 1974. February 16–22, pp. 1–7.

6. Sayeed, K. B. May 1972. 'The Breakdown of Pakistan's Political System', p. 3. Paper delivered at the University of Toronto.

7. Jones, P. n.d. 'Islam and Politics under Ayub and Bhutto: A Comparative Assessment', pp. 5–6. Paper delivered at the Seventh Wisconsin Conference on South Asia.

8. Ziring, Lawrence. 1979. 'The Phases of Pakistan's Political History'. In Naim, C. M., ed. *Iqbal, Jinnah and Pakistan: The Vision and the Reality*, p. 147. Syracuse.

9. Rahmat Ali, Choudhary. 1947. 3rd edn. *Pakistan: The Fatherland of the Pak Nation*. Cambridge.

10. The initial letters of Punjab, Afghanistan, Kashmir, and Sind, joined to the prefix *stan*, place of. The name also has meaning in that the word *pak* means pure.

11. Said, Edward. 1978. *Orientalism*. New York.

12. Papanek, Gustav F. 1967. *Pakistan's Development: Social Goals and Private Incentives*, p. 242. Cambridge.

13. Sayeed, 'The Breakdown of Pakistan's Political System', p. 29.

14. Mujahid, Sharif al. 1974. 'The Ideology is Still Supreme', *The Pakistan Times*, March 23. Emphasis added.

15. Jones, 'Islam and Politics under Ayub and Bhutto', p. 9.

16. Quoted in Russell, Ralph. 1967. 'Islam: Culture and Society in Pakistan Today'. Unpublished manuscript. [See also his *How not to Write the History of Urdu Literature* (1999).]

17. Gledhill, A. 'Dustur', *Encyclopedia of Islam*, 2nd edn, p. 670.

18. Gledhill, 'Dustur', p. 672.

19. Rahman, Fazlur. 1972. 'Some Islamic Issues in the Ayyub Khan Era', p. 2. University of Chicago, Muslim Studies Sub-committee Occasional Paper Series.

20. Rahman, Fazlur. 'Some Islamic Issues', pp. 3, 19–20.

21. Masud, M. Khalid. 1979. 'Failure of Islamic Reformism in Pakistan'. Unpublished manuscript.

22. Sayeed, Khalid bin. 1972. 'The Breakdown of Pakistan's Political System'; Jawed, Nasim A., 'Nationalism and Islamic Consciousness in Pakistan and Bangladesh'. University of Chicago, Muslim Studies Sub-committee Occasional Paper Series. [See also his *Islam's Political Culture: Religion and Politics in Pre-divided Pakistan* (1999).]

23. The immigrants who were not originally Urdu-speaking and who came to Sind tended to learn Urdu rather than Sindhi.

24. See Malik, Hafeez. 1975. 'Problems of Regionalism in Pakistan'. In Wriggins, W. H. ed. *Pakistan in Transition*, pp. 60–132. Islamabad.

25. Jones, P. 'Islam and Politics', includes a reproduction of an election poster of the PPP. Bhutto is dressed in a Western suit with a 'Jinnah cap' on his head, mounted on a caparisoned, leaping horse, the flag of Pakistan in his hand, and a sword and shield by his side. Across the top, under 'Zu'lfaqar-

i Haidari' is a picture of the sword, the width of the poster, emblazoned with the Qur'anic phrase, 'With the help of Allah, victory is near'. The dense epigraphy includes the attestation of faith; a quotation from a Bhutto speech promising he will sacrifice his life for the people; Bhutto's titles, 'The Pride of Asia', 'The Leader of the People', a prayer to the great Sindhi mystic Shahbaz Qalandar that Bhutto live a thousand years; a Punjabi denunciation of imperialism and the Indian foreign minister; and a couplet from Iqbal, 'China and Arabia is ours, Hindustan is ours; Every Muslim is our fellow countryman, the whole world is ours'.

26. Government of Pakistan, Ministry of Foreign Affairs, *Pakistan's Relations with the Islamic States: A Review*, 21 February 1977, p. 34.

27. Bhutto, Zulfikar Ali. 1979. '*If I am Assassinated...*' p. 223. New Delhi.

28. Dani, A. H. June 1974. Letter to the editor, *The Pakistan Times*.

29. Ewing, Katherine. 1980. 'The Pir or Sufi Saint in Pakistani Islam'. Doctoral dissertation, Department of Anthropology, University of Chicago. [See also her *Arguing Sainthood* (1997).]

30. Zia-ul-Haq, Mohammad. 1979. 'Introduction of Islamic Laws'. Address to the Nation, 10 February 1979. Published by Government of Pakistan, Ministry of Information and Broadcasting.

31. An estimate of 25–30 per cent appears in Ali, Salamat. 1979. 'Is Time Running out for Zia's Regime'?, *Far Eastern Economic Review*. 30 March: p. 17. The Shi'a protests were reported in *The San Francisco Chronicle*, 7 July 1980.

# 10

# Islamic Arguments in Contemporary Pakistan

The use of an Islamic vocabulary in political discussion in contemporary Pakistan is not unusual in the country's history. What is unusual is that, that language has come to dominate all discussion and that no alternative, whether Marxist, liberal, or other, exists as a counter to the dominant ideology. Whether supporter or opponent of the current regime, everyone has learned to argue with Islamic symbols and terminology. The current situation differs dramatically in intensity from the earlier use of Islamic symbols in political discussion in Pakistan. That earlier use of Islamic symbols, hardly surprising in a country created to protect Muslim interests, reminds us that there is no single 'Islamic politics'.

There have been, broadly speaking, three dominant interpretations of what Islamic symbols should mean in Pakistan. The first interpretation made Islam a focus of national unity, not a programme for government action. Political leaders in the first decades after Independence talked of Muslim interests and rallied the country, above all, by the cry of 'Islam in danger' in relation to India. Pakistan was to be a Muslim homeland, founded to protect business elites; and religious leaders, who had not been central to the movement to found the new state, had no autonomous base of power.[1] Pakistani leaders during the 1950s and 1960s were tied to Western military aid and influenced by American developmental theory. There were, of course, figures who wanted

Islamic principles to be more central to governmental concerns. But aside from a commitment that nothing should be undertaken repugnant to Islam and the decision that councils on Islamic ideology should be established to offer Islamic advice, religious issues were never central.[2]

In the early 1970s, a second interpretation arose as the dominant political language turned away from Western Europe and America and identified itself as Islamic and socialist. In 1971 the context of political life had changed dramatically in Pakistan when the civil war between the eastern and western wings led to the establishment of the independent state of Bangladesh. Under Zu'l-faqar Ali Bhutto, the leader with the most popular support of anyone after Jinnah, the loss of the eastern half of the country was weathered with perhaps surprising ease. A more homogenous country came to focus less on its origin as a homeland for Indian Muslims and more on its existence as a Muslim nation on the edge of the Middle East. This image of a Middle Eastern, Islamic identity was fostered by Bhutto's hosting an Islamic conference of heads of state in 1974. It was fuelled by the new found wealth and power of the oil rich and the desire on Pakistan's part to be identified with, and benefit from, that power. Pakistan called itself the *qila*, or fort, on the eastern edge of the Muslim heartland and offered military expertise and manpower to its fellow Muslims. Migrant labourers provided crucially important foreign exchange and further focused ties to Pakistan's west. Thus two sets of factors influenced a more self-conscious Islamic or Middle Eastern identity: one was internal, the loss of East Pakistan and with it a claim to legitimacy as a South Asian Muslim homeland; and second, an external set of factors, the new found wealth and power of the oil-rich Muslim states. Bhutto himself was not personally religious, was impatient of the religious leadership, and did not even pay lip service to Islamic standards of drinking, dress, or behaviour. But his programme for the country was to be called Islamic.

It was also to be socialist, symbolized by the Mao-like uniform adopted by the central leadership. Bhutto's Islamic socialism prom-ised a curb on vested interests in the country and a fairer distribu-tion of resources. It was meant to speak to the discontents of those who had not prospered during the earlier period of growth. Bhutto appealed directly to ordinary people, whose political consciousness and desire for direct involvement in government reached a peak in the early 1970s that had not existed before and has not continued since. As Bhutto felt his position challenged, however, his rule became more arbitrary and his concessions to the very vested interests he had hoped to eliminate more evident. In early 1977 he also made concessions to narrow Islamic interests, notably in a ban on alcoholic consumption and gambling and the establishment of a weekly Friday holiday.

The military leaders under General Zia'ul-Haqq who overthrew Bhutto on 5 July 1977 intended to create stability and order, but, very shortly after establishing themselves, their ambitions grew to use the opportunity they now had to attempt to establish what they called an Islamic order within the country.[3] Talk of 'Islamic socialism' disappeared overnight in favour of a third interpretation of Islamic symbols, that based on *nizam-i mustafa* ('the system of the Prophet'). Religious leaders still played little role in national politics. Although the *coup* had been supported by an alliance that included the explicitly Islamic party, the Jama'at-i Islami, along with parties of the ulama, that alliance was never an alternative to the military takeover. The alliance was a fragile one, challenging a long-time history of mutual opposition between the classically educated ulama and lay parties like the Jama'at. The formally educated religious leadership in Pakistan had nothing like the independent base of power it developed in a country like Iran. Religious influence within the new regime came from non-clerics, broadly speaking, influenced by the Jama'at, and not from the traditional religious leadership.

This regime benefited from several years of excellent weather, substantial foreign remittances, and the military aid and stimulus to unity provided by the Soviet invasion of Afghanistan in 1979.[4] The military in Pakistan is disproportionately large as a result of its historic situation, and the new regime readily established martial law as the fundamental law, with little attention given to individual liberties, fair trial, or freedom of expression. The regime, like the Jama'at, favoured the interests of private property. Pakistan is conservative, both socially and in external affairs, more like Saudi Arabia (which has patronized the Zia regime) than Iran. There appears to be little radical opposition within the country, though there are many who chafe at restraints on individual liberty. The greatest challenge to political stability has not been ideological but regional, above all in Sind.

Certain continuities are evident in these three political interpretations of Islam. One is the minor role of the religious leadership, even under the Zia regime. A second is the important influence on the ideologies (and on their longevity) played by external political realities: enmity to India; early dependence, economic and political, on the USA and its allies; growing ties to Middle Eastern oil producers; and support from both other Muslim states and the USA in the aftermath of the invasion of Afghanistan. Third, it appears that, despite the changes in ideology, there has been relatively little change in social relations and in the domination of the landed, business, commercial, and military elites. Although both Islamic socialism and the current Islamic reforms speak of the interests of the poor and oppressed and seek to dissociate themselves from the inequities of the early period of growth, neither has created policies to change the pattern of economic distribution or claims to political power. What studies there are confirm a preponderant continuity of the power of the old elites, softened only by unplanned changes like the earnings of migrant workers in the Gulf.

If the newly influential Islamic style in Pakistan, which this essay will explore, is not a vehicle of class interests, what does lend it its current salience? The external influences and internal political changes noted above may have influenced a more self-conscious Islamic identity, but not necessarily the one that has emerged. The question of the pre-eminence of this particular orientation is one to which we shall return after surveying the current movement and the programme of the Zia regime in more detail.

## Islamic Reforms: The Nizam-i Islami

Throughout Pakistan's history the most serious intellectual challenge to the various regimes has come from the Jama'at-i Islami, an organization long led by the late Maulana Abu'l-A'la Maududi (d. 1979).[5] The Jama'at had its origins before Partition when Maududi, then a journalist and politician, ended a long association with the Jami'atu'l-'Ulama-yi Hind because of its nationalist commitment to cooperation with non-Muslims in order to secure Independence. In the early 1930s he established a journal whose target was not political alliance as such but Western culture. His increasingly influential writings sought to show by rational argument the superiority of Islam to any other source of values or guide to behaviour.

From 1937 to 1941, as political competition intensified, he directed his writings against nationalism (whether of the Congress or the Muslim League) as one of the most serious threats of Western civilization to Islam, both because it fractured the *ummat* and because it based political life on alien theories. In 1941, with the demand for Pakistan explicit, Maududi founded the Jama'at-i Islami to embody an example of a disciplined Islamic society. He was influenced in this by the example of both Fascists and Communists in Europe where highly organized minorities, he felt, could influence a whole society. His society, whose members initially lived together, was to be thoroughly Islamic in ideas and conduct. This early opposition to the League discredited the Jama'at in later years in Pakistan; and reminders of that opposition continue to be articulated in controversies today.[6]

When Pakistan became a reality, Maududi, despite his earlier opposition, moved to the new country and soon became the most coherent voice arguing that the state should exist not only to protect Muslim interests but to embody Islamic principles. The Jama'at founded branches throughout Pakistan to do relief work and disseminate propaganda. The association was feared by early governments and accused of a central role in the anti-Ahmadi riots of 1953 when Maududi, personally deploring the violence, emerged as the spokesman of the ulama and thus established a reputation of authority. From this time on there were ulama prepared to accept Jama'at leadership on political questions.[7] With the first constitution of 1956, the Jama'at in fact acted as a political party; and since then, when parties have been permitted to exist, the Jama'at has regularly contested elections. It has never had major electoral success, but its influence has been widespread and pervasive in cities and among university students, for whom it has served as a significant source of meaning and identity at a particular stage in their lives. Its influence grew in the early 1970s, in part because of Saudi patronage and support.[8]

With the establishment of the new regime in 1977, members of the Jama'at felt that for the first time their values were being publicly proclaimed at the highest levels and that people they approved of were being appointed to influential roles. The terms that were being used by Zia and others—Islamic system, Islamic economy, Islamic education, Islam as a complete code of life (*mukammal zabita-i hayat*)—all had been honed in Jama'at scholarship and polemics over the years. Even though their ideal of an Islamic state did not permit a military dictator as leader, Jama'at members were prepared to offer their cooperation. In August 1978, Mian Tufail Muhammad, the *amir* of the Jama'at, said that this was 'a golden opportunity for the establishment of an Islamic system which should never be allowed to go unavailed of.'[9] In that month members of the Jama'at for the first time accepted positions in a federal cabinet. But even after they resigned eight months later, and even when the Jama'at was legally outlawed along with all other political parties, the ideology of the organization continued to be very influential informally.

Despite the widespread publicity and discussion given them, the Islamic changes since 1977 have been deemed 'cosmetic' by critics. An implicit judgement of these policies is given in a document prepared at the request of the Ministry of Finance in April 1980 to recommend basic policies for an Islamic state. The document focuses on ends that are truly Islamic, defining their goal as a better life for more people, moderate economic growth, and social justice. To achieve this goal, the report strongly recommends, for example, a policy of universal education, land redistribution, and limits on inherited wealth. It also argues that a focus on ending interest (said to be a misunderstanding of the meaning of *riba*) and a policy of levying *zakat* would work against the poor, when what is needed is a comprehensive and socially progressive tax policy. These economic recommendations have been largely ignored, although they could have been expected to ameliorate the very low level of social development (as measured by child and female welfare, life expectancy, and literacy) that persists, despite the overall growth in national product.[10]

In contrast to all this, the Islamic programme in Pakistan has called for certain policies, which have been undertaken throughout history by any ruler who wanted to gain religious legitimacy: prohibition of alcohol and gambling, changes in certain taxes (*zakat, ushr*) and in laws related to interest, and changes in the judicial system. Even the taxes and judicial changes, while highly visible, have not had far-reaching impact. The imposition of the corporal *hadd* penalties for certain criminal offences, for example, has attracted widespread attention, even shock, in the West.[11] Yet

242 ISLAMIC CONTESTATIONS

they are so limited in application that the current ruler himself has said they will not affect one in a thousand cases; they are those about which the Prophet said it was better for a pious Muslim not to give evidence.[12] Certain shari'a benches and religious courts have been established as a supplement to the existing judicial system to review a limited range of laws. Those associated with the new benches and courts are primarily those qualified to be judges (not the ulama); short courses for them are now offered in the new Islamic University.[13] A federal assembly was appointed, then elected, with only limited power. Although dignified with the title Majlis-i Shura in order to recall the earliest days of Islam, it can only with difficulty be described as an Islamic reform. Every provision and every debate raises, among other questions, sectarian issues, most dramatically so far in the unwillingness of Shi'a Muslims to accept Sunni directives on the alms tax (zakat). A major limitation on change has been the agreement to accept sectarian objections to any Islamic ordinance.

Issues related to women have perhaps attracted more attention than any others, although in fact almost nothing has changed the legal status of women or their opportunities. Women's opportunities are limited less by law than by long-standing customary practices and attitudes, above all those that result in no more than 13 per cent of the female population being literate. The most substantial institutional change has been the establishment of the Women's Division directly responsible to the President within the Cabinet Division in early 1979. It is charged with formulating public policies and laws to meet the needs of women, developing programmes to spread female education and employment opportunities, and protecting women's legal and other interests; the division is staffed by women with English, typically foreign, education. This institution exists, however, in an atmosphere that is not supportive of the goals it is meant to achieve.[14]

The general atmosphere, and the encouragement given to those who favour the immurement of women, has created widespread fear about the imposition of second class civil rights on women, the restriction of opportunities for paid employment, and the enforcement of gender segregation, notably by proposals to create a separate university for women. The phrase that has become current in recent years is *chadar aur char diwari* (the veil and the four walls): an orientation that one side seeks to extend and the other side seeks to resist. The prohibition on women athletes competing publicly in Pakistan or travelling abroad was particularly telling. Also significant has been recurring discussion about female dress and decorum, although in theory such presidential directives as those affecting the dress of civil servants have applied to both men and women.

Two issues affecting civil rights have in particular caused great public concern. One is talk of abolishing the Muslim Family Laws Ordinance of the early 1960s. This law provides certain minimal protection to women in relation to divorce, in consultation before a husband undertakes a second marriage, in securing the rights of grandchildren to inherit, and in procedures for securing rights to maintenance. Recent studies suggest that the actual utilization of those laws has been limited, but they remain a major symbol of women's attempts to secure their own interests, interests they insist Islam has guaranteed but local custom has thwarted. Despite talk to the contrary, the President himself appears to be committed to their protection and an appeal to the Shari'a Court exempted the laws from review on the grounds that they were part of the excluded area of personal law.[15]

The second issue that provoked great discussion about the legal position of women took place in the early 1980s over proposed modification of the Law of Evidence. Debate was raised in particular about the proposal to require two women witnesses as the equivalent of one male witness. Those in opposition have argued that the single instance in the Qur'an where this situation seems to prevail is limited to a case on financial matters, where women are presumably less experienced and a second woman is to provide help to the first if needed. The point therefore, it may be argued—if one looks at the essential meaning of the verse—is simply that attention must be given to the credibility and experience of the witness. The Majlis-i Shura, however, recommended that two women be required for each single male witness. The major exception to this was in *hadd* cases (whose legal provisions had already been in force for some time) where no woman could give evidence.

During the debate on this issue in February 1983, a procession of women in Lahore tried to present a petition in opposition to the High Court. The women, some one hundred fifty to two hundred, were attacked by police and riot control squads, and some thirty were arrested. Their protest was led by the Women's Action Forum, an association of women's organizations which seeks to protect women's rights. Women members of the Jama'at and others sharing their views, who had formed their own organization, the Majlis-i Khawatin-i Pakistan, held their own rally and offered their own statement, a mark of the kind of polarization that some expect to continue to grow.

The result of this confrontation, and of others like it, is that, even if there has been no substantial change in the actual laws, there has been far reaching change in discourse: everyone in public life is forced to think about certain issues, of which the position of women is a central one; and everyone has to address those issues in an Islamic language. This change has taken place in a context of Islamization from the top, not from broad popular demand. Its core support is the military and some segments of the literate urban population. It is instrumental in maintaining an authoritarian regime that seeks to preserve the existing structure of society and itself in power. Yet this ideology is intensely appealing to some segments of the population, and it is the character of that appeal to which we now turn.

## Arguments of the Jama'at-i Islam

The Jama'at has long been known for its extensive publication programme of clearly written pamphlets, which are inexpensive and widely distributed. Many characteristics of the movement are evident in even a single pamphlet like the one I shall now examine in some detail to provide an illustration of Jama'at arguments. I shall supplement the arguments of the pamphlet with comments taken from newspaper accounts and interviews that speak to the same issues. The pamphlet is entitled *Three Women, Three Cultures* and was written by Sayyid As'ad Gilani, chairman of the Lahore branch of the Jama'at, and published in 1982.[16] The supplementary comments date primarily from the winter of 1983 and many were stimulated by the dramatic controversy over the protest procession in Lahore noted above.

The pamphlet does not illuminate the systematic political theory of the Jama'at, which is simply taken for granted. According to this theory, the purpose of society is to foster a life obedient to God on the part of individuals, the same obedience that non-human creation embodies automatically, an obedience whose requirements are known to humans through the Qur'an and examples of which are evident in hadith and understood by human reason. Although concerned with the inculcation of individual moral virtues, members of the Jama'at, in contrast to many of the ulama, also insist on the transformation of the social order by political means. Most important to their programme is the control of society by the righteous who should wield power in a mono-lithic state, guided by the advice of people like themselves.

This concern with the overall social order is evident in the organization of the pamphlet. Thus the 'three women' are not three individuals, but are profiles of what are taken to be the characteristics of women in three different forms of society: the capitalist, the socialist, and the Islamic.[17] The capitalist is given more than twice the length of the socialist because the latter is regarded as the 'daughter' of the former: the capitalist system is also more alluring and more dangerous. Each of these cultures shapes what a woman is: it is the political order that is crucial. From this perspective, in contrast to what might be called 'reformist' movements that focus on individual change (like the Tablighi Jama'at and the Deoband movement in the subcontinent), change in the total socio-political environment is given prece-dence.[18] This concern with the total structure has made the word *nizam*, or system, central to the political discourse in Pakistan today, with the goal being the *nizam-i mustafa*, or, now more commonly, simply the *nizam-i islami*. The current desire for systematization is evident in the on-going discussion about codi-fying the shari'a and attempting to apply it by formal law to all aspects of life. It is also evident in the assertion, made in this pamphlet as elsewhere, that there is an equivalent to capitalism or socialism in an Islamic system and that system must be accepted as a whole. 'Whoever adheres to capitalist Western culture or socialist culture can go to its house and pursue it there.'

It is this focus that gives the contemporary movements, respond-ing as they do to the national states and social ideologies of the present century, characteristics that make them, as a Deobandi critic of the Jama'at once said to me, simply 'too modern'.[19] Earlier activists concerned with the state either wanted to place more pious rulers in power or envisaged some utopian community based on Islamic egalitarianism. The ulama in modern times have, like the

Jama'at, talked of a return to pristine teachings and of renewal, but their thought about society and politics has been limited to the assertion that they should guide and influence behaviour; they expect society to improve if the building blocks of individual lives are fully Islamic. Movements like the Jama'at diverge from such orientations because they want to control the machinery of a modern state themselves. In the internal debate, what defines them is that they deny the authenticity of the medieval schools of law and go directly to the revealed sources, they are *ghair-muqallid* (non-conformist), and can, they maintain, ignore trivia and custom to focus on what is understood to be truly important.

In their thought, however, relatively little attention is given to the economic organization of alternative systems, even though the terms used to describe societies—capitalist, socialist—are economic terms. The currently dominant ideologists in Pakistan are not concerned with far reaching structural changes to assure economic justice or redistribution; and unlike the Ikhwan al-Muslimun in Egypt and Syria, with which they are often compared, they have not even questioned the legality and morality of private enterprise. In the pamphlet under consideration here, for example, the only possible economic implication of the changes proposed would be to prohibit women from participating in much of the paid labour force. Women would still serve in professional and technical capacities, but only in institutions that serve other women. They would still have higher education, but ideally in separate facilities. It is such issues, relatively peripheral to change in the fundamental structure of society as it now exists, on which these thinkers have dwelt.

A second point, and an important corollary to this dominant concern with the organization of society, is the extent to which positions are formulated against what is called 'Western culture'. That culture must be known, rejected, and kept at bay by impermeable boundaries, whether it is represented by westerners themselves or by fellow countrymen tainted by exposure to it—particularly those who are seen to have dominated earlier Pakistani regimes. Again this characteristic contrasts significantly with the position of reformists of the Deobandi sort, who argue less with outsiders than with fellow Muslims who are not committed to a programme of reform.

Western culture is, however, only partially known and Islamic ideals are often contrasted with the worst of Western realities. An

upper class urban Islamic ideal is also contrasted with a working
class Western reality: in the case of women, leisured urban Muslim
women in seclusion are implicitly contrasted either with working
class Western women engaged in unskilled or manual labour or
with some vision of 'liberated women'. It is, in fact, descriptions
of the West that this particular pamphlet primarily undertakes, for
the author hopes to educate his readers who, he believes, are misled
by a false picture of Western life. The description, ironically, uses
many arguments of Western feminists concerning such matters as
crimes against women, wage differentials, and pornography.[20]

The author begins his work with reassurances to those women
who are, he claims, the victims of their husbands, becoming
westernized, and who have therefore panicked at the recent
discussion of women initiated by the concern with Islamic reforms.
These women, the author says, fear what they consider to be a
burden of dead teaching to the point that they say, 'Save us from
Islam'. But, the author warns them ('our "modern" sisters') that
they do not know how Western culture disgraces women. Its first
fruit is socialism, which turns women into beasts of labour.
'Shoulder to shoulder' is not strolling along Mall Road or Bunder
Road, he warns, but working heavy machines, excavating mines,
and driving tractors. In capitalist culture, woman is 'Eve's deprived
daughter'. In her youth she is the football of lustful male players.
In later years she lives with no husband to hold her hand; no son
to serve her; no family to protect her. Her final years bring the
torment and loneliness of an old people's home. Women come to
bear, the author calculates, three-quarters of the burdens of society.

Women are preyed on and are themselves criminals in such areas
as lewdness, sexual deviance, suicide, childhood vagrancy, oppression, theft, and adultery. The three checks on crime are undermined: an inner sense of morality; external punishment (which is
replaced by the theory of crime as 'psychological disease' or
*nafsiyati marz*); and fear of God's inquisition at the Last Day. To
show what happens in a mixed society 'with backward morals',
Gilani provides a chart of crimes committed in a single region of
the United States during one year, including the number of crimes
committed by women. He also gives descriptive examples of what
happens in a world with no restraints: women are in the army to
amuse men; houses are deserted and hotels and restaurants are full;
alcohol and drugs are used and led in the recent past to the 'mixed

battalions of hippies' where, as the Urdu has it, 'that was seen which should not be seen'.

'Dating', one of the thirty odd words in the pamphlet that are considered untranslatable into Urdu, is defined and explained.[21] The bond of marriage is taken so lightly, the author explains, that people have physical relations with scores of others, like animals. The 'fashion' of living together, a form of dating, means that a man can decide he is bored and leave with no responsibility for either the woman or the children. Everything is left to family planners and government orphanages; and one-third to one-half of the children in Europe, Gilani believes, are now born in these conditions.

The whole notion of 'fashion' in appearance and dress is one more way in which woman is the victim of this materialist, animal world. If a man wishes a woman to be thin, a bizarre notion in a society as poor as Pakistan, she starves herself, even takes poison. This is called 'dieting' and can result in palsy or even death. Women appear in bikinis so that men can be gratified while they themselves remain fully clothed. There are nude clubs and pools, advertisements showing scantily clad women, sports teams of women watched by men, magazines designed to incite passion. Gilani recalls Allama Iqbal, the modernist poet who is the only thinker the author cites, visiting London early in the century and asking a salesgirl, 'Daughter, why are you here?' Tears came to her eyes and she explained the hard circumstances which forced her to work. Iqbal said, 'This woman should have been the light of a house where she would give true nurture to her offspring; she should not be selling merchandise in a shop.'

Women in the West, far from finding freedom, cannot go out after dark. Police encourage them to carry whistles. Family planning offices work day and night. Women have to learn judo and karate. Women are nothing but shop-soiled 'girlfriends'. 'May God grant understanding to those sisters in our country who are fans and flag bearers of this impure culture; and may He protect Muslim women from their shadow!'

Women in socialist countries, 'Eve's daughters deprived of dignity and purpose' lead an even worse life. In these societies marriage is nothing and 'every woman is for every man'. Gilani tells the story of a refugee from Afghanistan whose son returned from schooling in the Soviet Union and wanted to marry his sister!

The old man killed his son and fled the country. Under the Soviets, the author explains, animal culture is joined to force.

Again, women suffer most. They do forced labour with no distinction. All wear thick blue clothes and live in barracks. Women do the heaviest work, and their physical and spiritual delicacy is ignored. Frequent abortions leave them barren. Their life is worse than that of animals. Their so-called equality exists only in work and trouble; they have no role in the governing councils or in any influential positions. All socialist countries are alike, the author says, and he links not only China and the USSR but such an unlikely candidate for socialism as Japan. The picture of the 'West', if factually shaky, is vividly drawn.

Basic to Gilani's argument, then, is, first, the conception of an Islamic system as distinct from the two competing systems and, second, the importance given to describing the inhuman and immoral organization of society in the West. As noted above, the Jama'at has not been led by the traditionally educated. Maulana Maududi, for example, although he wrote extensively on scholarly issues, did not have a proper madrasa education, nor did Dr Israr Ahmed, recently a leading spokesman for this orientation, who was trained as a physician in Western medicine.[22] Just as the leadership and organization of the Jama'at differ from the classical pattern, so does the style of writing. These thinkers do not pursue the traditional genres of religious writing, where an essay like this on Western customs would be wholly uncharacteristic.

Certain techniques or approaches make the presentation of this material particularly effective. In the remainder of this essay, I shall identify four points, evident in this pamphlet and in arguments given elsewhere, that are characteristic of the persuasive rhetoric that has been a hallmark of the Jama'at. First, as will have already been evident, the issues chosen are clearly visible ones that arouse highly charged reactions. Some of the intensity of feeling surrounding the topic of this pamphlet, for example, is evident in its opening line: 'Woman is the anchor of our life in society'. The word chosen for this key metaphor, *langar*, not only has root meaning with all its implications of harbour and a steadying foundation, but is used far more commonly to describe the food, sanctified by proximity to holiness, which is offered to the poor and the pilgrim at a saintly shrine. *Langar* is a refuge in a turbulent world. The insistence on the domestic role of women and the importance of limiting women's involvement in public life defines Muslim culture against something alien and also defines a sphere of safety, power, and control.[23]

A second characteristic of the presentation of the argument is the use of deductive logic. Reason here is used to show that Islam is conducive to human life, whereas Western culture makes men less human and more animal. The initial premise is based on Islamic understandings of human nature as distinct from animal nature. Evidence is then deduced from 'facts' about Western societies to show that they reflect and in turn shape the animal elements in humans. The argument is thus taken to be scientific and empirical. The language is logical and deductive, identifying principles, examining their implications, and illustrating them by what might be called a selected reality, although, as noted above, echoing in many cases issues of serious importance to Western feminists.

What is natural and what is revealed are identical. Classic Islamic theory sees man as unique in creation in combing angelic qualities (often summarized in the term 'aql) which foster rational adherence to a natural law which is also God's revelation, with a lower self (often identified as nafs) which is wilful, animal-like, and given to its own irrational appetites. The unique opportunity of humans is to cultivate 'aql in everyday life so that they live in accordance with their true nature. This theory is not explicit in the pamphlet in hand; it is implicit in its concern with latent animality and the need to control it.[24]

The argument that the Islamic way of life, as understood, is in harmony with nature is a strong one. By nature man is responsible for securing a livelihood for the family, providing for defence, working at industry and agriculture, and organizing social life. Women are responsible for the home and for bearing and nurturing the new generation. When humans thwart this law, they become animals. But the sense of nature as given is not only evident in gender roles. Dr Israr, for example, who, like his sometime mentor Maulana Maududi, had opposed Partition, even now insists that the problems of Pakistan are in part owing to the violation of nature effected by the vivisection of the Punjab.

Western ignorance of nature is evident in their development of an alternative theory which substitutes, it appears, a different view of man's created constitution. Darwin's theories are taken to confirm that it is the animal side of humans that Western culture develops. From the late nineteenth century on, it is worth recalling, Indian Muslims were fascinated by Darwinian theories and their implications for Western culture, a fascination epitomized in a couplet of the satirist Akbar Ilahabadi:[25]

Mansur in ecstacy cried, 'I am God';
Darwin's ecstatic cry is, 'I'm an ape'.

And the verse continues with the famous line of Hafez:

The thought of each man is in accord with the capacity of each.

The result of this, the author writes, is that Western philosophy sees man as evolving from animals, and rebelling against oppressive religion, and, in the end, against all religion. Man, free of religion, is animal-like and has no purpose, no feeling or quality of consciousness, no responsibility for his kind.

The author identifies three characteristics observed in the West that confirm this animality. First, Western man has adopted an animal nature because he seeks to destroy everything for the survival of his particular 'herd'. The evidence of this is found in nationalism, imperialism, materialism, and hedonism; there is no conception of worldwide brotherhood. Secondly, Western man has adopted 'such a foolish thought as secularism', an impossible quality for any human conscious of his true nature. Only animals can be secular. Secularism is negated by man's beliefs, feelings, sense of good and evil, and above all his solidarity with his fellows (his *qaum*). Third, Western man has started taking animals as an example for behaviour: in clothes, he shows no concern for covering his private parts; in food, he follows no distinction of what is prohibited and forbidden; in human interaction, he has no concept of human etiquette and standards. In the West, the author reports, they have a fashion of eating standing up, like animals. No limits are set in sexual matters. There are no norms of respect for the old or of kindness to the young, no chart of the rights of relatives and neighbours. The human understanding of rights and responsibilities is replaced by force. In such a society, it is the old and the weaker sex who suffer. 'Unable to stalk prey, their value is less in an animal herd.'

Other thinkers, sympathetic to this appraisal of the West, adduce Freudian theories. Dr Israr, for example, argues that Freud shows the basic soundness of the Muslim emphasis on human sexuality. This justifies 'Islamic' reforms controlling access to women; it explains the corruption of Western society where no social programme controls the sexual impulses that motivate everyday life. The familiarity of writers with Darwin and Freud, however limited, is a reminder that many of the current spokesmen are not traditionally educated but exposed to secular education or even, as in the case of Dr Israr, educated abroad.

The emphasis on Western animality, logically explicated, suggests the emotive edge to the arguments presented: what could be more feared than such degeneration? It is also one of many elements that fuel fierce anti-American feelings, evident, for example, in Pakistan in the incidents surrounding the burning of the US embassy in November 1979. Western opponents are, at least to some Pakistanis, something less than human.

A third characteristic of the argumentation is that it is bolstered on both sides by authority, by quotations from the scriptural texts of Islam. This element is present in all debate, for when introduced by any one party it has to be answered in kind by the others. In this pamphlet, it is particularly evident in the final section when Islamic society is described and hadith are enjoined to sanction it. This section, based as it is on a reading of sacred authorities, might well be summarized here.

Women in Islamic societies, in contrast to those of the West, are 'Eve's darling daughters', surrounded by comfort, satisfaction, and honour. Islam first put women in a place equal to men, equal in rights, but favoured and honoured. Because she is physically weaker, a woman has different duties from a man, a difference that is meaningful and purposeful. She is charged with the continuation of the human race.

Women are free of the struggle for survival. They are protected from evil glances, thanks to the veil. An Islamic society follows five rules:

(i) There is no mixed society.

(ii) Women avoid going out of the home.

(iii) If they need to go out, they do not adorn themselves and use a veil.

(iv) They avoid conversation with men who are not related to them.

(v) If they must speak, they speak briefly and directly, not gently and sweetly.

These rules produce a different social order (*nizam*) in which the mingling of men and women is limited and protected. These rules, Gilani explains, prevailed until the time of the British, when 'a special service class and the well-to-do' adopted a mental slavery and began distorting the clear orders of the Qur'an and the hadith. When seclusion was observed, he insists, society flourished; when it ended, it declined. Iqbal, quoted again, explained that freedom for women has invariably destroyed human society.

Gilani's list of 'women's rights' is not that of liberals. Islam, he notes, gives a woman the right to private property, to inheritance, and to the marriage portion. She has the right to maintenance. She has the right to leave her husband if he is oppressive or distasteful. She can choose her husband within the limits of modesty. When asked about the differential roles of women and men, the Prophet replied that to manage a house well, keep a husband happy, and behave appropriately was equal to anything men might do. Women are to stay at home; home is the best place for their prayer, it is their field of holy war. All the respect a woman earns ('*izzat, ihtiram*) depends on her attention to her domestic circle. To know the command of Islam is to find well-being, Gilani concludes. The other cultures will disappear, but Islam will last forever.

A fourth and final characteristic of the argument, running like a thread throughout the pamphlet and the debate, is what might be called an argument from status. I choose this phrase rather than 'an argument based on class' because it is necessary to avoid the easy assumption that the argument made has some direct sociological correlative. Gilani speaks of the rich and westernized as his opponents, but the least reflection will make it apparent that, despite such terms and even the more specific sociological terms he uses, the kind of argument he is making is one that describes a cultural perspective far more than any objective measure of occupation, educational experience, or income. Bhutto, in contrast, made specific appeals to the economic interests of peasants, workers, and the poor, although, in the end, he grew ever closer to the landlords and industrialists who had dominated Pakistan from the beginning.[26] The spokesmen for the *nizam-i mustafa* also speak a language of egalitarianism and seem to denounce the rich— but it is only the rich who do not share their values. There is no element in their programme to challenge the existing economic relations in society.

It is possible to make some sociological statements about Jama'at membership. Its leadership has come from academics, students, teachers, lawyers, and journalists. Its core supporters are urban and literate, and it has been strong in the universities. It does not include the rural or the very poor. However, it is hard to go beyond these statements. Particularly in the current situation, many are drawn to a Jama'at orientation because the national leadership is known to be sympathetic to it. Pakistan is a society where the elite, and people in general, defer to the authority in power and are likely to be very flexible—or realistic—ideologically. No one speaks now of 'Islamic socialism', the phrase current only a decade back. Beginning in the late 1970s, Pakistanis made enormous shifts in the political language they employed. Those now supporting the government's Islamic policies come from a very wide variety of backgrounds. Some may do so out of expediency, some may be motivated by a desire for order and stability, some many genuinely be committed to the current programme or to a vague longing for an Islamic programme of any kind.[27]

The appeal throughout the pamphlet is to true Muslims, and against the rich and westernized. The opposition are summed up by calling them the *apwa* (pl. *apwaee*), treating the English acronym for the All Pakistan Women's Association as an Urdu noun. APWA was founded after Partition as a voluntary organization of privileged women who engaged in a number of welfare activities, initially among refugees and then among the poor generally. APWA has attained international recognition as a social service organization. It is fundamentally conservative in that its programmes do nothing to change the structure of society but rather seek to alleviate misery among the poorest people. It has been outspoken in opposition to any talk of government action that would end the Family Laws Ordinance or hamper what mobility and public roles are open to women.

Gilani argues that the *apwaee* have taken up the false European belief that women and men are equal, denying their separate roles as separate wheels of a common enterprise. 'The begums of APWA [*begum* being another loaded term to describe the women of the social elites], whose work is to become second wives of their rich old husbands and to live in luxury and pomp, take up the role of showing off their glitter outside of the house all in the name of "progress" and "equality"'—the English words are used. The serious social work of APWA is thus completely ignored and its members are contrasted to 'innocent Muslim women', 'our God-fearing and good sisters who are obedient in the order of God and the Prophet'. He speaks of a struggle of principle between the voiceless Muslim well-born *shurafa* who are middle class and the *mutrafin*, defined as capitalists, the well-to-do, and high government servants. It is they who want to turn 'Muslim women' into 'foxes with their tails cut off' like themselves; it is they who will surely be defeated in a pure Islamic struggle, for they are nothing but mongrels. The point of this pamphlet is to show the true face of *sharafat*, of high birth, and to argue that it is not genealogical but moral.

The debate stimulated by the Lahore procession used the rhetoric of class. Women themselves, especially those influenced by the Jama'at, condemned the protesters as 'westernized and misled'.[28] A hundred ulama in Lahore stated, as reported in *The Pakistan Times*, 17 February 1983, that the women's agitation was 'a proclamation of war against God's commands'; they identified the women as those who 'either belonged to the upper stratum of society who were fond of Western culture and civilization or were the champions of secularism'. Maulana Sami'ul-Haqq Deobandi of Akora Khattak, a member of the Majlis and a well-known correspondent, writing in *Dawn*, 20 February 1983, said that the women were not representative 'of the toiling suffering women in the villages' but 'represented the rich urban and westernized elite'; they were people whose 'influence, wealth, and social status were threatened by Islamic social and legal justice'. In a long signed article in *The Pakistan Times* of 18 February 1983, another columnist, N. A. Khwaja, like the author of the pamphlet, made APWA responsible for the protest (although without ever naming the organization); in a phrase neatly combining Darwinian echoes of the rational theories and the status argument of the fundamentalists, he dismissed the protesters as 'influential begums eager to *ape* Western ways' (emphasis added).

As noted at the outset, Jama'at-style arguments have set the terms of the debate; answers to them have been piecemeal. At best opponents have tried to deny the appropriateness of the debate, as expressed, for example, in a somewhat baffled and bemused tone in a letter to *The Pakistan Times* of 21 February 1983 by one Lt. Col. (Retd) G. Dastgir:

By the grace of Almighty God I was born in a Muslim home like any other Pakistani Muslim but during my life of over 50 years I have never experienced so much controversy on Islam as I am experiencing now for the last 3-4 years. It has almost become a matter of routine to read in the Press, see on TV, and hear on Radio what is Islamic and what is not. One starts thinking whether our ancestors and we have so far been living an Islamic or un-Islamic life.

The writer identifies himself as a Muslim, but not with the Islam and the process of defining Islam current today; he presumably represents a position that wants religious matters left to individuals and to sects, and a society that is more open to participation and dissent. In a similar vein, S. K. Kauser, writing in *Dawn* of 10 February 1983, reviewed the restrictions on make-up on television, dress, and a separate university, and then asked.

A question stares us all 'why this obsession with women?' Correction please..., there are other questions: Doesn't the government have better things to do? Aren't there real problems in Pakistan? Despite utmost resistance, a thought forces itself out of the many queries that whirl within one's mind. Is the victimization of women related to their greater vulnerability? Or is it the case that men have become insecure and are willing to use any means to restore their status quo?

Such writers simply want the issues and, at times, the whole public appropriation of religious symbols, dropped.

Other writers adduce, even if they do not systematically present, liberal concepts in their disagreement with so-called Islamic policies. Those who refuse to accept a limited domestic sphere for women often draw on the language of Western egalitarianism. Here is a letter to *The Muslim* of 20 February 1983:

Being a working woman and supporting my parents, I fail to fathom why my legal position should be any different than that of any man....[The mullas] are not the *thaikadars* of Islam. No one has given them this contract.

An argument of gender equality is thus joined to one of the right of all believers to speak to Islamic issues. The language of Western constitutionalism was explicitly used in the petition of women lawyers to the Chief Justice of the Lahore High Court in speaking of a struggle 'to achieve full and justiciable rights' and to argue that if, as it happens, an oath of a woman is equal to an oath of a man, her evidence must also be equal.

The elite women who are outspoken on issues of their civil rights are also inspired, even if not consciously, by their dominant position in a deeply hierarchic society. They are used to power and respect. An aristocratic woman member of the Majlis cried out indignantly during the debate on the Law of Evidence: 'Am I then worth only half my manservant?' Perhaps no-one would articulate the presumptions behind that statement, but no-one would object to it either.

Most commonly, however, opponents of the current ideology draw on independent interpretations of Islam. Thus the women lawyers in the petition just noted insisted that their position was Islamic and that the advisory Council on Islamic Ideology should be reconstituted with men and women 'able to interpret the true spirit and intrinsic justice of Islam'.[29] Most common, and presumably most effective, are assertions that premise their arguments for women's right not on grounds of ability, necessity, local social structure, or universal rights, but rather on their own citation of Islamic authority.

One of the most eloquent of such interpretations was published in *The Pakistan Times* of 5 February 1983.[30] The author focuses her discussion on the Prophet's first wife, Khadija, and argues that she was a woman in the midst of public life, twice-widowed and managing her own business and family affairs. '[Descriptions of her] reveal a fair-minded businesswoman, with a sense of ethics and confident in her abilities. She had to be informed about business and market trends and to deal with many people. It was because of this, the author argues in detail, that she became an experienced judge of human nature, refused other offers of marriage, identified the superior moral qualities of her employee Muhammad, and married him despite his being 15 years her junior. It was this same acumen and experience—that no woman locked inside a room could ever have had—that gave her the insight to recognize at once the truth of the revelation he brought.' On the occasion of the attack on women in Lahore, the same author wrote of the incident as 'an assault on Qur'anic injunctions that are permanent and binding—the rights of women as human beings'. She also subtly redefined the boundaries of the four walls: 'The Pakistani women have a great responsibility in safeguarding their home, which is Pakistan'.[31] This kind of argument from scriptural authority attempts to see the context and implications of the behaviour of personages whom all regard as exemplary.

Other responses based on the texts include general claims to the 'Islamic rights of women',[32] and an insistence that the opposition cannot alone speak for Islam. In a reply to a statement by Dr Israr that he would rather be dead than ruled by a woman, one correspondent wrote in *The Muslim*, 18 February 1983:

The 'Islam' of these Pakistani Rasputins is but a concoction of alien and pagan beliefs mixed with their own small-time mentality and outlook. There is little patience left among women for their frivolous 'fatwas' on women's dress, women's hairstyles, women's make-up, women's jobs, in fact their total obsession with women....Dr Israr Ahmed deserves to be criticized for his irreverence in deliberately overlooking the example given by our Holy Prophet (Peace be upon Him).

A third kind of response based on authority is a technical one, in which many Pakistanis have become proficient, citing *ayat* and hadith on specific points. One of the most interesting exercises along these lines was the publication of a pamphlet by a woman, presumably Pakistan's only fully trained female Islamic legal scholar, who was educated by her father and was able to respond in legal detail to the discussion on the Law of Evidence and the Law of Retribution.[33] The pamphlet was written at the request of people associated with the Women's Division, and the scholar herself was reported to have been surprised that her serious, technical legal researches in fact led her to disagree with what was being put forth as Islamic.[34]

Such efforts, like the plan of the Women's Action Forum to start classes in Arabic, are meant to counter the common charge that women who oppose these policies are 'not conversant with the teachings of Islam'.[35] Charges against them go beyond that. After the procession in February 1983, groups of ulama informed the women that they were *kafir* and, seeking to strike terror into them, that unless they changed their ways their marriages would automatically be dissolved.

The incident of the attack on the procession made clear the extent to which there was a certain lack of consistency in the position of the petitioning women, a lack understandable in the face of violence, to be sure, but also a lack reflecting the dilemma of trying to speak both an Islamic and a liberal language and yet to avoid what are commonly taken to be the ultimate implications of both. Although insisting on equal civil rights for women, opportunities for employment, and generally lack of restrictions based on gender, even the women petitioning tend to share the general Pakistani assumption that the fundamental role of women is a domestic one and to accept the notion that women deserve particular respect. On this their attitudes coincided with supporters of the fundamentalist position, who disapproved of the petition but also disapproved of the attack: a typical headline, in *Dawn* February 1983, read 'Women's honour to be protected at all costs'. Even the burqa-clad president of the women's wing of the Jama'at student organization, the Jami'at-i Talabat, spoke in public to condemn the lathi-charge and the violence.[36] But support for the women in that sense blurred lack of support for their cause. The women themselves compounded this confusion by bringing a legal charge against the police on the grounds that, as unrelated men (*namahram*) who had laid hands on women, they had violated the principles of *chadar aur char diwari*! The women were, in fact, challenging those principles but, for short-sighted tactical reasons and, in fact, because of their acceptance of some aspects of women's traditional place, they were prepared to invoke them and thus give them weight.[37]

It is significant, perhaps in the long run decisive, that there emerged an opposition to the Islamic ideology espoused by the Zia regime. There are new organizations and new groups prepared to interpret Islam. In public, however, even if not always in private, it is arguments like the ones of the pamphlet described here that have held centre stage.

These arguments, I have suggested, are made persuasive by the choice of a single, riveting, salient topic that is seen sharply to distinguish Islamic culture from an alien 'other'; by deductive logic and empirical evidence that shows the superiority of what is Islamic in human cultural terms; by citations from authority that legitimize the argument; and by a redefinition of social standing so that Islamic behaviour, as defined here, is taken as the supreme marker of superior status. The appeal of this Islamic style, as it is presented here, is overwhelmingly personal and psychological. In this, the position of women and the continuation of the patriarchal family have become the central symbols of order and justice.

Such teachings offer a strong assertion of cultural and individual self-worth as defined by Islam and by adherence to a particular interpretation of Islam. As a 'system', it is the equivalent of alien systems, but, in its content, it is not merely equivalent but uniquely superior to all others. It offers not only individual well-being but, ultimately, social well-being by elimination of the injustices and inequities associated with what is defined as the West. In recent years, moreover, such an orientation has enhanced ties to other Muslim states, especially to the Saudi government, which is revered for the sanctity of its holy places and valued for its patronage.

Not all Pakistanis argue this way, not all accept the argument. But from the time of Zia, an Islamic language became dominant in public life, and there is no coherent, fully developed rival language to challenge it, whether couched in terms of Islam, or liberalism, or anything else. Those who accept it do not represent unquestioned 'tradition', but a self-conscious and deliberate reformulation of Islam by people who are literate, often professional, usually urban. They are part of a society characterized by rapid change where educational institutions fail to educate, bureaucracies are corrupt, justice does not prevail, and life often seems to lack dignity. For that society only a new order, in which the position of women is tightly defined, seems to offer hope. The Jama'at, and Islamic groups like them, are not traditional but modern—in their concerns, in their arguments, and, above all, in their goal of monopolizing the symbols and instruments of the modern state to organize a society on principles apart from the other modern systems which they despise, yet fear.

## Notes

1. The classic studies of the background of the Pakistan movement, representing the Indian Muslim and the Pakistani perspective respectively, are Mujeeb, Muhammad. 1967. *The Indian Muslims*. London: George Allen & Unwin; Qureshi, I. H. 1962. *The Muslim Community of the Indo-Pakistan Subcontinent*. The Hague: Mouton. See also Hardy, Peter. 1972. *The Muslims of British India*. Cambridge: Cambridge University Press. For the position of the religious leadership in the core area of what is now Pakistan, see Gilmartin, David. 1979. 'Religious Leadership and the Pakistan Movement in the Punjab'. *Modern Asian Studies*, 13: 485–93.

2. For a survey of these and other aspects of Pakistani history, see Sayeed, Khalid B. 1980. *Politics in Pakistan: The Nature and Direction of Change*.

New York: Praeger; Taylor, David. 1983. 'The Politics of Islam and Islamization in Pakistan'. In Piscatori, James P., ed. *Islam in the Political Process*, pp. 181-98. Cambridge: Cambridge University Press; and Metcalf, Barbara D. 1982. 'Religious Myth and Nationalism: The Case of Pakistan'. In Merkl Peter and Ninian Smart, eds. *Religion and Myth in Modern Times*. New York: New York University Press.

3. These generalizations about the Zia regime continued even after the announcement of a civilian government in 1986, with Zia himself continuing as president.

4. Burki, Shahid Javed. 1984. 'Pakistan's Sixth Plan: Helping the Country Climb Out of Poverty'. *Asian Survey*, 24: 400-22.

5. For the early history and ideology of the Jama'at, see the excellent article by Adams, 1966. The Jama'at currently exists in the two very different political contexts of a presumably Islamicizing military rule in Pakistan and a secular constitutional polity in India. Although beyond what I am able to do, a comparison of the two contemporary organizations would offer an excellent opportunity to investigate how a single movement has changed in two very different contexts.

6. Mintjes, H. 1980. 'Maulana Mawdudi's Last Years and the Resurgence of Fundamentalist Islam'. *Al-Mushir*, 22: II, 67-9, for the reinterpretation of Maududi's position in this period; in this reinterpretation Jinnah becomes more like Maududi and Maududi like Jinnah. In the debate over the proposed Law of Evidence, discussed below, opponents of the proposal challenge 'these mullas [who] spoke against Pakistan' (*The Muslim*, 18 February 1983).

7. The Ahmadi are a highly coherent and successful sect, dating from the late nineteenth century; their beliefs about their founder are said to deny the finality of the Prophet. In 1974 they were declared a non-Muslim minority within Pakistan.

8. Like the Ikhwan al-Muslimun in the Middle East, the Jama'at is in principle opposed to a kingly and feudal regime as un-Islamic. Both movements were drawn to the Saudis, however, because of their Wahhabi origin and because of the magnet of the holy places; the Ikhwan, moreover, found common ground with the Saudis in their shared opposition to Nasser. As the Saudis have used their new-found wealth for Islamic causes, criticism of them has subsided, see Mintjes, 1980: 57.

9. Quoted in Mintjes, op. cit., p. 48.

10. Burki, Shahid Javed. 1984. 'Economic Management within an Islamic Context'. Paper presented to the annual meeting of the Association of Asian Studies, Washington, DC, 23 March.

11. These are for fornication, theft, gang robbery, drinking, and false accusation of female fornication. Recent work by Daniela Breda, comparing the Hadd Ordinance to the Indian Penal Code, argues that the law was formulated 'through the filter of Western legal ideas'. In discussions in Paris, May 1986.

12. H. Mintjes, interview with author in Rawalpindi, 20 February 1983. Dr Mintjes has carefully monitored the Islamization programme in Pakistan over the last several years. If minimal, there have been, certainly, reported cases of *hadd* penalties, particularly lashing for 'fornication'.

13. Juridiction of the Shari'a benches excludes the constitution, fiscal law, Muslim personal law, court procedures, and law relating to financial matters. Carroll, Lucy. 1982. 'Nizam-i-Islam: Processes and Conflicts in Pakistan's Programme of Islamization, with Special Reference to the Position of Women'. *Journal of Commonwealth and Comparative Politics*, 20: 57–95.

14. For a more detailed treatment of this and related issues, see Maskiell, 1983.

15. Any change would have to be initiated as new legislation proposed by the Council on Islamic Ideology. Also see Carroll, op. cit.

16. The final page of the pamphlet lists other publications of the publisher, the Islami Akademi. There are publications about the Jama'at as indicated by the name *tahrik-i islam* in the title; there is also a biography of Maulana Maududi, as well as one of Imam Khumeini (so named).

17. Western capitalist culture is *sarmayadarana maghribi tahzib* and pagan socialist culture is *mulhidana ishtiraki tahzib*. Each culture is assigned a colour: white for capitalist, red for socialist, and green for Islamic.

18. Long the most widely respected Muslim leader in India, Maulana Abu'i-Hasan 'Ali Nadwi (d. 1999) criticized Maududi and the Jama'at on the grounds that they distorted Islam by emphasizing political issues to the neglect of acts of worship; all else, he insisted, was only a means to them. See his 1978 publication *'Asr-i hazir men din ki tafhim o tashrih*. Lucknow. This argument stimulated a debate in India with Nadwi answered by S. A. Qadri on behalf of the Jama'at. See Troll, Christian W. 1983. 'The Meaning of Din: Recent Views of Three Eminent Indian Ulama'. In Troll, Christian W. ed. *Islam in India: Studies and Commentaries*, pp. 168–77, Delhi. Vikas Publishers.

19. For the development of this argument, see Lapidus, Ira M. 1983. *Contemporary Movements in Historical Perspective*. Institute of International Studies: Policy Papers in International Affairs, No. 18, University of California, Berkeley.

20. For an example of extensive use of feminist writings, including many articles from the American journal *Signs* (Stanford University), see Ahmad, Anis and Muslim, Sajjad. 1982. *Muslim Women and Higher Education: A Case for Separate Institutions and Work Plan for Women's University*. Islamabad: Institute of Policy Studies.

21. The following words, set in quotes in the text, are among the untranslatable terms: fashion, dieting, girlfriend, herd, secular.

22. Dr Israr, once allied with the Jama'at but now independent, has opened a school in Lahore and admits only young men who have, like himself, completed university training in some aspect of modern science or technology (comments about Dr Israr are based on an extended interview in Lahore,

10 February 1983). Reflecting the same distance from the madrasas of the ulama, Zia'ul-Haqq talked of modernizing the madrasas and freeing them from 'the influence of the mullahs', *Dawn Overseas Weekly*, 8 January 1978. Quoted in Carroll 1982: 77.

23. One can compare the major reformist work on women, the *Bihishti Zewar*, circa 1900, whose genesis also owes something to this desire for a sphere of power and control untouched by political or social intrusions. This book, however, covered all kinds of topics in the religious law and in cultural deportment, meant to assimilate women to the high normative tradition. It was not focused on immurement and it was not written in explicitly oppositional terms.

24. This theory is discussed from many perspectives in Metcalf, Barbara D., ed. 1984. *Moral Conduct and Authority: The Place of Adab in South Asian Islam*. Berkeley and Los Angeles: University of California Press.

25. See Russell, Ralph and Khurshidul Islam. 1974. 'The Satirical Verse of Akbar Ilahabadi (1846–1921)'. *Modern Asian Studies*, 8: 1–58. The reference to Mansur in the verse is to a ninth century mystic who was executed for his presumed monistic views; the cry referred to, *ana'l haqq*, is known and quoted in many contexts.

26. Richter, William L. 1979. 'The Political Dynamics of Islamic Resurgence in Pakistan'. *Asian Survey*, 19: 547–57.

27. I am avoiding here the assumption usually made that 'fundamentalists' are to be found among the traditionally educated, the 'lower middle class', people suffering status deprivation or feeling cut off from the benefits of economic growth. Fadwa El Guindi made the same point about the Ikhwan, where at least the student movement 'ranges all the way to the upper socio-economic class'. See El Guindi, Fadwa. 1983. 'Contemporary Activism and the Current Islamic Debate in Egypt'. Paper presented to the conference, 'Law and Development in the Contemporary Societies of the Middle East', University of California at Berkeley, 28-29 May.

28. This is one Nazima Ala, speaking for the Jama'at-i Talabat, *The Muslim*, 17 February 1983.

29. *Dawn*, 14 February 1983.

30. Amera Saeed Hamid, 'Women's Role in Society'. The author herself served formerly in the Pakistani Foreign Service and is now a journalist and researcher. In conversation with her in February 1983, I asked how the Islamization policy, presumably in effect then for some five years, had affected her. She replied very thoughtfully that her own life had not changed in any way at all externally. She and other women and men like herself, however, had been forced to think about Islam, to learn about their religion in a way that most of those who had been educated in English had never done before. The article discussed here illustrates the fruit of this thinking. One of the most sustained arguments on women's legal rights in accordance with Islam (denying the legitimacy of polygamy and claiming women's right to initiate

# 264 ISLAMIC CONTESTATIONS

divorce, for example) is Patel, 1979. The author is herself a lawyer and the
book is detailed and meticulous.

31. 'Whither Chadar and Char Diwari?', *The Muslim*, 14 February 1983.

32. For example, Begum Ra'ana Liaqat 'Ali Khan, the articulate and
influential widow of Pakistan's first Prime Minister, quoted in *Dawn*, 14
February 1983.

33. The two laws raise parallel implications because of the payment of half
the amount of blood money in case of a woman.

34. Idris, 'Atiya (Daughter of 'Allama Khalil' Arab Ansari). 1982. *Qur'an
wa sunnat aur fiqh-i islami ki roshni men 'aurat ki shahadat aur diyat ka mas'ila*
(The problem of evidence and blood price in the light of the Qur'an, sunna,
and Islamic Law). Islamabad: Women's Division, Government of Pakistan.

35. A charge made, for example, by the Minister of State for Health and
Social Welfare, Begum Afifa Mamdot, the most prestigious woman to have
denounced the petitioner who opposed the Law of Evidence (*The Pakistan
Times*, 19 February 1983).

36. *Dawn*, 16 February 1983.

37. Nor does the government project a consistent image, as noted above
in the discussion of the Women's Division. Here is a small example of that
inconsistency in the context of another 'authority'—patriotism. A musical
interlude was shown from time to time during 1983 on the state controlled
television in which a singer offered a sentimental song on 'our Pakistan', 'our
garden', with scenes of the country flashed on the screen, among them a
woman, with head uncovered, gesticulating at a microphone and a woman
karate player flinging down what appeared to be a male opponent.

# 11

## 'Traditionalist' Islamic Activism
### Deoband, Tablighis, and Talibs

When the Afghan Taliban emerged into the international spotlight at the end of the twentieth century, no image was more central than what seemed to be their rigid and repressive control of individual behaviour, justified in the name of Islam. They set standards of dress and public behaviour that were particularly extreme in relation to women, limiting their movement in public space and their employment outside the home. They enforced their decrees through public corporal punishment. Their image was further damaged, particularly after the bombings of the East African American embassies in 1998, when they emerged as the 'hosts' of Osama bin Laden and other 'Arab Afghans' associated with him.[1]

Many commentators described the Taliban with generic, catch-all phrases like 'fanatic', 'medieval', and 'fundamentalist'.[2] The Taliban identified themselves, however, as part of a Sunni school of thought that has its origins in the late nineteenth century colonial period of India's history. The school is named after Deoband, the small country town north-east of Delhi, where the original madrasa or seminary of the movement was founded in 1867. Many of the Taliban had, indeed, studied in Deobandi schools, but one spokesman for the movement in its final months went so far as to declare 'Every Afghan is a Deobandi'.[3] This comment may be disconcerting to those familiar with the school in its Indian environment where its 'ulama—those learned in traditional subjects and typically addressed as 'maulana'—were not directly engaged in politics and were primarily occupied in teaching and providing both practical and spiritual guidance to their followers. The comment might be disconcerting as well, moreover, since it was suggestive of a regime shaped by ideals more than reality, given, for example, the substantial Shi'a element in the Afghan population.

Another movement linked to Deoband came to international attention at the same time, an apolitical, quietist movement of internal grassroots missionary renewal, the Tablighi Jama'at. It gained some notoriety when it appeared that a young American who had joined the Taliban first went to Pakistan through the encouragement of a Tablighi Jama'at missionary.[4] This movement was intriguing, in part by the very fact that it was so little known, yet, with no formal organization or paid staff, sustained networks of participants that stretched around the globe.

The variety of these movements is in itself instructive. Clearly, all Islamic activism is not alike, and each of these movements deserves attention on its own. Together, however, for all their variety, these Deoband movements were, in fact, alike in one crucial regard that set them apart from other well-known Islamic movements. What they shared was an overriding emphasis on encouraging a range of ritual and personal behavioural practices linked to worship, dress, and everyday behaviour. These were deemed central to shari'a—divinely ordained morality and practices, as understood in this case by measuring current practice against textual standards and traditions of Hanafi reasoning. The anthropologist Olivier Roy calls such movements 'neo-fundamentalist' to distinguish them from what can be seen as a different set of Islamic movements, often called 'Islamist'.[5] Limited, as he puts it, to 'mere implementation of the shari'a' in matters of ritual, dress, and behaviour, 'neo-fundamentalist' movements are distinguishable from Islamist parties primarily because, unlike them, they have neither a systematic ideology nor a global political agenda. A more precise label for them is, perhaps, 'traditionalist', because of their continuity with earlier institutions, above all those associated with the seminaries and with the 'ulama in general.

The contrasting Islamist movements include the Muslim Brothers in Egypt and other Arab countries, and the Jama'at-i Islami in the Indian subcontinent, as well as many thinkers involved in the Iranian revolution. All these movements constructed ideological systems and systematically built models for distinctive polities that challenged what they saw as the alternative systems: nationalism, capitalism, and Marxism.[6] Participants were Western educated, not seminary educated. They were engineers and others with technical training, lawyers, doctors, and university professors, and, generally speaking, they had little respect for the traditionally educated 'ulama. These 'Islamist' movements sought to 'do' modernity in ways that simultaneously asserted the cultural pride of the subjects and avoided the 'black' side of Western modernity. Many of the jihad movements that arose in Afghanistan in opposition to the Soviets were heirs of Islamist thought (although over time they also moved to define their Islamic politics primarily as encouragement of a narrow range of Islamic practices and symbols).[7] Participants in militant movements, including bin Laden's Al Qaeda, often belonged to extremist, breakaway factions of Islamist parties.

What is perhaps most striking about the Deoband-type movements is the extent to which politics is an empty 'box', filled expediently and pragmatically depending on what seems to work best in any given situation. Islam is often spoken of as 'a complete way of life'—arguably a modernist and misleading distinction from other historical religious traditions—so that political life must be informed by Islamic principles. In fact, as these Deobandi movements illustrate, virtually any strategy is accepted that allows the goal of encouraging what is defined as core shari'a-based individual practice, coupled with a range of mundane goals that may or may not be explicit—from protection of life and property to social honour and political power to the dignity that comes from pious adherence to what are taken as divine commands. Indeed, these movements often work well in the context of secular regimes where they can pursue their emphasis on disseminating adherence to correct practice with relative freedom.

Secondly, the movements illustrate another important corrective. A great deal is written about modern Muslim societies being consumed with antipathy toward America, American values, and American international political activities. No one, especially after 11 September 2001 would deny that anger exists. However, anger may well be very specific; for example, it may be directed at specific

American international policies and not at American 'freedom' or 'values' in general. Moreover, Islamic movements like the ones discussed here may have many goals and offer a range of social, moral, and spiritual satisfactions that are positive and not merely a reactionary rejection of modernity or 'the West'. Quite simply, these movements may, in the end, have much less to do with 'us' than is often thought. In all their complexity, the Deobandi movements serve as an example of one important model of contemporary Islamic thought and action, a major example of what can be called 'traditionalist' Islamic activism.

## The Daru'l-'Ulum and 'Cultural Strengthening'

The origin of the Deobandi school of thought is literally a school, a madrasa or seminary, founded in the late nineteenth century at the height of colonial rule in the Delhi region of northern India.[8] Indeed, the key institution of the movement would prove to be the seminary. The madrasa does not appear to have been a major institution in the pre-colonial period. Instead, those who wished to be specialists in the great classic disciplines studied through Arabic—Qur'an, Qur'anic recitation and interpretation, hadith, jurisprudential reasoning based on these holy sources, and ancillary sciences like logic, rhetoric, and grammar—would sit at the feet of one or more teachers, travelling often from place to place, seeking not a degree but a certificate of completion of particular books and studies. The modern madrasa, in contrast, as a formal institution, organized by classes, offering a sequential curriculum, staffed by a paid faculty, and supported by charitable campaigns, was a product of the colonial period and the result of familiarity with European educational institutions. The founders of the school gained support by utilizing all manner of new technologies—from printing presses to the post office to railroads—as they turned from reliance on increasingly constrained princely patronage to popularly based contributions. Deoband spun off some two dozen other seminaries across the subcontinent by the end of the nineteenth century.[9]

Boys who came to the school were provided their basic necessities. They lived modestly and were expected to adhere to a serious schedule of discipline. They did not learn English or other 'modern' subjects. They did use Urdu as a lingua franca, enhancing links among students from Bengal to Central Asia to the south. The 'ulama who founded this school were above all specialists in prophetic hadith, the narratives that constitute the Prophet Muhammad's sayings and practices and that serve either directly or analogously to guide every aspect of moral behaviour. Their lives were meant to embody their teachings. Through the giving of fatwa, they responded to inquiries with advisory opinions to guide their followers as well. By the end of the nineteenth century, Deoband formalized the position of a chief mufti at the school. Increasingly, the Deobandi fatwa, like the fatwa of other groups, were disseminated through print. Fatwa were judgments, attempts to fit sanctioned precedent to present circumstances, and it was well accepted that there could be differences of opinion about what was correct. Islamic law at its core is not rigid but profoundly contextual.

Focus on hadith was not only central to the desire to live in external conformity to certain behavioural patterns. It was also a route to cultivating a spiritual relationship through practice, love, and devotion to the Prophet Muhammad and, through the bonds of Sufism, to those guides and elders who were his heirs in chains of initiation that stretched back through time. Many of the teachers at Deoband shared Sufi bonds, and many students sought initiation into the charisma filled relationship of discipleship. The Deobandis cherished stories about the Sufis. They practised the disciplines and meditations that opened them to what was typically imagined as a relationship that developed from one focused on their teacher, to one engaged with the Prophet, and, ultimately, with the Divine. The bonds among students and teachers in this largely male world were profound and enduring, based on shared experience, commitments, and affection.

The 'ulama as a class were new in the modern period, much as the madrasas that produced them were. There of course had been learned people in Mughal times, but the emergence of a distinctive class, one that over time became professionalized (for example with 'degrees' recognized by state authorities), was very new. The role of the 'ulama was distinctive as well. Instead of being trained, as the learned had been in the past, for specific state functions in such areas as the judiciary, these scholars went out to take up positions as teachers themselves, writers, debaters with rival Muslims and non-Muslims, publishers in the expanding vernacular marketplace, prayer leaders, and guardians at mosques and shrines.

The Deobandis were 'reformist' in a way that, with broad strokes, was shared across a whole range of Muslim, Sikh, and Hindu movements in the colonial period. Characteristic were movements that recognized a lack of worldly power and looked to earlier periods or pristine texts as a source of cultural pride and a possible road-map to resurgence. Armed with their studies of hadith, the Deobandis, for example, deplored a range of customary celebrations and practices, including what they regarded as excesses at saints' tombs, elaborate life cycle celebrations, and practices attributed to the influence of the Shi'a.

There were rival Islamic reformist schools in the quest for true Islamic practice. One group, the Ahl-i Hadith, for example, in their extreme opposition to such practices as visiting the Prophet's grave, rivalled that of the Arabians typically labelled 'Wahhabi'. The Wahhabis were followers of an iconoclastic late eighteenth century reform movement associated with tribal unification who were to find renewed vigour in internal political competition within Arabia in the 1920s.[10] From colonial times until today, it is worth noting, the label 'Wahhabi' is often used to discredit any reformist or politically active Islamic group.

Another group that emerged in these same years was popularly known as 'Barelvi', and although engaged in the same process of measuring current practice against hadith, was more open to many customary practices. They called the others 'Wahhabi'. These orientations—'Deobandi', 'Barelvi' or 'Ahl-i Hadith'—would come to define sectarian divisions among Sunni Muslims of South Asian background to the present. Thus, 'ulama, mosques, and a wide range of political, educational, and missionary movements were known by these labels at the end of the twentieth century, both within the South Asian countries of India, Pakistan, and Bangladesh, as well as in places like Britain, where South Asian populations settled.[11] Beginning in the colonial era, 'ulama competed in public life to show themselves as the spokesmen or defenders of 'Islam' to their fellow Muslims. This was a new understanding of Islam, as a corporate identity in competition with others, and it created a new role in public life for religious leaders.

That role in the colonial period was not overtly political. The brutal repression of the so-called Mutiny of 1857 against the British had fallen very hard on north Indian Muslims. In the aftermath, the 'ulama, not surprisingly, adopted a stance of apolitical quietism. As the Indian nationalist movement became a mass movement after World War I, the Deobandi leadership did something of an about-face. They were never a political party as such, but, organized as the Association of the 'Ulama of India (Jamiat 'Ulama-i Hind), they threw in their lot with Gandhi and the Indian National Congress in opposition to British rule. Deobandi histories written before 1920 insisted that the ulama did not participate in the anti-colonial rebellion of 1857; those written after, give 'freedom fighters' pride of place. Like much of the orthodox Jewish leadership in the case of the Zionist movement, most Deobandis opposed the creation of what in 1947 would become the independent state of Pakistan—a separate state for Muslims to be led by a westernized, secular leadership.[12] They preferred operating in an officially secular context, apart from the government, in pursuit of their own goals.

Despite a serious dispute over control of the institution in the early 1980s, Deoband at the end of the twentieth century continued to thrive, with more than 3000 students enrolled, although in the mid-1990s the government of India terminated visas that allowed foreign students to enrol. The seminary's web page displays a monumental marble mosque, still being built and intended to accommodate more than 30,000 worshippers. Links provide further information in English, Hindi, Arabic, and Urdu.[13] Visitors to the school reported remarkable continuity in the content and mode of teaching characteristics of the school,[14] and the web page itself stresses its enduring role: the training 'of Ulama, Shaikhs, traditionalists, jurisconsults, authors and experts'. Its network of schools, moreover, are 'stars of this very solar system by the light of which every nook and corner of the religious and academic life of the Muslims of the subcontinent is radiant'. Among these, presumably would be the humble Deobandi madrasas along the Pakistan-Afghan frontier and in southern Afghanistan, which were the original Taliban base.[15] But within India at least, the ulama of Deoband continued their pre-Independence pattern: they did not become a political party and they justified political cooperation with non-Muslims as the best way to protect Muslim interests. For 'millions of Muslim families', the website writes, '[their] inferiority complex was removed'.

## Tablighi Jama'at

The Tablighi Jama'at was an offshoot of the Deoband movement. In some ways, it represented an intensification of the original Deobandi commitment to individual regeneration apart from any explicit political programme. All reform movements strike some balance between looking to individual regeneration on the one hand and intervention from above on the other. The Tablighis put their weight wholly at the end of reshaping individual lives. They were similar in this regard to an organization like Alcoholics Anonymous—to pick a familiar example which began at about the same period—in its rejection of progressive-era government politics in favour of individual bootstraps. Like AA, the heart of Tablighi Jama'at strategy was the belief that the best way to learn is to teach and encourage others.

Always closely tied to men with traditional learning and the holiness of Sufis, Tablighi Jama'at nonetheless took its impetus from a desire to move dissemination of Islamic teachings away from the madrasa, the heart of Deobandi activity, toward inviting 'lay' Muslims, high and low, learned and illiterate, to share the obligation of enjoining others to faithful practice. It also differed from the original movement because it eschewed debate with other Muslims over jurisprudential niceties and resultant details of practice. The movement began in the late 1920s when Maulana Muhammad Ilyas Kandhlawi (d. 1944), whose family had long associations with Deoband and its sister school in Saharanpur, the Mazaahiru'l-'Ulum, sought a way to reach nominally Muslim peasants who were being targeted by a Hindu conversion movement.

Maulana Ilyas's efforts took place in an atmosphere of religious violence and the beginnings of mass political organization. His strategy was to persuade Muslims that they themselves, however little book learning they had, could go out in groups, approaching even the ulama, to remind them to fulfil their fundamental ritual obligations. Participants were assured of divine blessing for this effort, and they understood that through the experiences of moving outside their normal everyday enmeshments and pressures, in the company of like-minded people bent on spending their time together in scrupulous adherence to Islamic behaviour, they themselves would emerge with new accomplishments, dignity, and spiritual blessing. Tablighis not only eschewed debate, but also emulated cherished stories, recalling prophetic hadith of withdrawing from any physical attack, an experience mission groups periodically encountered. No word resonates more in Tablighi reports of their experiences than *sukun*, the 'peace' they experience as a foretaste of the paradise they believe their efforts (jihad), in this path of Allah, help merit.

A pattern emerged of calling participants to spend one night a week, one weekend a month, forty continuous days a year, and ultimately a hundred and twenty days at least once in their lives engaged in tabligh missions. Women would work among other women or travel, occasionally, with their menfolk on longer tours.[16] Although Tablighis in principle preferred to use any mosque as their base while travelling, over time specific mosques throughout the world have come to be known as 'Tablighi mosques'. Periodic convocations also came to be held. With no formal bureaucracy or membership records, it is hard to calculate the number of participants over time, but at the end of the twentieth century, annual meetings of perhaps two million people would congregate for three-day meetings in Raiwind, Pakistan and Tungi, Bangladesh; large regional meetings were regularly held in India; and other convocations took place in North America and Europe, for example in Dewsbury, the site of a major seminary associated with Tablighi activities in the north of England. These convocations were considered moments of intense blessings as well as occasions to organize for tours. They also gave evidence of the vast numbers touched by the movement.

Even though there are publications specific to the movement, above all those associated with Maulana Muhammad Zakariyya Kandhlawi (d. 1982) of the Mazaahiru'l-'Ulum madrasa at Saharanpur, the stress in the movement was not at all on book learning but rather on face to face, or 'heart to heart', communication.[17] Their cherished books included topically arranged prophetic traditions, used as a stimulus to everyday behaviour. In invoking and embodying those traditions, participants felt themselves part of dense networks of Muslims, both dead and alive, and aspired to relive the Prophet's own time when he too was part of a faithful few among a population sunk in ignorance. Participation thus gave meaning and purpose to everyday life. It is important to see that participation in such a movement, often explained as a response to the failure of the corrupt, underdeveloped, or alienating societies in which Muslims perhaps find themselves, in fact offered a positive, modern solution to people who were geographically and socially mobile. Participants in principle made a 'lifestyle' choice; they found a stance of cultural dignity; they opted for a highly disciplined life of sacrifice; they found a moral community of mutual acceptance and purpose. That community would be reinvented and reformed in the course of missions, and replaced if participants themselves relocated. Other contemporary Islamic movements of the 'ulama or, indeed, of Sufi cults, provided many of the same satisfactions.

As noted above, the original Deobandis were both 'ulama and Sufis, offering 'a composite' form of religious leadership. Indeed Pnina Werbner has recently argued that the fact that Muslims in South Asia (in contrast to those in other parts of the Muslim world) have not had to choose between Sufism and a learned, often reformist, leadership in the modern period accounts for the vitality of Sufism and, indeed, for the continued role of the 'ulama.[18] Tablighis continued to offer the 'ulama a respected role. The place of Sufism was more complex. Although what were seen as deviant customs around holy men were discouraged, Sufism in no sense disappeared. Indeed, among Tablighis, the holiness associated with the Sufi *pir* was in many ways defused into the charismatic body of the jama'at so that the missionary group itself became a channel for divine intervention. The kind of story typically told about a saint—overcoming ordeals, being blessed with divine illumination, triumphantly encountering temporal authority—was in fact often told about a group engaged in a mission. Thus, as in the initial Deoband movement and in many other Sufi and sectarian movements in modern South Asia, it was not necessary to choose between the devotional power of Sufism and the conviction of reformist imitation of prophetic teaching.

Participants in tablighi activities define their efforts as jihad. This word is, of course, widely translated as 'holy war' but its root meaning is 'effort' or 'struggle'. Following prophetic hadith, jihad may be classified as 'the greater jihad', the inner struggle to discipline and moral purification that a person exerts upon the individual self, or as 'the lesser jihad' of militancy or violence. For both kinds of jihad, the focus transcends the nation state to a global *umma*. Tablighis use the same discourse of jihad as do those engaged in militant action. Their leaders are *amirs*, their outings are 'sorties' or 'patrols'; the merits for actions are exponentially multiplied as they are during a military campaign; a person who dies in the course of tabligh is a *shahiid*. Finally, the obligation to mission is not negotiable: on fulfilling it hinges nothing less than one's own ultimate fate at the Day of Judgment. Both militants and Tablighis, moreover, stress the obligation of the individual believer, not (in the case of mission) the ulama, nor (in the case of militancy) the state.[19] One of the fundamental characteristics of the reform movements of the colonial period and after was a diffusion of leadership and authority, a kind of 'laicization', evident here.

The key difference in the two kinds of jihad is, of course, that one is the jihad of personal purification, the other of warfare. In the words of an annual meeting organizer at Raiwind, 'Islam is in the world to guide people, not to kill them. We want to show the world the correct Islam.'[20] As noted above, the oft told tales of the movement are tales of meeting opposition, even violence, and of unfailingly withdrawing from conflict—and of so gaining divine intervention and blessing.

Effectively by this focus, as in the original Deoband movement, religion, in practice, became a matter of personal, private life, separate from politics. This division, albeit untheorized, has worked well in the context of a wide variety of state structures, including the modern liberal state. The Sufi tradition, moreover, here as elsewhere, always engages with, but imagines itself morally above, worldly power. This attitude further encourages an apolitical or detached stance toward government.

## The Taliban and their Teachers, the Jamiat Ulema-i Islam (JUI)

In the final years of colonial rule, a minority group among the Deobandi 'ulama dissented from support for the secular state and the privatization of religion espoused by the Indian nationalist movement. They organized, instead, as the Jamiat Ulema-i Islam to support the Muslim League and the demand for a separate Muslim state. In Independent Pakistan after 1947 they became a minor political party led by 'ulama and a voice in the ongoing debate over the nature of the Pakistani state. Should it be the secular state presumably intended by its founders, or a state meant to be shaped in accordance with Islam? The JUI has never had more than minute popular support, and the content of the party's programmes over the years, it is probably fair to say, has been a fairly simplistic call for the primacy of Islam in public life.[21]

Like other Pakistani parties, the JUI has been subject to factional splits coalescing around personalities more than issues, and there were perhaps a half-dozen factions and reorganizations over its first half century.[22] The JUI struck alliances with any party that would win them influence. In the 1970s, for example, they allied with a Pashtun regionalist party in opposition to Bhutto's Pakistan People's Party (PPP), a party that was, in principle, socialist. In the mid-1990s, in contrast, they allied with that same PPP, now led by Bhutto's Harvard and Oxford educated daughter. Its ulama were given to realpolitik with a vengeance and, like just about every party in Pakistan, not shielded from corruption, in this case because they were clerics. Their most famous leader at one point, for example, was referred to as 'Maulana Diesel' because of his reputed involvement in fuel smuggling earlier in the 1990s.[23] When the JUI was excluded from power, its Islamic rhetoric became a language of opposition, often invoking a discourse of 'democracy' and 'rights'.

At the same time, the 'ulama of the JUI were engaged with the madrasas that furthered Deobandi teachings. From the 1980s on, the number of seminaries in Pakistan soared, used as a tool of conservative influence by the military dictator Ziaul Haq (in power from 1977 through 1988), who was, in fact, particularly sympathetic to the Deobandi approach. The seminaries were not only a resource in domestic politics but at times found themselves engaged in a kind of 'surrogate' competition between Saudis and Iranis, as each patronized religious institutions likely to support their side.[24] It was in this atmosphere of politics and education that the origin of the Taliban is to be found.

The surge in the number of madrasas in the 1980s coincided with the influx of some three million Afghan refugees, for whose boys the madrasas located along the frontier frequently provided the only available education. One school in particular, the Madrasa Haqqaniya, in Akora Kathak near Peshawar, trained many of the top Taliban leaders. These sometime students (*talib*; plural, *taliban*) were shaped by many of the core Deobandi reformist causes, all of which were further encouraged by Arab volunteers in Afghanistan. These causes, as noted above, included rigorous concern with fulfilling rituals; opposition to custom laden ceremonies at weddings and pilgrimage to shrines, along with practices associated with the Shi'a minority; and a focus on seclusion of women as a central symbol of a morally ordered society. Theirs was, according to Ahmed Rashid, a long time observer, 'an extreme form of Deobandism, which was being preached by Pakistani Islamic parties in Afghan refugee camps in Pakistan.'[25] This focus on a fairly narrow range of shari'a law, which emphasized personal behaviour and ritual, was something the Taliban shared with other Deobandi movements, even while the severity of the Taliban approach made them unique.

The Taliban emerged as a local power in Afghanistan starting in 1994 because they were able to provide protection and stability in a context of warlordism, raping, and corruption. They found ready support from elements within the Pakistani state, which welcomed an ally likely to protect trade routes to Central Asia and to provide a friendly buffer on the frontier. Similarly, the Taliban also appeared, in the mid-1990s, to serve a range of US interests, above all in securing a route for an oil pipeline to the Central Asian oilfields outside Iranian control. The Taliban, on their part, like their teachers, were not ideologically driven as they determined with whom they were willing to work as allies and supporters. Indeed, the scholar Olivier Roy suggests that while they could not be manipulated easily—for example in relation to issues related to women—they were profoundly expedient when it came to securing a power base. They worked with the Pakistani state, the United States, and, anti-Shi'a or not, he argues, they would have dealt with Iran had it served their advantage.[26] The United States' interest in the Taliban shifted away from them, however, first because of what were seen as human rights abuses in relation to women, and second because the East African embassy bombings in August 1998 were linked to the presence of terrorist activists within Taliban controlled areas, with Osama bin Laden as their most visible supporter. That alliance would, after the World Trade Center bombing of 11 September 2001, be the Taliban's undoing. Bin Laden's charisma, his access to wealth, and his networks had been invaluable to the Taliban in achieving their success, and his anti-Americanism found fertile soil among the Taliban already inclined to disapproval of 'the West'. There is an irony in the fact that links to him brought the Taliban down, since the Taliban's driving force at core had *not* been abhorrence of Western culture but the specific goal of prevailing within Afghanistan, and, in so doing, fostering Islamic behaviour.

The Taliban, for all their extremism and the anomaly of their rise to power on the basis of dual levels of support from Pakistan and Arabs, nonetheless throw into relief an important dimension of Deobandi strategy in the school's early years and later. None of the Deobandi movements has a theoretical stance in relation to political life. They either expediently embrace the political culture of their time and place or withdraw from politics completely. For the Taliban, that meant engaging with the emerging ethnic polarities in the country and seeking allies wherever they could find them.[27] For the JUI, it meant playing the game of realpolitik in Pakistani political life. For the Deobandis in India and the Tablighi Jama'at, it meant fostering benign relations with existing regimes—necessary even in the latter case to receive permits for meetings, travel visas, and protection.

## Deobandis, Talibs, and Tablighis

Deobandis, Talibs, and Tablighis demonstrate pragmatic responses to the varying environments in which they find themselves. The Taliban surely represent an exceptional case both in their rigour—criticized, for example, in relation to women even by leading ulama of the JUI—and in the deal they struck with Arab extremists, who were like them in embracing Islamic rituals and social norms, but so unlike them in their vision of global jihad. Even the Taliban, arguably, had moderate voices, as well as pragmatism in their alliances, that might one day have made their society more acceptable in terms of international standards, had that possibility not been foreclosed by the attacks of 11 September and the American 'war on terrorism'.[28]

The other Deobandi movements—the JUH in India, the JUI in Pakistan, Tablighi Jama'at everywhere—although they tend to see the world in black and white, have in fact all played a largely moderate role by participating in or accepting ongoing political regimes. The recent exceptions were some students and teachers in the madrasas of Pakistan, as well as Pakistanis in other walks of life, who were drawn to the heady rhetoric, demonizing America and Jews on the one hand and imagining the triumph of global Islam on the other, symbolized by the jihad in Afghanistan.[29] Deobandi madrasas on the Pakistani Frontier at the turn of the twenty-first century periodically closed to allow their students to support Taliban efforts.[30]

Nevertheless, the historical pattern launched by the Deoband 'ulama for the most part treated political life on a primarily secular basis, typically, de facto if not de jure, identifying religion with the private sphere and in that sphere fostering Islamic teachings and interpretations that proved widely influential. Aside from Deoband's enduring influence, it exemplifies a pattern, represented in general terms in a range of Islamic movements outside South Asia as well, of 'traditionalist' cultural renewal on the one hand coupled with political adaptability on the other. This tradition, seen over time and across a wide geographic area, illustrates that there are widespread patterns of Islamic apoliticism that foster a modus vivendi with democratic and liberal traditions. It also demonstrates, most notably in the teaching and missionary dimensions of their activities, that the goals and satisfactions that come from participation in Islamic movements may well have little to do with opposition or resistance to non-Muslims or 'the West'. Their own debates or concerns may well focus on other Muslims—an internal foe, and not an external 'Other' at all.[31] And what they offer participants may be the fulfilment of desires for individual empowerment, transcendent meaning, and moral sociality that do not engage directly with national or global political life at all.

As for political life, recently the commentator Nicholas Lemann has argued that particularly in contexts of weak or non-existent states, alliances typically reflect estimates of who will prevail, not who is 'right'. As Lemann puts it, 'In the real world people choose to join not one side of a great clash of civilizations but what looks like the winning team in their village'.[32] The JUI would seem almost a textbook case of this kind of argument. In the fragmented, factionalized world of Pakistan's gasping democracy, the winning side seems to be whichever party—regional interest, secular, or Islamic—offers some leverage. In the aftermath of the terrorist attacks of 11 September along with the Jama'at-i Islami, the JUI

was at the forefront of anti-American protest. Were they motivated, particularly given their support base among Pashtuns along
the Afghan border, by the expectation that the 'winning team'
would be transnational Islamic militants (and their funding sources),
and, in the end, that they would gain the support of the presumed
majority of Pakistanis who do not support religious parties but do
resent American foreign policy? As for the Deobandis in India,
sometimes the winning team seemed to be the British colonial
power, sometimes the Indian National Congress, sometimes other
parties.

Tablighi Jama'at is particularly striking in regard to its accommo-
dationist strategy since it implicitly fosters the privatization of
religion associated with the modern liberal state. Political leaders
of all stripes in Pakistan and Bangladesh at least since the mid-1980s
have invariably appeared at the annual convocations and been
welcomed accordingly. Some observers and political figures claim
that the movement is in fact covertly political; others, that it is the
first stage on the way to militancy. This argument is made particularly in Pakistan, since the majority of Tabligh participants there
belong to the frontier province adjoining Afghanistan. All of this
is, however, speculation. What is clear is that the formally apolitical
missionary tours, gatherings in local mosques and homes, and
annual gatherings continue to be the routine of the movement, one
that clearly offers meaning and dignity to many who participate.
In the many goals fostered by these movements—social, psychological, moral, and spiritual—as well as in the political strategies adopted
with such virtuosity, Islamic movements, in the end, turn out to
be less distinctive than either they or outsiders often assume they
are.

## Notes

1. I am grateful to Muhammad Khalid Masud, Academic Director, and
Peter van der Veer, Co-Director, who invited me to give the annual lecture
of the Institute for the Study of Islam in the Modern World, Leiden University,
23 November 2001. This essay is based on the lecture I gave on that occasion.

2. An example of the typically imprecise discussion of 'Deobandism' is:
'A sect that propagates a belief that has inspired modern revivals of Islamic
fundamentalism.' Burns, John F. 2001. 'Adding Demands, Afghan Leaders
Show Little Willingness to Give up Bin Laden'. *The New York Times*, 19
September.

3. Conversation with 'the ambassador at large' of the Taliban, Rahmatullah Hashemi, Berkeley California, 6 March 2001, in the course of his tour through the Middle East, Europe, and the United States.

4. See for example 'A Long, Strange Trip to the Taliban'. In *Newsweek*, 17 December 2001, and Lattin, Don and Kevin Fagan. 2001. 'John Walker's Curious Quest: Still a Mystery How the Young Marine County Convert to Islam Made the Transition from Spiritual Scholar to Taliban Soldier'. *San Francisco Chronicle*, 13 December.

5. Roy, Olivier. 1998. 'Has Islamism a Future in Afghanistan?' In Maley, William. ed. *Fundamentalism Reborn? Afghanistan and the Taliban*, pp. 19–211. New York: NYU Press.

6. Here I differ from Salman Rushdie who uses the term too broadly: 'These Islamists [here he speaks of "radical political movements"] we must get used to this word, 'Islamists', meaning those who are engaged upon such political projects, and learn to distinguish it from the more general and politically neutral "Muslim".' Salman Rushdie, 'Yes, this is about Islam.' *The New York Times*, 2 November 2001.

7. The Jamiyyat-i Islami was formed by Burhanuddin Rabbani and others who had studied at Al Azhar; the Hezb-i Islami of Gulbuddin Hekmatyar was more influenced by the Pakistani Jama'at-i Islami. On the original movements, see Nasr, Seyyid Vali. 1994. *The Vanguard of the Islamic Revolution: The Jama'at-i Islami of Pakistan*. Berkeley: University of California Press, and Mitchell, Richard. 1969. *The Society of the Muslim Brothers*. London: Oxford University Press.

8. See Metcalf, Barabara, D. 1982. *Islamic Revival in British India: Deoband 1860–1900*. Princeton: Princeton University Press.

9. For an evocative picture of the education of an 'alim that, despite the Shi'a setting, resonates broadly with the kind of education briefly described here, see Mottahedeh, Roy P. 1985. *The Mantle of the Prophet: Religion and Politics in Iran*. New York: Simon and Schuster.

10. For a comparative view of the contexts of such movements, see Roff, William R. 1987. 'Islamic Movements: One or Many?' In Roff, William R., ed. *Islam and the Political Economy of Meaning*, pp. 31–52. London: Croom Helm and Berkeley: University of California Press.

11. For a general background to all these movements, see Metcalf. 1982. op. cit. On the 'Barelvis' (who call themselves Ahlu's-Sunnat wa'l-Jama'at in order to assert that they are true Muslims, not a sect), see Sanyal, Usha. 1996. *Devotional Islam and Politics in British India: Ahmad Riza Khan Barelwi and His Movement, 1870–1920*. New Delhi: Oxford University Press. For the experience of religious institutions in Pakistan, see Malik, Jamal. 1996. *Colonization of Islam: Dissolution of Traditional Institutions in Pakistan*. New Delhi: Manohar; and Zaman, Muhammad Qasim. 1990. 'Religious Education and the Rhetoric of Reform: The Madrasa in British India and Pakistan'. *Comparative Studies in Society and History* 41-2: 294–323 and Zaman. 1998.

'Sectarianism in Pakistan: The Radicalization of Shi'i and Sunni Identities'. *Modern Asian Studies* 32–3: pp. 689–716, as well as his forthcoming monograph from Princeton University Press. For the religious institutions of South Asian Muslims in Europe and North America, see Lewis, Philip. 1994. *Islamic Britain: Religion, Politics and Identity among British Muslims*. London: I. B. Tauris, and Metcalf, Barbara D., ed. 1995. *Making Muslim Space in North America and Europe*. Berkeley: University of California Press.

12. Friedmann, Yohanan. 1971. 'The Attitude of the Jam'iyyat-i 'Ulama'-i Hind to the Indian National Movement and Establishment of Pakistan'. In Baer, Gabriel, ed. *The Ulama in Modern History*, pp. 157–83. Jerusalem: Israeli Oriental Society, Asian and African Studies, VII.

13. www.darululoom-deoband.com. The estimate of numbers to be accommodated in the mosque is in Bedi, Rahul. 2001. 'Taliban Ideology Lives on in India'. On-line *Asia Times*. 12 December.

14. Many journalists travelled to Deoband in late 2001 in order to report on the source of Taliban religious training. See, for example, Harding, Luke. 2001. 'Out of India'. *The Guardian*. 2 November; Sharma, Kartikeya. 2001. 'Scholar's Getaway'. *The Week* (www.the-week.com/21jul01/life); Fathers, Michael. 2001. 'At the Birthplace of the Taliban'. *Time Magazine*. 21 September. Reprinted on www.foil.org/resources/9–11/Fathers010921-Deoband. On 29 December 2001 the search engine 'Google' listed approximately two thousand and five hundred sites for 'Deoband', many of them reporting on the links of the school to the Taliban.

15. The Madrasa Haqqania in Akhora Khatak trained the core Taliban leadership. See Goldberg, Jeffrey. 2000. 'Jihad U.: The Education of a Holy Warrior'. *The New York Times Magazine*. 25 June.

16. See Metcalf, Barbara, D. 1998. 'Women and Men in a Contemporary Pietist Movement: The Case of the Tablighi Jama'at'. In Basu, Amrita and Patricia Jeffery, eds, *Appropriating Gender: Women's Activism and Politicized Religion in South Asia*, pp. 107–21. New York: Routledge, and reprinted in 1999 in a re-titled volume, *Resisting the Sacred and the Secular: Women's Activism and Politicized Religion in South Asia*. Delhi: Kali for Women.

17. I discuss the movement's publications in my 1993 publication, 'Living Hadith in the Tablighi Jama'at'. *The Journal of Asian Studies* 52, 3: 584–608.

18. See her forthcoming study of the regional Sufi cult of Zindapir (2002. *Pilgrims of Love: The Anthropology of a Global Sufi Cult*. Bloomington: Indiana University Press). This study also exemplifies the positive accommodation to contemporary life offered by a transnational Sufi movement and explicitly distinguishes herself from those who explain Islamic religious movements as a reaction to frustration and failure.

19. A little noted aspect of Osama bin Laden's leadership was his claim to authority, despite his lack of a traditional education, to issue fatwa. His call to make jihad incumbent on all Muslims deployed a technical distinction

of Islamic legal thought, saying that jihad was an individual duty, *farz 'ain*, rather than a duty on some subset of the *umma* (e.g., political leaders, soldiers), *farz kifaya*.

20. Rone, Tempest. 2001. 'Huge Gathering of Moderate Muslims in Pakistan'. *San Francisco Chronicle*, 3 November. Also, Maulana Zubair-ul Hassan: '(The Holy Prophet) said it is not bravery to kill the non-believers but to preach [to] them is the real task'. Quoted in 'Tableeghi Ijtima Concludes'. *The Frontier Post* (Peshawar), 5 November 2001, (www. frontierpost. com.pk).

21. Seyyid Vali Reza Nasr, op. cit., makes the important argument that it is by welcoming Islamist parties into the democratic process, as happened in Pakistan in the mid-1980s, that they become political moderates.

22. See Pirazda, Sayyid A. S. 2000. *The Politics of the Jamiat Ulema-i-Islam Pakistan 1971–77*. Karachi: Oxford University Press.

23. The target of this is Fazlur Rahman, head of the JUI (F). See Bragg, Rick. 2001. 'A Pro-Taliban Rally Draws Angry Thousands in Pakistan, Then Melts Away'. *The New York Times*, 6 October.

24. See Nasr, Vali R. January 2000. 'International Politics, Domestic Imperatives, and Identity Mobilization: Sectarianism in Pakistan, 1979–98'. *Comparative Politics* 32-2: 171–90.

25. Rashid is the definitive source for the history of the Taliban. Rashid, Ahmed. 2000. *Taliban: Militant Islam, Oil and Fundamentalism in Central Asia*, p. 88. New Haven: Yale University Press.

26. Roy, op. cit., p. 211.

27. The phrase 'ethnic polarization' is Olivier Roy's. He uses this phrase to suggest that ethnic loyalties are complex and fluid, not ideologized. He further argues that these loyalties have shaped all parties in the Afghan competitions of recent years.

28. Hashemi for example attempted to establish common ground with his foreign interlocutors in the spring of 2001 (see note 3, above). He emphasized the desperate conditions inside his country, both the crisis of public order characterized by warlordism following the Soviet withdrawal in the early 1990s and the immediate extreme conditions produced by drought and famine, as partial explanation for the regime's severe policies. He insisted that the regime favoured public employment and education for women, but in the conditions of the time needed 'to protect' them. He tried to show that the destruction of the Bamian Buddhas was understandable if perhaps irrational; he almost suggested, as a reaction to offers of international aid to preserve antiquities rather than to avert starvation and disease.

29. For a sensitive analysis of the tension between the lure of this rhetoric and actual moderation in behaviour on the part of most British Muslims, see Werbner, Pnina. 2001. 'The Predicament of Diaspora and Millennial Islam'. *Times Higher Education Supplement*, 14 December. The argument is suggestive for the behaviour of many Muslims in a place like Pakistan as well.

30. See Friedman, Thomas L. 2001. 'In Pakistan, It's Jihad 101'. *The New York Times*, 13 November, and Goldberg, Jeffrey. 2000. 'Jihad U.: The Education of a Holy Warrior'. *The New York Times Magazine*, 25 June.

31. Mixed in with sites addressing current political issues among those referred to in note 5 above, are sites that primarily transfer the materials of polemical pamphlets to the web. Thus, a site posting 'Berelwi' perspectives excerpts Deobandi fatwa to show that they are guilty of the very insolence towards the Prophet that they condemn, the kind of condemnation current a hundred years ago. See www.schinan.com/jhangi. A particularly elaborate site, intended to show that Ahl-i Hadith beliefs alone are true, reviews the errors of many other groups, with a dozen and a half linked pages challenging issues of 'Tableegi-Jama'at'. See www.salaf.indiaaceess.com/tableegi-jamaat.

32. Leman, Nicholas. 2001. 'What Terrorists Want'. *The New Yorker*, 29 October, pp. 36–41.

# IV

# Islam, Society, and
the Imagination of the Self

# VI

Islam, Society, and
the Imagination of the Self

# 12

## Reflections on Iqbal's Mosque

In 1931 Muhammad Iqbal went to London to participate in the
Second Round Table Conference organized by the British Government to discuss further constitutional reforms in the Indian
Empire.[1] Iqbal's role was a minor one on that occasion, but on
his way home he stopped in Spain. There he sought out the
monuments that testified to the glorious past of Andalusia. He
was moved by his tour and found, above all else, the Mosque of
Cordoba to be a monument that riveted his thoughts and
emotions. He secured permission from the authorities of the
building, now a church, to perform the canonical prayers, and he
carried away from that moment a complex of emotions and
perceptions from which he was to forge one of the best-known and
beloved poems of his entire Urdu corpus.

The poem, 'The Mosque of Cordoba',[2] exemplifies many of
those qualities that have won Iqbal his popularity. The appeal of
the poem is often attributed to its subject. That alone, however,
does not explain the poem's magic, for the mosque alone could be
read about in Baedeker or a history of Spain. The subject is important only because of the way it is treated and the way it is embedded
in the poem. It is, therefore, important to examine the poem itself,
its stanzaic form and patterns of rhyme, and rhythm as well as its
content. Most studies of Iqbal take for granted the fact that Iqbal
is a poet and do not analyse his skill as craftsman and artist.
Treatments of his poetry typically extract from the verse aspects
of Iqbal's political or philosophic or religious thought without
attention to the context that gives them form and meaning.

The poem's ordering of line, metre, and rhyme on the one hand, and its patterning of metaphor and diction on the other, together are central to its effectiveness. Moreover, I would suggest, the meaning of the poem is inextricably linked to the fact that it is a structured and crafted expression. Iqbal in this poem not only celebrates a mosque, but literally builds in the verse a 'mosque' of his own. I should like, first, to look at the form of the poem; then, at the metaphor and diction that share its language; and, finally, at the meaning the structure embodies.

★ ★ ★

Iqbal, for all his modernist thought, did not deviate from classical forms when it came to poetry. His poems were written within well-defined patterns of metre and rhyme which he was able to manipulate masterfully. 'The Mosque of Cordoba' is a long poem. It consists of eight stanzas, each of sixteen lines of which the final two form an emphatic final couplet. The metric and rhyming pattern are basically that of the *ghazal*, a short lyric poem, here multiplied eight times. In this poem, however, each stanza has its own rhyme, and as typical in what is called *tarkib band*, each stanza concludes with a couplet whose importance is made clear by the fact that it does not include the common rhyme. Each line has a caesura, a break in the middle, and occasionally the common rhyme appears there as well. In the first stanza, for example, the rhyme appears not only in the first two lines and in alternate lines thereafter, but in the middle of three lines as well. The rhyme is particularly important. It resounds in each verse and its choice has a subtle influence on the reader or listener. Thus in the first stanza the end rhyme is *at*—a syllable which often indicates an Arabic plural; and I would suggest that its choice here strikes a tone of formality, of abstractness, of solemnity: *hadisat, hayat o mamat, sifat, mumkinat, ka'inat,* and so forth.

Within this structure, Iqbal chooses to create more patterns by using repetition and variations on recurrent phrases. He takes, again looking at the first stanza, a single phrase, *silsila-i roz o shab,* 'the chain (or succession) of day and night' and introduces five of the first eight lines with it. Moreover, in this stanza and throughout the poem he is particularly fond of parallel constructions. As many as four or five lines in a single stanza will have parallel forms in each of two phrases:

> *tujh ko parakhta hai yeh; mujh ko parakhta hai yeh*
> *maut hai teri barat; maut hai meri barat*
> *who bhi jalil o jamil; tu bhi jalil o jamil.*

The examples are many. Repetition of a phrase in the preceding couplet often appears in the first lines of a new stanza, making the transition effective.

The result of these patterns is that the poem sings. Fast-paced and flowing, it is hypnotic. Rhymes, repetitions, and parallels are mnemonic devices also and the listener remembers, soon predicts what comes next. This is true of all successful Urdu poetry, for this is a poetry primarily designed for recitation. Tempted to abstract from the poetry lofty thought on socialism or Sufism, we must not lose sight of the fact that Iqbal's skill in manipulating traditional poetic forms provided a foundation for his work. Poetry is not all craft, but craft certainly is an important part of poetry.

A further dimension of Iqbal's craftsmanship and skill is evident in the metaphoric images and diction of the poem. I should like, briefly, to describe the poem, stanza by stanza, pointing to prominent themes and selected examples of the poet's use of language.

The poem begins with a meditation on Time, on the succession of day and night. This succession itself is the delineator of all events; is the 'two coloured silk' from which God creates 'His robe of attributes'. In this one vivid image, Iqbal introduces the profound and complex issue of the relation between God and His creation. For the moment, he stresses human transience and he introduces the metaphor of music as a cry of pain from the endless succession of Time. Here, Time is personified as a *shroff* who weighs creation in the balance, finds it wanting and rewards it with death. Time, as noted above, is repeatedly described in the Persian phrase, *silsila-i roz o shab*. Against it, utilizing the rich options of vocabulary available in Urdu, Iqbal plays the humble everyday time of man for which he uses the common Hindi words of *din* and *rat*. That time, like all else associated with creation, is fleeting. The final emphatic couplet of the stanza insists on this nothingness: *manzil-i akhir fana*, a phrase which recalls the final stage pursued by the Sufi. Here that phrase resonates not with a sense of fulfilment but of emptiness.

The second stanza, echoing phrases from the first, continues the theme of the flow of Time, identifying it with water, with flood. But now *ishq* or dynamic love—to use Professor Schimmel's definition—is proclaimed as itself a tide able to stem all else. *Ishq* is characteristic of the special man, the Believer or Man of God. *Ishq* is equated in a series of cascading phrases with Gabriel's breath, the Prophet's heart, the envoy of God, God's word, the scholar, the noble, the vagabond. It is—returning to the question of the identity of man and God—the common link between man and some special segment of His creation. Again Iqbal speaks of music but now, no longer a cry of despair, it is the melody played on the strings of life plucked out by the plectrum of love. Throughout the stanza now plays an image of light, of radiance, of illumination, all owed to the presence of *ishq*.

In the third stanza, Iqbal develops the central meaning of the poem, the idea that the mosque, here introduced as the very embodiment of love, the product of the heart's blood, itself lives. The creative artifact, whether the stone of the mosque or the word of the poet, is thus transformed from death and mortality to life and immortality. Man's emotions transcend in value all else in creation, far surpassing the obedience of the angels which is given without cost. Of all men it is the poet—and this poet in particular— whose emotions are of such value. Iqbal calls himself *kafir-i hindi* whose passion is the passion of faith, made the stronger by the pride of the recent convert. In the final couplet he describes himself as an embodiment of the name of God. God the Creator, the Artist, and the Artist's artifact all are linked by the qualities which are introduced at the opening of the fourth stanza, those of *jalal* and *jamal* which are the qualities par excellence of God but are here shared by the mosque and by its architect. Iqbal revels in the beauties of the mosque and links it with other expressions of *ishq*, exulting in the Muslim past and again celebrating the faith in the final couplet which incorporates the first phrase of the *shahada*. Finally, in the fifth stanza, Iqbal pushes even further the question of the relation between the Creator and the artist when he says 'As is God's Hand, so [is his] hand'. He delineates the character of the Believer who is the truimph of God's creation, the slave whose qualities are in fact those of the Master.

In the sixth and seventh stanzas, Iqbal develops further his historical perspective, recalling the great moments of the Muslim past which now exist only in the memory of Muslim hearts. Muslim rule was humble, unlike European rule which was merely regal. Muslim rulers instructed the rest of the world. Echoes of that past live on in the warmth and openness of the people the poet sees before him. Andalusia's breezes waft the fragrance of Yemen; its songs retain the colouring of the Hejaz. But the poet wakes from this reverie to face the reality that Muslim worldly greatness is gone. He thinks of the Protestant Reformation and the French Revolution and hints that now the caravan of *ishq* has found its new halting place in the soul of Islam. What, he asks, will come surging from the ocean to change the whole colour of the cosmos?

In the final stanza Iqbal weaves together a synthesis of these images of the flow of time and water, of music, of colour and light, and of the crafted work. His opening note in this stanza is muted and nostalgic, set against neither day nor night but twilight. Music is now concrete, not abstract—the simple and affecting song of a peasant girl. Water is now no cosmic flood but the flowing Guadalquivir by whose banks he stands. But the music is transformed as the poet continues, for he announces that behind his eyes burns a new dawn. Latent within him is a song whose fire Europe will not be able to bear. Light is no longer twilight but the glow of his words. A people—not Time—must weigh its acts, he writes, and bring to life the fervour that passionate life requires. That fervour, the blood of the heart, alone makes a creative act like a poem perfect and whole.

Iqbal's poem at once describes and actualizes the power a poem can have. At one level, Iqbal writes to instruct the reader, to remind him of past glory, and future potential greatness. At another level, far more profound, he writes to embody his own spirit, to make it eternal. To achieve this latter objective he creates, as we have seen, an artifact—symmetric, highly structured, as classic as the mosque which is its analogue. Iqbal's stanzaic and imagistic pattern thus is important not only for creating a poem that sings, that resounds and allures the listener, but is intrinsic to creating the meaning of the poem as well.

★ ★ ★

'The Mosque of Cordoba' as a whole has salience, I would argue because it touches two concerns that have been central to thoughtful Muslims in this century: first, an interest in the glorious past of Muslim history; and second, a quest to understand the relation of man to God, an issue that has long roots in the intellectual history of Islamic, especially Sufi thought, and that finds in Iqbal a particularly interesting formulation. Underlying both themes is an orientation characteristic of modern Urdu literature, namely its didactic character. From the 'Musaddas' of Hali and the moral tales of Deputy Nazir Ahmad in the late nineteenth century through to the Progressive Movement of Iqbal's own day, Urdu literature has often taken as its mission that of the goal to instruct. Not all of Iqbal shares this concern, but this poem decidedly does.

Many of those intellectuals who wanted to change the attitudes and behaviour of their fellow Muslims turned to the past and identified a period of earlier glory that both reaffirmed the pride of a now subject people and provided a model toward which they might aspire. Such an emphasis was one response to the fundamental dilemma that confronted all thoughtful Indians in the nineteenth and twentieth centuries under British rule: why are we so weak, so powerless; why is the disparity between us and our rulers so substantial? In general the response, for Hindus and Muslims both, was to blame oneself for a failure to adhere to proper belief and behaviour and discipline, to find oneself wanting and to conclude that current subjection was deserved. Such a conclusion was profoundly troublesome. Yet it provided a programme for change and the solace that it was only human error, not something intrinsic to one's culture, that was at fault. Either by adhering to the texts of religion or by reviving the practice of the historical past, Indians could again be great. Among Muslims, for example, the *mujahidin* of the 1830s and the early Ahl-i Hadith, and, among Hindus, Roy and the early reformers in Bengal, all emphasized the revival of texts. They insisted that if one brushes away false accretions a shining truth could emerge that would put aright individual lives and the life of society as well. Later in the century, other reformers emphasized glorious ages in the past when one's people were subject to no one and one's science advanced. The Arya Samajis with their focus on the age of Vedic glory represented this stance and, among Muslims, the work of Hali, Amir Ali, and Shibli did so as well. For members of each community a pride in their past became only then a crucial strand in their identity.

In focusing on Cordoba, Iqbal found a symbol of past Muslim glory more evocative than any other. It represented the farthest reach of the great early empires, and, specifically, a time when Muslims ruled European soil and far surpassed Europeans in both morality and the arts and sciences of civilization. Iqbal claimed a tie to that past on the basis of religion. Indeed he explicitly raised in the poem the lurking anxiety of South Asian Muslims that they could not make that claim, that they were inadequate in their faith because of their distance from the Islamic heartland and their presence in an infidel land. He insisted that the emotion of his heart was proof irrefutable of his tie. Rather than let others accuse him of a tainted faith, he called himself a *kafir*, but insisted that the depth of his emotions linked him unquestionably to the truest currents of the faith.

Iqbal used the context of reflections on Cordoba and the past to raise what I have indicated to be a second central theme of the poem, namely the relation of man to God. Iqbal looked at the mosque as an artifact, a creation, a tangible expression of man's power at its peak. He celebrated the architect of the mosque; the warrior who made his work possible, and, in a daring leap, the poet, Iqbal himself, who before our eyes creates an artifact that will transcend time. In this, as in other poems, Iqbal celebrates man's power. The poem is an exciting statement of man's extraordinary potential and in this rests without question a major reason for the popularity of the poem.

The subject of the poem, the mosque, and the glories of the Islamic past, is one that has particular salience for South Asian Muslims. For Pakistanis, perpetually seeking to define a locus for their roots, its appeal is clear. But the treatment of the subject goes far beyond such particular issues to universal ones. At that level Iqbal transforms the idiom of mystic thought—of such profound concepts as *ishq* and *shauq*—to an original view of creative man's potential, a view that places a theory of aesthetics within the context of *tassawwuf*. Thus even when some day the historic romanticism of the late nineteenth and twentieth centuries will seem dated, the deeper currents of the poem will continue to have meaning. The poem—as Iqbal meant it to be—will be like the mosque itself: an artifact that has transcended time.

## Notes

1. I should like to thank Professors A. H. Dani and C. M. Naim for their helpful comments on an earlier draft of this paper. The latter will see some of his felicitous phrases incorporated intact.

2. Iqbal. 1969. *Bal-i Jabril*, pp. 92–101. Amritsar, trans. into English, Kiernan, V. G. 1955. *Poems from Iqbal*, pp. 37–42. London.

# 13

## The Pilgrimage Remembered
### South Asian Accounts of the Hajj

The pilgrimage to Mecca is unquestionably one of the great phenomena in the history of Muslim peoples. It has largely been studied from the perspectives of medieval travel and learning, of modern administrative issues, and of topics in the religious study of rituals.[1] These studies provide a context for yet another approach, that of eliciting meaning in the pilgrimage, examining not only uniformities in the experience of Muslims but differences over time. The accounts written by pilgrims themselves invite an analysis of individual experience against the background of the social and political world in which they were produced. They are accounts of journeys that are at once inner and outer; and they are guides for us, both to changing patterns of religious sensibilities and to a world in technological, social, and political transition.

The South Asian accounts[2] take shape initially in the period of British rule, a period of complex and extensive redefinition of Islam and of community life; they continue, since 1947, in an Islamic republic and in a secular state where Muslims live as a minority. Nowadays, they are written in a world where Islamic values and Muslim identity seem increasingly significant. The hajj accounts produced in all these contexts show us important dimensions of Islam as a modern religion, of modes of self-presentation, and of Muslim social and corporate life as recounted in distinctive individual lives.

## The Scope of the Accounts

The accounts of the hajj written by South Asians take many forms: travelogues, journals, letters, and guides.[3] They describe to different degrees and in different ways experiences of travel, judgements of other people and cultures, the meanings of the hajj, and other central symbols of Muslim religious life, and—in so doing—offer self-representations of the pilgrim authors themselves. The authors include some well-known figures: major religious thinkers like Maulana Siddiq Hassan Khan Bhopali (1872), the poet Shefta (1841), the Begum of Bhopal (1870), and the Nawab of Rampur (1872), and, in this century, literary figures from 'Abdu'l-Majid Daryabadi (1929) to Shorish Kashmiri (1967) as well as statesmen like Muhammad Zafrullah Khan (1967). A very substantial number of writers are from families touched by the institutions that emerged under British rule: they are well-born, literate in Urdu, of families with some mix of connections to government service, professions, and land.[4] But some are not from this type of background. Khwaja Hasan Nizami, himself scion of an illustrious Sufi family and a public figure in the first decades of this century, introduced, for example, the memoir of a craftsman, one Mistri Chiraghu'd-din Pasruri (1926), insisting on its usefulness and telling the reader that it was pointless to object to its Urdu—on the grounds that the author was, after all, from the Punjab! A handful of accounts have been written by women, from the wife of an army captain in Madras (Saba Mustafa 1979) to a former school principal from Lahore (Zainab Kakakhail 1976). In the late 1980s, the well-known writer Imdad Sabiri published the first of a proposed multi-volume series of collections of hajj accounts preserved in the records of his family. The accounts thus offer a very concrete and specific subject presented by a relatively wide range of observers over a considerable period of time.

Perhaps surprisingly, however, the accounts are concentrated in the years of British rule and after. Despite the splendid travelogues written in Arabic in the centuries after the 'Abbasids, there does not seem to be a continuous genre of travel writing in Muslim societies generally. In the Indian subcontinent, even travellers to the holy places of Mecca and Medina did not write about their travels before the late eighteenth century, except in so far as they recorded visions or wrote treatises while there.[5] In 1787, one

Maulana Rafi'u'd-din Muradabadi (1961 edn), a disciple of the great hadith scholar and reformer of Delhi, Shah Wali'u'llah, performed the hajj and later set down a record of his trip; his is generally taken by later Indian writers as the first such account to have been written from the Indian subcontinent. Only a few pilgrims were to do likewise for the next hundred years. Between 1870 and 1950, however, the pace quickens when several dozen published their accounts. Since then, even more people have written accounts, probably as many in the last four decades as in the eight decades before.[6] Many more, of course, wrote unpublished letters and accounts, known only to family and friends. Written accounts of the hajj thus seem a modern phenomenon. They share the impulse and context of other writing that emerges in this period, including travel accounts that range as far as Europe.[7]

## The Hajj Accounts as a Modern Genre

The impulse to write is clearly related to the changes engendered by British domination and Western technology, including the printing press, which permitted easy dissemination of writings, and new modes of transport, which permitted easier travel. Writers were discovering new worlds as they were discovering, or creating, new ways of thinking about themselves. The first two Indian Muslims to leave accounts of their trips to Europe, for example, were each from areas of intensive contact with the British in the late eighteenth century, Bengal and Oudh respectively. The traveller from Oudh, Mirza Abu Talib Khan, was a revenue official for the East India Company and wrote—at least in part—with a European audience in mind.[8] The hajj accounts share important characteristics with other new forms of modern literature which are, for example, increasingly conceived as occasions for constituting a persona, a representation of a self that focuses on individual experiences, perceptions, and feelings, much like the autobiographies that began at the same time. Authors began to present themselves not only as observers but as active participants in what they describe: the hajji and not the hajj takes centre stage.

Many accounts take on characteristics, if not the shape, of novels, including dramatic vignettes of episodes with directly quoted conversations. Some abandon what one might call the built-in pattern of a pilgrimage account—beginning with the departure, climaxing in arrival at the destined goal, and, on occasion, describing the journey home—in order to structure their story by some other principle.[9] In recent decades many of the most popular accounts have been written by literary figures. Thus the novelist Mumtaz Mufti in his opening apologia makes clear that he is writing neither an entertainment nor a religious treatise, but simply the life story (*ap biti*) of an 'unknown, ignorant, but sincere pilgrim' (not a hajji but a *za'ir*); he opens with a series of compelling vignettes that show what propelled him, as a sometime secular leftist, to undertake the journey (Mumtaz Mufti 1975: 10).

Studies of Persian and Southeast Asian travel literature, including hajj literature, suggest, broadly speaking, a similar pattern. Fragner (1979) finds the earliest Persian memoirs for the nineteenth century to be in fact travel accounts; only in the twentieth century does he find autobiography and what he calls attention to one's 'development and fate' (*Werdegang und Schicksal*) as characteristic of either travelogues or memoirs. Matheson and Milner analysing five Malay texts, identify as one theme an increased emphasis on personal experience in the most recent texts.[10]

The hajj accounts turn out not to be an isolated genre, a continuation of a static medieval form, but rather a genre that develops in ways broadly similar to the modern novel and autobiography. The accounts should be read, moreover, in the context of modern biographies, particularly the biographies of the Prophet Muhammad, a subject that has seen a virtual explosion from the late nineteenth century on. The representation of the central personal symbol of the faith has been increasingly emphasized as Muslim cultures have focused more on issues of individuality and personhood. This emphasis is evident not only in biography and poetry, but in a reformist emphasis on the hadith of the Prophet, and in increased celebration of devotional practices related to the Prophet's birthday (*mawlud*). Since the hajj to Mecca often included pilgrimage to the Prophet's grave in Medina, the accounts themselves may include reflections on the Prophet as well.[11] The accounts should be read as part of an enduring yet shifting constellation of three poles: changes in society generally, changes in concepts of individuality, and changes in the interpretation of central religious symbols, of which two, the hajj and the Prophet, are relevant here.[12]

The hajj does not decline in modern times. In contrast to European Christian pilgrimage, it is rarely called into question. It is a canonical duty, an unalloyed good; it is always better to go. Christian pilgrimage to Jerusalem or saints' shrines is always problematic, even in centuries when such practices flourished. Similarly suspect can be Muslim pilgrimage to saints' tombs whose devotees, from Morocco to Senegal to Baluchistan, may even identify a visit to a shrine as equivalent to the hajj.[13] What questioning there has been of the hajj has not been associated with modern change but with some streams of Sufi mysticism that deplore external duties with no focus on inner purification.[14]

There is, not surprisingly, lively cynicism about a practice so revered. The hajj can be seen as a cover for worldly greed—contacts for smuggling—or honour. But far from diminution, modern decades have seen the hajj grow, not only from South Asia but from all Muslim societies, until today the annual pilgrimage numbers up to two million. As Mary Byrne McDonnel shows, modern currents of reform have in fact encouraged the hajj and modern transportation has facilitated it.[15] Far from being seen as an alternative to ethical duties or piety, Islamic rituals like the hajj have been seen in periods of reform as essential to both.[16]

By the nineteenth century in Europe, however, travel accounts had little to do with pilgrimage. The image remained as metaphor, for pilgrimage had in fact often given way to exploration and quest.[17] The romantic quest, our most persistent mode of literary travel, made of pilgrimage a new image of a journey into the self, with the antagonist neither the exterior temptation of the Middle Ages nor the external nature of writers like Defoe; it was, instead, identity and selfhood that gave the challenge.[18] We now take for granted that travel, removing a person from local identities and ties, familiar languages and people, and placing him amid different ways of living and thinking will force at least the sensitive and thoughtful to reassess exactly who they are. As S. Naipaul puts it: 'All travel is a form of gradual self-extinction'.[19]

The hajj, however, even if it partakes of adventure, practical account, or inner exploration, remains a pilgrimage in the specific sense of the visitation of the Ka'ba at Mecca under prescribed circumstances as an essential duty of an able Muslim. 'Hajj' is not a metaphor as 'pilgrimage' is in English; even if used as a vehicle for a personal quest, the hajj in fact remains and is the structure for whatever experience the hajji creates. That experience, filtered by distance and literary conventions, becomes the remembered hajj of the written account and, for its readers, part of a shared understanding of religious symbols, self-expression, and interpretation of peoples and places.

## Perspectives on the Hajj

Travel accounts in general are richly revealing because they at once purport to describe an objective reality yet in fact reveal the cultural world through which the traveller filters what he sees. Sometimes it is possible to identify some central implicit set of issues that shapes an entire account.[20] Perhaps surprisingly in writings on a core religious ritual, many travellers in late nineteenth century British India, for example, wrote with a range of imperial issues close to the surface of their perceptions. Thus Mirza 'Irfan 'Ali Beg (1895-6) explicitly wrote to provide useful information and describe interesting events for the Anjuman-i Islamiyya, a voluntary association of Muslims—presumably well-born and educated urban professionals, landlords, government servants, and traders—with whom he was associated. Like many hajjis, he wanted, presumably in all sincerity, to pass on the blessings of a journey like his and to make such a journey easier for those who would follow. At the same time, however, as a deputy collector in the eastern United Provinces, as high a civil servant as any Indian in the imperial bureaucracy, he was clearly a person who had internalized British concerns for governance and had an identity as a British subject and functionary. He knew English, his tastes were English (from cricket to tea)—and he knew how a government ought to behave.

For him, the significant group in his journey was 'Indian Muslim', a category of increasing salience in the social and political context of his day, and one that takes on new meaning for him in the course of his travels. He looks for Indian Muslims and in a foreign context takes pride in what is special about them. He rejoices in their piety, describing, for example, their unceasing circumambulations and barefoot journeys to Medina. He remarks on their generosity in endowing hospices, gardens, and mosques. In the Haramayn and *en route*, he readily takes on the role of civic leader—whether acting as examiner at the Indian-founded

Madrasa-yi Saulatiyya in Mecca or meeting the pilgrim protectors in Bombay and Jidda to ascertain their role. At every point he reflects on the way in which government should act to provide order, protection, comfort, and cleanliness. He speaks to the imperial government of their responsibilities and addresses himself as well, in the Hijaz, to the Turks. The plight of the poor Indian Muslim—vulnerable, abused, and cheated—is his overwhelming concern. Two years after publishing his Urdu account, 'Irfan 'Ali personally translated and revised his journal in English, adding a table of each occasion when he found the situation amiss—his main goal being to influence the government of India to act responsibly to project their Muslim subjects on hajj.

There is more in his account than this. There are also his deep bonds with his friends, his kindness to his servant, his ready response to a holy and learned man he comes to know in Mecca, his cosmopolitan interest in touring, and his congenial relationships with non-Muslims as well as Muslims. However, his particular political perspective is central, and it is enhanced and made public by the very act of writing. Other writers in this period have a somewhat similar experience in the hajj and its recording, notably the Begum of Bhopal who so internalized the British ideals of an 'improving' ruler—committed to cultivating good character and installing drains—that she urged the Turks to withdraw and leave the running of the holy places to her![21]

Some of the accounts are shaped by a specific religious orientation. Muhammad Ma'shuq 'Ali (1909), for example, described his experience as a disciple of the great Sufi, Maulana Ashraf 'Ali Thanawi. His hajj followed residence at the hospice of this saint and was part of the training in ritual fidelity and personal formation that was set for him. Other accounts argue a sectarian perspective and use the hajj as a platform for asserting its validity.[22] Yet others are essentially scientific—written like government gazetteers to review history, local customs, the educational system, and the organization of the government (for example, Hasanu'd-din 1935). In each case, to present the hajj is to present a certain kind of self.

Many of the accounts in recent decades are explorations of the self in a more specific sense, looking to the great communal ritual as an occasion to test a person's place in relation to nothing less than Islam itself and to the Muslim *umma*. Somewhat like the quest for meaning, for authenticity, outside of one's own culture—such as we know in some forms of modern European or American travel—self-described secularists embark on the hajj to test themselves, to experience faith vicariously, perhaps in some sense to participate in that faith themselves.[23] Thus 'Abdu'llah Malik (late 1970s) explicitly calls himself a *tahzibi Muslim*—a cultural Muslim—who goes on hajj reluctantly: and sets out looking over his own shoulder as he learns, he says, a new vocabulary. He struggles to find an intellectual equivalence for his Communism and Islam. He finds himself ever more emotionally involved, but thanks to the structure of the travel narrative, in contrast to a more sustained kind of essay writing, he can savour a thought or emotion ('My eyes were moist and I wept—quite apart from what my beliefs were and what they weren't'), then just move on. Indeed, the formal structure of the travel account, it has been argued, makes it particularly appealing to a certain kind of modern personality which prefers not to resolve but to sample and explore.[24] Malik calls his account *Hadis-i dil*, the testimony of the heart and not of the canonical scripture. One characteristic of the self-conscious intellectual, playing off connection and lack of connection, is to find ways to assert his difference from those around him. One sometime secular leftist, for example, whose story I heard orally in 1985, made a point that in contrast to most hajjis who—as they are told over and over is normal—feel fear in Mecca but love in Medina, his experience was the reverse.

Whether as part of a re-identification with Islamic symbols or not, recent accounts tend to take as their central theme what one writer,[25] explaining her list of favourite accounts, calls 'matters of the heart' and 'inner experiences'. The freshness of hajj accounts, she explains, rests not only in their docu-menting actual changes to benefit the reader, but in their showing 'the singular and unique experiences', the individual heart and gaze, that refract the beauty of the Ka'ba—in every case in a distinctive way. For her, given her emphasis on feeling, it is not surprising that she draws her vocabulary for central religious symbols—God, Unity, the Ka'ba—from Sufism, distinguishing the hajj from other duties which are ethical in purpose and seeing the pilgrimage 'alone as a matter of the heart', 'easing the pain of separation', its customs those of the world of passionate longing ('*ishq*).

Zainab Kakakhail's account is not alone in using such language. In the past, however, the Sufi tradition was expressed by the insertion of couplets into the ongoing prose account. Indeed, to be able to quote aptly the Persian or Persianate Urdu couplets of the Sufi tradition has long been the mark of a refined and educated person in this culture. The recent accounts seem to demonstrate a convergence of what had been two levels of discourse: a prose discourse focused on external events; and a poetic discourse of passion, longing, and separation offered without comment and not claimed as one's own speech. Now the poetic language is appropriated as one's own.[26] As the content changes, the rhetoric and forms of the accounts change as well. If we take the accounts from the late eighteenth century on, they clearly become a continuing genre, building on each other, shaping each other. Do they develop in certain directions as possibilities of the form are simply played out?

Howard, in his study of the pre-Chaucerian accounts of the pilgrimage to Jerusalem, shows how certain 'built-in' possibilities of the pilgrimage genre—in that case, irony above all—do develop over time.[27] Do the accounts shape their own landscape, so that the traveller sees through lenses honed through literature? Fussell, in the case of British travellers to the continent, has particularly shown how reading creates the experience of travel; Kabbani has argued the significance of the European discourse of Orientalism, including travel accounts, in precluding a traveller like V. S. Naipaul from even seeing Muslim countries which he purports to describe.[28] Writers also learn from those who have gone before, at least in part, the form they must give their account, a form that changes over time—for example, from the conventional self-deprecation in Zardar's account,[29] to the now obligatory trope of denying that one ever intended to write at all.

Much that is in the accounts is, of course, implicit. Some aspects of the world of writers can be elicited by focusing on the audience, explicit or implied, in the accounts. The writers, while telling their stories, pursue conversations whether consciously or not, of which their written words form largely one side. Sometimes they present, in effect, a response to questions they know would be asked; sometimes they assert the kind of person they want to be known to be—in contrast to some alternative kind of person; sometimes they declare by their assessments and emphases a position in ongoing controversies of a religious or political nature. Sometimes they may not even be conscious that they are writing to a range of concerns, expressed in their societies and internalized in their psyches, shaping the experience which they create as they write.

## Visual Representations in the Texts

One way to elicit these themes is to look not only at the words but also at the physical presentation of the texts.[30] One need go no further than the title pages, for example, to see the increased tendency to make the author's experience central and to present each account as distinctive. Figure 7 juxtaposes two title pages, on the left that of Muhammad Zardar Khan (1873) published by the great Hindu Kayasth of Lucknow, Nawwal Kishur. Zardar shared with Nawwal Kishur the Persianate culture of the well-born, often, as in Zardar's case, typical of people employed by the government or a prince. Zardar's book was conventionally entitled *Safarnama-yi haramain* (A Travelogue to the Two Sanctuaries). Its lack of colour, its floral border, the medallion for the title, and the inscribed panels top and bottom present the immediately familiar cover of innumerable publications of the day. The top panel replicates in words the balance and symmetry of the page, setting out in the elegant calligraphic style, *nastaliq*, a two-part rhyming invocation, in Persian, that sets the tone of humility common to publications of the day: 'With the help of the Maker of the man (*makin*) and the place (*makan*) and the aid of the Shaper of the land (*zamin*) and the age (*zaman*)'. The author's name does not even appear on the cover, but only in the midst of the formulaic phrases of self-described abjection set out on the opening page.

The jacket on the right appeared some hundred years later (Mumtaz Mufti 1975), a three-colour design, with the one-word title *Labbaik*, ('I am here', the call of the hajji in Arabic as he enters Mecca). The background, yellow-green, significantly deepens to dark green, the Islamic colour *par excellence*, as field for the black Ka'ba centered at the top. The title is written in a swinging free form so that the first letter, *lam*, points to the shrine and the elongated final *kaf* encircles it: the calligraphy thus recalls drawings of the plan of the Ka'ba like those in Figure 9. The author's name, Mumtaz Mufti, is boldly written in the loop formed by the downward stroke of the same letter; the name is written at an upright angle that identifies it not with Persian but with the Arabic of the Qur'an and the larger Muslim world. The jacket makes the

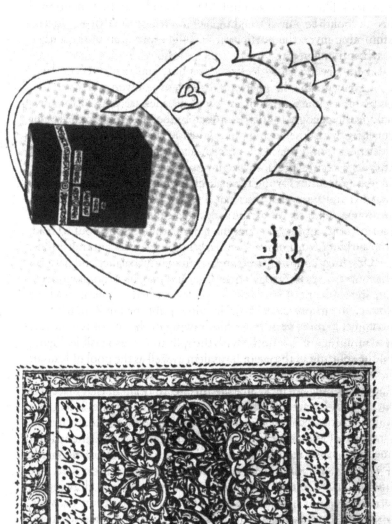

FIGURE 7: Book cover. (Left) Muhammad Zardar Khan (1873) *Safarnama-yi Haramain*; (right) Mumtaz Mufti (1975) *Labbaik.*

book look like a novel, and indeed the friend who first mentioned this account to me thought that it was just that—a logical assumption given the poetic title and the reputation of the author as a literary figure.

Like a novel, the goal of this account, and many recent ones, is to convey an immediacy of experience. Over and over, the successful accounts written in recent decades are praised for their making the hajj vivid and present before the reader's eye; the reader identifies with the writer and vicariously lives his experience. Readers' letters prefaced to the publication of Muhammad Riza Ansari's account (1965), for example, praise it for being a veritable cinema and avow that the reader feels he has made the hajj himself. The text itself serves as the hajj. Here *Labbaik*, the title, says, 'I am present' and its calligraphy circumambulates the Ka'ba just as the author's words will effect the hajj for the person about to read.

Drawings of monuments similarly suggest significant transitions. Early drawings published in the accounts show balance and patterning (reminiscent of Zardar's title page) and may incorporate miraculous elements presumed visible once or expected to appear in a time to come. Figures 8 and 9 show drawings published in Zardar's 1873 account. Figure 8, left, shows his drawing of the site of the miracle of the splitting of the moon, with the split moon also visible; Figure 9 shows the Aqsa mosque in Jerusalem as well as the pool of Kausar, the bridge, the balance, and the throne of God, all associated with the Day of Judgement, which is expected to begin in that place. He thus includes both visible and invisible reality. Figure 9, left, is a drawing of the Sacred Mosque (1880) depicted in a characteristic medieval style, seen from above with the side walls flattened out (Wazir Husain Khan 1880–1). Drawings like this are very schematic and patterned, almost mandala-like in their focus on the centre. The drawing on the right eschews formality for realism, drawing an accurate ground plan of the mosque without attention to walls, domes, and doors, and distinguishing by slashed lines what did not seem of interest before: the distinction between the old building and new additions (Sultan Da'ud 1963). The early author shows himself as part of a long historic and aesthetic tradition; the modern author gives us accuracy and new information.

The charming drawing in Figure 10 records the climactic event of the hajj, 'the standing' at 'Arafat ('Abdu'r-rahim 1915). The simple line drawing and design recall the block prints of northern

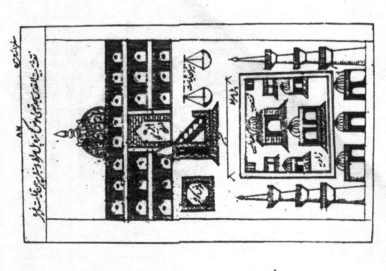

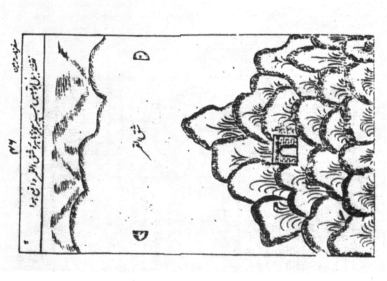

FIGURE 8: Drawings of sacred places and symbols (Muhammad Zardar Khan [1873] *Safarnama-i Haramain*).

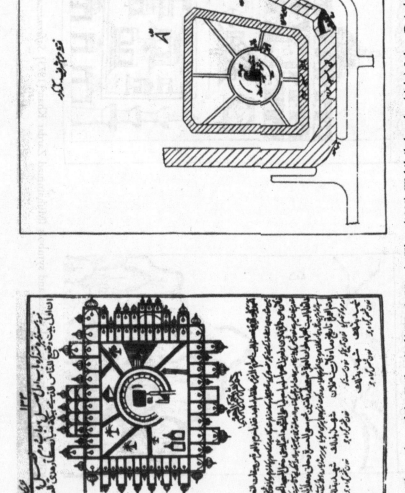

FIGURE 9: Floor plans of the Ka'ba. (Left) Wazir Husain Khan (1880) *Wakilu'l-ghuraba*; (right) Sultan Da'ud (1963) *Safarnama-yi hijaz.*

Indian textiles, as do the sketches of the ladies, who all wear saris. The repetitive camels, tents, and mounted pilgrims form a strong line across the bottom, the Turkish artillery in their modern military uniforms balance the two sides, and the hills provide the top frame for the central focus—the gathering, preaching, and prayer on the sacred hill. An account written in more recent decades would probably include an aerial photograph, rather than a balanced and patterned drawing of this sort.

Finally, Figure 11 offers two photographs of authors. Not many authors provide photographs, perhaps fearing to offend the sensibilities of those who find photographs suspect or who might think the author vain. But even from the limited number of photographs available, the contrasts are again suggestive of the increasing tendency to focus on what is individualistic. The photograph on the left shows a venerable figure dressed in *ihram* (Ghu'lamu'l-husnain 1935); the second, a wonderstruck woman, wife of a Madrasi army officer (Saba Mustafa 1979). Her photograph is meant to communicate the personal emotional quality of the hajj— the theme that her text as a whole is meant to demonstrate. The earlier photograph, in contrast, is as much a generic representation of a hajji as a photograph can possibly be.

## Conclusion

Travel to Mecca is travel of a very particular kind. To go to Mecca is to go home, to return to one's *ruhani watn*.[31] To go to Mecca is to perform an act of unquestioned value. Not only is the goal clear, but the place, in contrast to the destinations of some kinds of travel, is thoroughly known by vast resources of the culture in story and devotional song—now reinforced by techniques of reproduction and communication that make the Holy Places ever present.[32] Moreover, the journey moves on the invisible lines which believers create by every prayer, posture at sleep, and burial in the grave; on the day the hajjis perform the ritual sacrifice, fellow Muslims everywhere perform their sacrifice, and all are linked worldwide in celebration of the feast. By undertaking the hajj, the pilgrim in principle affirms his individual responsibility for obedience to God and claims his place among the community of faithful people. However much the pilgrim seeks in his experience and in his writing to explore a unique and self-conscious

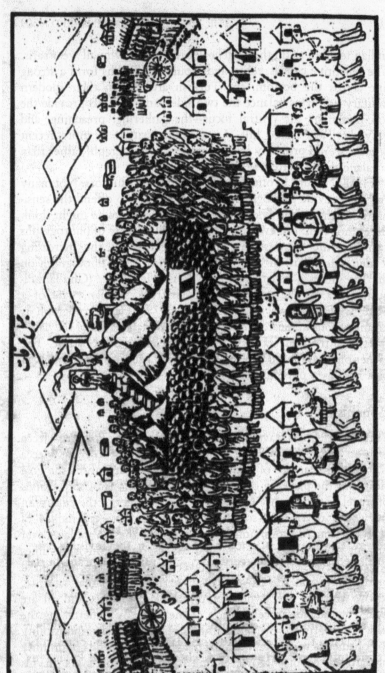

FIGURE 10: Mount 'Arafat ('Abdu'r-rahim [1915] *Safarnama-yi rahimi*).

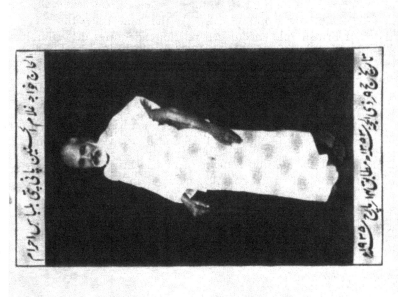

FIGURE 11: Photographs of authors. (Left) Ghulamu'l-Husnain (1935) *Safarnama;* (right) Saba Mustafa (1979) *Paharon ke daman men.*

self—the theme, as suggested, of many of the recent accounts—his undertaking must be in some tension to the normative programme of the hajj, and of all of mainstream Islam, to hone himself to the prophetic model, the person of the Prophet Muhammad, in whose footsteps on this occasion he can literally walk.

Such a context suggests that we have more than a simple mirroring of European individualism explored in alien settings as we trace changing patterns of self-representation in the hajj accounts. If a person is 'finding himself' he is doing so in a crowd, following a ritual programme of dress and behaviour meant precisely to obliterate the markers that make a believer distinct by class, race, or region. The accounts, even if imitative of European travel writing and made salient by the socio-political change engendered by European technology and domination, are written in the context of interaction with the core tradition of Islam.

All this would be true of any Muslim account. Those from South Asia share their own characteristics, which are rooted in the peculiarly plural character of Indian cultures and in the long experience of colonial rule. That rule provided a range of alternative values, so that indigenous cultures became self-conscious and, in Geertz's phrase, oppositional.[33] At the same time, the very idiom of British rule encouraged religious identities in a plural society. These experiences shape all forms of self-statement by South Asian Muslims, but accounts focused on such central symbols as those represented by the hajj present themes particularly suggestive of the specific issue of how being Muslim has been experienced and conceived. A Muslim identity has not been the only one significant to those we label South Asian Muslims, but it has, assuredly, been an important one. In the accounts we see something of the shifting content of that identity as well as its relation to competing and complementary strands—of occupation, moral formation, spiritual quest, gender, and territoriality. The texts let us hear people speak, telling us, in a wide variety of ways, what kind of people they are and how they think of Islam, the places they go to, and the people they meet.

## Acknowledgements

I am grateful to the John Simon Guggenheim Foundation for support during 1983–4 as well as to the American Institute of Pakistan Studies and the American Philosophical Society for grants to support travel, all of which enabled me to collect materials and undertake preliminary work on this project. I returned to the project in Autumn 1987, thanks to the Davis Humanities Institute which provided released time from teaching and the company of excellent colleagues.

## Notes

1. For an excellent introduction to these topics, see Lewis, Bernard. 1971. 'Hadjdj'. *The Encyclopedia of Islam*, 2nd edn, vol. III, pp. 31–8. Brill, Leiden and London. On administrative issues, see Long, David. 1979. *The Hajj Today: A Survey of the Contemporary Pilgrimage to Makkah*. Albany State University of New York Press and Roff, William R. 1975. 'The Conduct of the Hajj from Malaya and the first Malay Pilgrimage Officer'. National University of Malaysia, Institute of Malay Language, Literature, and Culture, Occasional Papers, no. 1, Kuala Lumpur, pp. 81–111. Roff, William R. 1982. 'Sanitation and Security: The Imperial Powers and the Nineteenth Century *Hajj*'. *Arabian Studies*, 6, pp. 143–60. On the hajj as ritual, see Roff, William R. 1985. 'Pilgrimage and the History of Religions: Theoretical Approaches to the *Hajj*'. In Martin, Richard A. ed. *Approaches to Islam in Religious Studies*, pp. 78–86. Tucson: University of Arizona Press; von Grunebaum, G.E. 1951. *Muhammadan Festivals*. New York: Henry Schuman; and Partin, Harry B. 1967. 'The Muslim Pilgrimage: Journey to the Center'. Unpublished Ph.D. dissertation, University of Chicago.

2. As will be clear in the discussion that follows, by South Asian I limit myself primarily to those written mostly in Urdu, a few in Persian, a handful written in or translated into English.

3. I currently have in hand, or have made use of, almost one hundred and fifty accounts. I have found these accounts in London (British Library, India Office Library), Lahore (Dayal Singh Trust Library, Oriental College Library, Punjab Public Library, and Punjab University Library), Islamabad (Islamic Research Institute [IRI], and the libraries of the University of California. I am grateful to the staffs of all these libraries and to Dr Muhammad Khalid Masud of the IRI for their generous help. I have also acquired books in shops in Lahore and Delhi as well as an excellent collection of accounts from old bookshops in Hyderabad, India, thanks to the skilled help of Dr Gail Minault. Dr Michael Fisher kindly provided an account by a Keralite; Dr Francis Robinson, one by a Farangi Mahalli. I have not yet had an opportunity to consult libraries in India where many more accounts are presumably to be found.

4. This 'sharif culture' is evoked for the late nineteenth century in Lelyveld, David S. 1979. *Aligarh's First Generation: Muslim Solidarity in British India*, chapter 2. Princeton, NJ: Princeton University Press.

5. See Pearson, Michael N. 1986. 'The *Hajj* (Pilgrimage) from Mughal India: Some Preliminary Observations'. *Indica*, 23, pp. 143–88; Pearson, Michael N. 1987a. 'Pious Passengers: Muslim Pilgrimages from India in the Early Modern Period'. A paper presented to the conference 'Sailing Ships and Sailing People', University of Western Australia, Perth and Pearson, Michael. 1987. 'Portuguese Records and Indian History: The Case of the "Hajj Market"'. Typescript. Pearson suggests that as many as ten thousand pilgrims a year may have undertaken the hajj during the period of Mughal rule [See also his *Pilgrimage to Mecca: The Indian Experience, 1500–1800* (1996) and *Pious Passengers: The Hajj in Earlier Times* (1994). The best-known example of early writing about experiences in the Hijaz is that of Shah Wali'u'llah (1730), the *Fuyuz al-haramain*, a collection of his visions.

6. This assumes that those I have identified are in proportion to the total written.

7. I am grateful to Dr J. P. S. Uberoi for reminding me of this and for presiding over a lively session on my work at the Sociological Research Colloquium, University of Delhi, on 11 December 1987.

8. The writers are Shaikh I'tisam al-Din from Bengal and Mirza Abu Talib Khan from Lucknow as noted in Lewis, op. cit.

9. Howard, Donald R. 1980. *Writers and Pilgrims: Medieval Pilgrimage Narratives and their Posterity*, p. 8. Berkeley: University of California Press, analysing the pilgrimage literature of pre-Chaucerian unknown pilgrims to Jerusalem, argues that the inclusion of the return journey—exemplified by a monk's account that touchingly ends with his welcome by the monastery dog—specifically points to an account that focuses on personal experience more than on the externals of the journey.

10. Matheson, Virginia and Anthony C. Milner. 1984. 'Perceptions of the *Haj*: Five Malay Texts'. Institute of Southeast Asian Studies, Research Notes and Discussion Paper no. 46, Singapore.

11. For excellent material on the whole range of expressions related to the Prophet in the modern period, see Schimmel, Annemarie. 1985. *And Muhammad is His Messenger: The Veneration of the Prophet in Islamic Piety*. Chapel Hill: The University of North Carolina Press.

12. See Brown, Peter. 1975. 'Society and the Supernatural: A Medieval Change'. *Daedalus*, 104, pp. 1–2 and pp. 133–51, for a discussion of eleventh and twelfth century AD changes in social structure, as communities became less coherent and intense; in relationships; and in conceptions of the supernatural 'as an upward extension of the individual'. Moris, Colin. 1972. *The Discovery of the Individual 1050–1200*. New York: Harper & Row delineates a new focus on inwardness in the twelfth century AD as shown in sermons describing personal experience, lyric poetry, ritual injunctions to confession with a focus on intention, and more personal portraits. New social roles and a new focus on personal relationships were the context for new interpretations of religious symbols, including a focus on the sufferings of Christ and devotion

to him and a new conception of the Virgin. See also Bynum, Caroline Walker. 1982. *Jesus as Mother: Studies in the Spirituality of the High Middle Ages*. Berkeley University of California Press. Other periods have, of course, seen this complex interplay in changes in society, religious symbols, and self, but this period is one that has been particularly well studied.

13. This is the case for the visit to Touba on the part of the Mourides of Senegal as it is for Demah on the part of Javanese. It is apparently the case also for the shrine of the Merinid sultan Abu Yusuf (AD 1258–86) in Rabat where tradition holds that seven circuits of the passageway around the *mihrab* give merit equivalent to the trip to Mecca. See Ellingham, Mark and Shaun McVeigh. 1985. *The Rough Guide to Morocco*. London: Routledge & Kegan Paul. The contemporary Zikri sect of the Baluch, studied by Dr Akbar S. Ahmed, identifies a local pilgrimage shrine in Makran with similar merit.

14. Thus the eighteenth century Punjabi poet Bulhe Shah, celebrating the love of Hir for Ranjha, the type of the soul's love for God, sang:

> The hajji go to Mecca, world by world,
> My Ranjhu is Mecca for me....
> The hajji is within
> The *ghazi* is within....
> I have become a fool.
> The hajjis go to Mecca.
> We must go to Takht-i mir [the birthplace of Ranjha].
> *This* is the road to Mecca.

(Provided by Dr Denys Matringe, Ecole des Hautes Etudes en Sciences Sociales, Paris, June 1986.)

In his poem, Bulhe Shah recalls themes that go back at least to Junaid (d. AH 298/AD 919) in insisting on an inner component to the external trip.

15. McDonnel, Mary Byrne. 1990. 'Patterns of Muslim Pilgrimage from Malaysia, 1885–1985', in Eickelman, Dale F. and James Piscatori, eds. *Muslim Travellers: Pilgrimage, Migration, and the Religions Imagination*, pp. 111–30. Berkeley: University of California Press.

16. For the 'reformational' quality of Islamic ritual, see Graham, William A. 1983. 'Islam in the Mirror of Ritual', in *Islam's Understanding of Itself*, pp. 53–71. Eds. Richard G. Hovannisian and Speros Vryonis, Jr, Malibu: Undena Publications.

17. This was true whether for well-known figures like Byron or a traveller like (Mrs) Parks, Fanny. 1975 (orig. 1850). *Wanderings of a Pilgrim in Search of the Picturesque*, p. 496. Karachi: Oxford University Press who travelled in India in the 1820s and 1830s. When Mrs Parks returned to London she concluded her two volumes by hanging up, she wrote, her long staff and stripping the scallop shell from her hat—the medieval emblems of the pilgrim to the shrine of Santiago in Compostella.

18. Howard, op. cit.

19. Naipaul, Shiva. 1984. *An Unfinished Journey*. New York: Viking Press. Naipaul begins his published account of a trip by recalling these opening words of his notebook: 'All journeys begin in the same way. All travel is a form of gradual self-extinction.'

20. In studying European travelogues to Latin America, Gonzalez-Echevarria, Roberto. 1987. 'A Lost World Re-discovered: Sarmiento's Facundo'. A paper presented at the conference 'Difference, Authority, Power'. University of California, Davis, 26 February 1987, is able to identify what he calls a shifting 'hegemonic discourse', so that travellers in one era, for example, will speak to legalistic concerns and use a legalistic vocabulary, travellers of another period will shape their account by science.

21. Sikander Begum 1870. 140–1

22. Abu'l-nur Muhammad. 1960.

23. Cohen, Erik. 1979. 'A Phenomenology of Tourist Experiences'. *Sociology*, 13: 179–201.

24. Bridgeman, Richard. 1986. *Travelling in Mark Twain*. Berkeley: University of California Press.

25. Zainab Kakakhail 1976: 6–7

26. For an analysis of the interplay of these two levels of diction in another context, see Abu-Lughod, Lila. 1986. *Veiled Sentiments: Honour and Poetry in a Bedouin Society*. Berkeley: University of California Press.

27. Howard, Donald R., op. cit.

28. Fussell, Paul. 1980. *Abroad: British Literary Travelling between the Wars*. New York: Oxford University Press. Kabbani, Rana. 1985. *Europe's Myth of Orient*. Bloomington: University of Indiana Press.

29. See Zardar, p. 93.

30. I am grateful to Dr Catherine Asher for pointing this out to me and for ably helping me, with her art historian's eye, to reflect on the visual materials presented here.

31. This is the phrase used by Gilani Kamran. 1979. '*Hajj ke safarnamon ki riwayat*'. In *1978 ke bahtarin maqalat*, ed. Sajad Taqwi, pp. 51–67. Sargodha: Maktaba Urdu Zaban. His is one of the few scholarly works that surveys the Urdu hajj accounts, and I have benefited from it as from the personal helpfulness of Professor Kamran.

32. Today the climax of the hajj is transmitted by television satellite and watched live throughout the world. Calendars and art of all kinds make the image of the holy shrine the most familiar distant building of many Muslims. Pakistan television, like the television of many countries, transmits special programmes during the hajj season, including a six-part mini-series, which I viewed in 1985, to prepare intending pilgrims for their trip.

33. Geertz, Clifford. 1968. *Islam Observed*. Chicago: University of Chicago Press.

# 14

# What Happened in Mecca
## Mumtaz Mufti's *Labbaik*

Travel often stimulates autobiographical reflection.[1] It offers marvellous potential for disjunction and irony as travellers move in
a world different from their own and confront the gap between
expectations and actuality.[2] Travellers not only move in space,
but often in time, to places whose history they seek, and even in
social hierarchy. In a new place they can abandon or question their
customary identity, and, Paul Fussell writes, 'among strangers a
new sense of selfhood can be tried on, like a costume'.[3] One well-
known type of travel writing is that of the European escaping the
modern, industrialized world in quest of an older simplicity or
authenticity. The subject of this paper, however, is a non-European
post-colonial 'bicultural' who nevertheless also is absorbed in
what is seen as the conflict between the old and the new—between
East and West, faith and doubt, the spiritual and the material. He
seeks what may be his roots, in no less a place than Mecca.[4] Travel
writing like this allows, above all, a personal exploration of the
perceived inconsistencies of modern life and gives occasion for
the fundamental modernist experience—that cultural truths are
inevitably contested.

In the mid-1960s Mumtaz Mufti, one of Pakistan's most
celebrated novelists and intellectuals, a self-proclaimed 'nominal
Muslim', encountered—or so he tells us—a series of disconcerting
events, not quite explicable, all of which worked together inexo-
rably to bring him to the point of undertaking the pilgrimage to

Mecca. Some time after he returned from Mecca, Mumtaz Mufti was prevailed on by friends to write out his experiences. They first appeared in sixteen instalments in an Urdu journal; a revised account was published as a book in 1975 and has been in print ever since.[5] Mufti used a simple and evocative one word title for the book version—*Labbaik*, 'I am here', the humble Arabic call of the pilgrim arrived at Mecca. He identifies his account as an *ap biti*, an autobiography or, literally 'what happened to oneself' (p. 10). He also repeatedly and somewhat disingenuously calls it *reportage*, transliterating a word known from English, perhaps to protest any suggestion that his account might be anything less than fact. The work is unconventional—at times phantasmagorical—vibrant and original.

The account opens with a story-like heading, 'The Madman of Fawara Square'. One evening as Mumtaz Mufti was crossing the square, a dark-skinned person with a frightening face, wild hair, and burning eyes suddenly accosted him. 'You will go on hajj, you will go on hajj', he cried. Taking him to be a *faqir*, Mumtaz offered him some change. But then—in a move that lifts the story from the predictable—the faqir turned the tables, reached into his pocket, and pressed money on *him*: 'Take this, take this, you will need money on hajj' (p. 24).

Other episodes glide imperceptibly from observation to the author's zany imagination. The middle of the night, finally on the PIA plane from Karachi to Jiddah, Mumtaz Mufti is sitting among the pious pilgrims in coach, dressed in their ritual garb, faces solemn, telling their beads. In first class the Pakistan Hockey Team, off to a match, periodically explodes in rollicking laughter. In Mumtaz Mufti's mind an alternate vision takes place: the hockey players are hijackers; the pilgrims, the hijacked; the laughter, the triumph of conspirators whose plans are working (pp. 50-1).

On finding himself in Jiddah, lodged in an absurdly luxurious hotel with every western-style amenity—when, as he mocks himself, his vision of being a pilgrim turns on deserts and camels—he entertains himself with a fantasy of his room as a *honimun swit* where a tall, long-haired beauty would glide into view saying 'Hi' (p. 57).

The continuum from strange episode to almost real fantasy reaches its culmination in the Ka'ba itself. Mumtaz, distressed at his lack of feeling as he passes through the marble outer courtyard, suddenly looks up at the roof of the plain stone building that is his goal and sees someone leaning out, a face looking at him, showing forth 'a storm of love, eyes moist with boundless sympathy, the face radiant, an affectionate smile on his lips'. As he watched, he writes, the house swelled and swelled until it filled all creation. The face, described with all the lexicon of Hindi or Punjabi idolatry, became the *but*, the idol of his devotion. He fled from the pilgrim guide leading him in the ritual prayers. He read the prayers from his own book until it too began to spread, covering everything—the mosque, the house, the smiling face—so that he threw it too away. Allah was before him, 'for my sake he had become a *but* so that my heart could delight in secret idolatry' (p. 82).

Days later, about to leave the sanctuary, Mumtaz knows the house now to be empty. He is riveted by the appearance of a procession of Africans, desperate at grief over departing, in humility exiting backwards from the shrine. It is, quite simply, the most moving spectacle he has ever seen in his life. He is not alone; every other pilgrim is fixed on the procession, too, 'as if by sorcery turned into stone'. Suddenly he thinks that perhaps Allah is leaving with the Africans. It is Allah, 'flowing from their eyes, distilled into tears, glowing from their foreheads, changed into light'. As they leave and the Ka'ba becomes, for him, nothing but a stone idol, he feels he must join them, find them so that he too can for a few minutes be 'soaked in God', 'become God'. He runs to the door, only to find the procession gone—and sinks down in despair. When he lifts his eyes, there is God, sitting on the outer stairs, his clothes in tatters, his face wrinkled. As every pilgrim leaves, God holds out his finger, he tugs at their skirt, asking to be taken along. 'Don't leave me, take me along, take my finger and take me along.... The house is empty. I am sitting here watching for you, waiting for you, wanting to go with you.' No one pays attention. And Mumtaz, too, turns him down. 'I am full of myself.... I have made a *but* of myself' (see Addenda, 'The African Procession').

Mufti has not given us a mainstream way of talking about God, or set himself in a heroic tale of triumph or conversion. Even these few episodes suggest the inconsistencies and ironies that make up the book. This is an account that defies both the religious scepticism of Mumtaz Mufti's coffee-house intellectual circles and the conventions of those he calls the *ijaaradaars* (The leaseholders/

monopolists) of Islam. The book is written by a cosmopolitan familiar with European literature—albeit with a time lag—and with an international world. Mumtaz Mufti can make an apt reference to Aristotle, William James, or H. Rider Haggard, as easily as he can to Shaikh Sa'di, the *Tazkiratu'l-ghausiyya*, or his son's letters from Prague. Here is a sceptic shaken by an encounter with a fortune-teller, a presumed pilgrim who fantasizes the pilgrimage as a hijacking, an irreligious person who more or less sees God. To write a travelogue whose goal is one's own presumably unscreened and discordant experiences is to participate in a cosmopolitan, Western-dominated genre of modern literature. At the same time, to go to Mecca is to say that one is a Muslim.

The authors of the other South Asian accounts of the pilgrimage to Mecca that I have been able to identify are often, broadly speaking, people like this. Even the practice of writing accounts, and of course publishing them, is very much a product of the colonial period, and many of those who write are involved in colonial institutions.[6] Not all are as sophisticated as the author presented here: indeed part of the appeal of this genre is that it includes relatively modest authors as well, people for whom the account of the hajj may be the only substantial document they ever write. But by and large those who write about the central religious symbol of the hajj do so from a position that suggests, to varying degrees, familiarity with multiple cultural values. Far from being a site where essential shared cultural characteristics remain untouched, the hajj is precisely the kind of cultural symbol where contestations and cultural negotiations take place. In the process of writing about the hajj, new cultural truths are constituted and explored.[7] It is the 'mongrels', as Salman Rushdie defiantly calls them, who have the most to contribute to these new cultural formations.[8]

If in this case the hajj account represents the experiences of someone familiar with Western institutions and literatures, it is at the same time a South Asian account. A modern mentality, engaged with cultural pluralism, finds expression in a distinctively non-European cultural milieu. The account has characteristics that differ from what seem to be widespread characteristics of life histories and autobiographies in European languages. These may help expand our sense of what the range of possibilities is in such writing and, indeed, in the way people think about themselves and their lives. Even in an account as unconventional as this, its three distinctive themes have long histories in biographical and autobiographical texts in the Urdu and, preceding it, the Persian traditions.

First, the definition of what is presented as part of life's experience is very inclusive. Put differently, magic is on the loose. There is a deep sense that reality is not limited to what is materially visible or subject to human control. An enduring model of dreams, for example, argues that any dream or vision involving God, prophets, or holy people is a visitation from beyond and not a product of one's own conscious or unconscious self[9] (see Addenda, 'A Conversation'). For example, one of the most celebrated books describing experiences in Mecca, the work of the great scholar of the eighteenth century, Shah Wali'ullah Dihlawi, is in no sense a travelogue but rather a compendium of visions and dreams.[10] What goes on in dreams is taken as fact and is intended to have continuity with waking life: thus a point in a dispute can be established by reference to an experience in a dream. In Shah Wali'ullah's case, his visions were taken as legitimation of his role as religious reformer. Here is an example of one of his visions:

I saw that the Two Imams, Hassan and Hussain, have come to my house. Imam Hassan is holding a pen which has a broken point. He held out his hand towards me as if he wanted to give me that pen, and said that the pen belonged to his grandparent, the Prophet of Allah (Peace be upon him). But he stopped for a moment, and asked Imam Hussain to mend the point of the pen for me, because it was no longer the same as it used to be.... I felt a great joy in my heart on this.

Another vision even more clearly confirms his calling; its image of expansion recalls Mufti's own vision in the same place: 'I was circumambulating the Ka'ba when I saw my own light before me and it was all majestic and magnificent. Then, I saw that this light covered everything—almost the whole of the world; and people living in lands, far and near, came under its brightness'.[11] Such visions in a great religious leader of the past do not surprise us as do, perhaps, the similar experiences of Western-educated bureaucrats and coffee-house intellectuals in Pakistan today.

The dreams and visions of Mumtaz Mufti's account are distinctive in their power and inventiveness, but such surreal experiences are part of the everyday life of many people of Mufti's background in this culture, people who are educated, travelled, and typically employed in what could be called the modern sector (Nazir Ahmad

uses the English word 'paranormal' to describe Mufti's experiences
in his introduction). Many, including Mufti, present these experiences as subject to interpretation. Unlike Shah Wali'ullah, they do
not simply accept them as fact. They may or may not be effective
interventions of the divine. Thus from the very first Mufti
distances himself from the traditional model of dreams. In describing his first dream he writes, 'I had the habit of writing down my
dreams, not because I thought they carried messages or gave
indications of the future, but simply because of an interest in the
unconscious (*nafs la sha'ur*, a neologism)' (p. 2). Over and over he
tells us that doubt, not faith, is the religious style (*maslak*, p. 33)
or occupation (*pesha*, p. 140) of intellectuals. In the central vision
of the *but* of the Ka'ba, however, no such caution or question is
asked. And Mufti alludes to the extraordinary experiences of
people he knows even in the course of retelling his own.[12]

*Fatwas* were pronounced against the book and some attempts
were made to have it banned. One might think that the condemnation of Mumtaz Mufti stems from the same mentality that
opposes Salman Rushdie. Both authors distance themselves from
religious leaders and their teachings, and both play rather exuberantly with 'reality'. Rushdie, unlike Mufti, however, writes in the
form that most alarms the absolutist, a form that denies that any
one voice is the author's own.[13] Moreover, he sets out to explore
the colonial Orientalist vision of Islam, and in so doing he has been
read as having sold out to it. Mumtaz Mufti, by contrast, however
much he creates an irony between his authorial omniscience and
the foibles of his protagonist, the Mumtaz Mufti of the account,
nonetheless claims to speak for himself.

Indeed, those who objected to his book did so not so much
because of its content per se, which in basic ways has a long
tradition, but because Mufti chose to tell what the pious often
believe should be kept secret, not least because it could be
misunderstood.[14] To tell any inner experience is problematic. Not
only can such experiences be misunderstood, but they should be
regarded as marks of divine favour likely to be withdrawn because
what is told publicly can be seen as boasting. Once, for example,
a university teacher told me extraordinary tales of his ability, over
a period of several years, to 'visit' the Ka'ba through meditation,
seeing in these visions details he had no other way of knowing.
He could tell me these experiences now, he explained, simply

because the experiences were behind him: he never would have told them while they were in process[15] (see Addenda, 'An Interview').

Mufti's play with multiple realities and his euphoric appropriation of a Hindu language for relationships to God, coupled with a scepticism of mainstream, ritually oriented religion, puts him squarely in the Sufi emphasis on interior religion. He flamboyantly identifies himself with what is local and mixed—the Sufism of pre-Partition Punjab—against those so prominent in Pakistan in recent years who have asserted an Islam meant to be universal and unalloyed. He is ambivalent throughout, yet mocks the scepticism he cannot escape. In one vignette he places God on church steps in Europe, just as he has put him on steps in Mecca. One day, he writes, the Europeans will discover God and take him East, and then we will adopt faith as the latest fashion just as now we have taken up miniskirts and irreligion (pp. 193–4). For all that, the thrust of the book, however ironically circumscribed, is to assert that Mumtaz Mufti is someone who confronts and is shaped by a dramatic series of what are taken as divine interventions into everyday life over a period of many years.

Besides this expanded sense of reality, a second striking feature of this account also has long roots in local tradition, namely a particularly pervasive way of thinking about the person, and, above all, an assumption of the givenness of personal qualities. In this model, which resonates with old Eurasian humoral theories, a person is endowed with certain qualities that persist throughout life. A biography then becomes an occasion for showing contexts in which those qualities are manifest. As one scholar has written, 'the telling of lives in much Islamic biographical material does not present events or cumulative reflections as constituting character. Rather, biographical notices serve to establish origins and display a person's type through his or her discrete actions and sayings.' The self is evident at any well chosen moment.[16]

Since character does not develop over time, there is no need for chronology or for dwelling particularly on childhood as autobiographers informed by Romantic individualism and subjectivism unfailingly do.[17] A biography may well be organized by categories of activities, for example, not by periods, so that a biography of a pious person might be divided into two parts, *shari'at* (describing activities demonstrating obedience to divine injunctions) and *tariqat* (describing manifestations of spiritual realization), with no concern for a single chronology.[18] Early episodes will be adduced only to illustrate what later become characteristic attitudes or activities. In this intensely personal account Mumtaz Mufti tells us virtually nothing about his childhood, his past, or even his present life except what is specifically relevant to the Mecca trip.

A recent study of Muslim conversion narratives, focusing on people who become part of reform organizations or movements that call for far-reaching change in behaviour and community, finds that even there Muslim accounts do not posit the radical break in self-perception that Christian narratives do. Muslims are not 'born again'.[19] What might be viewed as a cataclysmic spiritual experience, namely the hajj, can mark a deepening of faith, a change in everyday patterns, or the adoption of a new name, but it cannot be seen as a change in fundamental identity. At best one returns to one's real self in a religion that posits to human character not original sin but an essential Muslim nature (*fitrah*) and that focuses on assiduity in obedience, not on vicarious redemption, for salvation. Life stories are thus marked by continuity, not by breaks. Malcom X, in telling his life, draws on a model that is quintessentially American, not on this mainstream Muslim tradition.[20]

One of the favourite South Asian genres for showing personality, especially the personality of holy men, is that of *hikaayaat*, tales, or *malfuzaat*, 'table talk', where strings of little anecdotes are given that illuminate a personality from different angles. A personality is like a prism, held up to the light of multiple contexts so that its constant characteristics are revealed. In 'A Story', in the Addenda, I have included a typical anecdote, in this case meant to show not only the givenness but the social acceptance of a type of personality. A person is taken for what he is. Thus, presumably without wounding either, Mumtaz Mufti can refer to the authors of the two introductory essays in his account as Nazir Ahmad 'who is nothing but brains' and Zu'lfiqar Ahmad Tabish 'who is nothing but heart' (p. 10).

We can see, I believe, the author Mumtaz Mufti treating his protagonist Mumtaz Mufti as do the recounters of *hikaayaat*, placing himself in contexts where the characteristics of his nature are revealed, turning himself around to refract dimensions of an essential self. What kind of person is he? He is the unconventional idiosyncratic, a revealer of ironies, always finding ways to distance himself and surprise the conventional, even if they are his fellow intellectuals baffled by his journey. He explicitly employs the alternate European model of personal development, only to insist that it does not apply to him. He does not change in essence, and does not, he claims, change even in detail. He mocks his expectation that he will be venerated as an ideal hajji would be. He deserves nothing—he is the same. The headings of the final sections of his book make his point plain: *jaissee ga'ee waisee lautee*, 'back as I left', *wahiin mumtaz mufti*, 'the same Mumtaz Mufti'.

Mufti articulates one model of personal change, but in his claims exemplifies the old humoral model of personality. Is he not using this convention with some sense of irony? He is to be sure the same person who boasts a lively and critical eye on human behaviour and emotion, including his own. He is the same distanced critic of formal religion that he always was. But by the very act of choosing to go on hajj and writing about it, he has realized himself as part of the crowd. In a characteristically modern move, he has sought authenticity by showing himself part of popular culture expressed in a popular tongue. He is now a man of some kind of faith, even if it is idiosyncratic, unconventional, and embedded in ironic layers. He saves himself from commitments or expectations by claiming nothing at all—except the implicit claim to now be more than a 'nominal Muslim' made by the very fact of the pilgrimage and its record in this book.

Finally, a third characteristic of the account again draws on a long-standing Muslim model of human behaviour, namely that the subject does not shape events but responds to events that happen to him. This is a common emphasis in the representation of human behaviour in life histories. Again, the particularities of Mumtaz Mufti's case make this conventional structuring significant. One has to be called to go on hajj—ultimately the choice to go is beyond individual will. Moreover, the actual achievement of the hajj is often attributed to the grace or the prayers of someone else. Here, however, we have someone who, far from waiting for God's invitation or for the mediation of the pious, claims he never even thought of going on hajj and yet finds himself propelled into it. The convention of passivity gives this sceptic his excuse.

Mufti presents himself as someone upon whom religious experience is thrust. He places himself, or sees himself placed, in a succession of events and observes his reactions, measuring his feelings. His account is cinematic, as scene after scene is presented: at one key moment, in the Prophet's mosque in Medina, when (perhaps) the

Prophet himself emerges (*utarna*, incarnates, as the Hindi verb has it), Mufti resorts to the metaphor of a zoom lens to convey the power with which he sees him approach from afar (pp. 236, 247).

The book jolts open: 'No desire to go on hajj ever appeared in my heart. But strange things happened.' We are then bombarded with some half-dozen vignettes, partaking, or not partaking, of something more than normal, though no explicit claim is ever made. This is, after all, reportage. The first vignette, the encounter with the faqir, is told above. The next episode is a dream. This time an uncle, as much a superficial believer as he (*allah t'aala ko sirf munh zabaanii maantee thee*) appears with suitcases and a ticket for the hajj (p. 27). The dream is remarkable, apparently, for its lucidity and coherence as much as for the implausibility of linking an irreligious uncle and the hajj. Mufti tells the story and lets it hang; he never systematically resolves the tension between his scepticism and the tradition that says dreams are communications from God. There is a surprising encounter with a pious man, yet another dream, even another madman. But the critical element in his decision to go, and in the trip itself, is the presence of the second major character of the book, Qudratu'llah Shahab, a distinguished civil servant who, for Mumtaz Mufti, emerges as a veritable Shams Tabriz, a realized self to act as spiritual guide.[21]

In creating Shahab in this role, Mumtaz Mufti evokes a long and rich tradition, both Indic and Islamic, of transformative personal relationships. A recent study has argued that the relationship of teacher and disciple holds for South Asians the kind of centrality that romantic love holds in Europe from the twelfth century on.[22] Mufti is explicit that without Shahab as guide he would never have gone on hajj. The trip depends on him; Shahab is his *lathi*, his stave and support (pp. 139–40). Shahab is an unlikely guide. An advisor to President Ayyub, he fills no conventional religious role. He is shown moreover to have his own vulnerabilities, particularly an oppressive immobility at moments of religious intensity (pp. 76–8). He is, Mufti writes, a person who knows simultaneously both doubt and faith. But like a classic spiritual guide he intuits Mufti's own conditions (p. 90); he sends him on quests whose meaning is obscure (pp. 27–8); he offers only oblique answers to significant questions (pp. 29, 31–2); and he sets a model of humility (p. 32) and self-abnegation (pp. 216–17). He is at once in the world but detached from it, and is able to focus his attention (what Mufti calls *ganga jamni tawajjuh*, p. 90)[23] in any setting. He finds good in everyone. In the portrait of Shahab, as much as anything, the account resonates with central traditions of life accounts and life experiences in this culture, with the twist that Shahab is, again, such an unlikely guide.

It is possible, moreover, that Mumtaz Mufti is acted on by yet another spiritual leader, alluded to when he declines to take initiation at the hand of his mother's guide, who foretells that he will find another (pp. 196–7), a person possibly witnessed in one key episode when his scepticism about God is challenged in Lahore by an unknown passerby (pp. 70–1). Shahab himself suggests that the unknown person may have been the *bazorg* or elder through whose grace Mumtaz Mufti's journey takes place (p. 196). Mufti himself speculates on this, troubled at the thought that one's personality, one's attitude or shape (*rukh*) as he calls it, is not of one's own making but can be reoriented through the intervention of someone else. He now explicitly adduces a model of personal development in which personality is the sum of one's own efforts and striving. If an elder or even God can change you, what is your 'contribution'? he asks (p. 199). He clings to the Western notion of self-generated personal development, but plays with the possibility of external intervention. And, when it comes to everyday life, he entrusts himself wholly to Shahab.

A series of inexplicable events leads Mumtaz Mufti to the point of imploring Shahab to take him on hajj when he goes (p. 350). Then, once he has taken such an initiative, all his actions prove futile. Shahab takes up a European post as ambassador and is not free to leave. Mumtaz puts in his name for the hajj lottery—certain, he says, mocking himself, that Allah Miyan would personally pull it out—only to fail (p. 39). The mysterious advocate, whose intercession has or has not secured offspring for Shahab (pp. 42–3), who has seen 'the list' (not the lottery results but the heavenly list, pp. 41–2), tells him that his name is not there. Agency does not rest with the individual.

In the very telling of his story he makes clear the extent to which he conceives of his life as subject to outside influences. Indeed, even the act of writing is seen as outside his own initiative. Mumtaz Mufti, like virtually every writer of these accounts, insists that he had no intention of writing until pressed. This recalls the conventional modesty of Urdu orators who begin haltingly and apologetically only to warm up to their powerful style.[24] Mumtaz Mufti specifically insists that he lacked the courage to write, since he had neither the emotion nor the knowledge to justify writing. Mufti, recalling the conventional attributes of humility that authors use, calls himself ignorant (*jaahil*, *anjaan*) but insists, as a nineteenth century Urdu author would not feel constrained to do, that he is also sincere (*mukhlis*) (p. 10). He wrote, he explains, first, to keep a promise to an editor and friend, and second, because, having begun, God 'grabbed him' and he, 'not knowing what happened', kept on writing. God becomes yet one more person who impinges on his life.

The burden of his account is distance and ambivalence. He mocks himself for even being on the hajj. He holds up the pretensions of his fellow pilgrims, freighted with 'ritual' and mundane concerns. He celebrates feelings and inner experience—only to recognize their fragility and immaturity. He does not know how to evaluate supernatural happenings and refers to his initial imbroglio as fairy tales, *tuta mina kahaaniyaan* (tales of a parrot), or, alternatively, *alis aur wandarland*. The advocate's spiritual power, nurtured through ceaseless prayer, for example, is expended in securing a child for Shahab against all medical opinion. 'Yet', he concludes, '[the birth] was just a coincidence' (p. 43), knowing we cannot accept it as such, given its presentation.

His insistence on his own limitations makes his presentation of intense moments of spiritual encounter more powerful. He sees himself in ritual dress and calls himself a *bahrup*, a mimic, 'the person dressed in *ihram* looking at me from the mirror made me want to laugh' (p. 48). At every stage he fails to react as he thinks he should, finding each town no different from home, maybe even less lively: Jiddah airport looks like the one he had just left (p. 52); the inn en route to Mecca feels like the frontier (p. 69); Mecca reminds him of Siyalkot (p. 73) and Medina, again, seems like an ordinary qasba in Punjab (p. 212). Entering the sanctuary in Mecca, he writes, he found he had as little religious feeling as would a tourist surveying the Taj (p. 78).

At both Mecca and Medina he is unable to pray in areas of particular sanctity. In Mecca he is driven out by an overwhelming sense that a buzzing noise attacks him and that he is radiating an overwhelmingly offensive smell (pp. 106–10). In Medina he sees the special cell of revelation as a kind of sports arena where people are being knocked over, and he is unable to stand (pp. 220–3). He mocks other people for their distractions and falls victim to them himself. After describing each moment of illumination, moreover, he retreats in his prose to flat description as a way of deflating his euphoria, adducing such conventional tropes as the racial unity of the hajj, or reminding the pilgrim to bring along a good pair of scissors (pp. 83, 112, 176).

Mumtaz Mufti shows by the very act of writing that he is part of a plural intellectual world. Here the characteristics of Urdu come into play. Mumtaz is regarded today as one of the best living novelists in Urdu, a language known to linguists as Hindi-Urdu since it is written in two scripts, one based on Sanskrit (Hindi) and one on Perso-Arabic (Urdu).[25] Urdu lends itself to a wide variety of registers, drawing as it does on vocabulary and expressions from the local languages (in this case Punjabi), from Persian and Arabic, and from English. The capacity to utter a well-turned phrase is valued in this culture; to open your mouth is to convey who you are. Great value is placed on eloquence, and those whose Urdu is free from rustic vocabulary or accent hope to be known as *ahl-i zaban*, masters of language. Mumtaz Mufti flouts that standard and makes his virtuosity in exploiting the options available to Urdu part of his success.

His use of English loan words is telling. He turns to English for a vocabulary that describes much that is summed up by 'the West': science (micrometers, test tube, transmitter, receiver, neutrons); materialism; obsessive cleanliness (he mocks a pilgrim complaining of an unfulfilled promise of a *nit and klen bath*, p. 126); sex. When he complains of the writers of travelogues who focus only on externals, he has one, 'Shibli, B. Comm.', come into the sanctuary with his tape measure, saying *ai baig yur pardun* (p. 183).[26] At the same time, it is to an English vocabulary that he turns to explicate Shahab's psychology and religion. He speaks of his psychological *resistance*, of the problem of *reversion* (p. 165), of the goal of *divine unconcern* (p. 91), of *identification* as a key to worship (p. 71). What comes from the 'West' is not easily dismissed.

Yet simultaneously he seeks an identity with the ordinary pilgrim, an identity that the very act of coming on hajj permits. Again, his lexicon makes the point. At the sanctuary he persists in referring to God's house not with the conventional words: *bait* in Arabic, *khana* in Persian and in Urdu, or even *ghar* in ordinary

Hindustani. Instead he uses the Punjabi word for hut, *kotha*. When a companion finally protests that this is disrespectful (*be-adabi*), he answers that the word does not convey contempt. He is Punjabi, not *ahl-i zaban*, and for him the word is dear (*piyara*) and conveys a sense of belonging (*apnaaiyat*). To treat the whole creation of God as a *but* and to use a local vocabulary is self-consciously to make a claim to what is indigenous and not part of a cosmopolitan or high tradition.

Mumtaz Mufti thus pictures himself as torn between the styles of faith and scepticism. In Mecca, placed in his luxurious hotel, which he has peopled with relics of the *raj*, he says he feels like a man with two mistresses: one is the secluded, modest housewife of the Ka'ba, the other is the old 'mem' of the hotel who sits on his lap and says, '*darling dont be so superstishus*'. At the time of stoning the pillars (meant to represent the devils who tempted Abraham), he discovers that they are throwing stones at him. Are they telling him that he is the tempter to disobedience, that the enticer is within? he asks. He tries to shout out to everyone to make him the target of their stones: 'I am the one who led people astray, sowed doubts, planted seeds of infidelity and scepticism. I am an intellectual who makes doubt the foundation of knowledge.... I am an educated person who set infidelity as the foundation of culture and defined faith as the mark of ignorance' (pp. 175–6). He consoles himself that he does not come like a trader storing up merit, and he says he watches his fellow pilgrims treating the hajj like a booking office for paradise, a dry-cleaning factory for removing sins (p. 115). Now he uses a Hindu vocabulary to mock them: *jap*, *mala*, *puja*, their frolicking under the *mezab-i rahmat*, a veritable *holi* bacchanalia of reversals (pp. 116–18).

Is Mumtaz Mufti culturally marginal? He would be part of the masses but shrinks back in dismay. He finds anomalies, incongruities, and mixed motives everywhere, especially in himself. He travels intellectually to Europe, physically to Arabia. But if this is marginality, it is of a sort that is increasingly the mainstream in *our* ever more integrated world. Bharati Mukherjee, as an immigrant American, asks who speaks for 'us', but, addressing her *New York Times* reader, explains that 'who speaks for us' means 'who speaks for you'.[27]

Mumtaz Mufti may, at one point, say he has not even completed the hajj, caught up as he is in his vision at the Ka'ba. But if he does

not, his book does. He lays claim, by the very act of writing a
pilgrimage narrative, to a place within the religious tradition and
at the heart of his society. Mumtaz Mufti has, in a sense, now made
possible the pilgrimage for people like himself. He has found some
sort of God in Mecca and something like the Prophet incarnate
in Medina, even though he decides he must leave them behind. He
comes back knowing that somewhere—back there, out there—
there is a benign force that every now and then, in ways that are
unexpected, even bizarre, comes home. His account is a tutor to
the emotions and intellectual ambivalences of people—ever more
numerous— like himself. This is not a conceptual resolution, but
a resolution achieved by narrative art.

Conventionally, pilgrimage accounts have little to do with the
personality of the pilgrim. They are not written as occasions for
self discovery; if anything, the particularities of the writer are
suppressed.[28] The text itself is seen as a kind of ritual continuation
of the duty of pilgrimage. An aid to later pilgrims and a stimulus
to their piety, it is nothing less than a further act deserving reward,
*sawab*. As the reader, typically invited to do so in the text, prays
blessings on the author, that *sawab* continuously grows. If the goal
of authors of the classic accounts was humbly to seek *sawab*, in
the end Mumtaz Mufti does too. For the second edition of *Labbaik*,
as mutterings were still to be heard about its heresies, Mumtaz
Mufti turned to the then Minister of Religious Affairs, Maulana
Kausar Niyazi, a distinguished writer himself and a member of the
'fundamentalist' Jama'at-i Islami, to provide a kind of *nihil obstat*
in the form of a jacket blurb. This book, the Maulana wrote, far
from being heresy, would secure for the author nothing less than
paradise itself.[29] *Sawab* indeed. And again, Mufti, in the freedom
that comes from travel and art, takes a cultural chord that resonates
deep and claims it for his own.

## Addenda: Three Everyday Visions and a Teaching about Character

### The African Procession, from Labbaik

Everyone's gaze had shifted from the House of God to the
courtyard of the sanctuary (*harm sharif*). It was the first of the
farewell processions.

*An African procession*: The procession was made up of forty or fifty Africans, men as well as women, children too. They were all standing on the road that leads directly to the outer gate.

The faces of these Africans, engaged in making their farewells were distorted with disproportionate love and the pain of impending separation. Their eyes, flowing with tears, were fixed on the House of God; their foreheads virtually quivered to make prostrations. Every member of their body emanated humility, respect, and grief.

They were all going toward the outer door from the House of God backwards. With every step their emotions grew more intense and their longing increased. Depth in their grief and ever more tears. Their faces were oozing like sores from their anguish and the chants of separation. The procession, still going backwards, crept on and on.

All the pilgrims sitting in the sanctuary watched them struck dumb. In my life I have seen many profoundly moving sights but never such intensity as I saw that day in the sanctuary in the scene of farewell.

The pilgrims could not lift their gaze from this sight, as if by sorcery they were turned to stone.

*Soaked*: It seemed as if Allah had left his house to be absorbed in that procession.

Those fifty Africans at this point were soaked in Allah. Their faces had absorbed God's love as jalebis do sugar syrup. Allah was flowing from their eyes, distilled into tears, glowing from their foreheads, changed into light. At such humility Allah stood astonished, his finger in his mouth.

The procession kept creeping backwards. Centuries passed.

When the last person left from the outer gate, I started. I felt that they had taken Allah with them.

The whole sanctuary was empty and the house of the Ka'ba stood in the midst like an idol. An idol of stone.

I ran to the outer door.

Outside I found no trace of the African procession. Lost, I thought, lost. I had to join that African procession. I too would be soaked in God even for a few minutes: I would become God. Lost. Despairing, I sat down on a platform outside. I don't know how long I sat there, my head bowed.

*The house and its master (makaan aur makiin)*: Then when I lifted my eyes I saw him sitting on the stairs of the outer gate with his chin on his knee. His clothes were patched, his face wrinkled, his eyelids covering his eyes.

When anyone leaving came out of the door, he looked up with love-filled eyes, held out his finger and said, 'Don't leave me, take me along, take my finger and take me along. Don't sorrow over leaving the house (*kotha*). The house is empty. I am sitting here watching for you, waiting for you, wanting to go with you. Take my finger, take me along.' He tugged at the skirt of everyone leaving.

But no one looked at him. No one heard him. No one paid attention to him. All were fixed on the house of stone. They were motionless in sorrow at leaving it.

They were so lost in the house that they forgot the master.

And the master just gazed at them, astonished and helpless.

Then he looked at me with suppliant eyes and extended his finger.

'No, no, I cannot take you', I said. 'I am full of myself. I have grasped the finger of myself with both hands. I have made a *but* of myself. How can I take you along'? (pp. 189–92).

## A Conversation about Dreams at the Daru'l-'Ulum, 1970

In 1970 I was conducting research on a leading Muslim theological seminary, the Daru'l-'Ulum at Deoband, whose rector and other officials welcomed me generously. One day, seated at my table in the guest house, I was chatting with a few of the people connected with the school about political life immediately preceding Independence. At that time most of the school's scholars supported the Indian nationalist movement and opposed the movement for a separate Muslim state. One young man spoke of the fact that people's confidence in the veracity of these religious leaders was shaken when both the leader of the nationalist scholars, Maulana Husain Ahmad Madani, and the leader of the smaller group supporting Pakistan, Maulana Shabir Ahmad Usmani, both claimed to have had dreams of the Prophet sanctioning their respective positions.

Caught up in the conversation, and influenced by the fact that this young man regarded himself as a bit of a sceptic, I interjected that it was perfectly possible that each should have had such a dream, that anyone could have such a dream, that after all I myself had once even had a dramatic dream in which the Prophet appeared. The stunned silence that greeted my remarks made clear to me that an epistemological chasm divided us. But the respect for dreams was so great that a sincere appreciation for my dream seemed to erase my 'logical' gaffe—and earn me a status I felt undeserved.

### Paraphrase of an Interview with a Poet and Scholar, Lahore, 1985

Although I had no particular connection to religious practices, my family, Pathans from Miyanwali, were religious, offering *namaz*, etc. My paternal grandfather was close to the English but inclined to Sufism. My father was a policeman but kept a beard and would repeat *namaz* even if he had to do it while wearing his regulation boots! As for me, I felt distant from God but not from Muhammad. It is Muhammad who is the way to know God, for there is no other man like him.

We were ten or eleven children in our family, but my father especially loved me. My father particularly wanted to go on hajj but was never able to do it. He was a 'misfit' in the police. He died. Once he was dead I needed to know if he was finished, how I could continue to feel his love. I knew that Sufism (*tasawwuf*) was the only way for me to find out.... It could promote a meeting, a *real* meeting and not just thought, a meeting as real as all of us sitting here around this table. I began Sufi practices.... My father had had a spiritual guide (*pir*) who was very unattractive. Nonetheless, he had felt an immediate rapport with him.

A professor I knew, Naqwi Sahib, came to discuss socialism, etc., with me and I felt he was doing something to me. After a week I felt it even more. He was establishing some connection (*rabita*). He asked me if I wanted to meet Data Sahib (Data Ganj Bakhsh, a twelfth century Sufi buried in Lahore). I gave no answer but after he left I wept for no reason. When he came the next day we sat in a dark room, he on my right and I on his left, and he had me repeat the name of God (*zikr Allah*) with a pattern of breathing while paying attention to my heart. The breathing was fast and lasted about an hour. At the end I was very tired (though later when I got used to it I would not be). At the end I closed my eyes and lost all connection with the world. The room was filled with light although my eyes were closed; when I opened them, the room was dark. In this meditation (*muraqaba*) the light was ten times brighter than the sun. The light narrowed to a dot and came from Naqwi's heart directly to mine. I would awaken for the night prayer and meditate, often with him, until dawn. I wanted to meet my father more than I wanted to meet Data Sahib.

Although it was not necessary we went to my father's grave to secure this meeting. I was always on Naqwi Sahib's left, on the side of his heart. He told me to exert attention (*tawajjuh*) on my heart and told me to enter the grave. I sat with my father as I am sitting with you. There was no need for language. My heart felt the conversation which came directly from his heart to me. After that I could meet him anywhere. I consulted him, for example, on my sister's wedding.... Without *tasawwuf* no one is complete.

I met Naqwi Sahib's *pir* in Chakrala. He is a Naqshbandi, but very informal and does not require initiation. He keeps goats. He was in Allah Yar Khan. He was a *malik*, a *Jat*, and an 'alim. He never heard radio or TV nor did he read a newspaper, but he was very informed about the world. I met him often. He was very informal, we all sat on the ground. He is dead now....

The stages of meditation begin, first with *uluhiyat*, the divine essence, whose colour is white (I am not a Sufi).

Then he would say, 'Go to *ahdiyat*, oneness'. I felt myself leave myself and go up, and everyone present could feel the others doing it.

The next stage was *mai'yat*, companionship, whose colour is green. No one taught me these colours.

The next stage is *aqrabiyat*, nearness, whose colour is red.

The next stage is *fana*, extinction, whose motion is continually upward; one feels that all are finished.

There could be more than three hundred of us meditating at one time. It would be completely dark, all of us with our eyes closed.

The next stage is *baqa*, abiding, whose colour is white again.

When we reached it he would say *sair-i Ka'ba*, the trip or experience of the Ka'ba, and it was there, not just as a thought. Everything was before me, the water of Zamzam, Mina, everything, as if I were there. I had not even seen pictures of all this before. I would do this two times a day, at sunset and at the time of the supererogatory night prayer. It would take about two hours. I could do it myself or with a group.

I thus went on hajj thousands of times.

The *pir* himself had gone on hajj four times. He died at over eighty and in his whole life had never missed the prayer in community.

People say there is more pleasure (*maza*) in the hajj done during meditation than there is in the real hajj.

The final stage is *sair-i rasul*, experience of the Prophet, when I would feel myself in the Prophet's mosque in Medina. I cannot describe the feelings I would have afterward. The *pir* presented me to the Prophet. I put my knees toward him and could feel them touching him. I extended my hands and he took them. At the time of initiation, the Prophet gives a gift. I had not told the *pir* that I was a poet and for three years I had not even read a book. Yet he gave me a pen! The others sitting with me had the same experience and afterward when I asked them the colour of the pen they all knew that it had been blue!

## A Story Concerning the Eighteenth-Century Scholar and Sufi Maulana Muhammad Mazhar Jan-i Janan

One day one of the great notables of Delhi decided to test three of the most distinguished scholars of hadith, Shah Wali'ullah, Maulana Fakhru'd-din Chishti, and Hazrat Mirza Jan-i Janan, to see whose rank (*martaba*) was highest. He invited each to take the morning meal at his house, inviting them to come at half hour intervals. All accepted. The next day, as each arrived, he graciously escorted him to a separate room, assuring him that a meal would soon follow. The entire day passed. Finally, the host went to each and apologized profusely that problems in the

336 ISLAMIC CONTESTATIONS

household had made it impossible to prepare food; instead he offered each a gift of money. Shah Wali'ullah graciously accepted the gift, assured him that there was no need to be embarrassed, and departed. Similarly, Maulana Fakhru'd-din arose, insisted that he not worry, and ceremonially held out a handkerchief to receive the proffered gift. Mirza Mazhar Jan-i Janan, however, took the money, stuffed it in his pocket and told him, with a frown, 'No problem, but don't bother me again'. Then he left.

When this story was told to a group of scholars in the late nineteenth century, they are recorded as having pondered the three responses with a view to seeing who of the three emerged as the greatest. The narrator himself ranked Maulana Fakhru'd-din highest because he acted ceremonially, followed by Shah Wali'ullah who was also gracious, followed in turn by Maulana Mazhar Jan-i Janan who showed his displeasure. But the most revered of the scholars demurred. For him the greatest was none other then Jan-i Janan, a man endowed with such a brittle temperament (*nazuk mizaji*) that for him to have acted as he did required the greatest forbearance and self-control (paraphrased from Zuhuru'l-Hasan Kasoli, *Arwah-i salasa*, Saharanpur, 1950-1).

So you are what you are. You can and should hone your personality—above all by acts of obedience to divine teachings—but you cannot change essentials. The goal is to direct what you are given in ways ordained by God.

*Notes*

I have been interested in hajj accounts for several years and have accumulated innumerable debts to institutions and individuals. I would particularly like to thank Robert Folkenflik, for inviting me to participate in the conference that led to the volume in which this article was originally published in 1993, in *The Culture of Autobiography: Constructions of Self-Representation* (Stanford: Stanford University Press has as well as the National Humanities Centre, for providing a tranquil setting to write. My thanks also to John Sturrock, a participant in the conference, at whose suggestion a shortened version of the conference paper was published in the *Times Literary Supplement* (1–7 June 1990). I am particularly grateful to two fellow inhabitants of the Center, Morris Dickstein and Thomas Metcalf, and to three North Carolina neighbours, Katherine Ewing, David Gilmartin, and James Peacock, for many lively conversations during 1989–90.

1. See Spengemann, William C. 1974. 'Eternal Maps and Temporal Voyages'. *Exploration*, 2: 1–7.

2. On the subject of irony in travel writing, see Howard, Donald B. 1980. *Writers and Pilgrims: Medieval Pilgrimge Narratives and Their Posterity*. Berkeley: University of California Press.

3. Fussell, Paul. 1987. *The Norton Book of Travel*, introduction, p. 13. New York: Norton.

4. For a stimulating treatment of non-Western travel writing to Europe, see Mitchell, Timothy. 1987. *Colonizing Egypt*, chapter I. Cambridge: Cambridge University Press.

5. The journal, published in Lahore was *Siyara Da'ijast*. The edition of the book used here is Mufti, Mumtaz. 1975. *Labbaik*. Lahore: Al Tahrir, with introductions by Nazir Ahmad (pp. 11–16) and Zu'l-fiqar 'Tabash' (pp. 17–24).

6. There is no continuing genre of travel accounts, despite the well-known works of the Arab geographers up to the fourteenth century. Travel accounts became common from the late eighteenth century on, and seem to have been products of the same intellectual impulse that stimulated other new genres, like autobiography and, later, the novel. See Metcalf. 1990. 'The Pilgrimage Remembered: South Asian Accounts of the Hajj', in Eickelman, Dale and James Piscatori, eds. *Muslim Travellers: Pilgrimage, Migraton and the Religious Imagination*, Berkeley: University of California Press, pp. 85–107. (Chapter 13 in this volume.)

7. See Rosaldo, Renato. 1989. *Culture and Truth: The Remaking of Social Analysis*. Boston: Beacon Press.

8. Rushdie, Salman. 1990. 'In Good Faith: A Pen Against the Sword', pp. 52–4. *Newsweek*, 12 February.

9. See von Grunebaum, Gustav and Roger Callois, eds. 1966. *The Dream and Human Societies*. Berkeley: University of California Press. For a study specifically related to this milieu, see Ewing, Katherine P. February 1990. 'The Dream of Spiritual Initiation and the Organization of Self Representations among Pakistani Sufis'. *American Ethnologist*, 17: 56–74.

10. Shah Wali'ullah. n.d. *Mushahadat wa ma'arif tarjama Fayuzu'l-haramain* (Visions and Inspirations: A Translation of 'The excellencies of the two Holy Places'), trans. from Arabic into Urdu by Muhammad Sarwar. 3rd edn. n.d. Lahore: Sindh Sagar Akademi.

11. The translations are from Kamran, Gilani. 1980. *South Asian Muslim Creative Mind*, pp. 41–3. Lahore: National Book House.

12. For example, the Ko'ila Centre's Baba, pp. 59–60; Khawar's vision and transformation, pp. 68–9; and the return of the martyrs of Badr, pp. 209–10.

13. For a brief but powerful argument about why magic realism is 'offensive', see Dharwadker, Vinay. 1987. "Offensive Books" and the Rhetoric of Outrage'. *Public Culture*, I (Spring): 76–9.

14. 'Tabash'. Introduction to *Labbaik*, p. 22.

15. Interview with an academic and poet, Lahore, 1985.

16. Hermansen, Marcia. 1987. 'Interdisciplinary Approaches to Islamic Biographical Materials', p. 4. Typescript. See also Eickelman, Dale F. 'Traditional Islamic Learning and Ideas of the Person in the Twentieth Century'. In Kramer, Martin, ed., 1991. *Middle Eastern Lives: The Practice of Biography and Self-Narrative*. This of course does not mean that there is no notion of

338 ISLAMIC CONTESTATIONS

coming to maturity in these writings. Quite the contrary, and other accounts, if not this one, stress the hajj as an occasion for ethical reflection and moral growth. In English, for example, see Zafar, S. M. 1978. *Haj: A Journey in Obedience*. Lahore: Ripon Printing Press. Ira M. Lapidus suggests that Muslim (auto)biographies tend not to map life stages and transitions but see positive change as a deepening of or return to faith. See his 'Adulthood in Islam: Religious Maturity in the Islamic Tradition', 1976 *Daedalus*, 105, 93–107.

17. See Robert Folkenflik's Introduction (1993); it is important to note that the generalization about a post-Romantic emphasis on childhood may not be true everywhere.

18. See for example Mirathi, Muhammad Ashiq Ilahi. n.d. *Tazkiratu'r-rashid*, 2 vols. Meerut: n.p., which is divided into two sections, *shari'at* and *tariqat*, so that events are categorized as to whether they are primarily related to fulfilment of religious obligations or spiritual experience. See also Khan, Muhammad Ikramullah. 1925. *Viqar-i hayat*. Aligarh, where events are categorized in relation to fulfilment of the so-called pillars of Islam.

19. Peacock, James L. 1984. 'Religion and Life History: An Exploration in Cultural Psychology'. In Bruner, Edward M. ed. *Text, Play, and Story: The Construction and Reconstruction of Self and Society*, pp. 94–116. Washington, DC: American Ethnological Society; and idem, 'Dahlan and Rasul: Indonesian Muslim Reformers'. In Becker, A. L. and Aram A. Yengoyan, eds, 1979. *The Imagination of Reality: Essay in Southeast Asian Coherence Systems*, pp. 245–68. Norwood, NJ: Ablex.

20. For a study linking the structure of Malcolm's autobiography to such American classics as the autobiography of Benjamin Franklin, see Ohmann, Carol. 1970. 'The Autobiography of Malcolm X: A Revolutionary Use of the Franklin Tradition'. *American Quarterly*, 22 (Summer): 131–49.

21. For Qudratu'llah's own account (1987) of a hajj (not the same one), see his *Shahabnama*, pp. 557–612. Lahore: Sangmeel Publications. Shams-i Tabriz was the spiritual guide of the great thirteenth century mystic poet of Konya, Maulana Jalalu'd-din Rumi.

22. Vaidyanathan, T. G. 1989. 'Authority and Identity in India'. *Daedalus*, 'Another India', 118 (Fall): 147–70.

23. Again, a pre-Partition allusion, here to the confluence of the Ganges and Jumna, a symbol of dualism in unity, sacred to Hindus.

24. Lelyveld, David S. 1988. 'Eloquence and Authority in Urdu: Poetry, Oratory, and Film'. In Ewing, Katherine T. ed. *Shari'at and Ambiguity in South Asian Islam*, p. 108. Berkeley: University of California Press. This device, as Lelyveld points out, prevents the listener from questioning authority.

25. C. M. Naim calls him one of today's two most distinguished Urdu novelists. See Robinson, Francis, ed., 1989. *The Cambridge Encyclopedia of India, Pakistan, Bangladesh and Sri Lanka*, p. 426. Cambridge: Cambridge University Press.

26. The account is a real one. See Shibli, 'Abdu'r-rahim. 1972. *Rabb-i ka'ba ke huzur* (The noble presence of the Lord of the Ka'ba). Lahore: Qamr Taskin. His presumed B. Comm. degree is not noted in the text.

27. Mukherjee, Bharati. 1988. 'Immigrant Writing: Give Us Your Maximalists!' *New York Times Book Review*. 28 August, p. I.

28. Compare the treatment of Egeria's late fourth century *Pergegrinatio ad terram sanctam*, in Campbell, Mary B. 1988. *The Witness and the Other World: Exotic European Travel Writing*, 400–1600. Ithaca, N.Y.: Cornell University Press. Campbell argues that Egeria deflects interest in her personality in favour of showing each place as a stimulus to the memory of a historic event; her presence, her response, is essentially irrelevant to what is primarily a didactic goal of enhancing the meditation of the reader who, in a sense, becomes a second pilgrim.

29. Interview with Maulana Kausar Niyazi, Delhi, 14 February 1990.

# 15

## Narrating Lives
### A Mughal Empress, A French Nabob, A Nationalist Muslim Intellectual

*Nur Jahan: Empress of Mughal India.* By Ellison Banks Findly. New York: Oxford University Press, 1993. 407 pp.

*A Very Ingenious Man: Claude Martin in Early Colonial India.* By Rosie Llewellyn-Jones. New Delhi: Oxford University Press, 1992. xxi, 241 pp.

*Abul Kalam Azad: An Intellectual and Religious Biography.* By Ian Henderson Douglas. Edited by Gail Minault and Christian W. Troll. New Delhi: Oxford University Press, 1993. xii, 358 pp.

With some exaggeration, one could claim that these three biographies, despite their disparate subjects—a seventeenth-century aristocratic lady of the Mughal court, an eighteenth century French adventurer, and a twentieth-century Muslim intellectual and political figure—all tell the same story. In each case, a figure is born (as it happens, outside the Indian subcontinent) in relatively humble circumstances and emerges as a singular figure in some combination of the political, economic, intellectual life of the day. Each account proceeds chronologically, with the life presented as an unfolding, linear story, the fruit of 'developments' and 'influences', in which the protagonist independently takes action. These accounts fit, in short, the genre of biography or autobiography known to Americans from Benjamin Franklin to Malcolm X, of rags to riches—and, typically, lessons to impart.[1] Each is an example of the canonical form of male biography and autobiography that emerged in Europe from the eighteenth century.

An intriguing variation on this genre, common to all three volumes and perhaps a mark of our particular time or trade, is that all the authors chose to end on a poignant note, mulling over the failed social relationships of their subjects. Nur Jahan spent her final eighteen years 'in relative seclusion in her own personal house in [Lahore]', 'ironically' subject to her own brother whom she had long worked to promote and then to defeat (p. 285). Claude Martin, 'as a working-class foreigner, was never able to break through the barrier of protocol and snobbery to become accepted by the Establishment…. It was, perhaps, his most serious failing not to recognize that the rewards and affection he always sought lay not among the self-centred British but in the people with whom he was most intimately connected' (p. 220). As for Azad, the Muslim intellectual active in the Congress movement, Douglas concludes that he was 'a sadly misunderstood man' (p. 252). 'His was not one of the great success stories of the modern world, but great men have not always been honoured in their time' (p. 253).

These meta-narratives remind us that biographers' knowledge of their subject is forged in their often implicit understanding of the world and, indeed, of themselves—and this knowledge is culturally specific. All of these biographers utilize this 'common sense' structure and rhetoric of life stories without reflection. Rosie Llewellyn-Jones describes her own goal as an objective study. To be sure, she acknowledges that another person using the same materials would tell a different story. But, noting that all biographers are 'creatures of their time', she makes clear that her main concern is that time may bring to light new materials, not with how cultural differences shape interpretation.

Her subject, Claude Martin, lends himself well to the received model of biography. He was an eighteenth century adventurer, actively seizing opportunities and events, and achieving, in many ways, the success he sought. Using his letters and extensive East India Company documents, and drawing on her earlier study of Lucknow, Llewellyn-Jones tells a story that presumably is not untrue to the story Martin would have told of himself. His self-composed epitaph marks the trajectory of his achievement: lying here is a 'Major-General Claude Martin, who, arrived in India a common soldier' (p. 213).

Llewellyn-Jones has two particular interests in her subject. One is the extent to which he is a self-made man, 'a working-class foreigner' (p. 220) who became a nabob. A second, reflected in the title, is Martin as an 'ingenious' man (the phrase used of him by a contemporary): someone who could fight, survey, and design buildings, oversee silk production, cure his own bladder stones with a silver wire (duly communicated to a medical society in London), engage in amateur botany, and, above all, make money as a merchant trader with connections—a nostalgic vision of a 'renaissance' man of a sort our age cannot produce. In his later years, and in his will, Martin was magnanimous with his rather ill-gotten gains, not least in funding the schools that still flourish, each called 'La Martiniere', in Calcutta and Lucknow.

Llewellyn-Jones tells a good story. Here one finds the sixteen-year-old apprentice from Lyons off in the army of the French company, facing shipwrecks and brushes with tigers, glory on the battlefield, politics and corruption and Freemasons, intrigue in a princely court, and the purchase of slaves, one of whom is the nine-year-old daughter of noble birth whom he educates and raises until—imagine the movie—he takes her as his life long mistress. This is as close to a page-turner as one is likely to find in books on Indian history. It is intelligent and sensible, offering marvellous texture and detail, including attention to the architectural and urban settings that Llewellyn-Jones, as an architectural historian who has written a definitive study of Nawabi Lucknow, delineates particularly well. If it does not stretch our sense of human possibility as the rare few best biographies do, or give us a new sense of how even the European past is 'a foreign country',[2] neither does it indulge itself in undisciplined speculation backed up by nothing.

The remaining two biographies chart out more ambitious programmes, both pointing to important issues, but both, I think, flawed in their execution. Findly says that her study of Nur Jahan is 'a documentation of the early emergence of the Nur Jahan legend' (preface). In fact, she devotes much of the book to establishing a factual narrative of the empress's life, including the important issue of how such a powerful figure was seen at the time; she includes discussions of Jahangir, court politics, the English embassy, art and architecture, and religious policy and views. She draws on secondary studies, including the biography of Shujauddin and Shujauddin (1967),[3] uses writings by Europeans at the court extensively and, to a lesser extent, consults Persian histories in translation; there are no known writings by Nur Jahan herself. The book includes numerous black-and-white reproductions of court paintings and photographs of monuments. A clue that the story told is somewhat problematic is suggested by the inordinate number of phrases of speculation: thus on one page, 'some say', 'said to have been', 'probably because', 'presumably' (p. 255).

Findly largely takes her sources at face value. A study of 'the legend', however, should distinguish the different life stories that emerge, who tells them and when. Above all, there is no single legend: the contemporary Amar Chitra Katha comic book version, for example, produced for Indian children, includes 'legendary' events but develops its own theme of bourgeois wifely devotion. A more contextually situated study of the 'legends' needs to be done. And it needs to be done from the original languages as Chatterjee's devastating critique of Elliott and Dowson's translations, drawn on heavily here, makes clear.[4]

Findly tends, moreover, to take European views as facts as, for example in explaining European acceptance of reports of a murder on the grounds that 'it supported all that India [sic] was coming to know of imperial Mughal behaviour' (p. 29). The limits of European reporting are especially marked in relation to women's lives, given all that has been written about 'Orientalism'. What the Europeans tell us about women, the harem, despotism, and so forth may tell us more about Europe than about India.

A biographer in this field should equally, of course, be aware of the rhetoric of the distinctive Indo-Persian cultural and literary tradition with its own conventions of writing and thinking about life histories. Three significant characteristics of that tradition distinguish it. First, chronology is irrelevant since the essential personality is inherent from the start. Discrete actions and sayings are adduced to show how an individual approximates some category of 'person' as defined in that society.[5] Moreover, the essential personality is always present. Vincent Crapanzano, for example, using similar Moroccan material, describes a 'scrambled' chronology—a sense of time that follows a different logic.[6] Susan Wadley reports north Indians telling their life stories in terms of episodes of *dukh*, sorrow, which are not causally or developmentally linked.[7] I have found biographies of Muslim religious leaders organized not in a single chronology but by types of activity or experience (for example, the five pillars or *shari'a/tariqa*).[8]

Secondly, the person thus documented is seen not as notable for 'individuality' but precisely for representing a timeless pattern. Such a way of seeing the individual and history approximates long-enduring themes in Judaeo-Christian tradition as well.[9] Significance is found in similarity, not difference.

Third, the subject may well not be imagined as an individual actively conquering and shaping the world independently but as responding to, or even being the sport of, outside events.[10] Moreover, a biographer seeking to tell the story of a South Asian life would, presumably, seriously misinterpret that life by focusing on the individual subject, given recent work positing an 'Indian self' or a 'relational self'.[11] That life would have to be presented as embedded in networks and relationships, an approach also identified as critical in life stories of American and European women.[12]

Only close work with the relevant Persian texts—to the extent that they are available—would allow us to see how the lives of Jahangir and Nur Jahan were understood and represented. Instead of that, we have texts, Persian and European, read off as fact. As a result, in the case of Jahangir, for example, classic tropes are taken as idiosyncratic. Thus Jahangir's particular personality, following Edward Terry (chaplain to Sir Thomas Roe), is imputed a contradictory character, 'barbarously cruel and exceedingly fair and gentle' (p. 62). It is at least plausible that Terry was echoing the classic rhetoric of Persian kingship, whose locus classicus in Indo-Persian literature is the *Fatawa-yi Jahandari* of Barani. In a different vein, but again leading to a misleading imputation of singularity, Jahangir's conceptualization of his kingdom as a universal empire, not a state as demarcated by the Mercator map he was offered (p. 72), is a view characteristic of other pre-modern empires and not his peculiar megalomania.[13]

About Nur Jahan, Findly writes,

Nur Jahan was exemplary not because she perfectly fit established ideals for women, but precisely because she stood outside of the traditional Indian prototypes of circumstance, role, and sentiment. Her image did not inherently conform to enduring cultural models but rather came to be seen in the form of a distinct personality, singular in its talents, consuming in its ambitions, and passionate in its tastes (p. 4).

These are very large claims if one is talking about contemporaneous, or even later, indigenous views. To consider someone as being outside all cultural models, as 'distinct', and 'singular' (even if these are characteristics admired today) would be literally unthinkable in Indo-Persian culture in this period. Enemies or admirers would find the representative type or types and place Nur Jahan there. There are many ideal types for women or men; among those for court women, for example, one could be the celebrated Bilqis (whom Findly does not seem to recognize as a traditional figure, p. 94).

Instead of trying to determine how Nur Jahan conformed to enduring cultural models, whether good or bad, and elucidating the view of person and history that such 'typological' thinking entails, Findly imposes her own idea of cultural symbols that she assumes must have been relevant to Nur Jahan's power and influence (pp. 5, 84–7, 213–17, 287). These are the Prophet's wife Khadija; the Madonna, known through paintings and Christian clergy at the court; and the powerful local goddesses, whether bloodthirsty Kali or nurturing Parvati. But there is not a single item of evidence adduced from the histories, memoirs, poetry or even European reports suggesting that Nur Jahan was understood as embodying these models, let alone that she was unique in combining them and pushing their limits, as Findly suggests.

Nor is there any recognition on Findly's part that these are each profoundly polyvalent symbols. Thus, for her, Mary represents unidimensionally the mother-child bond and maternal nurturing. But Mary has a long and distinct tradition in Sufi thought where she is taken as a model of disciplined obedience to God: the 'fast of Mary', for example, is the silence she was bound to, and kept, when she went into the wilderness to bear her child, a prophet whose birth serves as a symbol of God's approval of her behaviour, not as the object of her attention.[14] We neither know if these symbols were relevant or what they would have meant for Nur Jahan.

The issue of culturally distinct ways of biographical/autobiographical telling is, again, striking in Douglas's biography of Azad. Douglas does not explicitly address the question of the structure or rhetoric of life stories in the Indo-Muslim tradition, but he does, implicitly, reject as flawed indigenous self-representation, and claims, again implicitly, an absolute value for his own. 'The meaning of [Azad's] life', he writes, 'can only be understood by taking into account the principle of development'. And he goes on to criticize writers like Ghulam Rasul Mihr, whose work he terms 'weak', on the very grounds that he fails to make distinctions among Azad's pronouncements at different times (p. 261). Douglas does not see that Mihr, and perhaps his subject, conceptualize both personality and life stories differently.

We nonetheless get occasional glimpses, from the point of view of Azad and his own world, of what Douglas calls the 'meaning' of his life. Thus when the autobiographical *Tazkira* was dragged out from him, Azad consistently denied the influences of family, teachers, and society. Douglas sees this as 'normal', instead of exploring the possibility that it reflects a different view of personality as God-given and innate (p. 29; also cf. p. 207). He is also puzzled by Azad's emphasis on the past. 'Although [sic] the *Tazkira* was intended to be an autobiography, Azad started with a description of one of his ancestors...and branched off into the story of other heroes' (p. 164). As Bernard Lewis notes, there was no other way to begin an Islamic autobiographic statement (p. 23).[15] Azad uses this structure to situate his life as a contemporary manifestation of an ideal of religious leadership, but Douglas sees this only as his being 'selective' in reviewing his ancestors (p. 31). Azad wants to be like the ideal reformers of the past; Douglas wants to show his distinct 'greatness'.

The case of Maulana Azad is in fact a challenging one since he was steeped in the received tradition of Islamic learning, as were people like Mihr who wrote about his life; yet he was also self-educated in English language and European texts. He discussed autobiographical writing by both Europeans and Muslims, and was interested in the 'creative individual' (p. 232). All this calls for analysis from Azad's own perspective.

For all this, Douglas's reading of Azad's works makes available a great deal of important material, for example the vision articulated in his journal between 1910 and 1922 of himself as the religious leader of his community and of that community organized to revive personal Islam. The editors, who complement each other perfectly for this project as a historian and an expert on religious thought, deserve our thanks for bringing this dissertation (1969) to posthumous publication. They provide an introduction, a conclusion, and notes and comments that offer additional material and correction, in part based on material that has become available since the original writing.

Douglas makes no claim to detachment. He cherishes Azad's lessons of an Islam distinguished by 'large-heartedness', of his not leaving politics to 'those ulama for whom religion is a matter of outward conformity and of bolstering their personal status', and for his simultaneous 'hospitality to Western learning and devotion to Islam' (pp. 277–9). Douglas, also trained in theology, engages with Azad, 'correcting' and judging his intellectual positions as fair or partial, puzzling over aspects of his character, identifying a stance or a spiritual position as 'genuine'. He ranks Azad as 'a major figure in twentieth century Indian History' (p. 1).

Douglas's moral judgments and stake in his subject seem very old fashioned. On the other hand, made explicit, they might have told us why he cared so very much about his fellow theologian. Had he let us know that he was imagining himself in Azad's place—perhaps down to the very bottom line of being misunderstood—he would have placed himself among the postmodernists, *avant la lettre*, in a style of biographical writing that at its best brings the author to literally 'inhabit' a subject (Simon 1994). Such an approach, with its assumption of a shared human imagination, would seem the opposite pole of the emphasis on distinctive cultural tradition, but biographers—one might venture—should aim for both, and *know* that this is what they are doing.

Life stories are fictions but they are fictions that matter in clarifying the conceptions and the valued activities of the cultures at hand. The metanarratives in the stories of the exceedingly disparate trio presented here are disconcertingly similar. This similarity suggests that there are more stories to be told—even about these very same lives—and, above all, that we limit our understanding of other lives (and times) if we make them too much like our own.

## Notes

1. Ohmann, Carol. 1970. '*The Autobiography of Malcom X*: A Revolutionary Use of the Franklin Tradition'. *American Quarterly* 22: 131–49.

2. Lowenthal, David. 1985. *The Past is a Foreign Country*. New York: Columbia University Press.

3. Shujauddin, Mohammad and Razia Shujauddin. 1967. *The Life and Times of Noor Jahan*. Lahore; The Caravan Book House; Simon, Linda. 1994. 'Review

of *Daisy Bates in the Desert* by Julia Blackburn'. *The New York Times Book Review.* 14 August 1994.

4. Chatterjee, Partha. 1993. *The Nation and Its Fragments: Colonial and Postcolonial Histories*, pp. 101–2. Princeton: Princeton University Press.

5. Eickelman, Dale F. 1991. 'Traditional Islamic Learning and Ideas of the Person in the Twentieth Century'. In Kramer, Martin, ed. *Middle Eastern Lives: The Practice of Biography and Self-Narrative*, pp. 35–69. Syracuse: Syracuse University Press; and Hermansen, Marcia. 1987. 'Interdisciplinary Approaches to Islamic Biographical Materials', p. 4, San Diego State University. Typescript.

6. Bruner, Jerome. 1993. 'The Autobiographical Process'. In Folkenflik, Robert, ed. *The Culture of Autobiography: Constructions of Self-Representation*, pp. 38–56. Stanford: Stanford University Press.

7. Wadley, Susan S. 1994. *Struggling with Destiny in Karimpur, 1925–1984*, pp. 17–21. Berkeley: University of California Press.

8. Metcalf, Barbara D. 1993. 'What Happened in Mecca: Mumtaz Mufti's "Labbaik", p. 261, fn. 18. In Folkenflik, Robert. ed. *The Culture of Autobiography: Constructions of Self-Representation*, pp. 149–67. Stanford: Stanford University Press (Chapter 14 in this volume.)

9. Frye, Northrop. 1981. *The Great Code: The Bible and Literature.* New York: Harcourt Brace Jovanovitch.

10. Wadley, op. cit; Bruner, op. cit; Metcalf, op. cit., p. 157.

11. For example, Roland, Alan. 1988. *In Search of Self in India and Japan: Toward a Cross-Cultural Psychology.* Princeton: Princeton University Press.

12. Barrett, Lindon. 1993. 'Self-knowledge, Law, and African American Autobiography: Lucy A. Delaney's *From the Darkness Cometh the Light*'. In Fokenflik, Robert, ed. *The Culture of Autobiography: Constructions of Self-Representation*, pp. 104–24. Stanford: Stanford University Press; Peterson, Linda H. 1993. 'Institutionalizing Women's Autobiography: Nineteenth-Century Editors and Shaping of an Autobiographical Tradition'. In Folkenflik, Robert, ed. *The Culture of Autobiography: Constructions of Self-Representation*, pp. 80–103. Stanford: Stanford University Press.

13. Anderson, Benedict. 1991. *Imagined Communities: Reflections on the Origin and Spread of Nationalism.* Rev. ed. New York: Verso.

14. Courtois, V. 1954. *Mary in Islam.* Calcutta: The Oriental Institute.

15. Lewis, Bernard. 1991. 'First-Person Narrative in the Middle East'. In Kramer, Martin, ed. *Middle Eastern Lives: The Practice of Biography and Self-Narrative*, pp. 20–34. Syracuse: Syracuse University Press.

# Index

358    INDEX

Mazāhir-i 'Ulūm, Saharanpur,
Uttar Pradesh 40, 51, 82, 272–3
Mazahiru'l-Ulum 83
Mc Donnel, Mary Byrne 299
Mecca 56, 186, 295–6, 299, 302,
309, 317–8, 320–1, 323, 328,
330–1
Medicine
indigenous system, revival by
Hakim Ajmal Khan 122–8,
145, 154–5, 157, 161, 163–9
professionalization 126
see also yūnānī tibb
medievalism 3
Medina 57, 59, 61, 68, 186, 296,
300, 325, 328
meditation (muraqaba) 334–5
meta-narrativeness 194, 341
Mewat
Tablighi Jama'at movement
175–7
conversions 181
Middle Ages 299
Middle East 1, 7, 13, 14, 20, 137,
198, 230, 233, 219
Pakistan relations 237, 239
migration 59
millat 186, 214n
Miller, Barbara Stoler 193
Miratu-l Arus, by Nazir Ahmad
115
Miskin 204, 206
missionary societies 31, 33
mleccha 201
modernist orientaion 224
modernity 10, 20, 173–87, 267
modernization theory 8
Mohammad, Prophet 220
Mohammad Shujauddin 342–3
Mohammadan Education
Conference 109
Mohī ud-Dīn Morādābādī 47
mohitimim 31, 32, 34–5, 43, 45
monogamy 111

monotheism 202
Montagu-Chelmsford
constitutional reforms 1919,
138, 161
moral formation and authority 4,
11, 312
morality 12, 114, 194
Morison, Theodore 129, 163
Moses 71
mosques 43
Mother India 187
motivations 1, 210
muftī 31, 63, 213n
Mughals 31
muhajir 227
Muhammad Ahmad, Maulānā
Hāfiz see Ahmad, Maulānā
Hāfiz Muhammad
Muhammad Ahmad, Maulānā
Hāfiz 35, 46, 48, 54n
Muhammad Ahmad Khan, Hakim
130
Muhammad Ahsān Nanautawī 45
Muhammad 'Ali 5, 140, 144, 174
Muhammad As'adu'llah, Maulana
75, 76, 89
Muhammad Ibn 'Abdul Wahhab
(1703–87) 59
Muhammad Ilyas Kandhalwi,
Maulana 69, 82, 88, 175–6, 179,
272
Muhammad Ismā'īl, Maulavī 48,
82
Muhammad Kichlu 144
Muhammad Ma'shuq 'Ali 301
Muhammad Mazhar Jan-i Janan,
Maulānā 335–6
Muhammad Munīr Nanautawī 35,
45
Muhammad, Prophet 68, 77, 78,
90, 106, 112, 298, 312
Muhammad Qāsim Nanautawī,
Maulānā 31, 34–5, 36, 40, 42,
43–8, 54n

Muhammad Sadiq 'Ali 133
Muhammad Sikandar Shah,
 Maulana 134–5
Muhammad Yahya 83
Muhammad Ya'qūb Nanautawī
 34
Muhammad Yusuf Kandhlawi,
 Maulana 79
Muhammad Zafrullah Khan 296
Muhammad Zakariyya Kandhlawi,
 Maulana (1897–1982) 67–91,
 273
Muhammad Zardar Khan 303–4,
 306
Muinu'd-Din Chishti, Shaikh,
 shrine of, Ajmer 135
Mujaddid, Hazrat 86
*mujahidin* 292
*Mujalla-yi tibbiya* (monthly) 157
Mujibu'r Rahman, Sheikh 229
Multan riots, 1923 144
multiculturalism 5
Mumtaz Kausar Niyazi 331
Mumtaz Mufti 23, 298, 304,
 317–36
Munawwar 'Ali Shah of Chishti
 Nizami order 134
Munē Shāh, Hazrat Mīyanī 44
Murtaza Khan, Hakim 171*n*
music 158, 170*n*
Mushtāq Ahmad, Hakīm 45
Mushtaq Hussain, Nawwab 134
Muslim(s) 42, 195, 200, 206, 208,
 210, 218, 220, 273–4
 architecture in India 42
 and British political relations
  127–30
 decline 153
 education institution 8, 10, 39,
  137
 identity in India before
  Partition 184–7
 role in Indian nationalist
  movement 2

movements 15
religious leaders 166
struggle for separate state 8
underrepresentation 141
women *see* women, Muslim
Muslim Brothers 266
Muslim League 134, 137, 138, 140,
 142, 159, 169, 174, 183, 240,
 274
 style of politics and Hakim
  Ajmal Khan 128–32, 146
Mutiny of 1857 34, 63, 162,
 270–1
Muzaffar Husain Kāndhlāvī,
 Maulānā 48
mysticism 14

Nadawatu'l-Ma'arif 136
Nadawatu'l-Ulama, Lucknow,
 Uttar Pradesh 136
Nadwa 140, 166
Naipaul, V. S. 197, 299, 303
Nair, Sir Shankaran 167
Naqshbandi Mujaddidi, lineage 57
Naqshbandis 7
Nargis 187
Nasser 261*n*
Nath yogic, 207
nationalism, nationalist movement
 4, 20, 101, 145, 151, 173–87,
 199, 200, 217–8, 240, 251, 267
 and Muslims, communal
  symbols and non-communal
  cooperation 136–46
nation-state 64, 173, 197, 218
Nawwal Kishur 304
Nazir Ahmad 109, 115, 324
Nehru, Jawaharlal 144, 180, 182–4,
 187
neo-fundamentalist 266
neologism 16
nepotism 47, 49
networks 273
Nihāl Ahmad, Shaikh 35

institutions 29, 276
religious leadership 42, 84, 237–
8, 274, 343
religious life 67, 141
nationalism in India 20, 193,
197, 232
obligation and obedience 65,
132, 141
orientation 58
reforms, Hakim Ajmal Khan
and 132–6
tradition, objectification 15
violence 178, 272
Renaissance 341
reputation 154
resecularization 125
resurgence 14
rights 11, 276
Roff, William 13
role models 25n
Rudolph, Lloyd 213n
ruling classes 10
Rushdie, Salman 23, 320
Russell, Ralph 7, 12
Russo-Turkish war 141

SSRC/ACLC's Joint Committee
11–4
Sa'di, Shaikh 320
Saba Mustafa 296
sadr modarris 31
Safarnama-yi haramain, by
Muhammad Zardar Khan 304
Safdar Hashmi Memorial Trust
(SAHMAT) 26n
Saharanpūrī, 'Alī 42
sāhib-i fatāwā 59
Said, Edward 222
Sami'ul-Haqq Deobandi, Maulana
255
sanad 30, 38
Sangathan 174
Sanskritization 176
sarparast 31, 34, 38, 40, 45, 50

Satanic Verses, The, by Salman
Rushdie 23
sati 99–100
Saudi Arabia
patronage and support to
Pakistan 21, 240
Saudis 261n, 276
Sayeed, Khalid bin 226
scepticism 161, 224, 319–20, 323,
326–7
'scripturalist' 69
seclusion see purdah
sectarianism 2, 21, 274
secularism 173, 197, 200, 218, 251
self, selfhood 11–2, 299, 250, 324, 344
self-abnegation 326
self-confidence 122
self-consciousness 10, 11, 24, 63,
178, 239, 302
self-control 11, 136
self-denial 84
self-esteem 122, 127, 154
self, imagination/perception 21–4,
324
self-improvement 2
self-justification 218, 219
self-realization 2, 4, 11, 13
self-representation 295–6, 312, 345
semitism 208
sensuality 196
Shabīr Ahmad Osmānī 40
Shabir Ahmad Usmani, Maulana 333
Shah Banu case 184
Shāh, Walīullāh see Dihlawi, Shah
Wali'ullah
Shaida Dihlawi, see Khan, Hakim
Ajmal (or Shahid)
shaikh 34, 46
shaikh ul-hadith 36
Shams Tabriz 326
Sharar 140
shari'a 36, 57, 60, 124, 141, 242–3,
267, 277
Shariat 103, 323